Faithfully Urban

Faithfully Urban
Pious Muslims in a German City

Petra Kuppinger

berghahn
NEW YORK · OXFORD
www.berghahnbooks.com

First published in 2015 by
Berghahn Books
www.berghahnbooks.com

© 2015, 2019 Petra Kuppinger
First paperback edition published in 2019

All rights reserved. Except for the quotation of short passages
for the purposes of criticism and review, no part of this book
may be reproduced in any form or by any means, electronic or
mechanical, including photocopying, recording, or any information
storage and retrieval system now known or to be invented,
without written permission of the publisher.

Library of Congress Cataloging-in-Publication Data
Kuppinger, Petra.
  Faithfully urban : pious Muslims in a German city / Petra Kuppinger.
    pages cm
  Includes bibliographical references and index.
  ISBN 978-1-78238-656-8 (hardback : alk. paper) -- ISBN 978-1-78238-657-5 (ebook)
 1. Muslims—Germany—Stuttgart. 2. Religious minorities—Germany—Stuttgart.
 3. Islam—Germany—Stuttgart. I. Title.
  BP65.G32S785 2015
  305.6'9709434715—dc23
                                                          2014039952

British Library Cataloguing in Publication Data
A catalogue record for this book is available from the British Library

ISBN 978-1-78238-656-8 hardback
ISBN 978-1-78920-504-6 paperback
ISBN 978-1-78238-657-5 ebook

In memory of my brother, Tom

Contents

Acknowledgments		ix
	Introduction	1
Chapter 1.	Arrival	34
Chapter 2.	Religiosities	64
Chapter 3.	Public Lives	101
Chapter 4.	Resentment	138
Chapter 5.	Our Mosque	156
Chapter 6.	In the Neighborhood	193
	Conclusion	236
Glossary		247
Bibliography		251
Index		275

Acknowledgments

This book is the result of a long intellectual and personal journey. It has been in the making for some time and many individuals have directly and indirectly contributed to its writing. There are those who helped and supported my earlier work in Cairo and those who were part of the work in Stuttgart. The work in Stuttgart could not have been done without my research and experiences in Egypt. My biggest gratitude goes to the many individuals and families in Cairo and Stuttgart who have accommodated my research and became close friends in the process. They have taught me invaluable lessons about their lives and life in general. They are too many to mention by name, but I would not be where I am today without any single one of them!

In terms of academic mentoring I owe much to Samir Akel (who first accommodated my interest in the Middle East when nobody else did). Thanks go to Asef Bayat who helped me find a home in urban anthropology (even though he is a sociologist). I am grateful to Lila Abu-Lughod who has provided much help and support over the years. Talal Asad greatly influenced my thinking about Islam and religion. Rayna Rapp often helped out with small things and support of all kinds when it was needed. Nicholas Hopkins took time to talk to me one day in May 1986 and then invited me to apply to the Department of Sociology/Anthropology at the American University in Cairo. This meeting changed my professional and private trajectory. I am grateful to Abdallah Cole for interesting courses and mentoring. I owe thanks to the late Janet Abu-Lughod, William Roseberry, and Cynthia Nelson who helped with guidance, independent studies, and detailed readings and commentaries on some of my work.

Over the years, many friends and colleagues have shared in discussions, participated in conferences and panels, invited me to workshops, read some of my work, collaborated on shared publications, and just made work and social life so much more fun and exciting. I am grateful that they crossed my path and shared my interests and life. I owe thanks to many who shared academic and other experiences in very different contexts, among them Nancy Abelmann, Berna Arabacioğlu, Sevgül Aydoğdu, Nadia Al-Bagdadi, Helga Baitenmann, Masooda Banu, Karin Beck, Sabine und Reinhold Eisenhut, Yasser Elsheshtawy, Mona Fawaz, Anita Fábos,

Achim Fingerle, Khaled Furani, John Gallagher, Jörg Gertel, Behrooz Ghamari-Tabrizi, Farha Ghannam, Peter Gotsch, Michael Guggenheim, Linda Herrera, Valerie Hoffman, Najib Hourani, Jayne Howell, Hilary Kalmbach, Ahmed Kanna, Petra Kaufmann, Kira Kosnick, Tassos Koumbourlis, Denise Lawrence-Zúñiga, Martina Lemke, Don Nonini, Petra Müller, Raj Pathania, Deborah Pellow, Guita Ranjbaran, Sabine, Aseel Sawalha, Serra, Suzanne Scheld, Oda Söderström, Dorothee Stahl, Ted Swedenburg, Mohammed Tabishat, Faedah Totah, Yasemin Yıldız, and Meryem Zaman.

Over the years a number of friends and colleagues have made small town life in Monmouth fun and vibrant. My gratitude to this group of people is enormous. They include Steve and Nancy Buban, Farhat Haq, Mohsin Masood, Hannah Schell, Martin Holland, Anne Mamary, Terri and Dan Ott, David and Polly Timmerman, Ira and Marge Smolensky, and Stacy and Simon Cordery. Nesli Sengül, Marie-Jo Descas and Alex Hervet, Badia Gabbour and Riad Al-Harithi who have since left Monmouth have helped in their time.

I am extremely grateful to the reviewers of the manuscript (who disclosed their identities after the fact): Esra Özyürek, Ahmed Kanna, and Riem Spielhaus. Their sharp eyes on the manuscript helped me to greatly improve my work. All remaining errors are solely mine. Finally I am grateful to Molly Mosher, Elizabeth Berg, and Duncan Ranslem at Berghahn Books for their help and patience publishing this book.

The fieldwork for this book was supported by a research grant from the Wenner Gren Foundation (2006–07) and an Enhancing Scholarly Agenda Grant from the Associated Colleges of the Midwest (ACM FaCE Project funded by the Andrew W. Mellon Foundation), and a Faculty Development Grant from Monmouth College.

I owe more than words can say to my parents, Gudrun and Helmut Kuppinger. My mother especially never tired to support my ideas and plans (even if she sometimes did not agree with them). My debt to her is enormous. My parents offered financial support for my projects when none was forthcoming elsewhere. My brother, Tom, my childhood companion, died in 1996 and I have thoroughly missed him every day since then. This book is for him (I hope you are proud of your little sister!). Finally, there are my daughters, Tamima and Tala, who lived through much of the research in Stuttgart, and at times were vitally involved in it. They were patient, and occasionally participated in activities and events that probably were not their first choice. From an early age they taught me a lot and made me humble with regard to all sorts of life's endeavors. I cannot even remotely imagine life without them.

Introduction

On a sunny Saturday morning in September 2007 the Park School celebrated its annual New First-Graders reception.[1] More than sixty proud six-year-olds with huge school bags, new clothes, and the obligatory colorful large cardboard cone stuffed with small gifts and sweets (*Schultüte*), accompanied by parents, relatives, and friends walked across the school yard toward the school's gym. More than 250 people crowded into the gym, many standing along the walls for lack of seating. As the crowd settled, the school's principal, Ms. Bauer, dressed in an elegant dark red suit with a necklace of matching large beads, greeted children, parents, and guests and emphasized the importance of the day. After her introductory remarks, she presented the next set of speakers: a Protestant Minister, a Muslim Imam, and a lay representative of the Catholic Church. The three religious representatives greeted the children and their families and said a few words about the importance of learning for life, and the special nature of this day as a turning point in the lives of the new first graders. The three men were dressed in suits and ties. After their brief remarks, each spoke a prayer and asked for God's/Allah's blessing for these young children in their new environment. Next the fourth graders performed a short play and sang some songs. Overall, this was an event like many others in Germany. Fanciful parties and receptions for first graders have in recent years gained social importance in Germany. Especially among the middle classes, they are celebrated with relatives and friends and often include an outing to a restaurant. In a highly secularized environment, where increasing numbers of the population officially left the churches, for some families these lavish celebrations replace earlier religious rites of passage such as first communion or confirmation. Traditionally in Germany, the first day of school starts with a non-obligatory church service in a local church. The service is followed by a festive reception in the school.

For many years the Park School, which is located in Stuttgart-Nordbahnhof, a multi-ethnic working-class neighborhood had a similar program with an ecumenical Christian service in a nearby church, and the school reception afterward. In 2006, however, less than ten people attended this service. This embarrassingly low attendance triggered a rethinking of the event and its religious components and resulted in a new mode of celebration. Instead of canceling the service, those in charge chose a different solution: religious elements were added to the (secular) school event. In the Nordbahnhof quarter, Muslims account for approximately one third of the population. Obviously, Muslims or atheists had no interest in a church service. German, Italian, Portuguese, Serbian, Croatian, Russian, and other Christians either lived at a distance to their religion, or did not feel represented by this particular church service. Others preferred to skip this 9 A.M. service and only attend the school celebration an hour later. The redesigned celebration in 2007 addressed Muslims needs and integrated religious elements into the secular celebration without overly stretching the patience of atheists, non-Protestant or non-Catholic Christians, and others. The new event represented a suitable compromise for most local families.[2]

The Park School's New First-Graders celebration is a cultural innovation negotiated in a multi-ethnic and multi-religious urban quarter. The presence of an Imam at this public school celebration exemplifies cultural changes that unfold in an urban quarter where successive waves of ever more diverse residents and immigrants have for more than a century been remaking local cultural forms and practices, and by extension elements of the larger urban culture. In recent decades Muslims have become an important constituency in Nordbahnhof. They have been playing a significant role in the quarter's cultural transformations. At a moment of rupture when the established practice of a Protestant/Catholic service in a local church was no longer viable, parents, teachers, the school's administration, and representative of churches and mosques negotiated a mode of celebration that reflected changing local constituencies and dynamics.

The reorganization of this First Grade celebration is not an isolated instance of creative cultural production, but exemplifies larger changes underway in Nordbahnhof and similar multi-ethnic working-class neighborhoods in Stuttgart and other German cities. In small urban spaces ordinary residents constantly remake local cultures to best accommodate their diverse habits, practices, beliefs, and sensitivities. The Imam's presence at the school celebration symbolizes larger dynamics of localization, cultural creativity, civic participation, and inclusion of Muslims and their lifeworlds in German cities. However, not all debates and negotiations involving Muslim needs are as smooth and successful as the Park School First Grade celebration. Other instances of Muslim participation are met with resentment and prejudice, or outright rejection and hostility. The question arises, why do some urban cultural transformations unfold smoothly, while other similar attempts end in bitter controversies? What are the elements and dynamics that account for the success of some negotiations and the failure of others? How does a religion become local? How do believers insert their beliefs and practices into contemporary cityscapes?

The dynamics of Muslim localization, participation, and inclusion in German cities unfold in multilayered contexts of national legal frameworks, specific forms of secularism, powerful landscapes of popular sentiments and media images, grass roots activities, global political and religious dynamics, and everyday urban practices and cultures. Reactions of dominant society and political elites to the presence of Muslims and the emergence of urban German Muslim identities, religiosities, and cultures alternate between neglect, ignorance, paternalistic accommodation, prejudice, resentment, hostility, support, recognition, and accommodation. Some Muslim communities were able to build a mosque without much opposition and debate. Others fought long and painful battles to build a mosque. Yet others were prevented from doing so altogether. A few pious Muslims have become recognized and respected participants in the urban public sphere; their interventions are heard and honored. Simultaneously, "Muslims" are frequently accused of a predictable list of shortcomings (forced marriages, oppression of women, blind following of Muslim law, putting Muslim law above national laws/constitutions, etc.) that are said to prevent them from becoming full-fledged citizens in a liberal democracy. What accounts for this highly unpredictable atmosphere with regard to Muslims and their religious, cultural, and civic role, needs, and demands? Why is it, on the one hand, so difficult for Muslims to build a mosque and become visible and vocal participants and cultural producers in Germany, when, on the other hand, Muslim localization is successfully underway in contexts like the Park School?

This book explores pious Muslim lifeworlds, religiosities, civic participation, and cultural production in the southern German state capital of Stuttgart (state of Baden-Württemberg). I illustrate that the localization and inclusion of pious Muslims is a complicated process that reacts to different dynamics and unfolds on a multitude of platforms. It is mediated by national debates about the role and rights of religion in general and Islam in particular in society, culture, and politics, discussions about the definition of citizenship, and controversies over the loyalty of Muslims to the German Constitution (*Grundgesetz*). These debates are politically charged and controversial. Concrete points of contention question if and how a "new" religion can be inserted into existing political, social, and religious structures. How much religion is good anyway? How is "good" religion practiced? What exactly is Islam? Who are Muslims? Can they be part of a secular liberal society? Can they live under the German constitution? How many mosques should be built? What is the place of Islam, Muslims, Muslim religiosities, and pious Muslim lifestyles and practices in the context of a twenty-first-century globalized metropolis? These abstract debates, local and global dynamics, and individual lifeworlds converge in concrete urban spaces where diverse individuals and groups try to create meaningful lives for themselves, their families, and communities. In order to understand the inclusion of immigrant cultures and religions it is paramount to examine the minutiae of everyday lives and transformations in spaces like the Park School where diverse individuals meet and create cultural compromises. Emerging urban practices, while rarely publicly recognized often become models for others to follow.

Since 9/11, debates about Islam in Germany and Europe have taken on an unprecedented urgency. In public debates, local issues (e.g. mosque construction, debates about the *hijab*/headscarf) are often conflated with global concerns about terrorism and militant Islam. The resulting atmosphere of fear, mistrust, and resentments has produced serious setbacks for Muslims' civic participation (Cesari 2010b; Monshipouri 2010; Spielhaus 2013; Yıldız 2009). At the same time, the precarious economic situation of some individuals and families as a result of the economic restructuring in Europe has produced a situation where immigrants or other seemingly "superfluous" populations are targeted as the scapegoats for various political, social, and economic ills (Bauman 2007: 29). Already caught on the margins of society, with lower than average incomes, education, and housing (Cesari 2010b: 19), many Muslims have in recent years felt the brunt of governments' and citizens' anger and resentment in the face of global political insecurity, and neoliberal economies' local fallout (Cesari 2010a; Bauman 2007; Yeğenoğlu 2012). Sharper immigration regulations, citizenship tests, discrimination, and prejudice are just a few of the issues Muslim immigrants and citizens have been facing in the early twenty-first century (Monshipouri 2010; Spielhaus 2011). As the overall picture often appears difficult for Muslims in Europe, the question arises whether different spaces and experiences exist? Are there moments and spaces of mutual respect, social and cultural recognition, civic participation, and creative cooperation? How are pious Muslims and their communities woven into existing urban cultural and religious geographies? Are there spaces that produce cultural transformations that reflect Muslim needs and participation? Do certain urban changes benefit pious Muslims? What concrete contributions, interventions, and models are being articulated in small urban spaces?

John Bowen (2010) asked "Can Islam be French?" and examined debates about Muslim law and its possible convergence with French secular law. He illustrates that Muslim legal scholars in France and Muslim majority contexts have engaged in lively discussions about the possibility of making Muslim law work for Muslims in France from within the "Muslim realm of justifications" (ibid.: 157). Bowen asks how individuals and communities can simultaneously abide by Muslim and French law. He identifies processes that would allow for a convergence of legal understandings where both sides could remain within their respective religious or philosophical realms of justification. Bowen concludes that such a convergence could be reached if all parties were willing to revisit legal debates with an open eye to social realities and intended legal consequences. He concludes that Muslim legal scholars in France and elsewhere have already gone a long way to address some legal problems and dilemmas that pious Muslims face in Muslim minority contexts. He encourages the French legal establishment to follow suit and do their homework of reworking, with their tools and justifications, a number of legal issues pertaining to current disputes that involves Muslims. In this book I ask related questions: How is Islam lived in German cities? How does Islam work as a guiding principle in urban lifeworlds and cultures? Under which conditions do Muslims and their communities join the larger landscape of urban religions? How is Islam made into a German religion in minute everyday interactions? What does a German Muslim urban culture look like? What processes and transformations are underway, which facilitate the creation of vibrant Muslim spaces, practices, and lifeworlds? What are the concrete steps, experiences, and contributions of pious Muslims and their communities to the making and remaking of urban cultures and public spheres? How are Muslims practices woven into an increasingly diverse urban cultural fabric? How do largely secularly defined cityscapes change in the process of such transformations? My central question is how do pious Muslims, as individuals and communities, negotiate meaningful urban lives, spaces, cultures, and public spheres that they can inhabit both as believers and involved citizens? How can spaces, events, identities, encounters, or civic activities be simultaneously piously Muslim (lived and legitimated within the Muslim tradition) and part of urban liberal cultural and public spheres?

In recent years, much ink has been spilled (and sound bites and images produced) in the German media about Islam and Muslims. Favorite topics include women and Islam (how oppressed are they?), political Islam (will Germany one day be run over by political Islam?), or the legal problems of being a Muslim in Germany (is *halal*—in accordance with Muslim law—butchering violating animal rights?). Debates about whether pious Muslims can be loyal German citizens, and whether they really intend to respect the *Grundgesetz* are in full swing. Simultaneously, there are debates and images circulating that aim to "disclose" aspects of Islam and Muslim lives that supposedly make it hard, if not impossible, for many pious Muslims to become loyal German citizens. Focusing on, or at times even obsessing with, subjects such as women, honor killings, forced marriages, terrorism, and the role of violence in Islam, popular media and often also serious media experts insist on being able to identify the dangerous features of Islam and Muslims, and hence warn non-Muslim society of the hidden dangers of Islam in Germany. Some pundits offer their expertise to distinguish between "good" Muslims (those who are not too insistent on their religious practices and affiliations) and "bad" Muslims (those who tightly hold on to religion and its supposedly anti-liberal features; see Mamdani 2004). Considerable parts of such debates remain stereotypical and ideological.[3] They feed on simplistic opposites of "us" versus "them," or "insiders" versus "outsiders" (see Shooman and Spielhaus 2010). Concerned citizens are provided with images that tend to enhance fears, and reinforce stereotypes and prejudices they were harboring all along. Differences are frequently stressed while relative silence prevails about commonalities and shared lifeworlds.

Ordinary pious Muslims, their lifeworlds, voices, civic participation, and cultural production rarely figure in public debates. Muslims are seldom depicted as active debaters of their own lifeworlds, traditions, subjectivities, and religiosities. Rarely are they identified as creative producers of local cultures. Muslims are seldom portrayed as regular citizens, workers, students, discussants in the public sphere, or individuals, who like everybody else suffer the consequences of environmental pollutions, increases in sales taxes, cuts in health insurance benefits, bad weather, or icy roads. Instead, occasional warnings are issued about the pending danger of ethnic ghettos where "generic" Muslims supposedly live lockstep by the outdated teachings of the Qur'an, or where Muslims might uncritically consume the hateful teachings of fanatic import-Imams. Muslims appear in public only with regard to Muslim issues (Spielhaus 2011: 156). If at the other end of the world a Muslim commits an atrocity, local Muslims are called in to explain, or worse to collectively apologize.

In this book I examine the lives of ordinary urban residents, neighborhoods, and mosque communities. I examine how they debate and configure subjectivities, religiosities, lifeworlds, and urban cultures. I analyze moments and spaces where Muslims and non-Muslims engage each other and create cultural forms and everyday practices that accommodate their respective needs and sensitivities. I ask: How have pious Muslims and their communities, in the face of resentment and discrimination, managed to create meaningful lifeworlds and become creative participants? How do Muslims participate in the city? What new forms, practices, and spaces have Muslims created to accommodate their needs and sensitivities? How have they inserted Islam into the urban religious topography? My central argument is that the localization of Islam and Muslims is a process rooted in concrete urban contexts where individuals, groups, associations, communities, and institutions debate ideas and practices, configure identities and religiosities, and create lifeworlds that reflect the needs of all involved constituencies. The point is not whether Islam is compatible with liberal German democracy or the German Constitution, but "rather under what conditions Muslims can *make* them compatible" (Bayat 2007: 4; emphasis in the original). I am interested in the concrete situations and processes where individuals and groups negotiate practical solutions and design ways to be involved citizens.

Instead of questioning whether Islam can have a space in German cities, I demonstrate that Islam and Muslim religiosities are already integral parts of German cities, as the process of their localization has been underway for decades. This localization can best be understood from a micro-level perspective. Like Lara Deeb noted for the case of a pious Shi'a community in Beirut, "we need ethnography to understand local dynamics of what has variously been called 'Islamization,' 'Islamic fundamentalism,' 'Islamism'" (2006: 5), the localization of Islam in German cities is best examined by way of ethnographic work. Considerable aspects of Muslim cultural negotiation and production are overlooked by dominant society, because they unfold in places that either go unnoticed or are not recognized as "public" spaces or locations of public debate. Moments of urban conflict, neighborhood talk, negotiations of individual identities, modes of participation, and associational lives illustrate the complex interactions of pious individuals with each other and with diverse urban constituencies.

While Islam does not have old historical roots in Germany, it has in recent decades become a constituent element of urban cultural and religious landscapes. In the process Islam and Muslims have become deeply and solidly rooted in cities and their cultural and religious geographies. Muslim participation and the creation of new urban cultures happened less by way of grand political projects, but by way of minute steps and compromises that paved the way for more visible and established religiously inspired practices. In their everyday encounters Muslims of diverse ethnicities and religiosities and their diverse neighbors, friends, and colleagues (ethnic German and others, Christians of varying denominations and religiosities, atheists, or individuals of other religious beliefs and backgrounds) negotiate individual identities and positions in society. Nobody remains unchanged, as new identities, modes of participation, and social and cultural configurations and practices emerge. Individual and collective everyday efforts, experiences, and transformations comprise the foundations of well-established and diverse lifeworlds, subjectivities, religiosities, everyday cultures, spatialities, and religious topographies (Göle and Ammann 2004; Jonker and Amiraux 2006; Al-Hamarneh and Thielmann 2008). The inclusion of the Imam in the Park School celebration bears witness to debates among parents, teachers, and students about how to best adjust the daily life of a school to accommodate the needs of diverse stakeholders. In such minute and mundane interactions, individuals, informal groups, and formal associations articulate practices, invent new forms, design compromises, discard some practices, and find friends and allies. The key concerns of the majority of urban dwellers are not philosophical questions of how state and religion relate to each other. Instead people strive to give religion the space in their lives and the city that they deem most desirable.

My goals in this book are to show that (1) Islam and Muslims are integral, inseparable, and creative parts of a city like Stuttgart. Pious Muslims do not stand or act apart from urban society, but are constituent members of the latter. They are insiders and act from within and not without. Like all urbanites, Muslims and Muslim communities shape the city and are shaped by it. (2) Muslim Stuttgart is not monolithic. It is a vastly diverse community with regard to ethnicity, culture, politics, education, gender, age, class, and religiosity. (3) Muslim Stuttgart is a dynamic religious and cultural field, where Islam, diverse lifestyles, practices, and religiosities are under constant debate. This field, in turn, is further engaged in complex processes of negotiating local pious Muslim identities and practices that interact with believers' countries of origin and the global *ummah* (community of believers). I illustrate that Muslim Stuttgart's social and cultural wealth, dynamics, and future potentials are rooted in its diversity, which sets the community apart from urban contexts in Muslim-majority contexts. (4) I demonstrate how public and media images continue to reproduce stereotypes about Islam and Muslims that burden and obstruct efforts of individuals and communities at equal and creative participation. Indeed these images considerably hinder the public recognition and subsequent appreciation of Islam, Muslims, and Muslim activities as constructive and constituent urban elements. (5) I unpack the complex nature of the ongoing construction and negotiation of urban pious Muslim lifeworlds, practices, and religiosities. These negotiations are situated at complex personal and communal intersections of multilayered local, regional, national, and global networks and dynamics. (6) The book portrays elements of the everyday lives of individuals and communities, their religiosities, debates about selves and identities, communities, society, and politics and their participation in the city. Pious Muslims in Stuttgart, like elsewhere in Europe, are engaged in debates about their role and future in the city, nation, and global *ummah*. (7) On a theoretical level, I seek to resituate debates about Islam in Germany in the context of discussions about urban religions. In recent years the discussion of Islam and Muslims in Germany (and Europe) has been conducted in isolation from emerging debates about urban religions, or religion in and *of* the city, creating a sense that Muslims are the only new religious group, or the only group that seeks to configure their urban participation in a religiously inspired manner. Similarly, I depart from debates about "integration" of Muslims, which imply the recent arrival and foreign nature of Islam and Muslims. My point is to analyze pious Muslim lifeworlds within a framework of contemporary urban religious studies. Central here is the understanding that pious Muslims are one among other (new and old) urban religious groups that vie for adequate spaces, respect, recognition, and participation in European cities in the early twenty-first century.

Migration, Culture, and Religion

Muslims have lived in Germany in small numbers for more than a century. King Friedrich Wilhelm I established the first documented Muslim prayer room almost 200 years ago in 1731 for Turkish soldiers in his troops (Ceylan 2006: 123). The first formal mosque was constructed and opened in Berlin in 1925 (Abdullah 1981: 29). In the 1950s increasing numbers of students from the Arab World, Iran, and Africa came to study at German universities. Many of them were Muslims. Plans for the first post–World War II mosque in Germany, the Islamic Center in Hamburg (Imam Ali Mosque, a predominantly Iranian Shi'a mosque), date back to this era. The cornerstone for this mosque (with a dome and two minarets) was laid in February 1961. The first prayers were held in 1963 (Kraft 2002: 91).

Starting from the mid-1950s Germany signed labor treaties with southern European and northern African states (e.g. Italy, Spain, Greece, Turkey, Morocco, Tunisia, and Yugoslavia). With the signing of a treaty between Germany and Turkey in 1961, thousands of Turkish men and some women arrived. Planning to stay for only a few years, most men left their wives and children back home. In the following years Moroccan, Tunisian, and Yugoslavian Muslims signed labor contracts in Germany.[4] By the mid-/late 1960s as some workers had already been in Germany for a few years and their initial dreams of a speedy return were increasingly put on hold, small groups of men organized themselves to accommodate their religious needs. Talking to older individuals, "founding" stories were often surprisingly similar. Planning for a short stay, informal groups rented premises that were first and foremost affordable and within the geographical reach of many men. Initially, the quality of facilities, their public visibility, or access to a larger public were of little concern to these groups (Schmitt 2003: 18; Ceylan 2006: 130).[5] They invariably ended up in backyards, defunct workshops, or the attics of workers' dormitories—out of sight of mainstream society (Schiffauer 2010: 36). In places that came to be referred to as *Hinterhofmoschee* (backyard mosque), men met for daily, Friday, and holiday prayers (Mandel 1996). Internal political or religious differences remained secondary in these small communities. Not very much in touch with their larger urban and social environments, the men were concerned with practicing their faith quietly and not attracting much attention (Schmitt 2003: 18; Kraft 2002). Interaction with dominant society, and political or social participation were not on their agenda (Ceylan 2006: 126; Jonker 2002: 119; Schiffauer 2000: 246). Regardless of their attempts at keeping a low profile, occasional smaller controversies emerged in some early prayer rooms. Neighbors were prone to complain about noise and traffic that resulted from tens of men coming for Friday or holiday prayers. "The neighbors complained and then we moved," is almost a standard element of narratives about early mosques. But tensions remained local and limited to particular facilities. In the political climate of the 1960s and early 1970s, a few "guest-workers" performing their prayers were seen as politically irrelevant, if they were noticed at all by dominant society. Many Muslim migrant workers had no contact with these religious spaces, as some men organized along ethnic or also political lines (e.g. in labor unions).

From the 1960s to the 1980s German authorities largely neglected the social, cultural, and religious affairs of migrants. The government relegated such questions to other institutions. For example, the Catholic Church provided services for Catholic migrants (e.g. from Italy, Spain, or Portugal). Many Italians joined local Catholic churches, which if there were sufficient numbers, would offer additional Italian language services.[6] In 1960, the Protestant Church in Baden-Württemberg entered an agreement with the Greek Orthodox Church to provide support for Greek migrants (*Diakonie Württemberg* 25.2.2010). Local chapters of the secular and leftist AWO (*Arbeiterwohlfahrt*; Workers' Welfare) provided some social services for Turkish workers in the 1960s. A religious vacuum remained for pious Turks, hence their informal religious associations.

The recruitment stop for foreign labor in 1973 dramatically remade the lifescapes of many migrants. Afraid that re-entry would be denied after summer vacations in their home countries, and still far from their ambitious goals of saving large sums of money, many workers decided to bring their families to Germany. Some Turkish, Moroccan, or Yugoslavian/Bosnian men had already spent a decade in Germany; and with the growing number of women and children, demands on religious spaces and services transformed. Whereas small, simple, and largely non-descript prayer spaces had been sufficient in the men's first decade in Germany, more was needed now. Ergun Can,[7] a member of the Stuttgart city council (*Gemeinderat*) and keen observer of the local mosque-scape argues that this early period indeed constituted a missed chance where authorities could have facilitated the construction of a larger mosque, which would have possibly avoided some of the subsequent segmentation into numerous smaller communities, and the spatially hidden nature of many mosques.[8]

In the 1970s many Muslim communities started to consolidate into larger and more organized congregations, which became increasingly differentiated in their theological outlook and also political loyalties. Among them were the communities that later organized as the VIKZ (*Verband der Islamischen Kulturzentren*; Association of Islamic Cultural Centers), and the Nurçuluk communities (Schiffauer 2000: 51; Jonker 2002: 91). Both were more mystically and spiritually inclined and at the time were illegal in Turkey (Schiffauer 2000: 52). In Stuttgart, the first such community, the predecessor of today's local VIKZ chapter, was founded in 1968. The outlines and organizational structure of what later became the Milli Görüş communities also emerged in the late 1960s (Schiffauer 2010: 63). These early processes of religious community formations in Germany irritated secular authorities in Ankara that controlled religious matters in Turkey. In 1984 the "Turkish-Islamic Union for Religious Affairs" (*Türkisch-Islamische Union der Anstalt für Religion e.V*; Turkish: *Diyanet İşleri Türk İslam Birliği*; short: DİTİB) was founded in Germany as a local extension of the Turkish Presidency for Religious Affairs, a government body under the direct control of the Prime Minister. Motivated by concerns about the spiritual lives of Turkish migrants, but also alarmed by the growing number of mosques and mosque associations in Europe that represented groups that were either illegal or watched with suspicion by the Turkish government, the German branch of DİTİB was to provide religious and cultural support, services, and guidance for Turks. Simultaneously DİTİB and its sponsoring agency in Ankara hoped to maintain a vague control over Turkish Muslim affairs in Germany. The existence of DİTİB absolved German authorities of the need to reflect about the spiritual needs of Turkish Muslims. DİTİB started to organize local mosque communities and the Turkish state sent and paid their Imams. More recently many mosques also include female theologians or teachers of religion sponsored by the Turkish state. Turkish consulates and DİTİB subsidiaries became informal representatives and partners of German public institutions and political bodies. At present DİTİB oversees almost 900 mosques in Germany.[9]

Based on the religio-political movement headed by Necmettin Erbakan (who was the Turkish Prime Minister in 1996/97; Schiffauer 2000, 2010), the Islamic

Community Milli Görüş (*Islamische Gemeinschaft Milli Görüş;* IGMIG) represents what could vaguely be termed Turkish nationalist Islam. Set on a political march through the institutions, Milli Görüş favors a strict interpretation of the Qur'an and a parliamentarian type of Islamic politics. The first communities vaguely based on Erbakan's ideas were founded in the mid-1970s in Germany (some used the initial name of Turkish Islamic Union). After a series of organizational and name changes, the community configured under the national umbrella organization of *Islamische Gemeinschaft Milli Görüş* (IGMG) in 1995.[10] Popularly known as Milli Görüş, the IGMG is viewed with suspicion by German authorities. The association is on the watch-list of state security (Schiffauer 2010). Therefore, the association and its individual mosques are often overlooked or outright boycotted with regard to inclusion in civic circuits and public events.

Consolidating Turkish mosque communities and emerging national umbrella associations increasingly came to reflect the outlines and controversies of Turkey's political and religious landscape (Tietze 2001: 36; Ceylan 2006: 139; Schiffauer 2000). Some older Turkish individuals related stories of veritable political "takeovers" or minor "mosque-wars" in this period of political and religious articulation (e.g. Ceylan 2006: 140; Schiffauer 2000, 2010).[11]

Arab, Bosnian, or later Afghan and other mosques similarly represent articulations of local, home country, and global dynamics. These developments unfolded quietly and never produced much public attention and debate. The largest predominantly Arab mosque association is the *Islamische Gemeinschaft in Deutschland* IGD (Islamic Community in Deutschland), which is part of the *Zentralrat der Muslime* (ZDM, Central Council of Muslims). Founded in Munich in 1958, the IGD is among the oldest German Muslim associations.[12] Loosely framed by aspects of the teaching of the Egyptian Muslim Brotherhood, the IGD is less invested in the national politics of any Arab country, and more focused on the construction of a German Islam, German Muslim platforms, the teaching of their theology and practices, and the construction of individual pious identities in the context of the global *ummah*. More than other associations the IGD attracts converts to Islam.

Under the umbrella of national organizations, local communities started to search for larger and more appropriate facilities (see Schmitt 2003: 18). They also recognized the material needs of their members and visitors with regard to ethnic and religious merchandise, such as *halal* food products (Ceylan 2006: 137; Haenni 2005; Mandel 1996: 151; Fischer 2009). Some new and larger mosque complexes started to include grocery stores and other businesses (e.g. barber stores, travel agents, undertakers). Becoming more settled and institutionalized, allowed communities a minimum of public recognition. Some gradually presented themselves as partners for municipal authorities and other civic associations (Tietze 2001: 36).[13] Becoming more established and locally rooted, growing in size, claiming a voice in public, and searching for better and possibly more visible spaces, mosque communities faced new problems. In their early years, mosque associations, as disenfranchised groups that largely consisted of (invisible) immigrants had produced few reactions from dominant society. Their attempts, however, to rent, and starting from the 1990s, buy larger premises were often met with opposition, prejudices, and rejection. At the same time the cast of players was changing in many mosque associations. Increasingly the leadership of mosque associations included members of the second generation with professional training or university degrees who were no longer willing to gratefully take handouts from dominant society. Instead, as educated and vocal citizens they were socially and legally savvy and claimed their legitimate right to acquire appropriate spaces to worship and adequate spaces from which to join and interact with the urban public.

These changes reflect larger European developments as many younger Muslims turned away from their parents' countries of origin toward participation in the societies where they had lived all or most of their lives (Ceylan 2006: 147, 2010; Schiffauer 2010). New political and religious issues emerged, like the shape and future of Muslim minority communities and the role of religious individuals and communities in civil society, culture, and politics (Nökel 2002: 160; Jonker and Amiraux 2006). This coincided with the emergence of a new cultural and intellectual pious Muslim elite and their increasing visibility (Göle 2004: 11; Klausen 2005; Schiffauer 2010; Kandemir 2005), and a new Muslim "public sphere and market" (Göle 2004: 13, Haenni 2005; Pink 2009; Kuppinger 2011a). Regardless of discrimination, disrespect, and ignorance about their existence and constructive participation in the last half century, pious Muslims made a home for themselves in German and European cities (Al-Hamarneh and Thielmann 2008; Nökel 2002; Mannitz 2006; Tietze 2001; Bowen 2007; Werbner 2002).

Belonging, Citizenship, and Identity

Discussions about belonging and citizenship in Germany are rooted in the nineteenth century when larger groups of labor migrants arrived in particular from Poland to work in newly established mines and factories, or in railroad or urban construction in the emerging German nation-state (Sassen 1999: 55). At a historical moment when hundreds of thousands of Germans left for the Americas, internal migration and increasingly migration from outside the consolidating borders of the new nation-state gained in importance. The new nation-state quickly drew a line between its nationals and incoming laborers, who were labeled as temporary (ibid.). Saskia Sassen explains that "long before any Turkish workers appeared on the German scene, these East European masses were treated as the nation's 'guest workers'" (ibid.: 57). The movement and settlement of incoming workers was closely controlled by residence and work permits (ibid.). The treatment of this first wave of im-/migrants reflects the conceptualization of the nation as a fixed community of "insiders" who share "a common 'blood,' as though a nation were a biological inheritance rather than a cultural acquisition" (ibid.: 61). *Jus sanguinis* (descent/blood-based law) became a basic tenet of German citizenship law, and very importantly also of political discourses and popular sentiments about migrant workers and immigrants. The myth of common descent became deeply engrained or naturalized into the understanding of Germanness. Consequently, it was easier for the children of past emigrants to regain German citizenship, than for long-term immigrants to receive citizenship. For much of the twentieth century, the notion of the German nation as a neatly circumscribed community of descent remained unchallenged in the political realm and popular imagination. Even after millions of migrant workers and their families had arrived starting in the 1950s, few observers asked for changes in citizenship laws until the 1990s. Even individuals who became German citizens were frequently reminded that they were not "as German" as ethnic Germans. Until recently, most politicians denied the reality of Germany being an immigrant nation. Rauf Ceylan noted, that Germany for too long has been an immigrant nation without an immigration policy (2006: 93).

In the 1990s, in particular with the arrival of waves of war refugees and political asylum seekers, debates about the unwieldy and discriminatory German citizenship laws became more pressing. In 2000 (under a Social Democrat and Green coalition), citizenship laws were reformed to ease the way into citizenship for long-term residents and their children (Ewing 2008: 16). Inserting aspects of *jus solis* legislation, the reformed law stipulates that children who have at least one (non-citizen) parent, who had lived for more than eight years legally in Germany, could automatically get German citizenship at birth. While much remains to be done with regard to allowing easier access to citizenship, first significant steps were taken with this law.

The adaption of legal contexts to existing realities, however, neither produces widespread knowledge of these changes, nor does it result in the automatic reconsideration of popular ideas about citizenship and belonging. For conservative politicians (who had opposed this legislation) and considerable segments of dominant society, this law did not alter their assumptions about the nature of the nation, its "legitimate" members, and the high stakes for those who wanted to join. Germany in this widespread understanding continued to be a nation of ethnic Germans. Those who wanted to become citizens would have to become "Germans" as defined by rather narrow characteristics. Citizenship in the popular imagination remained closely linked to an adherence to rather ill-defined notions of German culture.

On October 18, 2000, Friedrich Merz of the conservative Christian Democratic Union (CDU) announced in an interview that "immigrants who [want] to live here permanently must adapt to the evolved German *Leitkultur*" (quoted in Ewing 2008b: 212). His utterance and the concept of *Leitkultur* (guiding culture, main/dominant culture) sparked considerable debate. What was Germany's *Leitkultur*? Who defined the tenets of this culture? On the political left, Merz's statement produced surprise, which quickly turned into mockery and ridicule. Leftist commentators, blogs, and cyberspace debates were flooded with lists and images of this *Leitkultur* as a collage of beer, *Sauerkraut*, *Wurst* (sausages), soccer, Neuschwanstein, Goethe, and Beethoven. The term quickly deteriorated into the butt of jokes and was largely avoided in broader debates. An eager CDU bureaucrat in Baden-Württemberg, however, took the task of creating *Leitkultur*-tested new citizens to heart and designed a test to verify that those who applied for citizenship were indeed infused with the spirit of German culture. In 2006 this test was implemented in Baden-Württemberg.[14] Other federal states have since instituted similar tests. These tests have been criticized for their discriminatory contents such as questions that conflict with pious Muslim sensitivities.

In the face of the more self-conscious and outspoken presence of young and educated German Muslims and debates about Islam in the wake of 9/11, many otherwise secular individuals increasingly insisted that Germany was a Christian nation and as such part of a larger Christian-Jewish-European cultural context and civilization. The presence of large numbers of Muslims not only intensified debates about citizenship and cultural belonging but also kindled debates about the role of religion in the secular state. Ensuing discussions incited considerable fears of Islam and Muslims, which produced further resentment with regard to legal inclusion and participation of Muslims (see e.g. Ammann 2004: 66; Modood 2007: 128).

From *Gastarbeiter* to Migrant to Muslim

When Southern European and North African workers first arrived in the 1950s and 1960s, their stay was deemed temporary and they were subsequently called *Gastarbeiter* (guest worker), a designation that stresses the temporal limits of their stay and their distinct outsider position. Guests do not belong and should not overstay their welcome.[15] The term guest implies the clear lack of rights to interfere with the lives of hosts, demand major cultural accommodations, become active participants in society, or creatively shape local culture (Yeğenoğlu 2012; Derrida 1992). Once the myth of the temporary stay of migrant workers was debunked (at least for those with a willingness to recognize and understand political realities), and the sons and daughters of the first generation became more outspoken and increasingly demanded their rights of inclusion and creative participation in society, the term *Gastarbeiter* was reluctantly replaced by *Ausländer* (foreigner, often used in a derogatory way) in general, or Turks, Italians, and Greeks in particular starting in the mid to late 1970s. Once more this set of terms drew clear lines of exclusion. Foreigners might live in Germany, but they did not belong and could not claim the same right as citizens. Simultaneously, a silent social contract existed that gave migrant workers and their families full access to health insurance, retirement, schooling, and other social benefits, at the price of not asking for political rights and relevant civic participation. In this earlier phase in the construction of a multi-ethnic society, religion took a backseat. Individuals and groups were largely identified by their nationalities. They were Turks, Italian, Portuguese, Moroccans, or Yugoslavians, and as such, separate from and outside of the German nation.

Starting in the 1990s growing numbers of immigrants, among them many Turks, started acquiring German citizenship which triggered yet another relabeling of groups of immigrants and increasingly also citizens. The term *ausländische Mitbürger* (foreign co-residents or co-citizens) made an appearance. Faced with a wave of immigrants from eastern European countries and war refugees from the former Yugoslavia, Iraq, and Afghanistan labeling became increasingly difficult. Understanding national and especially immigration affairs progressively more in larger European terms (the Schengen Agreement went into effect in 1995), terminologies across Europe also became increasingly similar. In the late 1990s the term migrant (and increasingly also immigrant) came to describe the vastly diverse population of non-ethnic German residents. The constant German quest or obsession to define, label, and re-label the latter groups signifies a concern with maintaining clear boundaries between "us" and "them." Labels betray the sense that "outsiders" become ever closer to be "insiders," a circumstance that many politicians and ethnic German deeply resented. These labels and the boundaries drawn by them illustrate irrational fears of outsiders becoming equals in the nation-state. Hence ever-changing labels first and foremost served to maintain lines of difference and exclusion. The third or even fourth generation of descendants of the *Gastarbeiter* continued to be labeled as outsiders in ever more hair-splitting and often demeaning ways.

The change of German citizenship law in 2000 made it much easier for long-term residents to acquire German citizenship, and for the first time allowed children born in Germany to automatically receive a German passport. This first shift away from an almost exclusively *jus sanguinis* to a mixed form of *jus soli* (born in the country) and *jus sanguinis* citizenship further complicated the position and terminology with regard to the new German citizens. Instead of simply referring to naturalized citizens as Germans or German-Turks or Greek-Germans, more terms were invented to signify the fine-tuned exclusion of what were now national citizens. The label of individuals *mit Migrationshintergrund* (with a background of migration or migratory roots) was invented to refer in particular to the younger generations of naturalized citizens, but also those of mixed parentage. An individual *mit Migrationshintergrund* is a person who either was not born in Germany, or has at least one parent that was not born in Germany.[16] In 2012, about 20 percent of the country's population (about 16.3 million out of 81.9 million) was identified as having migratory roots (Statistisches Bundesamt 2013: 7).

Twenty-first century ongoing processes of exclusionary labeling coincided with a dramatic wave of Islamophobia after 9/11. A dramatically diverse population of migrants, refugees, and (long) naturalized citizens who were from Muslim majority countries were rapidly re-labeled once more: this time as "Muslims" (Peter 2010: 127). At the same time the citizenship law of 2000 and ongoing processes of naturalization were producing ever larger numbers of German Muslims, a circumstance that struck segments of the dominant population as problematic.

Religion, which in the 1970s and 1980s had played a negligible role in debates about migration, suddenly moved to the forefront of public and political debates. Italians, Portuguese, Serbians, or Croatians largely remained "migrants" and their religions secondary. Turks, Moroccans, Egyptians, or Bosnians, in contrast, were increasingly and indiscriminately labeled as Muslims. The label "Muslim" came with resentment, fear, suspicion, and the assumption that Muslims were inherently different; and often unwilling to become loyal citizens in a liberal democracy. The term furthermore drew yet another line between ("real") Germans and Muslim Germans. The emergence of "Muslims" as a constituency and simultaneously as a "problem" is a national and European phenomenon.

Religion, Religiosity, and Ethnicity

Muslims practice their religion and traditions in a multitude of ways from a very committed religiosity to atheism. For some, every letter of the religion must be respected, while others do not care at all. Some practice their religion because their families have always practiced. Others practice by their own personal decision, and seek to learn more about Islam and become more pious. Yet others were born Muslims and do not practice on a daily basis, but celebrate Muslim holidays. For some being Muslim is a cultural aspect of their lives, for others it is a political commitment. There are no dividing lines between these diverse individuals. Regardless of this vast specter of possibilities and blurred lines, there are individuals and groups who, in particular in the last two decades, have increasingly adopted Islam, Muslim theology and practices as defining elements of their lives, and very importantly also their public identities and engagements (Deeb 2006; Ismail 2006; Keaton 2006; Bullock 2005; Werbner 2002; Tarlo 2010; Backer 2009; Kandemir 2005; Wilson 2010). Political adversity toward all things Muslim has led some individuals to re-/claim Muslim cultural and religious identities (Modood 2007: 134).

In addition to diverse religiosities, concrete lifeworlds unfold on the background of specific ethno-cultural traditions which are in constant flux (Werbner 2002; Nökel 2002; Gerlach 2006). To be a Turkish Muslim in an Anatolian village in the 1960s differed from being the grandchild of that person in Germany in the twenty-first century (Schiffauer 1987, 1991, 1992, 2000). These lifeworlds, in turn, differ from those of war refugees from Afghanistan, Bosnia, Iraq, or Syria. Each individual or group is involved in cultural, religious, and social negotiations and transformations as they encounter concrete lifeworlds and situations. Living in a society which views Muslims with suspicion, even the most secular and atheist Muslims who might care little about Islam, its teachings and practices are routinely reminded of their (ill-defined) Muslim identity. The category "Muslim" sticks to individuals and they have to maneuver its assigned characteristics.[17] Being Muslim in Germany is a complex position, where assigned, inherited, and chosen elements of identity and religiosity interact in intricate manners (Brubaker 2012).

Dominant German media and political discourses have little understanding of Muslim diversity and the complexity of Muslim identities and religiosities. One frequently reads reports about *der Islam* ("the" Islam)[18] and *die Muslime* ("the" Muslims). *Der Islam* is often depicted as a stagnant religion, that tends to foster violence and war (the little understood concept of *jihad* is said to be central here), that oppresses women, and resists change and modernization.[19] *Die Muslime* are said to often be unwilling to integrate into German society (*integrationsunwillig*), occasionally practice forced marriage (*Zwangsheirat*), sometimes they are even suspects to terrorism. Some Muslims are said to conspire to Islamize Germany and set up an Islamic state based on the *sharia* (Muslim law/legal system).[20] Such simplistic representations and arguments create images of Muslims as a surprisingly coherent or monolithic group that blindly and lock-step follows Islam—however defined—and is thus hard to "integrate" into liberal German society. These images suggest that Muslim lives are narrowly circumscribed by religious laws and customs and leave little room for individual religiosities, religious transformation, and cultural creativity. Some pundits insist that Muslims withdraw into isolated and socially disconnected *Parallelgesellschaften* (parallel societies). Nothing could be further from the reality of ordinary Muslims' lives. In fact, in German cities there are no ethnic or religious ghettos where one ethnicity or religion dominate all else. There are multi-ethnic quarters like Nordbahnhof in Stuttgart, Hochfeld in Duisburg (Ceylan 2006), Wilhelmsburg in Hamburg (Tietze 2001), or most famously Kreuzberg and Neukölln in Berlin (Mandel 2008; Ewing 2008b; Kaya 2001),[21] which in the popular imagination might be the homes of Muslim "parallel societies," but in reality are multi-ethnic quarters that include ethnic German and diverse other residents. In Stuttgart, quarters like Hallschlag, Nordbahnhof, Zuffenhausen, or Bad Cannstatt are sometimes referred to as problematic. What sets these quarters apart from others is their larger percentage of migrant populations (51.3 and 49.1 percent for the latter two quarters; Landeshauptstadt Stuttgart 2013: 300; 96),[22] their working-class histories (less so for Bad Cannstatt), and their relatively larger number of families with children, lower average household incomes, and higher rate of recipients of social welfare (ibid.). None of these quarters are self-contained or disconnected from other quarters and urban circuits.

Contrary to such simplistic images, Islam, Muslims, and Muslim practices and religiosities constitute a religious and cultural field that is part of a larger discursive tradition (T. Asad 1986) where individuals, formal, and informal groups inter-/act on many stages. In daily encounters, these participants formulate the outlines of a Muslim public sphere, which overlaps and is linked with other spheres, such as ethnically based ones (e.g. Turkish, Arab, or Bosnian), those based on shared histories of migration (cross-ethnic associations), and those based on non-religious and non-ethnic issues (e.g. sports, unions, professional associations). People of diverse backgrounds interact in these fields in planned and unplanned, conscious and unconscious, harmonious and confrontational ways. In minute encounters, ordinary people configure identities and practices; they voice content or discontent, argue and formulate compromises.

The boundaries of religiously inspired civic participation and cultural production are blurred. When does an encounter include religion? Do Muslims exclusively interact as Muslims? When does Islam become a factor in a situation or interaction? Certainly, there are central actors (Imams, mosque association members, active mosque goers) and spaces (mosques), but there are many others who are much harder to categorize. Pious individuals are citizens, workers, students, housewives, parents, and neighbors and they spend more time in these capacities than in their houses of worship and religious centers. Obviously, not all Muslims are mosque goers. Some never set foot in mosques. There are those who are pious, but practice their faith at home. And there are those who are neither pious nor attend mosques, and prefer spaces of popular entertainments like soccer fields and bars. Anybody who claims to be a Muslim, or claims to have been born Muslim vaguely falls into this field of interaction. Non-Muslims play a role as interlocutors of Muslims. When Muslims bring gifts of food to non-Muslim neighbors for holidays, and receive gifts in return for Christian feasts, this is an important interaction that affects both parties. When a non-Muslim woman complains that she feels embarrassed about sitting on her balcony in her bikini in the summer, as the Muslim neighbor whose wife wears a headscarf, or even the wife herself, might peek over, then this encounter is similarly situated in the larger urban cultural field of Islam, as Muslim notions (modesty) and practices (to cover the female body) are at stake.

Understanding that the field of Islam, Muslims, and Muslim cultures and religiosities is a vast one with blurred boundaries, I will in the following largely limit my analysis to individuals and groups who take religion and religiosities as central features of their lives. My interest more specifically is in the creation and negotiation of urban religious lives, spaces, interactions, and identities. My goal is not to chronicle the "integration" of Muslims, but the configuration of urban Islam and Muslim lives as part of a larger geography of urban religions and religiosities.

Urban Religions

The study of urban religions, urban religious cultures, immigrant religions, the role of religiosity in the lives of ordinary urban dwellers, and the overall role of religion in cities, has gained momentum since the turn of the twenty-first century.

Based on earlier work, often conducted by scholars of religion and cultural geographers, a growing number of scholars of a variety of disciplinary backgrounds have in the last decade taken a keen interest in religion, and the contribution of faith-based organizations to urban cultures and transformations.

Robert Orsi (1985, 1999, 2005), a historian of religion, insists on the significance of religion, religiosity, and religious practices for many ordinary urbanites, and identifies the role of religion as a critical element in urban processes. Orsi's *The Madonna of 115th Street* (1985) inserts religion into debates of urban cultures. Similarly, the contributors to *Gods of the City* (Orsi 1999; among them two urban anthropologists, Brown 1999; Kugelmass 1999) assert that religion is not only *in*, but very crucially *of* the city. Orsi points to the importance of religion beyond houses of worship noting that urban religions "do not exist in a sacred space apart, but in the midst of social life" (1999a: 57). Lily Kong, an urban geographer, has been instrumental in "mapping new geographies of religion" pointing to the role of religion in contemporary cities (2001; see also 1990, 2010). She argues that religion, religiosities, and religious practices are dynamic components in the negotiation of urban lives and spaces (Kong 1993).

More recently, a number of anthropologists have studied the role of Islam in urban transformations in contemporary Muslim-majority cities (Deeb 2006; Deeb and Harb 2013; White 2002; BouAkar 2012; Henkel 2007; Fawaz 2009; Harb and Deeb 2011, 2013). Others analyze Muslim religiosities and everyday religious practices and their spatial impact on cities (Desplat and Schulz 2012), paying attention to social tension and conflict (Keaton 2006; Asher 2012; Zöller 2012). Some examine the role of Muslim communities in recent transformations in European cities (Ghodsee 2010; Ceylan 2006; Mattausch and Yildiz 2009). In Europe announcements to construct a mosque have frequently caused controversies about the role of Islam in cities and Europe at large (Cesari 2005; McLoughlin 2005; Astor 2012; Hüttermann 2006; Lauterbach and Lottermoser 2009). Such controversies often initiate broader debates about Islam and religion in secular cities (Beaumont and Baker 2011; Molendijk et al. 2010; Wilford 2010; Olson et al. 2013).

Debates about the position of Islam have in recent years dominated popular and scholarly debates about religion in many European cities. Less has been said and written about other (immigrant) religious communities. In order to analyze the inclusion of Muslims into German cityscapes, it is helpful to take a broader analytical look at urban religious transformations. In the process of large-scale immigration, German cities have experienced considerable religious transformations that are largely neglected and have not been sufficiently analyzed. If urban religions are discussed in the case of Germany, the debates focus on the declining membership of traditional Christian churches (Lutheran-Protestant and Catholic) and the rise of Islam. Little attention is paid to the broader transformations of the urban religious topography that include the arrival and localization of other religions, like Hinduism, the recent growth in Jewish communities (immigrants from the former Soviet Union), and the rapidly growing numbers of Orthodox and other Christian churches (Costabel 2009).

Since the turn of the twenty-first century, a growing number of scholars have explored immigrant religious associations in Europe and North America (Badillo 2006; Foley and Hodge 2007; Jeung 2004; Cesari 2010; Bowen 2010). They asked questions about the role of religion in (secular) cities (Stepick et al. 2009; ter Haar 1998; Livezey 2000; Tweed 2002), reflected about the neglected role of space in the study of religion (Knott 2005; Tweed 2008), and analyzed place-making aspects of religious practices (Smith 1987). Drawing on theoretical debates about the history, definition, and validity of the concept of the secular (T. Asad 1993, 2003; Calhoun et al. 2011; Habermas 2006; Casanova 1994; Butler et al. 2011), and discussions about the role of religion in urban processes (Cloke and Beaumont 2010; Kong 2001; Hervieu-Léger 2002), researchers examine faith-based associations and their impact on urban spatialities and transformations. Examining especially the expanding landscapes of immigrant faith-based organizations, some voice doubts about the (imagined) secular nature of US and European cities. However, to speak of post-secular cities and spaces, does not imply "an epochal shift from a *secular* age . . . to a *postsecular* age" (Cloke and Beaumont 2012:3; emphasis in the original), but "might usefully be understood as marking some limitations of the secularization thesis" (ibid.). The growing number of faith-based organizations (including soup kitchens or food banks) represents broader negotiations of post-secular cityscapes. Faith-based associations and their religiously inspired place-making and participation (e.g. Levitt 2008) need to be examined in the broader framework of the "encroachment" of the religious onto dominant (often incompletely) secularly defined European cityscapes (Butler et al. 2011). This is not a new phenomenon, but represents the renewed and more self-conscious acts of religiously inspired actors and faith-based institutions which have always existed in western cities, but have gained new prominence in the face of large scale immigration. Comparing the experiences of different immigrant religious communities (e.g. Shah et al. 2012; Peach and Gale 2003) it becomes quickly apparent that some problems that Muslim communities face (especially with regard to mosque constructions) are not unique but are shared with other new urban religions.

Taking evidence and inspiration from vibrant debates in the study of urban religions, I seek to reposition the study of Islam and Muslims in Stuttgart in these debates. Instead of focusing on Islam as the singular "foreign" religion that impinges of an otherwise religiously well settled cityscape, I understand pious Muslims as one group of believers that configure a place and home for themselves in a dynamic urban religious topography where many different groups and congregations work to define their spaces, practices, and forms of participation.

Urban Culture and Small Spaces

In his otherwise pessimistic account about the "liquid times" of the early twenty-first century, Zygmunt Bauman identifies cities and in particular neighborhoods and small urban spaces as possible sites of hope and inspiration (2007: 79). Urban quarters, and here especially, multi-ethnic working-class neighborhoods, which often carry a heavy share of social problems, nonetheless are always communities "in the making" (P.M. Smith quoted in Bauman 2007: 79). In neighborhood spaces, global trends and dynamics are lived and negotiated by ordinary people in minute encounters. It is worth quoting Bauman's understanding of such spaces at length:

> It is around places that human experience tends to be formed and gleaned, that life-sharing is attempted to be managed, that life meanings are conceived, absorbed and negotiated. And it is *in* places that human urges and desires are gestated and incubated, that they live in the hope of fulfillment, run the risk of frustration—and are indeed, more often than not, frustrated and strangled.
> Contemporary cities are for that reason the stages or battlegrounds on which global powers and stubbornly local meanings and identities meet, clash, struggle and seek a satisfactory, or just bearable, settlement—a mode of cohabitation that is hoped to be a lasting peace but as a rule proves to be only an armistice; brief interval to repair broken defences and redeploy fighting units (2007: 81, emphasis in the original).

In a world of global links and processes, the lives of most people remain surprisingly local and indeed neighborhood and small urban spaces remain the most feasible for individuals and groups to participate in and to possibly change. Bauman explains: "For most of us and for most of the time, local issues seem to be *the only* ones we can 'do something about'—influence, repair, improve, redirect. It is only in local matters that our actions or inaction can be credited with 'making a difference,' since for the state of those other 'superlocal' affairs there is (or so we are repeatedly told by our political leaders and all other 'people in the know') 'no alternative'" (ibid.: 82; emphasis in the original).

Neighborhoods, where strangers share permanent and transient spaces (apartment buildings, streets, stores, public transportation) harbor great potentials for cultural negotiations and changes. Constant proximity and interaction with neighbors and strangers is a "permanent modus vivendi" (Bauman 2007:86), where participants constantly observe each other. Old and new forms and practices are "experimented with, tested and retested, and (hopefully) put into a shape that will make cohabitation with strangers palatable and life in their company livable" (ibid.). Arguing for urban spaces and processes that foster "mixophilia" (versus "mixophobia"; ibid.), Bauman hopes for shared experiences and creative encounters of difference.

Resented Inclusion

Examining pious Muslim participation and citizenship, and the cultural creativity of multicultural neighborhoods, it is paramount to recognize the reality of everyday discrimination, adversity and prejudices that Muslims often face.[23] I am acutely aware of the existence of xenophobia, racism, and Islamophobia in Germany—on private, public, and institutional levels. Without exception, Muslims (and other migrants) who I worked with had stories about negative, offensive, and hateful experiences. From being spat at, to rude remarks ("why do you people have so many children?"), to insulting ignorance/curiosity ("why do you wear a headscarf?"), to continued questions about their origins ("no, really what country are you from?"), being a (visible) Muslim/a in the German public sphere can be a daunting experience. Several individuals related particularly harsh experiences when looking for apartments ("no headscarves in this building," or "if your wife wears a headscarf, you cannot move in here"). Several scholars have chronicled the at times deeply humiliating and offensive experiences of in particular Turkish immigrants (Ewing 2008a, 2008b; Mandel 2008; Partridge 2012). My intention is not to add another account about discrimination and xenophobia in Germany. Instead I examine creative, yet at times painful processes of inclusion, participation, and cultural production. Examining inclusion and participation, necessarily illustrates processes of exclusion. Turkish immigrants in particular, but pious Muslims at large have often been targeted for their alleged unwillingness to integrate and participate.[24] There is no blame for social ills that would not be piled onto Turks and Muslims. Whether taking jobs away from native populations, abusing the welfare system, fostering Islamic extremism, militancy, and fanaticism, abusing and locking up their wives and daughters, forcing their daughters to marry obscure cousins, refusing to learn German, not supporting their children's schoolwork, raising sons prone to violence and crime, withdrawing into parallel societies, or practicing animal cruelty, Muslims are blamed for numerous social problems. Despite this flood of blame, accusation, disrespect, resentment, suspicion, rejection, and discrimination, there are tens of thousands individuals who disregard such sentiments and wholeheartedly plunge into work places, schools, universities, institutions, and the public sphere and participate in a plethora of activities and debates.

Islam is a German religion and an integral part of complex cityscapes (Ceylan 2006; Schiffauer 2008; Mannitz 2006; Tietze 2001: 219). The central lens through which to understand diverse Muslims is not "integration," but participation and citizenship (T. Ramadan 2003a, 2003b; Modood 2005). Thus my analysis proceeds from the assumption that societies are dynamic fields where actors and concepts are under constant negotiations (see Modood 2007: 146). Nations, national identities, and notions of good citizenship are flexible and often most successful when they are able to respond to social transformations and global challenges (ibid.).

Citizenship is not written in stone as a priori characteristic of some individuals (e.g. those who carry the national passport) but is up for grabs for all those who share the fate of the community and wish to responsibly participate in the making of a shared future. While passports play a role in the making of national politics, on the level of local participation and debates, the actual dedication, involvement, and participation in the locality, in this case the city, are more important.

Equal participation is based on recognition. With regard to Muslims this means that differences that are often viewed with suspicion and fear need to be recognized as legitimate and positive differences. Recognition would ideally turn negatively perceived difference into positive difference that could be instrumentalized for the benefit of society (Modood 2007). Recognition can be manifold and might imply different aspects for diverse constituencies. For Muslims, this implies not only the creation of yet another space that duplicates those created for other groups, but also involves the rethinking of the concept of the secular (ibid.). This will not happen overnight. Instead "recognition . . . must be pragmatically and experimentally handled, and civil society must share the burden of representation" (ibid.: 82). Notions of citizenship need to include engagements with society that transcend ownership of passports and voting in elections (Soysal 1994; Sassen 1999). Active citizenship is the conscious sharing of the responsibility to maintain and improve society (Modood 2005, 2007). Social or cultural citizenship (Sassen 1999: 123) is lived in multiple relationships and civic participation.

Small transformations like the Imam's presence in the New First-Graders celebration need to be analyzed in their larger urban, national, and global framework. There are dominant and much-celebrated images of globalizing cities and their high-tech and globally linked landscapes and super-productive upscale generic modern citizens (Sassen 2001). These cities are caught in an ever faster race for global recognition and financial investments. In order to become or remain a valued location, cities have to invest in infrastructure and very importantly also in cultural features. They need to join the circus of national and global spectacles to prove that they can live up to globalized standards of organization and representation. Cities spend millions to accommodate first rate theaters, art shows, film or music festivals, and very importantly also global sports events. In addition to fulfilling this catalogue of cultural and financial conditions, a "truly" globalized city needs to flaunt its cultural vibrancy, and the diversity of its citizenry. This diversity is celebrated in politicians' statements or municipal brochures. International cultural fairs, visiting artists and official cultural exchanges are the pride of municipalities and urban elites (Schuster 2006). These often provide a sanitized and depoliticized version of diversity, in which the difficult reality of multi-ethnic neighborhoods does not play a role (Modan 2007, 2008; Cahill 2007; Newman 2011; Ingram 2009). Official celebrations of cultures and diversity contrast the lived realities of neighborhoods like Nordbahnhof where every apartment building, classroom, or line at the supermarket's cash register is globalized or multicultural. Thus an Imam might easily fit into a local (if not to say quaint) celebration. Nobody would object to that. Indeed Nordbahnhof as a multi-ethnic neighborhood might be a perfect location for such an event, but most observers would not take this as a model for dominant society. The glittery globalized city of international fairs and artists is heralded as the multicultural or global future, whereas existing globalized neighborhoods or institutions like backyard mosques are relegated to the (ironic) status of local and hence not worthy of being a model for the (globalized) future. Places like Nordbahnhof are central sites in the making of multi-ethnic twenty-first-century German cities. An Imam at a public celebration is not a quaint expression of an irrelevant local quarter or a dangerous parallel society, but a cultural detail that foreshadows tomorrow's cityscape. Inclusion of pious Muslims might be an increasingly normalized feature in small contexts and localized platforms. Yet, it remains rare on larger political and cultural stages.[25]

(Muslim) Stuttgart

The city of Stuttgart is one of the wealthiest in Germany. The larger Stuttgart Metropolitan Area, the so-called Mittlerer Neckarraum, counts among the wealthier urban regions in Europe. With 600,000 residents Stuttgart is the sixth largest city in Germany after Berlin (3.4 million), Hamburg (1.75 million), Munich (1.3 million), Cologne (1 million), and Frankfurt (680,000). Stuttgart does not have the concentration of political power and innovative cultural production like Berlin, the financial power and centrality of Frankfurt, or the powerful fashion and film industries like Munich, or an ocean port and a concentration of the press like Hamburg, instead it is a high-tech, car, and banking city. In the early twenty-first century, Stuttgart—in the competition of German cities—scores by its global industries (most famously Mercedes, Porsche, and Bosch) and growing banking sector (second only to Frankfurt). Overall unemployment rates (5.8 percent, only Munich's rates is lower; Borgmann SZ 28.6.2008) are among the lowest in Germany and social programs and projects receive, not lavish, but good funding. While Stuttgarters experience considerable differences in wealth, income, and size and quality of housing, the differences are less pronounced than in other Germany cities (e.g. Berlin), and indeed seem benign when compared to many global cities.

At the turn of the twenty-first century, Stuttgart is the German metropolis with the largest share of residents who are either immigrants themselves or have backgrounds of migration (*Migrationshintergrund*).[26] In 2012, 39.9 percent of all Stuttgarters had a *Migrationshintergrund*. For those under the age of three years, the figure was 57.5 percent (Landeshauptstadt Stuttgart 2013: 12). About one fifth of Stuttgart's residents are foreign nationals (ibid.).

Examining the localization of Islam in Stuttgart, economic aspects without doubt play a role, but this process is not centrally marked by a fierce struggle over economic resources. It is much more of a cultural and political struggle. For instance, controversies over the construction of mosques are not about whether or not a community owns the funds to buy adequate real estate, but whether this real estate is made available to them. The position of Islam and Muslims in Stuttgart is neither characterized by ghettoization and grossly substandard housing conditions, nor dramatically high rates of unemployment. While some Muslims occupy the lower end of Stuttgart's rental market and experience higher rates of unemployment, Stuttgart does not share the social problems of some Parisian housing projects or British cities (e.g. Keaton 2006). In addition to the relative absence of severe poverty, Stuttgart has a reasonably well-funded landscape of social and cultural projects. Some cultural and social neighborhood centers are model projects that bespeak the city's financial circumstances and an overall willingness to support intercultural projects.

Despite its considerable Muslim population (almost 10 percent of the population, that is almost 60,000 people; Baden-Württemberg 2005: 10), Stuttgart, unlike other regional (e.g. Sindelfingen, Mannheim), German (e.g. Cologne, Duisburg), or European (e.g. Dublin, Rotterdam) cities, does not have a purpose built mosque. None of the city's mosques remotely has the exterior architecture of a mosque. Mosque architecture does not require many special features, indeed only a *mihrab* (niche to indicate the direction of prayer) and a possibly a *minbar* (pulpit) are necessary (Serageldin 1996a: 9). Yet, mosques in the Muslim world and in Muslim minority contexts frequently use an architectural grammar that makes mosques recognizable as such. Holod and Khan noted that mosques in the West often become symbolic statements that bespeak "the Muslim presence in non-Muslim countries" (1997: 227), and thus are distinct from their counterparts in the Muslim world. While prayer spaces can be arranged almost anywhere, mosques nonetheless are symbols of political contexts, history, community, and of money and power in both Muslim majority and minority contexts. Stuttgart's mosques offer little in terms of exterior architectural beauty, symbolic representation, or prestige. Situated in less than attractive quarters or industrial zones, these mosques are neither recognizable as such, nor can they serve as physical markers of communal pride or foster social recognition.

Over the years Stuttgart's Muslim spiritual geography has consolidated. Starting from late 1980 and gaining momentum in the 1990s some communities bought facilities. Stuttgart's mosques are predominantly located in defunct industrial facilities in marginal, distant and largely non-residential areas; many use less than perfect spaces. The search for the best-possible facilities continues to create a certain movement among communities. For instance, in 2007 a Moroccan community moved from rented to owned premises. In 2008, a Bosnian association moved from a smaller owned to a larger owned location. Another Bosnian association moved to larger facilities in the same year. A look at the metropolitan region indicates that Stuttgart might be a particularly resilient location with regard to mosque constructions, because several regional towns and cities boost purpose-built mosques. One of the largest mosques in the state is located in Sindelfingen, not far from the central Mercedes-Benz plant where migrant/immigrant workers have been employed for over half a century (Buchmeier SZ 15.12.2006). On a regular Friday about 1,000 men pray in this mosque's large prayer room (830 square meters), which is topped by a dome (14 meters in height; ibid.). The town of Schorndorf also has a purpose-built mosque complete with a minaret and 1,500 square meters of facilities (ibid.).

The topography of Stuttgart's mosques illustrates the position of Islam and Muslims in the city. At present the city has about twenty-five mosque associations. The mosque count remains imprecise as smaller associations come and go, and other associations avoid terms like Islam, Muslim, and mosque in their names. For example, one (Sufi-based) group is officially known as "Association of Turkish Parents." There is a core of about a dozen well-established communities (some in their third or fourth decades of operation) with larger premises and an array of services, activities, and programs for members and non-members. Marking these twenty-five associations on the map, one finds the not surprising pattern that, with one exception, they are located on the vague crescent of older industrial, now turned multi-ethnic quarters that curve around downtown.[27] Bad Cannstatt is the undisputed center of Muslim Stuttgart with eight mosques. Feuerbach has three, Zuffenhausen, Obertürkheim, Ost, Wangen, Süd, Mitte each have two. Stuttgart-Nord has one, which is located in the dense urban part of the quarter and not in its upscale hill section (Killesberg). Only an Afghan mosque, situated in Stuttgart-West, is outside the crescent pattern. Wealthier quarters like Sillenbuch, Möhringen, or Degerloch do not have mosques.[28] Stuttgart's mosques are almost exclusively situated in multi-ethnic working-class quarters. Of the six city quarters with the highest purchasing power, five did not have mosques. Of the eight quarters with the lowest purchasing power, six had mosques. Seven of the eight quarters with the highest rates of unemployment had mosques; the eight quarters with the lowest rates of unemployment did not have mosques. Similarly, the quarters with mosques have higher rate of social welfare recipients and lower rates of transfer to schools that prepare for university studies (Landeshauptstadt Stuttgart 2013). The quarters with mosques are the socially and economically more disadvantaged ones.

Stuttgart's mosque associations are registered legal associations (*Verein*). This status conveys advantages as German law favors this format of public organization. Associations are given certain privileges (e.g. access to facilities, possibilities of funding). Stuttgart's largest mosque (by space/size) is the Salam Mosque complex in Stuttgart-Feuerbach (Kuppinger 2010a, 2011b). Administered by the Turkish Presidency for Religious Affairs, this mosque is funded and organized by the Presidency's subsidiary, the DİTİB. Imams and female theologians or teachers of Islamic studies are sent and paid by the Turkish state. With its superior funding and vast spatial complex that yields considerable rental income from numerous stores, the Salam Mosque can—more than any other local mosque—engage in civic activities, invite visitors and delegations, and participate in the public sphere. Because of its size, activities, relative visibility, and its politically uncontroversial affiliation with the Turkish state, the Salam Mosque has emerged as "the" mosque in Stuttgart.

The Medina Mosque, run by the Milli Görüş (IGMG) association, claims to be the largest association (by membership) in Stuttgart. Because the IGMG is on the watch list of state security (Schiffauer 2010), the Medina Mosque is largely overlooked or outright boycotted with regard to inclusion in civic activities and events. Less political is the *Verein Islamischer Kulturzentren* VIKZ (Association of Islamic Cultural Centers). This association favors personal piety situating itself in a broader mystic tradition. The VIKZ or its regional LVIKZ (*Landesverband Verein Islamischer Kulturzentren*) provide the frame for the Hussein and the Takva Mosques.

Stuttgart has two Moroccan mosques, which in part has to do with the early and numerous arrivals of Moroccan workers in the 1960s. These mosques are not affiliated with national mosque associations. The largest Arab, but increasingly international mosque, is the Al-Nour Mosque. With a core of Palestinian, Egyptian, Syrian, and Lebanese members, this community is organizationally linked to the *Islamische Gemeinschaft in Deutschland* IGD (Islamic Community in Deutschland). The fourth Arab mosque, the Yassin Mosque, has common origins with the Al-Nour Mosque, but the two eventually split over theological questions. The Yassin Mosque, which is predominantly frequented by North Africans, in particular Algerians, tends to be stricter in some of their theological interpretations (e.g. with regard to gender segregation). Some of its members self-identify as *Salafi*. Their aim is to closely and literally follow the live and practices of the Prophet Muhammad in all aspects of their lives. The Yassin Mosque is not part of a national mosque association.

There are smaller congregations: some are well established (e.g. a Bosnian mosque), others are more recent (e.g. an Afghan mosque). Some only maintain a prayer room for men (e.g. a group from Bangladesh). Some communities are in flux as they articulate, improve, and enlarge their communities, activities, and facilities. One smaller Bosnian community recently moved to more spacious premises, which some of my interlocutors (in different contexts) agreed had been nicely renovated considering that this former warehouse facility had no windows. Figuring a well-liked ethnic German preacher, several people remarked in late 2008, that they liked to go there especially for holiday prayers. A small but growing number of younger, more savvy, mobile, and ethnically flexible individuals attend activities in two, three, or even four mosques (not including prayers that they might attend anywhere they happen to be).

In the wake of 9/11, Muslims were identified as a group that needed to be watched. In 2002 the Stuttgart police (*Polizeipräsidium Stuttgart*), added a special unit for Islamic affairs. In addition to regular criminal affairs, this unit was supposed to maintain contacts with mosques, identify problems, and cooperate with congregations. Simultaneously, local police departments established ties with mosques, where they offered programs about juvenile delinquency, drugs, or the dangers for youth on the Internet.

Even before 9/11, Muslims and non-Muslims, who worried about widespread Islamophobia formed platforms for more respectful dialogue. The Christian-Islamic Society (*Christlich-Islamische Gesellschaft Stuttgart e.V.*, CIG was founded in 1998. This society folded in 2013 as leading members thought that some of their goals had been achieved, but even more so because these activists had moved on to other engagements, and there continued to play central roles in debates about Islam and religion in Stuttgart. In 1999 the Society for Christian-Muslim Meeting and Cooperation (*Gesellschaft für Christlich-Islamische Begegnung und Zusammenarbeit e.V.*, CIBZ) followed. In 2003, the Coordination Council for Christian-Muslim Dialog was founded in the Stuttgart region (*Koordinationsrat des christlich-islamischen Dialogs e.V.*) which was to function as a national umbrella organization for Christian-Muslim interfaith dialog. There is an overlap of activists between these organizations.

These organizations organize activities, meetings, and lecture programs to disseminate information, and bring Muslims and non-Muslims together. Members or representatives of DİTİB, the LVIKZ mosques, the Al-Nour Mosque, the Milli Görüş Mosque, and the larger Bosnian mosque are involved in interfaith dialogue activities like a revolving *iftar* cycle (organized by CIBZ). Some mosque representatives and other activists are very visible and known in Muslim and non-Muslim circles and are frequently invited to public events and debates. They form the small informal core of the local pious Muslim public sphere and operate as Muslim contacts or spokespeople on cultural or political platforms. Most know each other.

Urban Fieldwork

This research is part of a longer intellectual and personal journey. I grew up in, what was in the 1960s and 1970s, a rural village that has since turned into a suburban town outside Stuttgart. I left the area in the 1980s to study and live first in Egypt and later in the United States. In Egypt I conducted many years of research on questions of urban communities, urban cultures, colonial urban histories, and globalizing urban transformations (e.g. 1998; 2001; 2004; 2006a, 2006b; 2014). I have also worked on emerging global Muslim consumer cultures (2009). In the summer of 2005 on a visit to my parents, I met up with three classmates with whom I had gone to school in the 1970s. We spent a long evening in a coffee shop under the open summer skies discussing all sorts of things, among them the role of Islam in Germany. As we stayed—past the coffee shop's closing time—I realized how urgent this debate was. I decided to refocus the project for my upcoming sabbatical from urban issues in Cairo to questions of Islam in Germany, or more specifically in nearby Stuttgart which combined my interest in urban cultures and my newfound quest to reconnect to political and cultural debates in Germany after an absence of twenty years.

To examine a phenomenon as complex as processes of participation and cultural creativity of pious Muslims in Stuttgart, multiple methodological tools and a number of research sites are necessary. I chose several central and more permanent field sites and some others where I conducted occasional or random observations, or where I attended specific events or activities. In these research venues I met many individuals. Some became close interlocutors, others became friends, and a few became very close friends. By way of these many helpful and open-hearted people, I met yet others and gained access to additional groups and spaces. Ultimately I was in the field wherever I was and went in the city at all times.

Before I moved to Stuttgart I conducted preliminary research to find the most suitable neighborhood to live in, and take as a central research site. My conditions were that it had to be a multi-ethnic neighborhood with available rental apartments. I narrowed my choice down to Nordbahnhof and Bad Cannstatt. In January 2006 I went to tour both neighborhoods and decided to go with Nordbahnhof as it was smaller and seemed more child-friendly, especially with regard to traffic, street spaces, and available greenery. In September 2006 we moved to Nordbahnhof. I registered my daughters, Tamima and Tala (eight and five years old in 2006) at the Park School. Several people warned me against sending them there, as the Park School had a "bad" reputation and middle-class parents are wary of this institution. This wariness in part bespeaks middle-class fears of immigrants (more than 80 percent of the school's students have backgrounds of migration). The girls started their German school career in September 2006 and had an excellent experience at the Park School. Nordbahnhof, its residents, its streets, playgrounds, stores, apartment buildings, the Park School, and the "Kulturhaus" (a successful multicultural neighborhood center) became some of my central field sites. Through the girls it was easy to meet some of their friends' parents. Early on I informed individuals and institutions that I was not only living in this neighborhood, but also conducting research about the neighborhood. In the Park School I served for one year as the parents' representative in Tala's class which gave me a better understanding of the school, and also allowed me to contribute and help with some school activities. I joined the Kulturhaus as a tutor in the afternoon homework program for students from fifth to ninth grades. Through this volunteer work I became familiar with the center's work and was later invited to help with other projects.

My arrival in Nordbahnhof coincided with the beginning of Ramadan. In search of public Ramadan events (mosques have some), I started calling mosques. As local mosques do not employ permanent personnel, this was not an easy task. I was lucky to establish a few contacts, had a first longer meeting with the president of a mosque association which eventually led to an invitation to an *iftar* (evening meal to break the fast). From this first contact and people I had met at this *iftar*, more contacts developed. For a while I worked to further all initial contacts, until three mosques emerged as particularly suitable research sites. I chose the Salam Mosque, the Hussein Mosque, and the Al-Nour Mosque as central research sites. These communities cover a broad specter of ethnic, religious, political, and local aspects, different types of spatial settings and contexts, and types of local involvement and participation. While these mosques and their congregations are not representative of all mosques, they provide a broad overview of sites, communities, and activities. In each mosque I focused my research on different aspects of communal lives and activities.

In addition to my neighborhood and mosque research, I tried to attend all/most larger public events to do with Islam and Muslim issues. At numerous lectures, panels, and conferences I met more individuals (Muslims and non-Muslims) who shared my interests. They guided me to other events, venues, and individuals. After a year of fieldwork I knew most of the central actors in the Muslim public sphere and non-Muslim activists involved in interfaith dialogue.

Overview

In the following chapters I analyze pious Muslim Stuttgart. I describe and examine individuals I met and spaces that I regularly visited. In each chapter I take a concrete urban context and analyze one element of Muslim lifeworlds, participation, and cultural production.

Chapter 1 chronicles the conflict over a planned mosque project in Stuttgart-Heslach. In 1999 the VIKZ bought a defunct factory and planned to convert it into a mosque complex. The announcement of these plans sparked a bitter controversy that involved numerous urban, regional, and even national constituencies. As Stuttgart's first mosque conflict, this encounter constitutes the first larger public debate about the role and position of pious Muslims in the city. Residents did not want a mosque in their neighborhood. The mosque association, used to decades of relative neglect, was ill-prepared to handle such public attention and controversy. Ultimately, despite the project's failure, this conflict made pious Muslims visible as a constituency and stakeholders in Stuttgart.

Chapter 2 focuses on the Al-Nour Mosque and examines experiences of pious individuals who are strengthening their faith, improving their pious and mundane lives and activities in the context of the mosque and beyond. I show how piety for most does not imply a withdrawal into a private world of mosques and worship, but involves the construction of a visibly pious persona and distinctly pious mode of public engagement. The construction of pious selves is not a hidden exercise.

Ensuing practices are eventually carried into public spaces (e.g. school, work) where they are lived and defended against prejudices in the secular public sphere.

Chapter 3 introduces six individuals who act as pious Muslims in their daily lives and different public contexts. Often unnoticed by dominant society, pious Muslims have carved out spaces for themselves, their families, and communities that are locally shaped and connected. I challenge stereotypes of "the Muslim" who stands at a distance to mainstream society. The men and women introduced in this chapter represent the diversity of Muslim Stuttgart with regard to gender, age, class, education, ethnicity, religiosity, and types of social and political engagement and participation. These individuals illustrate that Islam is a German religion, and that many pious Muslims are engaged civic participants.

Chapter 4 examines widespread fears and resentment of Islam. I describe and analyze an exhibition entitled "The Abused Religion: Islamists in Germany" that was on display in Stuttgart in 2007. This exhibition claimed not to speak about ordinary Muslims, but only aimed to depict the dangers of Islamists. However, its design and implicit message were more far-reaching. The chapter chronicles a walk through the exhibition and analyzes its overt and subtle messages. Examining the fine-tuning of the exhibition, I demonstrate the powerful nature of such informational tools. I further discuss the controversial remark of the German President that "Islam is part of Germany" which caused considerable debate and controversy in the fall of 2010. Analyzing these concrete examples I illustrate how pervasive Islamophobia is in Germany, and how easily anti-Muslim sentiments can be mobilized in the public sphere.

Chapter 5 examines the localization of the Hussein Mosque. I introduce the old village of Zuffenhausen and illustrate how it has over the centuries witnessed travelers and armies passing through, and absorbed diverse newcomers. I chronicle the village's transformation in the late nineteenth century into an urban industrial quarter. I introduce the Hussein Mosque, its larger historical and religious context, and some of its activities. I describe how the mosque came to be seen as "our mosque" by many in the quarter. I illustrate how processes of localization were neatly negotiated to ensure long-term acceptance and civic inclusion. I argue that the Hussein Mosque's success is not based on a dramatically altered public opinion about Muslims and mosques, but on the mosque president's, board members,' and community members' close cooperation with the local council and active participation in the quarter.

Chapter 6 introduces the neighborhood of Nordbahnhof and illustrates how this multi-ethnic working-class quarter has for more than 100 years been a place where new cultural practices were initiated, and notions of what it means to be a Stuttgarter were negotiated to become more inclusive. Urban quarters bring diverse residents together as neighbors, shoppers, parents of school children, and users of public spaces. "Talking" and "testing" Islamic practices on a neighborhood level is an overlooked crucial element in the configuration of pious Muslim lifeworlds. I introduce and examine mundane moments of cultural negotiation and production where Muslims and others remake existing neighborhood cultures.

As a conclusion I examine the role of individual mobilities in the articulation of the city's pious Muslim geography. I illustrate how younger individuals by way of their mobilities create multilayered connections, moments of cooperation, and shared platforms that consolidate nascent urban Muslim spiritual geographies. The urban mobility of these young people brings the earlier globalized mobility of their migrant parents and grandparents full-circle as they inscribe pious Muslim practices and circuits into the contemporary cityscape. While still a work in progress, pious Muslims have found a home and space for themselves in Stuttgart. They have become Muslim Stuttgarters.

Notes

1. All personal, place, and mosque names (unless otherwise indicated) are pseudonyms. I use the real names of city quarters.
2. The remade celebration was a success and became normalized. I attended another such celebration in 2010.
3. An example of such writing is Thilo Sarrazin's *Deutschland schafft sich ab* [Germany eliminates itself, 2010].
4. David McMurray (2000) neatly chronicles the experiences of a Moroccan migrant in Germany, and his family back home in Morocco.
5. Haider noted for a makeshift arrangement in England "it was the practice that mattered" (1996: 36).
6. A Catholic church close to Nordbahnhof for several decades had both German and Italian services. Only recently they "reunited" the two communities for lack of sufficient members on both sides.
7. Not a pseudonym. Interview July 30, 2007.
8. A visit to the large mosque in Dublin proves Mr. Can right: on the *Eid al-Fitr* holiday I encountered thousands of multicultural worshippers at this mosque located in a middle-class residential neighborhood.
9. http://www.ditib.de.
10. http://www.igmg.de.
11. I am grateful to Ayşe Almila Akça for providing examples of this.
12. http://www.igd-online.de.
13. This representation has not been undisputed. Many—less pious—Muslims resent the relative monopoly of mosques and mosque associations to speak for (all) Muslims.
14. The Green and Social Democratic state government that took office in 2011 abolished the test in the same year.
15. The following discussion centrally draws on the works of Riem Spielhaus (2011, 2013) and Yasemin Yıldız (1999, 2009).
16. The bureaucratic definition of an individual mit Migrationshintergrund reads: "alle nach 1949 auf das heutige Gebiet der Bundesrepublik Deutschland Zugewanderten, sowie alle in Deutschland geborenen Ausländer und alle in Deutschland als Deutsche Geborenen mit zumindest einem zugewanderten oder als Ausländer in Deutschland geborenen Elternteil" (Statistisches Bundesamt 2013: 6).

17. The Chair of the Green Party, Cem Özdemir, is a good example. Starting his career on a distinctly secular platform, he has over the years, nevertheless, been consulted or interviewed on topics concerning Islam. (See also Özdemir 1997, 1999, 2002.)
18. Religions take a definite article in German, hence *der Islam*, also *das Christemtum* (Christianity) und *das Judentum* (Judaism).
19. Udo Ulfkotte has been notorious for fostering such fears. The titles of some of his books *Prophets of Terror* 2001; *The War in our Cities* 2003; *Holy War in Europe* 2007) speak for themselves.
20. See the cover of *Der Spiegel* No.13 on March 26, 2007, which reads: "Mecca Germany: The Silent Islamization."
21. Kreuzberg has in recent years undergone rapid gentrification.
22. Nordbahnhof and Hallschlag are subsections of larger quarters (*Bezirk*). No numbers for individuals with migratory backgrounds are available for these quarters. There are however figures for the share of foreign residents. In Hallschlag 45.8 percent of the residents hold foreign passports, in Nordbahnhof the figure is 48.9 percent. The figure for Stuttgart is 16.7 percent (Landeshauptstadt Stuttgart 2006: 107; 59; 16).
23. Damani Partridge coined the term "exclusionary incorporation" (2012: 21). Conceptually I follow his lead, but I prefer to use the term "resented inclusion."
24. Trica Keaton uses the term "suitable enemies" for the case of French Muslims of North/West African descent (2006: 7).
25. Jytte Klausen's (2005) study about the new European Muslim elite (political and other) predominantly includes more secularly inclined individuals. There are numerous Muslims (e.g. Cem Özdemir, Lale Akgün) in German politics, arts, and public life (e.g. Fatih Akin, Feridun Zaimoğlu, Serdar Somonçu,), but most operate on a secular platform. (See also Akgün 2008; Zaimoğlu 1998, 2000, 2003, 2005; Somonçu 2004, and Akin's well known movies, e.g., *Kurz und schmerzlos*, 1998; *Gegen die Wand*, 2004; *Auf der anderen Seite*, 2007).
26. While this category (*mit Migrationshintergrund*) remains problematic, it is frequently used in public debates.
27. This mapping is based on locations in 2007.
28. In 2008 a smaller Bosnian mosque moved to the outskirts of the wealthier quarter of Botnang, which constitutes a break with the crescent patterns of the local mosque-scape.

CHAPTER 1

Arrival

In December 1999, the Association of Islamic Cultural Centers (*Verband der Islamischen Kulturzentren*, VIKZ) bought an old factory compound in the multi-ethnic neighborhood of Stuttgart-Heslach. The association paid DM 4.6 million for the industrial facility and planned to remodel the large structure into an extensive mosque and community complex. Within weeks of this real estate transaction, part of the local population was up in arms against the proposed project. Residents feared that the mosque project might turn Heslach into "a ghetto for institutions that nobody liked" (Osswald SZ 27.1.2000). Some residents threatened to sell their houses and leave the quarter, if the mosque complex materialized. Local politicians voiced fears about the "social balance" of the quarter (ibid.). The local council (*Bezirksbeirat*) quickly announced that it would discuss this project at its next meeting (ibid.). The purchase of the defunct industrial complex and the mosque association's plans to create an extensive community complex, including educational and meeting facilities, marked the beginning of a bitter conflict that soon engulfed not only the local community and council, but became a citywide, indeed state-wide, affair.

The conflict erupted suddenly and caught local constituencies by surprise. The mosque association, which had been in contact with municipal bodies before the purchase of the factory, had naively assumed that once the real estate transaction was complete, they could quickly handle obligatory bureaucratic hurdles necessary to transform the former factory into a religious community center, and soon after start to renovate the complex. The respective municipal bodies similarly foresaw no problems and accommodated the purchase of the factory. Most residents, however, were completely surprised by the project. They questioned the need for a mosque complex and indeed for any mosque facility regardless of its type or size in their quarter. Some quickly took up their rhetorical arms and vehemently opposed the project before they had seen any details, or learned much about the mosque association. The ensuing public debate was marked by considerable prejudice and resentment against Muslims and their communities. Ignorant, crude, and often offensive statements characterized the arguments of some mosque opponents. For many residents, a mosque was utterly out of the question as a neighbor, regardless of the specific circumstances, or characteristics of the sponsoring mosque association. For the next three years the mosque association, its national umbrella association, the local council, individual citizens, community associations, political parties, the city council, the mayor of Stuttgart, media, and courts fought passionate rhetorical, administrational, and legal battles about whether this mosque complex could be realized. In the end the mosque association was defeated and the city bought the compound. The mosque never materialized.

The Heslach mosque controversy revolved around concrete local, spatial, and larger political questions: If a mosque complex was to be built, what would be its adequate size? What was a local mosque and what was a regional community center? What kind of activities and programs would turn a local mosque into a regional center (which would be against building codes in a largely residential neighborhood)? Was a local mosque necessary in Heslach? How many mosques did a city like Stuttgart need? For some residents, the proposed project was an immediate object of contention, which they wanted to prevent at any price—without a second look or further questions. Beyond this not-in-my-backyard attitude, many mosque adversaries had little interest in political or philosophical reflection. For other residents, local and urban groups, and some representatives of political parties and the media, the Heslach controversy triggered long overdue debates about the localization of Islam, the civic participation of Muslims in urban public and cultural spheres, and larger transformations in a multi-ethnic and multi-religious city. In addition to questions about the role and place of a mosque in Heslach, and more generally mosques in Stuttgart, these discussants pointed to the changing demographics of the city and the resulting necessity of serious engagement with local Muslim communities, their civic rights, and religious needs. Together with the arguments of the mosque association, these critical voices countered anti-Muslim sentiments and attempted to direct the debate into a more analytical and constructive direction. This small but growing number of discussants understood that this controversy was not simply about the size of a specific mosque or the concrete local or regional outreach of one concrete Muslim community, but about the role and position of pious Muslims and their communities in the city. After half a century of presence in Stuttgart, Muslim communities were striving for more suitable and very importantly permanent homes in the city. Such a home would not only accommodate the spiritual, social, and cultural needs of community members, but would also serve as a home space from which communities would enter and engage the urban public sphere.

As a result of the Heslach conflict, questions concerning the visibility, civic participation, cultural production and citizenship of pious Muslims were permanently installed in public debates and municipal politics. Muslims had entered the urban public sphere, even if their roles remained contested. Emerging from disputes about the concrete nature and function of one mosque, some non-Muslim individuals and constituencies tried to understand Muslim communal needs and activities. In the conflict's aftermath concrete activities and resources for Muslim localization were hesitantly designed and implemented. The needs of Muslims were, on a larger scale, for the first time publically discussed and acknowledged. Additional and more detailed questions entered the urban public sphere und debates. What indeed were the functions of a mosque in a German city? Who is entitled to speak for Muslims and their needs in public debates? What are the legitimate rights of Muslims and their communities in a neighborhood and city? How can Muslim communities become visible, respected, and engaged urban constituencies? How can Muslim communities interact and cooperate with other religious communities and civic associations?

This chapter examines the Heslach mosque conflict that unfolded between 1999 and 2002. I chronicle the conflict, analyze arguments of mosque proponents and opponents, and illustrate how Islam emerged as a topic of urban debate. The Heslach controversy illustrates that after fifty years of residence, pious Muslims and their communities still face considerable obstacles and resentments when they voice plans to purchase premises, and even worse, they encounter outright hostility when they plan to build a "real" mosque (including architectural features such as domes or minarets). Having a space in which to live one's communal life and to negotiate a local role is essential to meaningful civic participation. Permanent spaces signify not only control over one's limited spaces, but denote a sense of arrival, home, and participation. The Heslach controversy, combined with global and national issues, made pious Muslims and organized Muslim communities more visible in Stuttgart. Some who had hitherto ignored them reluctantly acknowledged their permanent presence. Yet the appropriate mode of participation for pious Muslims, and the accommodation of Muslim religious needs remained controversial. As a first broader urban debate about Muslim communal needs, the Heslach conflict represented a (painful) milestone in the localization of Islam and Muslims in Stuttgart. Until the announcement of the Heslach mosque project, many ethnic German residents in Heslach and Stuttgart had perceived their longtime (predominantly Turkish) Muslim neighbors as atomized individuals with little interest in local politics, and indeed little legitimacy or need for urban participation. In the 1970s, 1980s, and well into the 1990s most Muslims of the first generation of labor migrants conducted their lives quietly, formulated few political demands, and for the most part shunned public activities and involvement.

New Arrivals, Place-Making, and Urban Recognition

Globalization, migration, mobility, mobile forms, and hybrid forms have in recent decades remade cities around the globe (e.g. Appadurai 1996; Smith 2001;

AlSayyad 2001; Urry 2007; Guggenheim and Söderström 2010; Gupta and Ferguson 1992; Sassen 1999, 2002). New spaces and spatial formations were added to existing cityscapes as cities entered the ever-stiffer race for global recognition, investment, and tourism revenues (Davis 1992; Harvey 2006, 1989; Caldeira 2000; McDonogh 2012; Harms 2009; Kanna 2010, 2011; Low 2003; Sorkin 1992; Abaza 2001, 2006, 2011; Kuppinger 2004, 2006a, 2006b). New or hybrid urban forms, spaces, and practices, however, are not exclusively the product of ambitious and profit-oriented large-scale plans, but also emerge from ordinary urban residents and their communities that strive to reshape urban spaces and cultures to best accommodate their lifestyles and cultures (Bayat 2010; Holston 2008; Deeb 2006; BouAkar 2012; Newman 2011; Truitt 2012; Sawalha 2010; Ghannam 2002; White 2002). These are "unplanned" spaces that evade or oppose official planning strategies and bespeak ordinary citizens' claims to their "right to the city" (Mitchell 2003). Such place-making activities include the tactics of excluded or neglected urban constituencies (de Certeau 1984; Lefebvre 1991; Zukin 2010; Hayden 1996; Loukaitou-Sideris and Ehrenfeucht 2009) and symbolize what Asef Bayat (2010) calls "the art of presence" of disenfranchised groups.

The construction of new spatialities and introduction of spatial practices by ordinary residents, new arrivals, or disenfranchised urban groups is a multilayered phenomenon where complex urban, spatial, and cultural dynamics intersect as residents inhabit spaces, move through spaces, and with their daily acts challenge and renegotiate planned spaces (Loukaitou-Sideris and Ehrenfeucht 2009; Zukin 2010; Lin 1998; Duneier 2000) and dominant social and cultural universes (Chauncey 1994). De Certeau points to the "microbe-like, singular and plural practices" and "swarming activities" (1984: 96) of urbanites who challenge dominant urban forms, trajectories, and visions. He identifies a "contradiction between the collective mode of administration and an individual mode or reappropriation" (ibid.) when residents insert their practices, spatial forms, and uses into the urban fabric. De Certeau points to the tension between large-scale urban plans and the daily acts and movements of "ordinary practitioners of the city [who] live 'down below' the threshold at which visibility begins" (ibid.: 93). The sum total of people's movements and daily acts "compose a manifold story that has neither author nor spectator" and is "shaped out of fragments of trajectories and alternations of spaces," which in contrast to dominant urban imaginaries often remain "daily and indefinitely other" (ibid.). Such ordinary and minute spaces can change use patterns of existing spaces, but also in more comprehensive efforts add new spaces to existing cityscapes.

De Certeau and Lefebvre's urban spaces are secular spaces. Both have little use for religion or religiosity as relevant urban dynamics, or as frameworks for urban lives. They associate religion ("the Church") almost exclusively as a (by-gone) seat of power (Lefebvre 1991: 254). Lefebvre identifies "religio-political" spaces (ibid.: 35), but has little to say about spatial or everyday practices inspired by individuals' religiosities. Indeed, de Certeau chronicles the replacement of the religious by the political (1984: 177). Yet, houses of worship are often central sites in which ethnic and religious communities invest time, energy, and money to localize and where they carefully tend to their growing local roots (Metcalf 1996; Haddad 2002; Orsi 1999; Livezey 2000; Warner and Wittner 1998; Ebaugh and Chafetz 2000; Peach and Gale 2003; Garbin 2012, 2013; Arab 2013; Eade 2012; Verkaaik 2012, 2013).

This localization of ideas, cultural forms, religiosities, and practices of new urban groups constitutes what Sharon Zukin (2010) calls "urban beginnings" that symbolize paramount elements of future cityscapes. Such processes can produce authentic, that is locally rooted and negotiated urban elements (versus abstract or globally available models). Their origins among ordinary, often powerless, disenfranchised, or new and underrepresented urban populations make them difficult to realize, as municipalities initially show little interest in and support for what they see as "foreign," unnecessary, or unsuitable spaces. Frequently, efforts are made to prevent such places from being constructed, or they are relegated to marginal spaces, out of view of dominant society.

New urban populations, often without resources to construct their own edifices, frequently inhabit spaces discarded by dominant or wealthier classes (e.g. storefront churches or warehouse mosques). Using much time, energy, and resources, immigrant groups appropriate, renovate, and remake such spaces and imbue them with new practices and meanings (Garbin 2013; Mandel 1996). They inscribe their cultural aspirations into these spaces, and their wish for a permanent home and presence in the city (Warner and Wittner 1998). Much of the material and emotional labor that is invested in such place-making escapes dominant societies (Kuppinger 2010a). Inherent in the appropriation of seemingly insignificant spaces is a struggle for recognition. Individuals and groups that are spatially rooted have a better position from which to act and contribute to urban public culture (Shah et al. 2012; Lewis 2006; Stepick et al. 2009a). From a secure spatial position diverse constituencies can articulate their role and mode of participation in the city (Zukin 2010). From their "home" space they can venture into the urban public sphere, and can invite other groups to be their guests. They become part of the urban symphony, which includes cooperation, contestation, dissonance, and rupture. Because urban culture is neither fixed nor monolithic, the insertion of new spaces, voices, practices, and modes of being is an ordinary feature of urban cultures. Sharon Zukin explains: "If we apply to cities a sense of culture as a dialogue in which there are many parts, we are forced to speak of the *cultures* of cities rather than of either a unified culture of the whole city or a diversity of exotic subcultures. It is not multiculturalism or the diversity of cultures that is to be grasped; it is the fluidity, the fusion, the negotiation" (1995: 290; emphasis in the original).

Mosques have long since become permanent features of twenty-first-century German cities. They were "new" at one point; their stories, to use Zukin's term, were/are those of beginnings. Beginnings are not moments of alienation or rupture for the existing cityscape, but are ordinary processes that articulate future urban forms and practices. Beginnings as such are not new, but have always been crucial features of urban dynamics. Zukin concludes that "these beginnings mark emerging spaces of urban authenticity" (2010: 20). As much as neighbors and urban administrations struggle with what they perceive as the foreign nature of mosques, the latter represent ordinary dynamics of urban beginnings. As they become recognized and rooted, they add their voices to the urban public sphere, which will be remade, and made to be more inclusive in the process.

Processes of urban beginnings and cultural negotiations are not easy. Participants make mistakes. Some are guided by cultural knowledge that is based on experiences in different times and places (Shah et al. 2012; Arab 2013). Through controversies and debates, opponents who had hitherto barely acknowledged or engaged each other, become familiar with each other and their respective needs and arguments. In the process they become actors on shared platforms. While interactions are shared, they are far from equal. Urban beginnings are characterized by the unequal interaction of political, cultural, and economic power. This power works in favor of established groups, their political interests and cultural visions (Zukin 2010; Mitchell 2003). Elites defend "their" city and the way they imagine it to be, against those who they define as neither belonging nor entitled to the right to equal cultural or political participation. The unequal distribution of power overall, and the power to define concrete spaces and their uses turns the struggles of newer urban constituencies into a steep uphill battle. The defining power of existing elite groups and political bodies keeps migrants locked in the recent arrival category for decades after they have settled in the city. The dominant narrative about the characteristics and roles of newcomers and outsiders is hard to deconstruct and counter, even once the "newcomers" have been settled for several generations (Spielhaus 2011, 2013; Brubaker 2012; Allievi 2005; Yıldız 1999). Even after decades of local residence, "immigrants" and their children are often not recognized as legitimate urban participants and cultural producers. Their ideas and visions continue to be labeled as foreign and inappropriate.

Mosque Conflicts

In the 1960s and 1970s, when small groups of men rented invisible backyard spaces (*Hinterhofmoschee*) to conduct their prayers, they remained below the radar screen of dominant society and political elites (Beinhauer-Köhler and Leggewie 2009: 25; Ceylan 2006: 123; Schiffauer 2000). As quiet uneducated *Gastarbeiter* they posed no threat to the existing political and urban order. Most of the new prayer spaces were established quietly in invisible spaces and sparked only occasional controversies. Such conflicts with neighbors often centered on parking (too many cars on Friday) or noise (too many visitors on holidays; see also Mandel 1996).[1] They were usually locally solved and sometimes ended in the termination of leases, or communities voluntarily left and settled elsewhere ("and then there were problems and we left," or "we had to move because the neighbors complained," several older people remarked when asked about early prayer facilities). These early controversies did not turn into larger urban issues as there was little public interest in the affairs of small prayer room communities. Conflicts remained local and rarely transcended their immediate urban contexts.

Early prayer room or small mosque projects unfolded against the background of a political and media landscape that was oblivious to migrants' religious needs. Simultaneously, emerging mosque communities and their leaders of the first generation were often not well informed about German politics, municipal rules, and regulations. Many had developed modes of operation that were inspired by political and legal contexts in their home countries and mediated by years of official neglect in Germany (Ceylan 2006: 133; Schiffauer 2010). Early timid interventions by mosque communities were often marked by the communities' and their representatives' inexperience in urban politics and debates. Small prayer rooms and mosques were quietly run to the best of their leaders' organizational abilities. They were increasingly organized as *Vereine* (registered civic association), but rarely participated in civic activities. Leaders and community members quickly learned a few essentials lessons, most centrally, that excessive noise and parking chaos outside their premises should be avoided, and that the less public attention a mosque community attracted, the more peaceful and smooth its existence became. Understanding that encounters with the urban public were predominantly negative and contentious, mosque communities shied away from public engagements and oriented their activities inward (Kuppinger 2011b). The more inconspicuous communities were, the less neighbors and authorities took issue with their existence. Neither public relations activities, nor the quest for urban rights and recognition were high on the early mosque associations' agendas. Ensuing forms and practices reflected the official neglect of Muslims affairs, and the unspoken arrangements that Muslims, as a disenfranchised group, were left on their own, so long as they did not interfere with dominant lifeworlds.

Starting in the 1970s many male migrant workers brought their families and permanently settled in Germany. Former prayer room groups turned into larger communities (Schiffauer 2010; Jonker 2002). Parents sought Islamic instruction for their children, youths and women wanted to meet, and community members increasingly saw the mosque not only as a place for prayer, but as a religious, social, and cultural center. By the 1980s many former *Hinterhofmoscheen* had outlived their purpose. When communities started to acquire or wished to acquire better and larger spaces of worship, disputes started to unfold more frequently (Cesari 2005a, 2005b; Jonker 2005; Manço and Kanmaz 2005; Schmitt 2003; Hüttermann 2006; McLoughlin 2005).

The growth of mosque communities and the emergence of a second and third generation of pious Muslims, many of whom were German citizens and some who had university degrees, changed the position of mosque communities and subsequently the nature of controversies (Göle and Ammann 2004; Jonker and Amiraux 2006; Schiffauer 2010; Klausen 2005). In need of more spacious facilities, some communities hoped to build "real" mosques with domes and minarets (Kessner 2004; Welzbacher 2008; Kraft 2002). Muslims and their communities surfaced with increased frequency in public debates in the 1990s. Discussions about the role of pious Muslims as ordinary social actors and civic participants only slowly gained momentum. Islam had de facto become a local religion, but was a long way from being recognized as such. For many ethnic Germans debates about Islam and Muslims occurred on distant platforms and had little bearings on their everyday lives. The announcement of a local mosque project, however, was different. It brought debates about Islam closer to home for those who had not paid attention to abstract debates and knew little about Islam, despite the fact that they lived in proximity to Muslim neighbors (see e.g. Crolly 2010).

In the 1990s political elites and large segments of dominant society had not yet recognized Muslims as permanent urban constituencies that had legitimate rights guaranteed to them by the *Grundgesetz*. For many ethnic Germans, Turks or Muslims had conveniently remained *Gastarbeiter* or *Ausländer* (foreigners) and hence were not entitled to a political voice (Holub 2002: 178; Spielhaus 2011, 2013; Yıldız 1999, 2009). Many Germans still thought or hoped that immigrants would return to their home countries. Whether or not their ethnic German neighbors acknowledged these transformations, over the years diverse Muslims had grown roots, formed mosque associations, some had taken German citizenship, and others had become engaged civic participants. The advent of a second, third, and fourth generation of practicing Muslims (including a small but growing number of ethnic German converts), increased their visibility, as much as educational and professional achievements, the growing cohesion of organized communities, and many Muslims' recognition of their rights as urban residents and national citizens altered the mode of interaction between Muslims, dominant society, and political bodies (Jonker 2006: 148; Göle 2006: 23; Kandemir 2005; Verkaaik 2012; Bowen 2007, 2010: 24).

Since the 1990s many German cities have experienced mosque conflicts in which residents and authorities used every conceivable argument, administrative procedure, and legal possibility to prevent the construction of mosques (Hüttermann 2006; Bahr 2006; Lauterbach and Lottermoser 2009: 51; Killguss et al. 2008; Jonker 2005). By 2000 such controversies slowly changed as increasing numbers of residents became reluctantly aware that Muslims were here to stay. Global political events and developments like 9/11 and the wars in Iraq and Afghanistan influenced local debates. While mosque projects had hitherto been largely dealt with as isolated urban conflicts, they suddenly turned into larger political issues that imported national and global politics into neighborhood disputes.² Conflicts became more frequent and arguments against mosques more resentful and hostile. Bärbel Beinhauer-Köhler and Claus Leggewie estimate that in the first decade of the twenty-first century about 200 mosque conflicts were underway in German cities (2009: 117). Treading on new territory, debates, interactions, and interventions were marked by trial and error strategies as individuals and groups negotiated one step or one statement at a time. Local resentment mixed with global political hostilities. Politicians, pundits, and the media used global events to produce local fears and intensify stereotypes and anxieties (Yıldız 2009). At the same time, mosque communities were no longer willing to quietly move from one backyard location to the next. And, as one mosque association official in Stuttgart so aptly noted, "the more the public is talking about Muslims, the more self-confident Muslims become."

Leaders and representatives of mosque associations changed as the first generation of largely uneducated migrants were replaced by the second generation of often academically educated and professionally successful individuals who no longer timidly asked for hand-outs, but politely requested their constitutionally guaranteed rights as a religious community. As citizens and participants in the urban public, they insist on their right to freedom of religion, and ask to practice their religion in adequate spaces like their neighboring church communities. Dominant society, frequently still caught in a 1960s discourse about *Gastarbeiter* who took the hand-me-downs from dominant society, was ill-prepared for this new generation of outspoken, visible, educated, and informed pious Muslim citizens, their well-established communities, and national, European and global networks (Jonker and Amiraux 2006; Färber 2006; Schiffauer 2010). They had for too long ignored the emergence of organized mosque communities whose invisible spaces had grown roots in cityscapes and whose members were citizens and civic participants (Nökel 2002; Idriz 2010; Spielhaus and Färber 2006; Kandemir 2005).

Since the 1960s mosque associations have created about 2,500 meeting spaces in Germany using mostly invisible backyard rooms, former workshops, warehouses, factories, office suites, defunct churches, or other Christian community facilities (Bahr 2006: 80; Beinhauer-Köhler and Leggewie 2009: 117). Only very few communities constructed mosques with domes and minarets (Kraft 2002; Welzbacher 2008). Some hotly debated German mosque projects, like the Cologne mosque made headlines beyond Germany (Landler *NYT* 5.7.2007; Wellershoff 2007; Bozay 2008). Others like the first mosque in the former East Germany, built by an Ahmadi community (designed by an Ahmadi woman architect) in Berlin weathered some controversies, but were eventually completed (Kurzlechner 2008). Some, like the large mosque in Duisburg-Marxloh, or a smaller one in the southern town of Hechingen were realized with little controversy and subsequently became icons of the possibility of peaceful mosque-building and successful multi-religious urban life (Jenkner 2008; Schilder 2008; *Welt Online* 12.8.2008; Idriz 2010; Günnewig

2008; Buchmeier *SZ* 12.12.2006). Regardless of the few success stories of purpose-built mosques, the majority of German mosques remain invisible. Invisibility, as mosques communities had learned, provided a certain peace of mind and quiet daily existence. Yet is does not allow for broad urban recognition and participation in the urban public sphere.

Two dynamics intersect in mosques projects. First, there is the process whereby Muslim communities translate their needs into available spaces, when they rent or buy spaces and remake them to suit their purposes. In a careful manner they insert their needs, ideas, and practices into existing urban spatialities. Their steps and projects are slowly woven into the urban fabric. Second, there are popular, media, and political dynamics, and anti-Islamic sentiments that come to the fore in the outspoken opposition to mosques (Schiffer 2005, 2008; Welzbacher 2008: 20; Häusler 2008; Spielhaus 2011; Lauterbach and Lottermoser 2009). They reflect widespread suspicions and resentment against Islam and Muslim activities (Hippler and Lueg 2001; Shooman and Spielhaus 2010). Unwilling to recognize or accommodate Muslim quests for equal rights and civic participation, this pervasive popular, political, and media discourse routinely challenges, frustrates, obstructs, and derails mosque projects.

Mosque controversies typically operate on several levels. There is the struggle over material facilities. More crucially, however, as individuals and groups voice their support or opposition to mosque projects, they formulate opinions on the position of Muslims and their communities in urban quarters, cities, and the nation. Mosque conflicts, especially the first larger such conflict in a city, transcend the context of the respective mosque and launch local debates about the position of Islam in a city. Heated debates about mosque projects invariably address the question of whether a particular mosque is meant to be a symbol of the larger Muslim presence in the city (nation) or a modest neighborhood prayer space (Bowen 2010: 31).[3] With the quest for larger and more visible facilities, Muslim communities move toward a different mode of urban engagement and seek to create a more permanent and respected urban position. Mosque conflicts ultimately localize communities as they become more visible, and their needs are inserted in public agendas. They teach their communities valuable lessons about urban political landscapes, sharpen their political and rhetorical skills, and establish important contacts and alliances. They trace the outlines of urban Muslim public spheres as Muslims of different ethnicities, religiosities, and political orientations engage each other in the city. Struggles over mosque projects transcend spatial, architectural, and economic concerns that mark other urban conflicts. As such politicians, the media, and other Muslim communities carefully monitor such controversies. Segments of dominant society are unwilling to easily concede recognition and equal rights to Muslims and their communities. These sentiments turn mosque conflicts into lively platforms where fears and prejudices against Muslims and their increasingly visible and self-confident presence are voiced.

Scripted Conflicts?

Many mosque controversies unfold in an almost predictable manner, involving "standard" casts of actors and repertoires of arguments (Hüttermann 2006; Lauterbach and Lottermoser 2009). While details of these conflicts seem unprecedented to most of the respective local residents, they are a new version of an "old" script to Muslims and informed observers. Announcements of mosque projects bring debates about Islam closer to home for local residents, and put concrete forms to detached political debates.

When news spreads that a mosque community intends to rent or buy concrete premises, opposition quickly emerges in neighborhoods (Leggewie and Beinhauer-Köhler 2009: 117).[4] The course of the ensuing activities is highly predictable. Letters to municipalities are written, local meetings are held, petitions sent to higher-up places, and neighborhood associations are formed. Lists of complaints and reasons why a mosque cannot be built or established are surprisingly uniform. Noise, traffic, lack of parking along with loss of real estate values are the most frequently used objections (see Bölsche 2008: 74). These are followed by concerns like the fear of Islamist politics and the accusation that mosque are places where women are discriminated against (Yıldız 2009). Questions of whether mosque associations really operate within the confines of the *Grundgesetz* are often added. Mosque opponents and municipal authorities formulate spatial arguments to express broader issues of urban rights, cultural production, and citizenship. Explicitly arguing over zoning and fire codes, discussants in fact debate the "zoning" of Islam in liberal democracies. The question about how many meters a minaret could measure concretely spells the question of how Islam is positioned in a European state, and also versus Christianity. Mosque conflicts are frequently and eagerly picked up by right-wing groups to spread their xenophobic and anti-Islamic agendas. These groups further heat or even poison local debates (Häusler 2008). They often manage to mobilize resentments and hostility against Muslims among broader segments of the population (Killguss et al. 2008; Shooman and Spielhaus 2010).

While many urban residents oppose mosque projects, only few, other than openly right-wing individuals or groups, are willing to outright state their opposition to mosques for fear of being seen as xenophobic (Bozay 2008). Struggles thus shift onto technical territories. Residents and municipalities complain about noise, lack of parking spaces, size of a project, height of a minaret, or zoning mismatches. Many mosque opponents, who see their struggle as genuine and unique quests, are unaware that they employ a standard list of arguments. For Muslim communities these circumstances are readily apparent, as they are ardent observers of similar debates and struggles in other cities.

The quest for adequate spaces and representation of Muslim communities almost predictably evokes irrational sentiments among mosque opponents who sense cultural invasion and a pending "take-over" (*Art Landnahme*; Bölsche 2008: 74). Other critics complain about "the demonstration of power and the creation of Islamic enclaves" (ibid.: 76). Some opponents see mosques not only as spaces of worship, but as jumping boards for unwanted extremist activities. Critics, of what Bölsche calls "only the beginning of a Europe-wide mosque construction boom" (ibid.), fear the construction of "veritable exterritorial defense castles (*Trutzburgen*) and propaganda centers of totalitarian parallel societies" (ibid: 73). Fears of a "creeping Islamization" of Germany and Europe are expressed (ibid.: 73/74). The "place, size and number" of new mosque constructions turn into central features of public debates (ibid.).[5] While there is the legitimate question of how ordinary citizens and believers might be utilized in "political projects that deploy religious idioms," as Ismail (2006: 83/84) noted for the case of Egypt, images of a Muslim "takeover" or pending Islamization in Germany are mere fear-mongering.

The Heslach Case

By the late 1990s tens of thousands of Muslims of diverse ethnic and national backgrounds, religiosities, and political orientations had settled in Stuttgart. Individuals and groups wished to participate in shaping their city. Whereas numerous individuals started to participate in local social, cultural, and political activities, organized Muslim communities remained relatively invisible throughout the 1990s. The Heslach controversy abruptly changed this, as the presence, needs, and civic participation of Muslim communities suddenly attracted considerable public attention.

Heslach is part of the *Bezirk* (urban district) of Stuttgart-Süd. In 2006, 38.9 percent of the district's population had migratory roots (Landeshauptstadt Stuttgart 2006: 76, 83). When the VIKZ bought the Heslach complex in 1999, there were already a number of mosques in the city, including the sizable Salam Mosque complex. These mosques, however, remained hidden from public view, either because of their small sizes or marginal locations in industrial quarters. The larger Heslach project, located in a predominantly residential neighborhood, departed from established patterns. It would be more visible (yet not visibly recognizable as a mosque) and situated in close proximity to dominant lifeworlds. This new visibility reflected the emerging organization and cohesion, and the permanent nature of Muslim communities in Stuttgart. This visibility was largely coincidental, as this particular industrial complex had been for sale and was identified by the VIKZ as most suitable for its purposes. For those who knew little about the size and complexity of local Muslim communities, the project seemed oversized. In 1999, established images of Stuttgart as the quiet Swabian capital, that were maintained and nurtured by politicians and the media, neither included multi-ethnic and multi-religious neighborhoods, nor mosques as urban elements. Rudely awoken, many ethnic German residents perceived the mosque project as a threat to their lifeworlds.

When the purchase of the Heslach factory compound became public in January 2000, different stakeholders quickly took their positions in the developing controversy.[6] The local VIKZ chapter, as the owner of the factory, opposing local residents, the local council, and by extension municipal bodies and institutions were core participants. Additional groups joined as the conflict gained in intensity. By mid-February 2000, the Turkish Consul General in Stuttgart issued a statement that there were "enough prayer places in the city for the religious needs of the Turks" (*Stuttgarter Nachrichten* 11.2.2000). This statement of the Turkish Consul General was the utterance of somebody who saw himself as the legitimate representative of Turkish Muslims and who had been treated as such for years by German officials. The fact that Turkish religious and political rivalries were involved in his words escaped the German public. Indeed at the time, Turkish officials had little interest in another VIKZ mosque in Stuttgart (the VIKZ already had two smaller facilities), as it was a declared opponent of the community/movement. For the German public, however, the Consul seemed to speak as the legitimate representative of all Turkish Muslims (the fact that not all Muslims are Turks was conveniently neglected). Turkish national and religious rivalries further complicated the Heslach project.

Meanwhile the head of the local council (*Bezirksvorsteher*) asked the municipal administration to "prevent a large mosque here" (*Stuttgarter Nachrichten* 11.2.2000). He gave no reasons why a mosque could not be built in Heslach. The city was repeatedly asked to employ its right of first sale (*Vorkaufsrecht*), but legal experts insisted that there was no way that this could legitimately be done after the fact. In this initial phase of the controversy, central opponents aimed to quickly defeat the project without any debate or engagement with the mosque association. Questions about the mosque's legitimacy or Muslim citizens' constitutional rights were not posed. Seeing no way to reverse the real estate transaction by legal means, city officials pointed to the proposed size of the project as an issue of contention. Was the center suitable for a quarter like Heslach? What indeed were the outlines and outreach of the planned center? What activities were planned to take place in what type of facilities? In its earlier statement about the project, the VIKZ had remained vague about the dimensions and outreach of the project. Informed by decades of disinterest, the mosque association had entered the public arena unprepared. They had no press releases or public relation agents to "market" their plans, which emerged piecemeal, not by design, but by way of the unfolding circumstances. Residents and local politicians worried about the size of the project and whether it would serve people from beyond the neighborhood. A senior city official (*Städtebaubürgermeister*) asked for a "dimension of the project that is suitable for the quarter" (Bienzle *SN* 12.2.2000).

On February 22 the local council called a public meeting to discuss the project. In the face of mounting tension the local VIKZ chapter had asked its national headquarters in Cologne (the nominal buyer of the factory) to send a representative. At the meeting the national representative announced plans for an extensive complex with prayer rooms, library, archives, a student dormitory for sixty residents, and forty-four parking spaces (Schwarz *SN* 23.2.2000). Meanwhile local citizens had collected 586 signatures against the project, which they handed over to the council at this meeting. They cited "fear of over-alienation" (*Überfremdung*)[7] as a central concern (ibid.). No evidence of "over-alienation" was presented. One city council member pointed to the large size of the project and pronounced it inappropriate for a residential community. The VIKZ representative from Cologne stressed that the association did not expect visitors from other cities, even less from other federal states. He emphasized that the association harbored no political goals. The mosque was conceptualized as a center for the southern part of the city. The association wanted to use the facilities to teach Islam and provide social services like tutoring for students. One local council member did not see "any need for instruction in the Koran" at all, as it had, in his view, no positive influence on youth (ibid.). This statement bears witness to the state of debates about Islam at the turn of the twenty-first century when a minor public figure could pronounce a devastating judgment on an entire religious tradition. Another local council member added, "I suppose that they want to create a radical Islamist center" (ibid.). This remark similarly bespeaks irrational fears and images of Islam as a dark, unpredictable, and possibly violent religion. A Christian Democratic city council member suspected "a study institution for Imams and not an inner-city" communal space in the proposed plan (ibid.). The VIKZ representative's words went unheard as residents and officials continued to formulate their positions based on their irrational fears and preconceived notions.

At the February 22 meeting, the national representative of the VIKZ also addressed the Turkish Consul General's statement that there were enough prayer spaces in Stuttgart. He asked "why should I care what the Turkish Consul General says, when I am a German citizen?" (Schwarz *SN* 23.2.2000). This remark is easily understood in the context of the Turkish state's resentments against Suleyman Tunahan (the founder of the movement which gave birth to the VIKZ, see also chapter 5) and his followers, and its policy of control over religious affairs. The statement reflects the perspective of the growing number of Muslim German citizens who for decades have been working to localize Islam. However, it makes little (positive) sense to the uninitiated. Yet, if Germany practiced freedom of religion within its borders, why would the estimation of a foreign consul be of relevance to the religious practices of local Muslim communities? The VIKZ representative insinuated that Islam had become a German religion whose problems needed to be negotiated by Germans in German contexts. Dominant society, however, had not recognized processes of Muslim localization. The representative's words thus were taken as inappropriate and impertinent. Whether or not he was a German citizen, he was not recognized as an equal player (Yıldız 1999). In the end his words created more resentment. Not surprisingly, his remark made its appearance as a (negative) quote in newspapers and was repeatedly quoted thereafter. Years later, a local VIKZ official remarked that to bring in a national representative might have made sense in terms of the organizational structure of the VIKZ, but had not been beneficial. On the contrary his intervention, reflecting the more abstract context of a national headquarter, had hurt the local cause. Subsequently, the local council (Stuttgart-Süd) unanimously voted against the mosque project (Schwarz *SN* 23.02.2000).

The February 22 meeting had been called to clarify issues and calm opponents, but produced the opposite effect. The national representative's remark was quoted a day later again as an example of the supposedly insensitive and arrogant ways of the Muslim side (Osswald *SZ* 24.2.2000). Even though the local council had voted against the mosque, this did not produce any immediate consequences. The VIKZ remained the legitimate owner of the old factory and could continue the legal procedures to turn the compound into a community center. Therefore, opposing residents left the February 22 meeting with a "sense of having been left alone with their fears" (ibid.). What exactly their fears were and what had caused them was not made clear. The residents' long held fears proved to be resilient regardless of the explanations of the VIKZ. A quick look at the history, context, and teaching of Suleyman Tunahan and his later lay community could have helped local residents to develop a better understanding of the community and decrease their inexplicable fears. It is hard to imagine the followers of Suleyman Tunahan as being inspired to violence and extremism when their spiritual guide/leader had "fought" the oppression by the secular Turkish government in the mid-twentieth century by becoming an itinerant preacher in the Turkish countryside.

Opponents' interventions continued to be marked by irrational fears of Islam. Decades of peaceful neighborly co-existence had made little difference to their assumptions about the threatening nature of Islam and Muslims. On the VIKZ side, the national representative had not operated in close communication with the local chapter and had shown little awareness of the local political situation (Osswald *SZ* 24.2.2000). His appearance and a certain lack of transparency on his part worked against the mosque project. Local residents continued to think that the project was a regional or larger "radical" center (ibid.). Arguments could not convince them otherwise.

As a next step officials and opponents closely weighed the project against building codes, in the hope of finding flaws that would provide technical reasons to reject it. The technical committee of the city council (*Technikausschuss des Gemeinderats*) met behind closed doors, but could find no technical fault in the proposed plan (*Stuttgarter Zeitung* 1.3.2001). One observer concluded, "by way of building codes the mosque complex cannot be prevented" (ibid.). This utterance illustrates how the committee had not met to examine a renovation project, but to find faults with the project to prevent its realization. Members of the committee were not pleased with this result. One Christian Democrat committee member felt that the question of parking spaces had not been sufficiently examined. Furthermore, the Christian Democratic faction inquired about issues of fire codes and if legal aspects of assembly rights were being honored. This faction also complained about administrational procedures and suggested that such issues should in the future be dealt with at a higher administrational level (ibid.). The technical route would have been a convenient one to deal with "uncomfortable" neighbors, and indeed this procedure remains the most favored in German mosque conflicts. Few constituencies (other than those on the far right) openly state that they object to a mosque per se. Most others recognize such a remark as xenophobic. The awareness of German history dictates the avoidance of such a discourse. This, however, does not turn local residents and their political representatives into defenders of (religious) minorities. Instead it pushes mosque opponents to formulate their arguments in carefully groomed technical terms and hair-splitting legal arguments. Some discussants were willing to disclose their relative ignorance of Muslim affairs and were hoping to learn more about them. Representatives of the Social Democrats, for example, asked for a round table discussion between Muslims and local residents, and for the local council to visit a mosque (ibid.), as many/most political actors had never set foot in a mosque.

A week after the controversial meeting, a citizens' forum, "Pro-Heslach," was founded to protest the mosque (Hamann *SN* 3.3.2000). It is interesting to note that there is a larger scene of movements in Germany that use the prefix "Pro" in conjunction with a neighborhood or city's name. These movements (the most well-known is "Pro-Cologne"; Killguss et al. 2008; Bozay 2008) often quickly emerge in the process of mosque controversies. "Pro" platforms or associations are frequently characterized by right-wing leadership, organization, networks, and rhetoric (Shooman and Spielhaus 2010; Andreasch 2008; Lauterbach and Lottermoser 2009: 100). "Pro" groups, like the inquiry into buildings codes and parking spaces, are central features of mosque controversies (Geber 2010). Almost uniformly, they state that their goals are communal welfare and beautification. They insist that their organization at the moment of a mosque controversy is purely accidental. Pro-X platforms usually "argue that political parties do not speak for the local population, so they have to congregate and speak for themselves" (Shooman and Spielhaus 2010: 203). Often connected to right-wing and neo-Nazi circles and websites, spokespeople of "Pro"-platforms often thrive on xenophobic and anti-Islamic claims and resentments (Killguss et al. 2008; Peters et al. 2008; Sager and Peters 2008; Jentsch 2008).

"Pro-Heslach" predates many similar platforms, and there is no indication that the group was directly linked to right-wing platforms or parties. Nonetheless,

Pro-Heslach initiators insisted that "their anger was not aimed against Turkish fellow citizens, but against the city administration who did not exercise its first sales rights" (Hamann *SN* 3.3.2000). The logic here is that Turkish/Muslim fellow citizens should not be allowed to proceed as far as purchasing such a large complex. For this spokesperson the city had failed its (non-Muslim) citizens by not keeping a closer tab on the activities of the mosque association. The municipality, in this argumentation, is understood as the exclusive representative of non-Muslim residents. Predictably, the forum announced that its goal was the general improvement of the quarter, "but for now the initiative was concerned with only one thing: to prevent the proposed Islamic Cultural Center" (Hamann *SN* 3.3.2000). While a "moderate" group of citizens around a local minister and Christian Democrat council member hoped to engage in a dialogue with the VIKZ, Pro-Heslach saw little use in such an engagement. Pro-Heslach's aim was not dialogue with Muslims, but their defeat. In the eyes of Pro-Heslach members/participants it was the task of the city administration to prevent any visible expression of Muslim life in the quarter. "Turkish fellow citizens" could live in Heslach, so long as they were neither visible nor made political demands. The task of officials was to maintain existing cultural expressions, regardless of unfolding urban transformations. In this case, forum members insisted that the city should have bought the factory once it came to officials' attention that a mosque association was going to buy it. The city had failed its citizens—so Pro-Heslach—as it saw no reason to object to this real estate deal. Worse, the city had dealt with the VIKZ much like with any other real estate investor. Muslims and their representatives, so Pro-Heslach, however, were not like other urban actors. Pro-Heslach members argued that the exercise of the city's right to buy the compound would have been called for because of the type of project. While the group's spokesperson was not against "Turkish fellow citizens," he accused the city of having neglected its tasks by allowing a Muslim association to conduct a legitimate real estate transaction. The underlying assumption was that sneaky city officials, who either supported the wrong constituency or were tricked by them, had betrayed "German" citizens.

By early March the battle lines had hardened and the national VIKZ representative's impudent, but ultimately irrelevant, remark with regard to the Turkish Consul General turned into a centerpiece and was quoted once more in the *Stuttgarter Nachrichten* (Hamann *SN* 4.3.2000). Underlying was a considerable irritation at the representative's references at being both German and a Muslim, a circumstance that was beyond the imagination of many at the time. Moreover, citizens were enraged about the mosque, which the Mayor of Stuttgart, Wolfgang Schuster, noted was not a real mosque, as "external signs like a dome and minarets were not planned" (ibid.). At stake were the size of the project and the question of whether it served only the quarter, or was a regional or larger center. This point still had not been sufficiently clarified by the VIKZ. Pro-Heslach once more announced that it wanted to prevent the project "but avoid xenophobic tendencies" (ibid.). The mood in the quarter was heated.

In the meanwhile, eight neighbors had submitted legal objections to the project based on the argument that a larger center was neither feasible nor legal in the quarter (Osswald *SZ* 15.3.2000). A round table discussion of all involved parties was announced for March 22. The local council asked for the project to be shrunk to the size of a local center. The council had met with VIKZ representatives and discussed their existing facilities in Stuttgart and plans for the future—should the Heslach project materialize. VIKZ representatives explained that in addition to prayer and meeting rooms for up to 220 persons, they were interested in youth programs. The dormitory with sixty spaces was planned to accommodate local and other school and university students. This, they emphasized, was an appropriate way to support immigrant children some of whom seriously struggled in the local school system. National VIKZ representatives mentioned the founding of an Islamic academy in Heslach and insisted that the association was well within the confines of the *Grundgesetz*. They distanced themselves "from whatever fundamentalism" (ibid.). Two weeks later Adrian Zielcke wrote in the *Stuttgarter Zeitung*: "It [the affair, PK] has turned into a teaching piece (*Lehrstück*) of how not to do it. The controversy over a house of worship (*Gotteshaus*) in Heslach has not been conducted—from all sides—in the open. Only honest dialogue can make it possible that Germans, Swabians, German and Turkish Turks can continue to co-exist in peace in the future" (Zielcke *SZ* 29.3.2000).

Zielcke noted that it had not been initially disclosed by the VIKZ that the center was designed as a regional or larger institution. With regard to the city, Zielcke noted that it had been asleep and only too late had the Mayor realized the outlines of the project. The "Swabian residents," he added, never openly stated that they simply did not want a mosque in the old factory complex. They operated under the pretense of concerns about parking and noise. None of this, Zielcke concluded, could be the basis of an open and honest debate. Several things had to be reconsidered. First, the city needed to address issues of co-existence (*Zusammenleben*) with the Turkish population. Former *Gastarbeiter* had become citizens and their needs had to be recognized. Zielcke's appeal, illustrated how far Muslim and/or Turkish affairs were out of dominant society's radar screen. Zielcke raised the question of why Stuttgart, unlike some of its smaller peers (e.g Mannheim), still did not have a purpose-built mosque. He asked: "Should in the future more and more spaces of prayer be established quietly and out of view in backyards and defunct factories? Or, will we be able to establish a grand mosque with all that is necessary? It is against all dignity (*unwürdig*) that Muslims have to hide their places of worship" (ibid.). Zielcke concluded, "Islam has found a home here and it should receive an appropriate house of worship" (ibid.). To situate this mosque in a residential neighborhood might not be the best idea and play into the agendas of right-wing movements. The compromise would be a mosque in a representative space elsewhere in the city (ibid.).

By the end of March, two months after the controversy had started, the *Stuttgarter Zeitung* published an interview with two local VIKZ representatives (Mack and

Honecker *SZ* 29.3.2000). The representatives explained their concept of an Islamic Academy modeled after educational institutions like the Catholic Academy which maintains a lively program of conferences and debates about theological, cultural, and social themes, including interfaith dialogue. The representatives stressed that their new academy would operate on a much more modest scale with fewer events. They pointed to the existing VIKZ academies in Cologne and Bavaria as models. They emphasized their efforts to work with young people and teach them the foundations of Islam. The interviewing journalists voiced popular concerns about Saudi-Arabian funding, and the teaching of "old Qur'anic rules" that define the role of women differently from that spelled out in the *Grundgesetz* (ibid.). The representatives disclosed their financing (members' contributions and a bank credit) and explained that much like other religious institutions their aim was to teach their religion to the younger generation. Furthermore, they explained the mishap with the national representative as the result of their fear as ordinary citizens to present their cause to a large audience and the media. They brought in the national representative thinking that he might be better equipped for such a platform. They realized that they had been wrong. The subsequent restructuring and foundation of the regional VIKZ association, the LVIKZ (*Landesverband der Islamischen Kulturzentren*) is an indirect result of this experience, as the community understood that they were best situated to articulate their own cause. One of the representatives noted that they eventually founded the regional association so that they can "find people locally who can do this" (i.e. represent their cause in public; ibid.).

In early April the *Gemeinderat* (city council) decided against the project and suggested the VIKZ either considerably shrink the proposed project, or realize it elsewhere (Mack *SZ* 7.4.2000). The city quickly introduced a new local master plan (*Bebauungsplan*) that identified the old factory complex as part of a general residential area. Only the Green Party faction voted against this plan, because they thought that the city "moved on the borderline to illegality," as the plan was designed for only a very small area because a religious minority wanted to establish a prayer space there (ibid.). Others talked of "legal crutches" that were used in this case (ibid.). The Social Democrats asked the city to buy the factory and offer the VIKZ other facilities elsewhere for a smaller place of worship. The central point of contention remained the student dormitory for sixty boarders. A second round table for all parties was supposed to further discuss the conflict. In the meanwhile the VIKZ announced that it considered shrinking the complex (*SZ* 19.4.2000). Pro-Heslach appealed to the Mayor and noted that the possible use of the factory by the mosque association was "hard to control" (*nur schwer kontrollierbar*; *Stuttgarter Nachrichten* 3.5.2000). They did not specify what exactly needed to be controlled in a mosque.

By mid-June Mayor Schuster met with Pro-Heslach and promised that the mosque would be prevented, and a residential and commercial complex built to replace the factory compound (Hamann *SN* 14.6.2000). A representative of the forum noted that unlike in earlier stages of the conflict, the Mayor had now entered the debate in an "open" (*aufgeschlossen*) manner and been adequately prepared for this meeting (ibid.). This implies that the Mayor's former position, when he had portrayed the mosque project as not disturbing, had been based on a closed mindset and lack of information. It further means that the Mayor had been mistaken in supporting the rights and needs of a mosque community, because in the perspective of Pro-Heslach and its constituency a mosque community was not a legitimate urban stakeholder.

In August the VIKZ submitted a new plan to the city. The association had eliminated the dormitory and only proposed prayer facilities, a kitchen, a library, and an apartment using only the first and second floor. The third floor, which in the original plan had housed the student dormitory, would be left a warehouse facility (Osswald *SZ* 11.8.2000). This plan coincided with the building code for residential areas that does allow for religious facilities that cater to more than neighborhood constituencies. With the ball in the city's court, the municipality had until December to decide about the revised plan (ibid.). In December the technical commission of the city council unanimously decided for the city to buy the factory. The city offered to provide an additional 400 square meters for the community to rent in one of its other existing locations in Stuttgart. Legally, the city council noted there was little to object to in this second plan (*Stuttgarter Zeitung* 13.12.2000).

Pro-Heslach immediately called another public meeting to "underline their No to a mosque in their quarter" (*Stuttgarter Zeitung* 14.12.2000). While arguments in the early months of the controversy had focused on the size and possible regional outreach of the center, the forum now voiced its rejection of any mosque—big or small. One resident remarked: "Heslach is not a xenophobic place, but we simply are afraid" (ibid.). Precisely what the fear was, that had grasped many citizens was not spelled out. Another resident explained: "We fear a radicalization," which is equally vague (ibid.). There were no known cases of "radicalization" in VIKZ mosques. Another person noted that the VIKZ "was not at all an integration-fostering sect" (ibid.). The use of the notion of a sect implies extreme behavior, secrecy, and tightly closed quarters. Sects are thought to pull in individuals and often forcefully keep them, even if they wish to leave. The VIKZ refused the city's offer to buy back the factory complex and accept additional space at their existing Takva Mosque (ibid.).

As the conflict went into its second year, the city council's technical commission had to decide about the revised plan for the smaller mosque facility. The plan foresaw that the VIKZ would rent all unused space back to the city for the next five years (Schwarz *SN* 16.1.2001). This was not enough for many city council members who feared that the dormitory plans would resurface after these five years. Yet, at this point, the city had no legal reasons to object to the revised plan. The VIKZ, aware of these circumstances and getting impatient with this long process, announced, "if our proposed project will be denied, we will immediately sue and insist on a speedy process (*Eilverfahren*), as we have high financial obligations" (ibid.). On January

30 the Christian Democrat majority of the technical commission rejected the revised proposal (Osswald *SZ* 31.1.2001). Social Democrat, Liberal (FDP), and Green representatives opposed the rejection. One Green commission member saw in the pending legal procedures a "catastrophic situation for a 'future-able' Stuttgart (*zukunftsfähiges Stuttgart*)" (ibid.). Others bemoaned the political damage for the city if differences were made between Christian and Muslim building permits (ibid.). Under the heading "dead end street," Konstantin Schwarz commented on the city's rejection of the revised plan which transferred the controversy from a local political to a legal platform (*SN* 31.1.2001). Those opposed to this solution feared that "the reputation of Stuttgart as a liberal city could suffer from the possibly lengthy procedures" (ibid.). Interestingly, these liberal voices were more concerned with the city's reputation than with the rights of the mosque community. Schwarz added that it was noteworthy that the city administration had been incapable for the entire year to curb the escalation of this conflict (ibid.). The VIKZ had honored the city's and opponents' objections and requests. Regardless, the conflict continued, indicating that most opponents were neither interested in dialogue, nor an appropriately sized mosque. They wanted no mosque whatsoever. The proposed discussion circle with Muslim participation about the general citywide need for prayer facilities never met (Osswald *SZ* 31.1.2001).

In February the Christian Democrats in the city council proposed that the city look for alternative sites to offer to the VIKZ. Where and what those could be, the faction did not specify. In the meanwhile, the VIKZ—still the owner of the factory—announced that they would start renovating the complex in February (Osswald *SZ* 6.2.2001). The Christian Democrats asked for more involvement in Heslach and proposed for the city to buy the compound and combine its area with another defunct industrial complex across the street, which had been awaiting reconstruction for years (ibid.). Months passed and the case remained hanging. Pro-Heslach organized the occasional meeting (*Stammtisch*), but never met with representatives or community members of the VIKZ (*Stuttgarter Nachrichten* 15.11.2001). In May the Christian Democrat faction in the city council proposed alternative sites for the VIKZ mosque. One site was a defunct industrial site that was, however, privately owned. The faction suggested for the city to contact the owner about a possible sale. They proposed a second site in the larger area of the main train station that was part of the controversial *Stuttgart 21* project (CDU-Gemeinderatsfraktion, Antrag Nr.219/2001).[8]

At this moment of impasse, when the city could find no legal fault with the project, and overt or covert anti-Muslim feelings marked the opponents' discourse, the tragedy of 9/11, dramatically altered this hitherto local conflict. By the middle of December 2001, a full two years after the purchase of the complex, the next higher administrative body (*Regierungspräsidium*) decided in favor of the city against the proposed mosque (Borgmann *SZ* 15.12.2001). The decision noted that "the building permit submitted by the VIKZ for the construction of a cultural center with prayer and cafeteria facilities is in opposition to the limits of transformation as agreed upon by the city council" (ibid.). The *Regierungspräsidium* pointed out that the VIKZ plans countered those of the city, because they did not "constitute use that is subordinated (*untergeordnet*) to residential use, and in addition this use was not limited to the needs of Heslach" (ibid.). The association's plans were not in tune with the priorities of residential use as the city had proposed in its most recent plan. This plan, it is important to note, had been conceived in the process of the mosque controversy (ibid.).

Almost simultaneous to this decision, authorities closed down two unlicensed student dormitories run by the VIKZ elsewhere in Stuttgart, which dramatically hurt the further proceeding of the Heslach case (*Stuttgarter Zeitung* 19.12.2001). It was certainly not a wise decision by the VIKZ to run dormitories without licenses. The decision to do so had been controversial among the local leadership, which was split—along generational lines—about such projects (see chapter 5). The younger members, aware of legal regulations and possible consequences, had advised against this endeavor. The older generation, who looked to similar successful projects in Turkey as models, was used to decades of neglect of their affairs by municipal institutions and hence saw no reason why this would be different now. The older generations' maneuvering was marked by a naïveté with regard to local politics and unfolding global politics. Regardless, the regular procedure for closing down an unlicensed student dormitory, which falls under the responsibility of the municipal child welfare agency (*Jugendamt*), would have been for this agency to initiate appropriate steps and close the facilities. Running an unlicensed student dormitory is an offense against child protection laws, but not a criminal offense. In the fall of 2001, however, in an atmosphere of heightened fear and suspicion, a small unlicensed student dormitory with less than ten students in the Hussein Mosque, turned into a matter of national security. Instead of *Jugendamt* officials, police and state security became involved as the affair quickly escalated. Only because Mr. Serdar, the President of the Hussein Mosque, had cultivated close relations with the local council and other neighborhood institutions, the affair took a more civil shape. Instead of state security and uniformed police driving up in large police vehicles and entering the mosque and producing a public scandal in this residential neighborhood, Mr. Serdar was informed of the now political "case." In the end, the head of the local council and a police official in plain clothes, accompanied by Mr. Serdar, went to inspect the dormitory. The students were dismissed and the case seemed over. A few days later, however, the police, this time with more personnel in official cars and uniforms, visited the now empty dormitory. After these incidents, the VIKZ quickly submitted plans for the legal establishment of a student dormitory and the necessary renovations (Höfle and Osswald *SZ* 15.5.2002). Soon after, the Hussein Mosque dormitory was first provisionally and later permanently approved (see chapter 5). By 2013 it had been in operation for a decade and never experienced any further problems. The public hype over the dormitories, however, had considerably damaged the ongoing Heslach controversy.

In March 2002 the VIKZ submitted a forty-page complaint to the administrational court (*Verwaltungsgericht*) against the city (Pazarkaya *SN* 18.3.2002). The dormitory plans were no longer part of the project. The administrative court announced a decision for July 17 (Höfle and Osswald *SZ* 9.7.2002). The case had come down to two central questions: First, was the project really only for the use of the neighborhood, or was it conceptualized for a much larger constituency? Second, was the ban on transformations as issued by the city until a final building plan was devised, legal or not? The lawyer of the VIKZ argued that without the dormitory, the project was local in nature (ibid.). Yet the unlicensed dormitories' affair had hardened the front lines between the city and the mosque association. The complaint of the VIKZ was rejected and the VIKZ subsequently sold the factory to the city. The city council decided in a closed meeting in September 2002 to turn the compound into a residential complex (*Stuttgarter Nachrichten* 18.9.2002). Almost five years after the VIKZ first purchased the old factory, the Mayor, local residents, and representatives of the VIKZ met once more at the controversial site, this time for the first "bulldozer bite" (*Baggerbiss*) for the destruction of the old factory that would be replaced by a residential complex with fifty apartments (Osswald *SZ* 7.10.2004). Mayor Schuster called it an "important project" for the quarter; another official called it a "milestone in the revitalization of Heslach" (ibid.).

Visibly Defeated

Why was the VIKZ defeated in this controversy? Was its leadership too uninformed or naïve? Not really. In fact, the VIKZ had worked with officials as the real estate transaction developed, because the association was aware of the sensitive nature of the project. Unlike their opponents, they had monitored and analyzed similar conflicts elsewhere. Officials, including Mayor Schuster, had initially not anticipated major problems. The municipality accommodated the purchase. Nobody foresaw obstacles, as this was a renovation project and not the construction of a "real" mosque. However, when the residents' opposition became more vocal, officials slowly withdrew from their former position. Local residents' prejudices, fears, and resentments dominated debates, possibly fostered by right-wing agitators from the sidelines. The VIKZ with its initially vague project description nurtured some confusion. The association's ambiguous announcement, however, was not meant to mislead the public. Rather it was the result of decades of local public indifference toward the lives and needs of Turks and/or Muslims. Years of negligence and lack of interest in the affairs of migrants in general and pious Muslims' affairs in particular had taught mosque associations to solve their problems alone. There had been few occasions to introduce their needs to the public or engage in debates with municipal officials. The association's public relations skills were clumsy and in the initial phase of the controversy even self-defeating. Regardless, the association quickly recognized points of contention and sources of local residents' concerns. They clarified their project and eventually shrunk it to a more acceptable size. But even after the plans were explained in more detail and modified in size, opposition did not subside. Many residents did not want a mosque—big or small—in their neighborhood. In the minds of opponents, a mosque was alien to their lifeworlds and deemed unnecessary. They were unable or unwilling to recognize the city's changing demographics and resulting needs, and spatial and cultural transformations.

Initial discussions about the size and appropriate nature of the mosque complex reflect reasonable concerns about the scope of a possibly regional or even national institution in a residential quarter. But, what about the outright rejection of a mosque in a quarter with a long-standing Muslim population? It seems that many of the outspoken residents had paid little attention to their Turkish and other Muslim neighbors and the fact that the latter had grown roots and become integral parts of the neighborhood and cityscape. In the absence of contact and relationship with their Muslim neighbors, mainstream ideas about Muslim affairs originated in stereotypes and media images of Muslims as prone to radicalism, militancy, and fanaticism (see chapter 4). Such prejudices further described Muslims as oppressing women, disregarding democratic processes, and being deceitful. In short: Muslims could not be trusted, and thus could not be good neighbors. Regardless of decades of peaceful co-existence in the neighborhood, and the VIKZ's attempt to explain and reshape their plans, an insurmountable wall of mistrust and suspicion remained.

In hindsight the conflict appears like a series of misunderstandings, ignorance, and naïvety on all parts. There are elements of irrational and uninformed fear of Islam and Muslims, and the use of rhetorically powerful terms such as "alienation," "radicalization," or "radical-Islamic center" that employed readily available images and resentments. The arguments of the mosque's opponents were surprisingly similar, if not outright identical, to those used in other mosque controversies. They included the standard repertoire of arguments: parking, noise,[9] the fear of cultural "alienation" in the local community, the possible radicalization of the mosque community, and the conviction that mosques teach outdated and hyper-conservative ideas and thus seriously "damage" and heavily indoctrinate innocent youths.

The passionate struggle over the Heslach mosque project exemplifies the dynamics of an urban and national political landscape in which Muslims at the turn of the twenty-first century had to fight for recognition, participation, and a material space in Germany. There is the incongruence of having lived in Stuttgart for decades, and in the case of the VIKZ as an organized community for three decades, yet not having been recognized as urban citizens and stakeholders. Subsequently the quest for communal facilities surprised dominant society. To be fair, many residents did not object to the mosque plans, some indeed supported the project, but mosque opponents were loud and shrill. In particular after 9/11, opponents linked local and urban concerns to global politics and tried to portray local Muslim associations as possible fronts for (ill-defined) radical or militant movements. It was impossible for a small local association (even with the help of its national umbrella organization) to single-handedly counter this onslaught of deep-seated prejudices, resentment, rejection, and mistrust.

The VIKZ's initial miscommunication and the two unlicensed dormitories did not help their cause. However, these mistakes did not lead to the demise of the project, as the official side produced equally or even more seriously flawed moments, like the small-size local master plan initiated after the mosque conflict had unfolded. Ultimately the mosque project was doomed as the urban political landscape was heavily weighed against it. Without much public recognition, few political ties, and weak alliances in the urban public sphere, the VIKZ was fighting a lonely battle. Regardless of constitutionally guaranteed rights of religious freedom, the local public and political environment at the turn of the twenty-first century was not ready to convert these rights into a larger and more visible material presence. However, in the course of the lengthy controversy, the city recognized that the VIKZ deserved better spaces in the city.

Years Later

Adnan Ömer, a VIKZ representative who had been centrally involved in the Heslach controversy, was one of my first interlocutors in the fall of 2006. For a first meeting Mr. Ömer invited me to the spacious premises of his company in a nice hillside location not far from downtown Stuttgart. We met in the conference facilities of his office. By then around forty, Mr. Ömer wore an elegant suit. He spoke in a soft voice with a Swabian accent. Among other issues, we talked about Islam and Muslim affairs in Stuttgart and quickly came to speak about the Heslach case. Mr. Ömer voiced his disappointment about the municipality which had known about the purchase of the factory ("Believe me, I know about such things and would never agree to buy such a large complex without being in touch with the city"). On a different occasion, Mr. Ömer noted, "up until today I still do not completely understand what made this opposition so fierce." Many of the involved actors, including some of the city officials, were startled by the fierce reactions. This surprise is illustrated by the reaction of the Mayor who was initially hesitant to interfere. As the noise of the opposition did not subside and indeed increased with time, the city had to react. "By the end," Mr. Ömer added, "it is this kind of noise that is most heard, and we had no chance against it. Of course, we were also quite naïve at the time and did not know how to best represent our case in public." When I mentioned the imbalance of voices in the numerous articles in the local press, Mr. Ömer explained: "We were complete lay people with regard to the public and journalistic aspects, when the controversy started. It is hard to speak to a journalist on the phone and then find that only particular aspects were reproduced in a newspaper article. There were times when I felt that journalists were only keen to hear what they wanted and then write things that they had thought all along, regardless of our words." In the end, he added, he tried to write down things before he said them in interviews to better control journalistic (mis-)representations. He also remarked on the imbalanced and neglectful reporting with regard to their efforts. For example, the VIKZ had collected 400 signatures of Muslim residents in Heslach about the need for a local mosque, "but nobody bothered to ever write about this." Ultimately, Mr. Ömer noted, he and his colleagues learned a lot in those years.

Mosque opponents successfully used dominant images of Stuttgart that described the city as "German" in ways that might have reflected the reality of decades ago, but were now outdated. They did not recognize pious Muslims and mosque associations as legitimate urban actors and stakeholders with a claim to participation, and more importantly a role in the negotiation and construction of the urban future. The mosque opponents who employed these static images of urban culture, belonging, and participation were better organized than those residents who might have been neutral or in favor of the project. One woman remarked to me about this project: "but you have to understand that Heslach is an old Stuttgarter working class quarter," (hence the fierce opposition to the "foreign" mosque) implying its continued existence as a quarter populated exclusively by ethnic Germans. Yet, in actual reality, the quarter like other inner-city quarters, had transformed into a multi-ethnic neighborhood. In fact, all Stuttgarter working-class quarters of the twenty-first century are multi-ethnic.

Despite its earlier implicit support for the mosque, the city gave in to loud popular demands. It was next to impossible for a small mosque association, even with the, in this case less than helpful, support of a national representative to counter the overwhelming organization, noise, and publicity of their opponents. As newcomers to urban public debates, the association could mobilize only few resources and even fewer individuals who could smoothly participate on local political platforms. "For our members," Mr. Ömer continued, "this was all new. Most of them do not read the newspaper. Ultimately, what they care about is a place where they can pray and send their children for religious instruction." Many of the opponents' arguments, including accusations of radical Islam or Saudi funding, were far removed from these ordinary people's lives.

The decision against the mosque project was a political decision. "There was nothing we could do," Mr. Ömer concluded. The city bought the factory at the price the VIKZ had paid which meant a considerable loss for the association as they had paid debt services, taxes, and insurance on the property for the duration of the conflict. "Nonetheless, after it was all over, the city was cooperative in finding a solution and a place for us," Mr. Ömer related. After the city offered a few other possibilities and renewed the offer of granting more space to the community in the existing Takva Mosque facilities, the association accepted the additional space in this location, which they ended up buying in its entirety. This transaction made them the owners of the large old industrial facility (3,000 square meters). For the past two decades they had occupied only a small part of this old factory. Mr. Ömer remarked: "This is somewhat ironic. Previous boards and presidents had for twenty years sent letters every year to the Mayor asking to buy parts of the building. Yet their quests were routinely rejected. It took the Heslach controversy for us to finally be able to buy our 'old' building. Sometimes we joke about these odd circumstances."

When I asked him how he felt today about this controversy and its outcome, he laughed and said "today we are actually very happy with the Takva facilities and now I would say it all worked out for the better." Because of the considerable loss through the Heslach project, the community has been slow with the renovation of the Takva Mosque. It took the community almost a decade to turn at least part of the vast production halls into a comfortable community center. By 2010 central elements of the renovation of the Takva Mosque were in place. With a glossy brochure (put into the mailboxes of residents with Turkish names in the larger vicinity of the mosque) the mosque celebrated its work and achievements. Years of dedicated labor (the premises had finally been bought in December 2003) resulted in multipurpose facilities including, among others, prayer rooms for men and women, classrooms for religious instruction, a library, kitchen, cafeteria, seminar rooms, administrative quarters, and multipurpose halls. The mosque offers programs like lessons for children and adults, preparation for the *hajj* (pilgrimage) and *umra* (lesser pilgrimage), the possibility to give alms, and funeral services (ritual washing, transfer of the deceased to Turkey). Moreover, the center has larger halls where families can celebrate boys' circumcisions, engagements, and weddings. The brochure proudly indicates that the total area of the mosque facilities amounts to more than 900 square meters. The centerpiece of the Takva Mosque, the men's prayer room—kept in soft beige and grey tones—among others pieces features an impressive intricately carved grey marble *minbar*, and a matching elaborately embellished large marble *mihrab*. Eleven years after the purchase of the factory in Heslach, the community had created a home for itself, at least as far as the interior of the Takva Mosque is concerned. From the outside the premises are not recognizable as a mosque.

Beginnings

Without belittling the expanded energy, and experienced frustration of different constituencies in mosque conflicts, it is important to understand that such conflicts are important public platforms where Muslim communities and their non-Muslim neighbors, fellow citizens, and urban administrators often encounter each other as partners (or opponents) for the first time. By way of planning to acquire and renovate larger premises, mosque communities take an important step out of their previous backyard locations. Their wish for adequate facilities symbolizes their arrival in the city and urban public sphere, as much as it is a visible indicator of their advanced localization. To run a prayer room for a small number of migrant workers in relative isolation in an industrial backyard with few or no ties to the surrounding urban environment is vastly different from administering a multi-generational, mixed sex, multi-class, and possibly multi-ethnic mosque that strives to be part of a quarter's public and cultural sphere. The move from the an all-male *Hinterhofmoschee* to the purchase of "better" facilities often coincides with generational transitions and the reworking of a community's central focus away from the country of origin toward a local urban and national public and political sphere. That mosque communities (especially under the leadership of first-generation migrants) did not always perfectly manage all aspects of such difficult transformations should come as no surprise. Faced with multiple challenges, communities worked hard to face these tasks and articulate their position in society. Examining the case of the Heslach mosque conflict, it is clear that the association was not prepared in 1999 for the struggle that unfolded. Yet, they learned and made the best of an at-times offensive and unfair conflict. In the process the association further developed its existing communities and learned the discourse and practices of urban public and political debates and media cultures.

As much as the Heslach case remains a painful memory for some of the involved parties, it constitutes a crucial moment in the localization of pious Muslims in Stuttgart. For the first time since their arrival decades earlier, Muslims and their communities had become the subject of urban public debates. While many members of dominant society categorically denied pious Muslims any rights and role in the city, a growing number of observers, discussants, and commentators understood the changing urban demographics, and cultural make-up. Muslims had entered the public and municipal consciousness, even if central actors and constituencies could not agree what exactly their rights and roles were. The municipality—without creating much of a public stir—eventually gave the VIKZ an alternative facility, ironically one that the association had for years been asking for. In the wake of the Heslach case, but also triggered by the events of 9/11, the city, other institutions, and civic associations in quick succession issued diverse programs of getting-to-know-each-other and cooperation with local mosques. Long-seated barriers were slowly and sometimes reluctantly addressed and sparse new links and networks cautiously initiated. Over the years, a few individuals, like Mr. Serdar, have become well-known and respected members of the Stuttgart's religious and cultural sphere. Whether in his own mosque community or neighborhood activities, in Christian-Muslim dialogue events, or the New Year's reception of Stuttgart's Jewish community, Mr. Serdar is now a sought-after guest and panelist in the Muslim and larger urban public sphere. After he made his first larger public appearances in the Heslach case, his interlocutors quickly understood his role within his community, his integrity, and enthusiastic willingness to participate and cooperate. His participation in the controversy solidly established Mr. Serdar as a public actor on multiple urban platforms.

In the meanwhile the Stuttgart mosque-scape remains a work in progress as mosque communities struggle to acquire better spaces or improve those they inhabit. Everyday realities, economic circumstances, political considerations, and a vaguely circumscribed but very real mistrust from members of dominant society and the authorities continue to create complicated encounters and negotiations. The municipality is both supportive and opposed to mosque associations' spatial projects, depending on these projects' locations, respective mosque organization, and interaction with other constituencies.[10] Understanding their precarious situation, most mosque communities do not search for exterior aesthetics or specific building plans. Their central objective remains access to space—any space that works or can be adapted to serve the needs of communities. Ending up in industrial or similar facilities, communities often spend years renovating these spaces. Individual spaces reflect what Gerdien Jonker and Valérie Amiraux called larger "urban trajectories" of Muslims and their communities (2006: 15). Many communities are engaged in lengthy renovation activities. Carpets are laid, mosaic wall designs realized, chandeliers hung up, kitchens taken out or added, multi-function rooms and halls created, and classrooms arranged—visiting Stuttgart's mosques at times feels like a veritable tour of home improvement. Mosque spaces and their social communities are a "work in progress" (ibid.: 18). Working on their "homes," communities become local. This does not mean that communities would not like to have more representative structures that partake in the broader grammar of conventional mosque architecture. Recognizing the cost and even more so the predictable struggles and possibilities of rejection, most communities shy away from planning ambitious projects. Whether and how projects unfold depends on details that cannot be planned up front. In their search for viable strategies, mosque communities and in particular their presidents and board members are keen observers of other communities' struggles and most importantly other mosques' successes. One board members of the Salam Mosque noted in a conversation about the conflict over the large Cologne mosque project: "of course we are watching what is happening in Cologne. What we learn might one day be useful for us here in Stuttgart."

As pious Muslims and mosque communities become urban actors and more visible and recognized urban constituencies, it is not only important for mosque communities to build mosques and community centers. It is equally important for the pious to articulate urban subjectivities, communal arrangements, and individual lifeworlds that best accommodate their religiosities. I will turn to these in the next chapter.

Notes

1. One man remembered how his mosque lost their facilities over a controversy involving one parking space.
2. Miriam Gazzah (2010) observed similar developments in the Netherlands.
3. Such conflicts are not limited to mosque communities. See the similar experiences of a Jain Temple on the outskirts of London (Shah et al. 2012).
4. Other new religious communities often experience similar resentments. A Hindu Temple in Stuttgart lost its lease over a dispute with neighbors about noise and kitchen smells (Sattler *SZ* 21.11.2007).
5. Bölsche notes that there are currently 163 "classic mosques" in Germany in addition to 2,600 mosques in a variety of buildings. In 2008, another 184 mosques are under planning or construction (2008: 74).
6. A much shorter description of the Heslach mosque controversy was first published in Kuppinger 2014e.
7. *Überfremdung* refers to a vaguely defined fear of too much foreign/alien elements in a community or country that would endanger the cultural integrity of the native residents.
8. The proposal is available at http://www.domino1.stuttgart.de/grat/cdu.nsf/520dd28abcee19ad41256717006476ce/412567210029d4cb41256a4d005e29c1?OpenDocument. The Stuttgart 21 site is particularly ironic, as the larger project had not even been approved by then. In 2014 the proposed area was still a vast construction site.
9. Arguments about excessive noise and too many cars are not limited to mosques. See the experiences of a Jain Temple in London (Shah et al. 2012).
10. The city prevented a Milli Görüş mosque project in Wangen in 2007 (Höfle and Brand *SZ* 6.12.2007). A Bosnian community successfully bought and renovated a commercial facility in Hedelfingen in 2009/10.

CHAPTER 2

Religiosities

In March 2007 a note in the women's suite of the Al-Nour Mosque announced a celebration for women and children on the occasion of *Mulid An-Nabi* (the Prophet's birthday). When I told my neighbor Fahime, who was not part of the Al-Nour community, about this celebration, she immediately asked whether I could take her daughter, Ayşe, along. The next Saturday Tamima, Tala, Ayşe, and I went to the Al-Nour Mosque. We arrived at the mosque at 3 P.M. and about forty women were sitting in the women's prayer room. Some older women sat on chairs lined up along the walls, the rest sat on the floor. We found a space on the floor. Most of the women were busy talking in small groups. After a while an older girl came and announced there would be games downstairs for the children. Ayşe, Tamima, and Tala went with the younger crowd. More women kept arriving. It was getting crowded and little seating space was left on the floor. Soon Zeinab Abdallah and Sabiha Abdel-Rahman, two of the mosque's active female members, brought a TV and VCR, which they set up in a corner. The formal part of the celebration was about to start. It took Zeinab some time and voice power to calm down about 100 loudly chatting women. More women kept coming in and each arrival caused new commotion as those already present greeted newcomers. Finally Zeinab was able to speak her greetings despite a persistent noise level. Next Sabiha did a beautiful Qur'an recitation which somewhat quieted down the chatter. Zeinab, dressed in a simple and elegant black *abayah* (Gulf-style Islamic dress), continued with a short lecture/sermon about the Prophet. She emphasized that in all situations we could hope for the help of the Prophet. This was particularly important for raising children. She related how well the Prophet treated children, always greeting them, and how he hugged and kissed his grandsons, Hassan and Hussein. She stressed that it was good to praise the Prophet, which was done anyway many times in the daily prayers. Throughout Zeinab's short sermon, Hebba her young daughter, kept wrapping herself in and out of the fabric of her mother's *abayah*. Showing her usual calm and quiet, and acting gracefully in line with her words about love and patience for children, Zeinab let her play. Minutes into Zeinab's talk, many women returned to their conversations and the noise level increased again. Newcomers, who were barely able to walk through the crowd of seated women, were greeted with "*Salam Aleikum*s." Smaller children ran in and out, here and there a baby cried. Even though I sat fairly close to Zeinab, it became increasingly difficult to understand her. Conversations were largely in Arabic (I heard Iraqi, Egyptian, and Palestinian dialects). Chats were lively, loud, and there was some laughter.

The crowd was diverse with regard to age, clothing, and to a lesser extent ethnicity. There were older women in traditional Palestinian dresses, younger women who wore black *abayah*s, others wore simple long dresses, or *gallabeya*s (Egyptian-style Islamic dress), a few had donned South Asian–style *shalwar-qamis* combinations, others wore tight jeans and long T-shirts. There were a few women with improvised scarves, like my own, which always seemed to be in danger of slipping down. At one point a women in a black *abayah*, decorated with red and glittery gold, stepped in. She wore heavy make-up and numerous golden bracelets on her arms. Some of her dyed blond hair escaped from under her *hijab*. Suddenly, most eyes were on her. The newcomer said her *salam*s. As she tried to cross the room under many watchful eyes, she kept her hands in front of her chest to allow a view on some massive golden rings. Her sleeves were pushed back enough for a full view of the plentiful golden bracelets. She walked across the room and greeted people as if Zeinab was not talking. In the face of this easily distracted and inattentive audience, Zeinab wrapped up her talk, faster than planned, it seemed. She quickly moved to the screening of a video about the revelations of the Prophet, but the VCR did not work. Some women tried to fix the technology, but gave up after about fifteen minutes. Many of the women barely noticed all of this, as they were deeply involved in their conversations.

Sometime later older girls and young women sang songs that praised the Prophet. The mood shifted from talkative to celebratory, as many women, including the older Iraqi woman who sat behind me, knew the songs and happily sang along. In some songs the girls sang the verses and the audience joined in the chorus. The audience gained momentum and many started clapping. The mood was increasingly joyful as in particular the older women seemed to return to their youth, their hometowns or villages and wholeheartedly brought their memories alive in their singing. There was more singing back and forth: the young women sang and the audience sang their response. The clapping grew louder. The mood became ever livelier and happier. After a while everybody was rhythmically singing "*Muhammad, sala wa salam.*" By now almost 100 women had to be in this large room and it was getting hot. The two open windows brought no relief. The singing lasted for about twenty minutes.

After a short break when conversations once more dominated the room, Sheikh Saleh, the Imam of the Al-Nour Mosque, appeared at about 4:20 p.m., wearing his regular "imam-outfit" of a long *gallabeya*, a wide cloak and a small cap. He was supposed to deliver a sermon. Zeinab and Sheikh Saleh had a hard time getting the room quiet. The women chatted, children ran in and out, babies cried. To get the women's attention, Zeinab called "*takbir*," (call to praise Allah) but few women noticed and only a weak "*Allahu Akbar*" came back from the audience. Zeinab was stressed and annoyed by the situation. She tried to make herself heard and appealed to the women's moral senses. Zeinab, who usually translated all her words into German, did not translate the next part. She shouted in Arabic that for an occasion like this, it was necessary to show *adab* (manners, behavior) and *ihtiram* (respect). Without the two this would not work. In near despair, she repeated these keywords three times, but to little avail. Sheikh Saleh stepped in and called for another *takbir*. His louder male voice yielded more audible results. He started his sermon. He talked in Arabic and Zeinab translated in five-minute installments. He also talked about how the Prophet treated children. He told the *hadith* (saying/lesson of the Prophet) of how the Prophet visited the son of a Jew who had been making fun of him. When the Prophet asked the boy to say the *shahada* (creed, declaration of belief), the boy questioningly looked to his father who then said to him "yes, say it." Sheikh Saleh noted how only by serious effort and blood (Zeinab did not translate the term blood) today's 1.2 billion Muslims got to where they were. The audience remained talkative. Suddenly commotion started behind Zeinab and the Sheikh.

An older woman approached Zeinab and whispered something in her ear and gestured toward the back. A few women slowly pushed a young ethnic German woman with a *hijab* toward Zeinab and the Sheikh. Zeinab was puzzled and turned to the Sheikh who at first was somewhat irritated, but then relieved to be able to end his sermon to this inattentive community. The scene was clear now: a *shahada* would be spoken (the young woman was going to convert to Islam). The young woman stood waiting and fighting back tears in the background as the Sheikh finished his sermon. Zeinab announced: "A new sister has found Islam. She wants to say the *shahada*."

The young woman moved to the middle of the room. Suddenly, the noise level subsided significantly. Still a little teary-voiced, the woman introduced herself: "My name Sophie and I am twenty-four years old." She called a woman from the audience who came and stood next to her and continued: "This is the cousin of my husband, who has helped me along this way." Zeinab and the cousin took Sophie in the middle and held her hands. After a few introductory words, Sheikh Saleh arrived at the *shahada*. The room was quiet. An excited but also serene tension had taken hold of the assembled women. Sheikh Saleh slowly started:

"*Ashhad inu,*" and Sophie repeated the words in a strong but tearful voice.

"*la allah,*" the Sheik said and Sophie repeated.

"*Ila Allah,*" the Sheikh continued and Sophie repeated.

"*Wa-Muhammad,*" the Sheikh continued and Sophie repeated.

"*Rasul Allah,*" the Sheikh finished and Sophie repeated.

All eyes were on Sophie in this solemn and intense moment, as she finished professing that there was no God but Allah and the Muhammad was his Prophet. Peace and quiet marked the atmosphere that only minutes earlier had been so boisterous and inattentive. The audience was moved. There was a short silence after Sophie spoke her last word. Then there were the first cries of joy (*zaghata*), which were followed by more and louder ones. The solemn tension gave way to celebration. Zeinab quickly called in Arabic "do not do *zaghrata*, do *takbir*!" Cries of "*Allahu Akbar!*" "*Allahu Abkar!*" now sounded from all over the room. Those around Sophie congratulated and hugged her. Still shaken, she moved to the far end of the room, where she was hugged and kissed by more women.

After this emotional and spiritual climax, it was impossible for Zeinab to get the audience to be quiet and listen once more. Clearly the event had come to an unexpected, but appropriate climax and needed no further talk, sermon, or explanations. The new sister was a highlight, and a seal to the success of the event. No words could express this more suitably. It was time to return to one's conversation. Before everything disintegrated, a professionally dressed woman with an elegant jacket (the only woman without a *hijab*) approached Zeinab. One last time Zeinab turned to the audience and announced/screamed that this woman was a Muslim midwife who advertised her services for whoever might need them now or in the future. The woman handed out her card. Several women took one. Judging by her name the midwife was of Iranian background. After Zeinab was done with this final announcement, our eyes met. I smiled and she came over to me. I said, "I admire your endurance and patience. It must be hard to speak to this audience."

She looked exhausted, irritated, and disappointed. She agreed about how demanding this was. To encourage her I suggested, "You need to get a microphone, otherwise this will not work." "We have tried to get one," she responded "but could not find anything affordable. They said new ones would arrive by late April. It is impossible without. It is too hard. Nobody listens." I agreed and added, "Did you expect such a large crowd?" Zeinab said no, and explained, "We only put a few small signs in the mosque and so many people came, many women came from other mosques. We never expected that many visitors."

I briefly talked to Susanne, another friend, and then decided to look for the girls. On my way out I encountered Zeinab again who was talking to Manuela, who complained about the behavior of the women and their rudeness toward the speakers. Manuela was annoyed. For her a religious ceremony was something different; this here, she noted was alien to her. Moments later Susanne joined Manuela, Zeinab, and me. She similarly pointed to the messy nature of the event and that it was rather un-Islamic. Zeinab was exhausted and frustrated with how things had developed. She said: "Next time one should give the women some calming tea so that they quiet down." Then she added, "Next time I will invite them for an hour before the event and serve them this calming tea." I added: "If you do that they will also have enough time to chat up front. This was simply a *mulid* in the word's popular sense."[1] Zeinab agreed. Slowly Manuela and I moved to the hallway to get tea. Pouring my tea, I saw Tamima, Tala, and Ayşe arriving from downstairs. Together we left the stuffy suite and sat down on the steps in the crowded stairways. It was enjoyably cool there. A constant traffic of women and children moved in and out of the suite. A man shouted from below to a boy that he should stop riding the elevator up and down as this was annoying. Nobody paid much attention. We decided to leave and as we walked down the main street, Sheik Saleh passed us at the next traffic light. Now dressed in a suit and long fashionable beige trench coat, he was busy talking on his cell phone but interrupted his flow of words for an exchange of pleasantries as we stood next to him. When the light turned green, he quickly took off and the sides of his open coat moved in the wind.

In this chapter I examine the negotiation of individual and communal religiosities and lifeworlds in the Al-Nour Mosque, where individuals like Sophie, Zeinab, Sabiha, Susanne, and Manuela (recent and established converts, born Muslims who turned to Islamic piety, and long-term believers) daily work and learn to improve their Islamic knowledge, refine their religious and social practices, and outline suitable public roles and engagements for themselves, others, and the community at large. Analyzing individual trajectories, group debates, and moments of learning and engagement, I illustrate that the *mulid*, Sophie's conversion, and other events and dynamics at the Al-Nour Mosque are integral parts of urban culture. While some observers would view Sophie's conversion as a step out, or even against mainstream society, I argue that this turn to Islamic piety and resulting changes in lifestyles, social engagements, and civic participation constitute a repositioning of an individual in society and not their departure from, or worse betrayal of local society. Islamic piety and its lifestyles, personal religiosities, and pious practices form an integral part of a multi-ethnic and multi-religious urban culture. The quest of diverse pious individuals to learn more about Islam, refine their religious practices, and locate their social life predominantly in a mosque community does not result in the creation of a parallel society. Instead, since mosques have become established elements of the urban public sphere, activities and engagements in mosques are ordinary cultural and civic activities like those in churches, clubs, and associations. Encounters and debates in mosques, and resulting practices and lifestyles contribute to the negotiation of local Muslim cultural and public spheres and the urban public sphere at large, as individuals carry Islamic knowledge, practices, sentiments, and modes of sociality into their neighborhoods or places of work and study, and as they participate in diverse Muslim or secular civic activities.

In the following I examine how individual mosque members or visitors strive to improve their religiosity with the help of groups, events, and other believers, and how they debate what it means to be a pious Muslim in a secular urban environment. Discussions and personal struggles focus on how simultaneously to be a pious Muslim and worthy member of the global *ummah*, and to live and participate as a pious individual in the city (Lubeck 2002: 77; Kandemir 2005). Learning about Islam and improving pious practices are crucial, not only for recent converts, but for most pious individuals (Deeb 2006; Mahmood 2005; Hirschkind 2006). Mosques play a central role for many believers as places to debate religiosities, and cultivate relationships with like-minded individuals (Bowen 2010: 37; Schiffauer 2000; Tietze 2001). Here believers create a spatiality and sociality that is marked by Islamic practices and sentiments that allow them to practice and live, what they define as, religiously correct lives and relationships. They experiment with and learn pious practices, and socialize children into religiosity. Considerable attention and labor is geared toward the refinement of pious practices and the creation of religiously correct spaces, activities, and encounters (Hirschkind 2006; Mahmood 2005; Jouili 2008). Yet, these efforts are not isolated from urban society (Nökel 2002; Gerlach 2006). As individuals and groups discuss and define (internal) religious practices, they do so with an eye on their lives outside the mosque (Fadil 2006; Lewis 2006; Backer 2009; Uhlemayr 2010). "Talking Islam" further helps individuals to reflect and analyze stories of exclusion and discrimination and refine and strengthen their pious identities in the process (Göle 2004: 21; Deeb 2006).

As the most international mosque in Stuttgart, the Al-Nour Mosque plays a crucial role in the articulation of local Muslim religiosities and Muslim cultural and public spheres. This mosque is a meeting space for diverse Muslims and a site for religious learning, debate, and experiments with practices, sentiments, and relationships (for a similar mosque in Munich, see Kandemir 2005). The mosque, its members, visitors, and groups constitute a loosely circumscribed field where activities, engagements, and varying religiosities unfold, which contribute to the construction of Muslim German lifeworlds, local pious subjectivities, and the localization of Islam and Muslims in Stuttgart (Fadil 2006: 75). Examining individual experiences and communal activities in the Al-Nour Mosque, I ask a number of questions: What are the issues, transformations, trends, and practices that are negotiated in this mosque? What questions and concerns do individuals bring to the mosque? What are guiding influences and dynamics? How do individuals learn and internalize practices? What is the position of this mosque versus others in the city? How do individuals insert their religiosities and the practices they learned and negotiated in the Al-Nour Mosque into different aspects and spheres of their daily lives?

Religiosities

Historically, most people were socialized into religiosities and their concomitant everyday practices. Few questioned the role and practice of their religion, chose not to practice it, or left it altogether. Since the nineteenth century, complex and often forceful dynamics of imperialism, modernity, and globalization thoroughly remade religious cultures, and the role of religion in individual and communal lives. While most people the world over are still born into specific religions or religious communities, whether or how they practice their religion has increasingly become a matter of choice and circumstances. For many Muslims, forced relocation (Ghannam 2002), displacement by war und unrest (Deeb 2006), rural to urban migration (White 2002), political upheaval and dramatic changes (Ghodsee 2010), and international migration (Ewing 2008; Silverstein 2004; Killian 2006; Mandel 2008; Mannitz 2006; Lewis 1994; Werbner 2002; Abbas 2005) crucially affected personal religiosities and transformed religious communities and individual lifeworlds and religiosities. Globalization and migration widen the range of religious choices and possible religiosities (Sassen 1999; Modood 2007; Castles and Davidson 2000: 134; Soysal 1994: 114). Individuals who were born Muslims and live in non-Muslims societies can position themselves on a range of possibilities vis-à-vis Islam and Muslim and local contexts. Some renounce Islam altogether.[2] Some live thoroughly secular lifestyles (Somunçu 2004; Akgün 2008; Özdemir 1997). Others might intermarry and have Christian or Jewish children. Yet others become high-holiday Muslims, cultural Muslims, or join a mosque only to make sure that their children learn the basics of Islam. Some drink alcohol during the year and fast for Ramadan (Akgün 2008). Individuals might combine Islam with Indian wisdom or Buddhism, or design eclectic practices they deem best for their purposes (Sezgin 2006: 109). Others remain or become pious and practice their religion alone. Yet others make religion the center of their lives and social lives. They join mosque communities and spend considerable parts of their time in the mosque and participate in groups, events, and celebrations at their mosque. Individuals pick and choose their religious practices, involvements, and affiliations. Individual life histories combine secular with religious chapters (Kandemir 2005; Uhlemayr 2010; Bullock 2005; Saktanber 2002). While (ethnic) social and cultural customs and practices constitute larger frames of reference in Muslim and/or migrant families, these frames vary considerably with the length of residence in Germany, rural or urban location, intermarriage, or other lifestyle changes and choices (Ewing 2008; Mandel 2008, 1996).

To be or become pious, especially in Muslim minority contexts, requires a conscious decision that engenders practical consequences and often results in a reorientation toward other pious individuals and possibly (but not necessarily) a mosque community (Baumann 2004; Jouili 2008; Uhlemayr 2010; Özelsel 2005). As Islamic religiosity becomes a choice, subsequent individual transformations are marked by further choices about practices and affiliations preferred by the pious. In a landscape of religious possibilities and plurality, such choices are not limited to those who were born Muslim. Islamic religiosities have in recent decades attracted numerous non-Muslims. Cat Stevens turned Yusuf Islam is probably the most well-known recent convert, but there are many others (Backer 2009; Bullock

2005a; Lang 1994; Wilson 2010; Hoffmann 1995, 1996a,b; Rouse 2004; Wadud 1999, 2006; Spohr 1998; Özyürek 2009, 2014).³ Joining new Muslims in their efforts to define their pious lifestyles are Muslims who "revert" to Islam. Reversion refers to the re-/turn of a Muslim to Islam—when a "cultural" Muslim or a person of Muslim descent transforms into a newly pious and more observant and practicing Muslim (van Nieuwkerk 2006; Kandemir 2005; Uhlemayr 2010). Like conversion, reversion entails reconstructing a person's identity and practices, and the negotiation of a transformed public persona. Converts, reverts, and the small but growing number of young believers who grew up in (very consciously) pious households find themselves in similar positions where, given different possibilities of pious lifestyles, they have to choose one for themselves, as there are no clear givens (Tietze 2001; Gerlach 2006; Tarlo 2010; Deeb and Harb 2013).

Sophie's conversion is situated in a larger framework of Muslim localization, local Muslim subjectivities and lifestyles, local mosque communities, and global Islamic networks. The actual moment of conversion is only one step and (most likely) results in a long learning process and the subsequent remaking of aspects of Sophie's subjectivity and public persona, everyday practices, social relations, and lifeworld (Asad 2003; Deeb 2006). In the process of such transformations, individuals insert themselves in local and global networks and circuits. Many (born) Muslims face similar challenges when they turn from a less religious lifestyle toward piety. Even those who have been pious for years or all their lives (growing up in pious families) are continuously confronted with the task to acquire more knowledge and improve their pious practices and lifestyles. One challenge is the careful examination of Muslim practices, whether they are "truly" Islamic, or the product of popular culture and social traditions (Amir-Moazami 2010: 193; Jouili and Amir-Moazami 2006; Bowen 2010: 70). Pious individuals and groups search for guidelines for practices of what Deeb (2006) called "authenticated Islam." In the process believers distance themselves from practices of "traditional" Muslims, and those of dominant secular societies. The negotiation of local pious selves unfolds with reference and in opposition to these two fields, as the pious situate themselves both in the Muslim tradition and in liberal democracies (Göle 2004: 28). They become owners, participants, and shapers of the Muslim tradition and the local cityscape (Boender 2006: 112; Henkel 2007). New forms and practices emerge that confirm and reject aspects of both socio-cultural traditions associated with Islam and liberal secular culture. In a fine-tuned and critical encounter with traditional or popular Islam, more orthodox and textual interpretations gain currency. Being able to read the Qur'an and other relevant sources by themselves, without the mediation of theologians and preachers, especially women challenge existing social and religious practices, in particular gender roles and relations (Barlas 2002; Wadud 2006). They differentiate between the teachings of Islam and patriarchal social and cultural universes (Barazangi 2004, 2005). Such reasoning challenges existing power structures in many mosques and pushes some women to search for avenues of learning, debate, and activities beyond mosque communities (Backer 2009; Özelsel 2005; Klausing 2009).

When individuals turn to Islam and construct their individual spiritualities and religiosities, their trajectories are open-ended (Baumann 2004; Filter 2008; Spohr 1998; Kandemir 2005). New believers engage more or less intensely with their faith and fellow believers. They might momentarily withdraw from society to reappear later with a renegotiated public persona and practices. Over time individuals decide whether to become more engaged, further develop their pious lifestyle, join a mosque community, or construct a circle of similarly minded friends. Some depart again from their faith, like a former member of the women's Qur'an study group at the Al-Nour Mosque about whom the other women noted that she "had lost her faith" *(vom Glauben abgefallen)*.[4] Others remain religious but relax some of their practices ("a very occasional glass of wine cannot be that wrong," one woman remarked).

The decision to live a pious life for most individuals marks the beginning of a learning process that involves engagement with Qur'an, *Sunna* (wisdom/experience of the Prophet), and theological texts, and the constant review and revision of one's life and practices. Just to pray, fast, give alms, and do the pilgrimage is not enough. The decision to become pious is not an ending point or arrival but a transitional moment for a new identity, subjectivity, lifestyle, and practices and their ensuing constant improvement (Hirschkind 2006). As individuals engage in learning processes and experiences they make decisions about concrete pious practices, lifestyles, theological preferences, and communal affiliations. Like in Muslim majority contexts (Deeb 2006; White 2002; Hirschkind 2006; Deeb and Harb 2013), pious individuals in minority contexts are faced with shades of religiosities, and an array of pious practices (Bowen 2007, 2010; Ghodsee 2010; Keaton 2006; Nökel 2002, 2004; Tietze 2001). When pious individuals encounter each other in mosques and beyond, they often "talk Islam" (Deeb 2006:99), debate their pieties, concrete religious and mundane practices, and share notes about resources (e.g. books, websites, lectures, meetings, stores; see also Haenni 2005; Pink 2009; Tarlo 2010). Friends compare notes about mosques, preachers, sermons, Qur'an study groups, Islamic singers, *halal* supermarkets, YouTube clips of events and sermons, Islamic websites, or experiences of discrimination in dominant society.

Believers who are part of formal or informal pious communities often adopt practices that are deemed appropriate in these communities (e.g. How much gender mixing is allowed or appropriate? Is it acceptable to eat chicken that was slaughtered in a non-*halal* manner?). Individual trajectories can evolve into different identities, and positions in Muslim and non-Muslim contexts. A person might live a more observant lifestyle (e.g. complete segregation of genders; avoid all places and gatherings where alcohol is served), or choose less strict interpretations on some issues (e.g. locally slaughtered, i.e. non-*halal* beef or chicken can be consumed, visit a bar but without consuming alcohol). Believers debate rules to do with religious practices and worship (*ibadat*; e.g. Should women wear socks to pray? How long after the call to prayer should one pray?), but also those to do with social and cultural practices (*mu'amalat*; e.g. Should one attend a Christian funeral service? Can Muslims sign the papers for their Christian relatives to be cremated? Should one go to restaurants where alcohol is served?). In their everyday lives pious individuals make choices about their diverse practices, religious involvements, lifestyles (Which mosque to go to? What headscarf to wear? What [religious or secular] events to attend?), and consumption (Which food products include *haram* substances? How to deal with interest payments on bank accounts? Is it acceptable to buy an apartment using conventional bank loans?). While the acceptance of divine teachings as spelled out in the Qur'an is paramount to the pious, there is leeway in mundane applications. Much of the intellectual and practical learning involved in these processes unfolds in spaces that have, as Bowen (2010: 105) termed it, an "Islamic ambiance" (see also Göle 2004: 32; Kömeçoğlu 2004: 163; Harb and Deeb 2013).

The Al-Nour Mosque

If one does not know the exact location of the Al-Nour Mosque, it is hard to find.[5] The mosque is located in a nondescript 1970s residential and commercial complex that is situated on the corner of a loud and busy main thoroughfare, which cuts across a densely populated multi-ethnic quarter of Stuttgart. The Al-Nour community occupies three suites on three different floors in this building, which includes five floors with three units/suites each. Two small signs by the corner and at the entrance to the building indicate the presence of a mosque. Next to this building on the main and side streets are older apartment buildings. To the back of the complex is a parking lot. A short street leads from this parking lot into a side street. Until November 2007, the large defunct premises of an old textile factory were located across the dead-end street. In 2007/08 these last remnants of the quarter's industrial past were torn down to make room for an inner-city urban development of residential units and social services. In 2009 the site was a huge "hole" in the urban fabric. Construction gained momentum in 2010, and in 2011 residents moved into the new apartments. Hundreds of residents brought new life to the former industrial city block. South of this new development, a number of old factories had in recent years been replaced by a mall and expansive office complex. After the closure of a large freight train station and adjacent industrial facilities further to the southwest, this area transitioned into a commercial and residential quarter. Located on the northern fringes of this transforming area, the Al-Nour Mosque is lucky to have spacious premises in the middle of a commercial and residential quarter with easy access to public transportation. The building itself is a mixed blessing with its assembly of private and commercial tenants, including a Hindu Temple, a doctor's office, a medical lab, an import-export firm, a few residential apartments, and a domina/SM studio.[6]

The Al-Nour Mosque is situated in an interesting spiritual corner of its neighborhood where established and more recent religious institutions are concentrated within a few blocks. In the same building as the mosque, sandwiched between the mosque's ground floor and second floor suites, is a Tamil Hindu temple. The combination of the mosque and Hindu temple occasionally makes for a remarkable (interior) soundscape when Hindu services and celebrations often accompanied by bells coincide with Qur'an recitations or the call for prayer. Across the main street is the impressive building of a Catholic continuing education facility. Diagonal across the side street are the meeting rooms of a Pietist Protestant group. At a short distance to the east lies the old Protestant church with its tree-shaded cemetery, founded centuries ago—by then located at a distance to this formerly independent town. Not far from the cemetery is the first Catholic church in the quarter built at the turn of the twentieth century. In the other direction in a small backyard, not very visible, but sometimes audible is a small Hare Krishna temple. At a further distance was, until 2006, the office of the Polish Catholic mission. These diverse religious spaces reflect ongoing urban cultural transformations.

Through a narrow passage between two buildings, one reaches the entrance to the building that houses the Al-Nour Mosque. In the late 1980s, the community first rented one suite in this complex. Over the years, the community purchased this and two more units in the building. Passing a set of mailboxes one enters a second door. A few meters down to the left is the entrance to the men's prayer room, the library, and the Imam's office. The neatly renovated large prayer room can hold about 200 worshippers, and is occasionally used for all-community events, like lectures, information events of general interest, or events for the larger public, like the annual day of the open mosque. The prayer room has a long row of windows toward the main street, and windows and a large balcony facing the parking lot in the back (south). The room includes a beautifully tiled *mihrab* and a wooden *minbar*. In the middle of the room, the ceiling has a large circle that is lit by green light. From the center of this circle an elaborate glass chandelier is suspended. The Imam's office is located off the prayer room. Because it is located in the interior of the men's section, this office is uncomfortable for women to enter.

Since 2006 the fourth floor suite serves as the women's and children's quarter. It includes a prayer room (large, but considerably smaller than the men's), small kitchen, tiny clothes store (open upon demand), and three classrooms. Men, other than the Imam or those engaged in renovation or maintenance work, do not enter this suite. Even when the door to the suite is open, men ring the doorbell for women to register their presence, and for somebody to come to the door and relay their message to whoever they are looking for. On busy days or special occasions, young boys often shuttle back and forth between the men's and women's quarters to relay messages, or more conveniently husbands and wives call or text each other on cell phones to avoid running stairs and the embarrassment of standing and waiting outside the respective other quarter. The men's prayer room is open for all daily prayers. The women's suite is supposed to be open, but there is occasional confusion about the key and it remains locked on some days. Numerous women congregate to listen to the Friday sermon, which is transmitted by loudspeaker from the men's prayer room, and to participate in the prayer. On weekends, Arabic and Islamic studies lessons are taught to young boys and girls, and teenage girls in the women's suite (older boys study in the men's prayer room). When children's classes are in session, waiting mothers often sit in the prayer room chatting and socializing. During Ramadan, there are weekly *iftar* events where communal meals are prepared in the third floor kitchen. Men eat and socialize on the third and women on the fourth floor.

The third-floor suite, which formerly served as the women's quarter, was renovated in 2008 to house the community's central kitchen, a multipurpose meeting room, two classrooms, and a tiny grocery store (open upon demand). Spatially located between the male and females suites, this unit constitutes a liminal space. No longer used as a prayer space, the suite has tiled floors, which means that visitors do not need to take their shoes off upon entering. For some social occasions, this suite is used as an extension of the male quarter. It is also used for smaller public events, like the public *iftar* in the annual Ramadan series of one of the local Christian-Muslim dialogue associations. A mixed-sex biweekly German language Qur'an study and discussion group for "Muslims and non-Muslims" (one of the oldest of its kind in Stuttgart), which is not formally part of the mosque, also uses this suite. This is the only adult group in the mosque, in which men and women participate together. The third floor suite accommodates public activities or mixed-sex events that are not easily accommodated by either male or female spaces. However, because of the suite's smaller size, large mixed-sex or public events are held in the men's prayer room where gender segregation is upheld (not always successfully) by separate seating blocks for men and women. Some of the weekend classes for children in Arabic and Islamic studies use the two classrooms on the third floor. When the women's Qur'an study group and other women regulars organized an *iftar* for their families, the event, after initial confusion, moved to this suite. We ended up putting the food on tables in the main meeting room, where both men and women served themselves. The men then went to eat in one classroom, and the women in the other. The mosque's spatiality of three separate suites neatly accommodates the community's gender-segregated activities, but also causes occasional problems when, for example, the staircase of the building turns into a busy and loud human highway on Fridays and holidays.

Communal Affairs

The Al-Nour Mosque operates under the umbrella of the *Islamische Gemeinschaft in Deutschland* (Islamic Community in Germany; IGD). Founded in 1958 by Arab exiles including Said Ramadan (the son-in-law of Hassan Al-Banna), the IGD is among the oldest Muslim associations in Germany. With only twenty to thirty communities, it is one of the smaller German mosque associations. The IGD defines itself as a German association that intensely focuses on the construction of German Muslim communities.[7] For decades the IGD has been publishing books and pamphlets in German.[8] The IGD operates in the very vague orbit of the Egyptian Muslim Brotherhood. Without much evidence, other than the vague association with the Muslim Brotherhood, which as such is defined to be "dangerous," the IGD, their national leadership, and local mosques remain under the watch of German state security (*Verfassungsschutz*). These circumstances make activities and cooperation difficult for individual mosques.

The majority of the Al-Nour Mosque's members/visitors are from Egypt, Palestine, Jordan, Syria, and Lebanon. There are other Arabs and other nationals, such as Turks, Afghans, or Somalis,[9] in addition to a growing number of converts, most of whom are ethnic Germans, but there are also Italians, Russians, and Greeks. Despite its central location and diverse community, the Al-Nour Mosque is rather isolated in its urban quarter. Because the mosque has been on the watch list of state security for years, it is effectively banned from civic participation as public institutions and civic associations avoid contact with the community. Continued accusations of anti-state activities, albeit never spelled out in detail, and mistrust, hostility, and resentment on the part of the public have produced a sense of frustration among, in particular, the older generation in the mosque. As a consequence, the Al-Nour community concentrates on internal issues.

The localization of the Al-Nour Mosque was severely disturbed in December 2002 when police searched the mosque as part of post–9/11 state security activities. No evidence of suspicious activities was found, yet the community was marked for years to come (*Esslinger Zeitung* 23.12.2002; *Südkurier* 17.12.2002; *Islam.de*. 16.12.2002). Local participation is further complicated since board members, regular members, and visitors live all over the city and in surrounding counties (e.g. Esslingen and Ludwigsburg). In Stuttgart, Moroccans are the only Arab community sizable enough to maintain a nationally homogenous (and organizationally independent) mosque. The small numbers and spatially dispersed nature of Arabs and Arab Germans leads to a faster loss of language abilities among the younger generation who cannot fall back on larger groups of relatives and friends who speak their language, as Turks can. This contributes to the increasing prevalence of the use of German in mosque programs and activities, especially those for the young.

The Al-Nour Mosque operates in a loosely circumscribed national and global theological field, that includes individuals, platforms, and institutions like Yusuf Al-Qaradawi, the European Council for Fatwa and Research, the Central Council for Muslims in Germany (*Zentralrat der Muslime in Deutschland*), Federation of Muslim Organizations in Europe, Muslim Youth of Germany (MJD), Tariq Ramadan (e.g. 1998, 1999, 2003a, 2003b; 2004), Amr Khaled (2004, 2005a, 2005b, 2006),

Sami Yusuf, or the German Islamic newspaper *Islamische Zeitung* (e.g Kuppinger 2011a; Pond 2006; Alim 2005). National "celebrities" within the IGD orbit include Ayman Mazyek, Murad Hofmann (1995, 1996a, 1996b), the rapper Ammar114, and the singer Hülya Kandemir (Kuppinger 2011c).

Because of its more international membership, growing numbers of ethnic German members, the use of the German language in some group settings, and the importance placed on *da'wa* (the call to Islam), the Al-Nour Mosque has for years attracted converts or those interested in Islam or converting. While Friday sermons remain in Arabic (summarized in German), some teaching activities, lectures, and events are in German, or include German language aspects or translations. Parts of the Islamic studies programs for children, two teenage girls' groups, and a women's Qur'an study group are conducted in German. The Al-Nour Mosque is not unique among Arab mosques with regard to convert members. Many accounts by or about converts (and some Muslim reverts) report finding homes in Arab mosques and social networks (Kandemir 2005; Baumann 2004). Some turn to Sufi contexts (Backer 2009; Özelsel 2005). Women, who converted to Islam because of their husbands,[10] tend to be married to Arab (and occasionally South-Asian) men (Baumann 2004; Filter 2008). Male or female converts who marry born-Muslims after their conversion often choose Arab (or to a lesser extent South-Asian) spouses (Backer 2009; Filter 2008: 111, 145, 222; Wohlrab-Sahr 1999: 145, 152). Few non-Turkish newly pious individuals turn to Turkish mosques.

The Al-Nour Mosque offers many groups and activities and gets busiest on weekends. Starting with the Friday prayer there are numerous activities. On Saturdays and Sundays a host of Arabic and Islamic studies classes for children and youth take place. Some individuals and families spent considerable parts of their weekends in the mosque. Among the older children, girls are overrepresented with two teenage girls' groups, one for thirteen- to sixteen-year-olds, and another for girls seventeen and above. There is only one group for boys aged thirteen to twenty-four, but the group meets only irregularly, as the Imam is often pressed for time. One mother remarked: "this is an unfortunate set up with regard to age. What does a thirteen-year-old have [in] common with a twenty-four-year-old? What kinds of things can they really do together?" Another mother added: "only recently, after some lengthy debate, I convinced my son to go to this group again. He went, but the Sheikh did not show up and nothing really happened. I was frustrated after all the energy I spent talking to my son." The two girls' groups in contrast are lively with many dedicated members. The community also offers Arabic classes for adults and three Qur'an study groups for women (two in Arabic and one in German). Regardless of its uncomfortable political position and local isolation, the Al-Nour Mosque is a dynamic community that maintains many (indirect) links with urban society, and occupies a unique position of religious and cultural mediation. It is a node for debates about what it means to be a Muslim in Germany, a Muslim German, or a German Muslim.

Through individuals and groups, the community is linked to other organizations and events. Youth groups participate in regional or national meetings of the Muslim Youth of Germany (*Muslimische Jugend Deutschland*; MJD). Individuals are involved with the Muslim Student Union (*Muslimische Studenten Union*; MSU), which organizes the annual "Week of Islam" (*Islamwoche*) at the University of Stuttgart. This event (the sixteenth of its kind in 2010) includes five speakers (theologians and public Muslim figures) who speak in a large lecture hall. Some individuals attend Islamic discussion groups in other mosques or public venues, or participate in other Muslim activities (e.g. a Muslim women's sports club). Several individuals occasionally lecture about Islam and Muslim concerns at public events or join panels and discussions in similar venues in the city.

Articulating Religiosities or How Susanne Became Samiha

Sophie's acceptance of Islam signifies a transitional moment in the open-ended construction of a new pious self, public persona, modes of communal involvement, and public participation. Sophie's public conversion is different from many others.[11] For example, Ulrike, never formally said the *shahada*, but slowly grew into pious lifestyles and practices (see chapter 6). Amna said the *shahada* alone in her room (see chapter 3). Andrea was married to Mahmoud for years before they together turned more religious and she converted along the way. Regina converted early in her marriage with a Muslim, and slowly, with her husband turned pious (see chapter 3). Elke converted after several visits to Morocco where she had been fascinated with the culture and Islam. She professed the *shahada* in the Imam's office of the Al-Nour Mosque in front of two witnesses.

For several years, Susanne Berger-Kilic was among the core members of the Al-Nour Mosque's women's German language Qur'an study group. Susanne stood out for her profound knowledge of theology. In complicated discussions, Susanne often clarified issues to the group. Occasionally, she slightly repositioned statements that Sheikh Saleh made. I quickly came to appreciate Susanne's sharp insights. After I had known Susanne for several months and had spent time with her in the mosque and beyond, I asked her for an interview. The following account is based on this interview and notes from other encounters.

Susanne was born in 1967 into a Catholic environment in a town northeast of Stuttgart. Under pressure from her family, she did her confirmation when she was fourteen years old. On the whole, Susanne felt alienated from the Catholic Church. She sensed a gap between what Christianity taught and everyday lives and practices around her. When she was eighteen years old, she met Andi, who was much older than her. A paraplegic since birth, Andi was a teacher and active in the MLPD (Marxist-Leninist Party of Germany). Andi's activism, his group of friends, and their political ideas and debates intrigued Susanne. They talked about

Religiosities | 79

a new world and how they would build it. They discussed issues of grassroots democracy and the rights of workers. In 1988 Susanne and Andi married. On the day of her wedding, Susanne officially left the Catholic Church. While never as active as Andi, Susanne sympathized with the MLPD. During her marriage, Susanne participated in numerous activities including a short engagement with a theater group. At the same time she was training to become a pharmaceutical technician. While still intrigued by the comrades' political debates, she slowly started to feel they were lacking a certain depth that she was longing for. She also noticed that their ideologies and everyday lifestyles did not match, as they did not always act according to what they said (*handeln nicht danach*). After Andi had an affair, she separated from him in 1991. Simultaneously, Susanne separated from politics.

A year later she met Dirk who was a nurse in a senior citizen's residence. Like Andi he was much older than Susanne and loved to discuss and philosophize. Dirk was a recovering alcoholic and had grown up in more than a dozen orphanages and children's institutions, where he had also been sexually abused. He had suffered deep emotional injuries. When Susanne listed all of Dirk's problems, she looked at me and smiled: "Yes, I have some sort of helper's syndrome, I guess." Dirk and Susanne talked about God and the world. Religious thoughts and considerations re-entered her world with these debates. In everyday life, Dirk was a difficult partner. He had no sense of money and was a spendthrift. He was a heavy smoker, occasionally smoked hashish, and had addictive tendencies in many aspects of life. He was a workaholic. After Dirk had an affair, and based on personality difference, Susanne felt they were drifting apart. Dirk had a few alcoholic interludes and the relationship became increasingly unbearable as Dirk unloaded his suffering onto Susanne. She remembered, "of course I kept listening to him. What else could I do? I always saw him as a potential candidate for suicide." She felt incredibly burdened by this traumatic relationship. Dirk remained a steady feature in her life through the 1990s, even though they no longer lived together.

To get back on her emotional feet and stabilize her own self, Susanne started to do Zen meditation. "I needed to get up again" *(mich selbst aufrichten)*. She added "the everyday witnessing of immediate and immense human suffering, the sense that trust can be broken or abused so much [sexual abuse of children] is very hard to bear. You simply suffer along with the other person." She continued to struggle with Dirk but gradually lost hope. Any time he might come or call with ever more desperate thoughts. She feared for his life, but was at a total loss of what to do, as she had exhausted her emotional energy. One day she received a suicidal call from Dirk at work: "All of a sudden I knew that there was nothing left that I could do for him. I was completely empty from the inside. I had reached the end of my knowledge and energy. There was no way that I could offer him any more help. Either he would commit suicide that day or he would not. There was nothing I felt I could do." After she put down the receiver, a long-lost verse from her Catholic past suddenly resounded in her mind. On his way to crucifixion, Jesus had said "Father into your hands I commend my spirit" (Luke 23: 46). From the depth of her heart, Susanne repeated these words, which were to stay with her. Susanne started to engage again with religion. She read about Christianity and Buddhism. She attended a spiritual retreat at a monastery, but could not re-immerse herself into Christianity. Yet the fateful verse remained her spiritual signpost or companion. She kept searching for Christianity or a Christian life in her own lifeworld, but with little success. By the late 1990s she completely separated from Dirk.

On a beautiful Sunday afternoon in March of 2000, Susanne walked alone through the city. She felt an immense inner peace, the kind of peace she remembers, "where one wants to hug everybody who comes along." Out of nothing she decided to say "hello" to the next passing person. This happened to be a young man who turned around, somewhat surprised as she said hello to him. Something had happened between the two in this moment. They started to talk and agreed to meet again the next day. Both showed up at the agreed time and place. The young man, Enver, was a refugee from a former Yugoslavian republic. About ten years her junior, Enver had come to Germany only months before this encounter and barely spoke German. He had run away from the army, had been in prison in his country, was sent to the army again, and ran away again. Enver was the youngest of ten children of a Muslim family that had little relations to its religion. "They drink alcohol," Susanne added, and "one brother converted to Catholicism in order to get married." Enver spent his teenage years in a situation of war. War experiences had shaped him. "My helper's syndrome, once more," Susanne dryly added. Susanne and Enver started dating. Enver, while living at a distance to Islam, nevertheless had some knowledge of Islam which he shared with Susanne, who became curious about Islam as their relationship unfolded. Up until then "Islam had been a religion of foreigners to me. It had never been a concern of mine. Indeed it had been totally alien to me." Six month later Susanne and Enver were married.

With her newfound interest in Islam, Susanne tried to learn more about this religion. She looked for books and pamphlets on book tables at events. Enver gave her a Qur'an in his language. Susanne read the Qur'an in German. She came across a *tafsir* (Qur'an interpretation) by Ahmed von Denffer, a convert and rather established actor and writer in the German Muslim scene. Reading this text in late 2000 Susanne had a kind of awakening (*Gongerlebnis*). Soon afterward she started to join the biweekly meetings of the discussion circle for Muslim and non-Muslim men and women in the Al-Nour Mosque. Reading and hearing more about Islam, Susanne perceived of her new knowledge more and more in terms of an answer to her earlier search and questions. She felt like saying "why did nobody ever tell me this before?" Or, "this is exactly what I have been looking for all along." In August 2001, Susanne, who had not yet formally converted to Islam, had a strange dream: "I was on my way somewhere on a grey day. I was looking into the sky and saw an airplane that all of a sudden fell down, crashed and broke apart. In that moment I found myself reciting the *fatiha* [opening chapter of the Qur'an]. I ran to the airplane and tried to enter it. I saw an infant that smiled at me. Turning back I saw some dogs surrounding the plane. At the time I could not completely make sense of this dream."

A few weeks later Susanne witnessed 9/11 at her workplace. Watching in horror, she said to herself "this cannot be; this is not how I came to know Muslims." Thrown into a whirlwind of emotions that resulted from this experience and how it strangely connected to her dream about the plane and her recitation of the *fatiha*, Susanne's engagement with Islam intensified. She felt compelled to make a public statement. On October 5, 2001, she converted in the Al-Nour Mosque. Enver who had initiated her interest in Islam, but did not share her growing involvement with Islam, refused to witness her conversion because he had vowed never to enter a mosque.

Susanne was happy with her conversion and new found religiosity and enthusiastically embarked on the journey of remaking her life. She started to pray, "first only twice a day but then soon five time a day." As she worked on herself she hoped that Enver would join her on her journey, but her hopes were in vain. Intensifying her contacts and involvements in the mosque, and relationships with individual members, Susanne quickly learned the basics of Islam and relevant religious and social practices. She started to experiment with more visible changes in her everyday life. One day, as she and Enver went to see his brother who had converted to Catholicism in order to marry, she decided to wear a headscarf. "We had a huge fight in the car, but I did not take the scarf off," Susanne remembered. At the brother's house, Enver and his relatives made fun of Susanne. She was puzzled as her husband had introduced her to Islam and had defended Islam in front of her. Now he showed no respect for Islam or her conversion and growing religiosity: "I felt increasingly that I was married without a marriage (*ohne Ehe verheiratet*) as my husband continued his lifestyle, which included plenty of alcohol, while I continued my journey." She started to fast in Ramadan 2002 hoping that Enver would join her. Instead he made fun of Muslims. He also stopped working.

Over the next few years Susanne diligently worked on "improving my *iman* (faith)." At the same time her lifeworld slowly repositioned itself into the city's pious Muslim circuits. She attended the women's Qur'an study group and later also seminars of the Islamology Institute.[12] She attended lectures and informally met with her new found pious friends. As she improved her theological knowledge, she adjusted her everyday life and practices. First she only wore a headscarf in the mosque. "I was too intimidated (*ich habe mich nicht getraut*) to wear it even on the S-Bahn (suburban train)." After some time she started to put the headscarf on at home and rode public transportation with it to the mosque. In the summer of 2003, Enver and Susanne drove to Sweden to attend the wedding of one of his relatives. On this trip, Susanne for the first time wore a headscarf the entire time. The wedding itself, while it included a mosque ceremony, was a disappointment for her new Islamic sensitivities. "I was the only woman who wore a headscarf at this

Muslim wedding. There was plenty of alcohol; even the old grandmother drank some. The only Muslim thing was that they did not serve pork." Susanne decided that "when I go home, I will leave on the headscarf for good," which she did.

Susanne had never informed her mother about her conversion. Now that she wore the headscarf she could no longer hide this fact. Not surprisingly, however, her mother had figured out her transformation as Susanne had refused to consume pork and alcohol. As a result her mother had started to read in newspapers about issues to do with Islam. Still, her daughter wearing the headscarf made her concerned, "do you women have to do this?" she asked in minor distress. Susanne's father, in contrast, who "does not like foreigners," ignored her conversion and avoided any direct confrontation. Susanne continued her pious trajectory, learned more about Islam, and shifted most of her social life into pious Muslim circles. She added a German language mixed-sex discussion group, which meets in a public venue, to her sites of learning and debate. As she became more occupied with Islamic activities, her husband became more problematic and settled into the pleasurable existence of the well-maintained unemployed spouse. He partied with friends and spent much time at car shows. In December 2005 Susanne went on the *hajj* (pilgrimage) to Mecca as a sign of her complete arrival to the life of a pious Muslima. Susanne's and Enver's lifestyles were now light-years apart. Sometime later, after a careful search, Susanne adopted the Muslim name Samiha. Her friends tried hard to use her new name, but it remained a challenge for many. Some referred to her as Susanne-Samiha. She signed emails with Susanne-Samiha.

Visible Piety

Susanne-Samiha's turn to Islamic piety was smooth. She herself decided the speed and details of these transformations. Some of her worst moments of frustration were the refusal and outright ridicule by her (nominally) Muslim husband. She kept hoping for Enver to change his perspective (and also everyday lifestyle) and join her pious journey. But to no avail. Susanne worked on the construction of her new pious self, public persona, and lifeworld. As her piety became visible to her environment, a second source of tension emerged: the public sphere and especially her place of work.

Susanne had worked for many years in the same pharmacy. Her job included contact with customers at the front counter, and office and laboratory tasks in the back. After she decided to wear the headscarf "full-time," she did not dare to show up at work with her scarf. She rode her bicycle wearing her headscarf to the pharmacy, took it off before she entered the premises, and worked all day without. When she left she put the headscarf back on. If she went out for lunch, she wore the headscarf during her break. While not to her best liking, Susanne thought this was a compromise—for the time being. She never asked her boss whether she could work with a headscarf. Everybody at work knew she was wearing a headscarf outside. "Nobody," Susanne remembered, "said anything to suggest that I could keep wearing the headscarf at work." Susanne prayed in a backroom. Some of her twenty colleagues were willing to switch break times for her to pray on time. The atmosphere remained tense over her pious transformations. Susanne unhappily settled into this state of affairs. She worked less in the front and took on more administrative tasks. While nobody openly objected to her unfolding new persona, appearance, and lifestyle, Susanne sensed that her boss was irritated and would not have minded for her to quit her job. Since she had been with the company for almost twenty years, he could only wish for her to leave, but had no legal ways to fire her.

When Suzanne returned from the *hajj* in January 2006, she started to wear a headscarf (tied in the back) to work, combined with turtlenecks or a scarf wrapped around her neck. By then she had taken over an administrative job and was in charge of the organization, preparation, and delivery of the medication for a nearby hospital. Nobody openly contested her headscarf, but her work atmosphere remained uncomfortable. Her new task was demanding, but Susanne with her experience managed and was happy to be left alone in her office. With time the atmosphere eased and Susanne knew that her efforts of running an entire branch of the pharmacy's business were appreciated. Her piety, however, was never openly debated. In 2009 Susanne's company started a new line of production, preparing larger quantities of medication for their customers. The company added a laboratory facility in a suburban location. Producing medications in a germ-free environment, lab workers were required to wear specific uniforms, which included complete head-coverings. Susanne jumped to the opportunity and transferred to this lab even though it necessitated a longer commute on public transportation ("but with the head-covering, the job is perfect for a Muslima").

After considerable tension, professional issues worked out for Susanne-Samiha. Most women are not that lucky. For example, Dzamila, who had worked in Bosnia (prior to the war) as a preschool teacher, never found work in her field. She explained: "I wrote tens of applications, I helped out in several places on a voluntary basis . . . anything . . . in the kitchen or whatever was needed, just to get a foot in the door. The local preschool had me on their list for sick replacements, and they called me to replace people occasionally, but nobody would hire me for good. They don't want women with headscarves in preschools and schools." Dzamila, who is in her mid-forties, eventually took on a part-time job cleaning and later worked for two hours every morning preparing clothes in two boutiques in a mall. She would love to return to her profession, but has given up hope. Yet, she recognizes the minimal changes in employment opportunities for women with headscarves. Like many other women she can list the slowly growing number of places in the city (e.g. OBI—home supplies chain; Burger King; H&M—fashion chain; LIDL—food discounter; a few bakeries, pharmacies, doctor's offices) that employ women with headscarves.

Upon Susanne-Samiha's return from the *hajj* in January 2006, in addition to wearing a headscarf to work she wanted to change other aspects of her life, especially her marriage. "I wanted to have a partner who also lived a Muslim life." With her husband's deteriorating behavior ("he spent his life in bars, with friends or cars"), she felt they had little left in common. Triggered by one especially outrageous incident, she separated from Enver soon after. Subsequently, she wholeheartedly plunged into Islamic activities.

Everyday Pious Lifeworlds

After Susanne-Samiha and I had spent over three hours on the interview, she sent an email the next day, where she noted that there was more about her life that she wanted to share. She explained some of these details. I include her note to illustrate some (mundane) aspects or challenges that many Muslims face. Responding to an interview question about how her everyday life differed from that before she turned pious, she wrote:

> My everyday life actually is much like it was before, as it remains foremost structured through my job/work hours. In addition, the five daily prayers have become very important for me; which considerably shapes my everyday life, and I plan my daily program accordingly. I schedule my lunch break of two hours in a way that I can perform the mid-day prayer in a relaxed manner. In fall/winter I even manage to include the afternoon prayer. In the evening I make sure that I perform the evening prayer on time, which then partially decides my evening activities. For example, if I go out I make sure that I can pray wherever I am, and how/where I can do the ritual washing. Shopping trips or visits to the movie theater are of little interest to for me at this point. I do not miss these things. Even so to perform the washing and prayer are easy and unproblematic, I noticed that I have become more of a home body, although I spent many evenings in the mosque or at Islamic meetings (here washing and praying are unproblematic).
>
> I don't feel that my new daily schedule with the five prayers is in any way limiting. On the contrary I would miss something basic or existential if I did not search out this daily connection to my Creator. In my initial time as a Muslima, I had problems to accept the monthly "prayer-free" times for women [i.e. during menstruation, PK]. I was missing prayer. I felt lost during that time. Today this has changed. I have developed a different attitude toward this time in the life of a woman and fill this time with (a) activities and errands that I otherwise do not get around doing, and (b) there are plenty of other pious (*gottesdienstliche*) things which one can do as a woman that can also gain God's favor (*Wohlgefallen*) and which are meaningful for my religious life (e.g. to read and learn). Already in my non-Muslim life, I had experienced that the time of menstruation can put a woman into a creative and spiritual position/circumstances, if she positively accepts this context. When I was still with my husband, he was the

(positive or negative) center of my life (*war er natürlich der Fixpunkt in meinem Leben*) in additional to my Islamic activities in the community. Of course I miss this now very much, regardless of the fact that he mostly annoyed me. Only when I found myself again, gained joy in life again, and when I put my strength and energy again into my religious activities, things improved for me. In this psychological crisis I fought with myself and sensed even more intensely that Islam IS my way.

Susanne-Samiha's joys and challenges bespeak ongoing transformations as she improved her pious knowledge, practices, and communal engagements.

Since her separation from Dirk, Susanne had embarked on a spiritual search, but did not find what she longed for in the places she initially sought out. Upon meeting Enver, Susanne learned about Islam and started to read more about the religion. Within a year, she converted. She entered a new social world and made new friends. She participated in groups and activities that gave her a new outlook on life and fulfilled her spiritual needs. She hoped for Enver to recognize her joy in this newfound religiosity and to join her pious trajectory. As she grew more committed to this marriage as part of her piety, Enver (literally and otherwise) cashed in on her piety. Nevertheless, Susanne-Samiha remained committed until a devastating incident left her little choice but to leave him.

Alongside her quest for piety, Susanne-Samiha remade her public persona. Her circles of friends and activities changed, as did her types and modes of engagements. While her struggle to wear a headscarf is only one among many aspects of her changing lifestyle and persona, it was a highly symbolic one, in part because it was contested in the public sphere, as the ensuing tensions at Susanne's workplace illustrate. Her trajectory toward a pious identity and lifestyle had its up and downs, the most difficult challenges were her husband and workplace. Struggling through extended painful episodes on both accounts, Susanne-Samiha was lucky to overcome or solve both conflicts.

In her transition to becoming a pious Muslima and a theologically knowledgeable person, Susanne-Samiha predominantly drew on local resources like the Al-Nour Mosque, other formal groups, and informal circles of friends. She remade herself, keeping such cornerstones of her life like her work, her relationship with her mother, and as long as possible her marriage to Enver in place. In her pious quest, Susanne-Samiha plunged into Islamic learning and took several of the intellectually challenging weekend courses with the Islamology Institute (*Islamologisches Institut*) run by Amir Zaidan (1999) and the German theologian and anthropologist Abdelrahman Reidegeld (2005). This Vienna-based organization offers theological weekend courses in German, Austrian, and Swiss cities. Many consider the Institute to offer the most sophisticated Islamic studies programs in German. Keeping with some of her earlier political or social engagements, Susanne-Samiha eventually returned to a variety of civic engagements, only now as a pious Muslima. She participates in public activities and debates where she represents Islamic points of view. With her turn to piety her private social circles became larger and her geographical networks global. Over the years, she traveled several times to Egypt to visit women from the Al-Nour Mosque who had moved there. Overall the women's Qur'an study group at the Al-Nour Mosque has played a central role in Susanne's process of becoming a Muslima.

Debating Islam

Every other week a group of women meets in the Al-Nour Mosque to learn about and discuss theological topics and questions of personal religiosity. Group sessions are conducted in German, which means that Arabic-speaking Imams teach the lessons together with Zeinab Abdallah (see above) who translates from them. Zeinab is of Syrian descent and has lived in Stuttgart for decades. While she has no official job or function at the Al-Nour Mosque, Zeinab is a central figure among the community's women.

The women's Qur'an study group meets in the women's prayer room or an adjacent smaller room. The group has a core of six or seven women (between thirty-five and fifty years old), some of whom have been attending for years. Most are German converts married to Arab men of different nationalities. The group on and off includes younger women of Arab descent who prefer German-language classes, as well as a number of changing young women, some of whom have recently converted as they married Muslims. Some disappear from the group within a year or two, once they have a baby. Finally there are women who are considering converting. Some are currently dating Arab Muslim men and want to learn more about their religion. These women sometimes come for weeks or months and then leave, a few eventually convert. Occasionally women of Turkish descent who prefer German teaching or hold vague grudges against Turkish mosques join the group. Most of the core group are formal (that is dues-paying) members of the community. Permanent, occasional, and short-term group members form a pleasant sociable setting. New participants receive a warm welcome. Coffee, tea, cakes, and cookies are often served at meetings. As I became friends with group members, I also socialized with some of the women outside the mosque. We met in homes, attended events in the mosque and elsewhere, had coffee in the nearby mall, or went to see movies with Islamic themes (e.g. the Turkish film *Takva*). Until the end of 2010 the Imam (first Sheikh Saleh, then his successor, Sheikh Anwar) taught the women. In January 2011, Sheikh Anwar stopped teaching the group for lack of time, as he explained. Since then the women run their own program. They have been trying to convince Sheikh Anwar to teach at least some sessions. So far, their attempts have been in vain. In 2012 Sheikh Anwar established his own women's group that meets separately.

When Sheikh Saleh was running the group, he covered varying topics, some he repeated in annual cycles. He also addressed themes on demand. Group meetings were a little tedious as translations back and forth between Arabic and German took time, prevented spontaneity, and sometimes obscured the fine details of lectures and discussions. Since I started attending this group in late 2006, we covered topics, like The Way to Paradise, The Pleasures of Paradise, Belief and Life, Allah's Mercifulness, Ramadan, The Prayer, or The Pilgrimage. In the winter 2006/07 we discussed "Death, Grave and Judgment" over several sessions. The Sheikh illustrated, using verses from the Qur'an and some *hadith*s, the stations between death and the final destination of either paradise or hell, including some indicators that would allow the dead person to anticipate the direction of their travel. He described the pains that await people for minor sins such as malignant gossip. Sheikh Saleh compared life to a hotel where everybody had booked a brief stay, and established fleeting relationships in superficial encounters. What really counted came afterward. He emphasized that one should never lose sight of the next world, especially since our deeds in this world impacted our entry to the next. Nonetheless, this world had its tasks and attractions. Believers had to live their earthly lives in modesty and help others, always keeping an eye on the next world. "With one foot on the earth and the eye directed toward Allah and the heaven," he described the best attitude for living in this world. Sheikh Saleh emphasized that the awareness of one's sins and the constant pleading for Allah's forgiveness were fundamental. Only then would believers be blessed with paradise. He finished a lecture about the topic of afterlife listing the four elements that were proof of afterlife. First, humans are given the ability to distinguish between good and evil; second, the changing annual seasons illustrate the ever-returning cycle between growth and harvest, and life and death; third the existence of a deep faith in Allah and his almighty nature. Finally, to reflect about our own mortality, he suggested that we visit a cemetery for deeper engagement with the topic. The next topic was judgment. My first group meetings were characterized by gloomy, depressing, or at times almost scary topics: judgment day, pains in the grave, and later in hell. Punishments played a central role in the Sheikh's elaborations. Yet, sessions were framed by warm and cheerful chatting at the beginning and end.

After several sessions on the trials and tribulations of dying, death, grave, judgment, hell, and hell fires, Sheikh Saleh arrived at the pleasures of paradise and gave a detailed description of this place. The soil there was made of saffron. Stones and construction materials were made of musk and trees of gold. The water was pure, and rivers were full of milk or wine, which however was not the type of the worldly intoxicating wine. In paradise, one was able to eat wonderful fruits directly from trees. Plates were made of gold and silver, yet see-through like glass. Clothes were made of silk, and jewelry of gold, silver, and precious stones. Everyone had a house made of glass, where one could see inside the house and all its rooms from the outside. Doors remained open at all times. Angels came to greet residents in their luxuriously furnished houses. People lived in communities and nobody aged beyond the age of thirty-three years. People could visit all those they longed for. Paradise was a place of ultimate safety. Sheikh Saleh described paradise as in stark contrast to this world. There were no secrets (glass houses), loneliness, disease, and aging. In some aspects paradise was a site of upscale consumption with exclusive jewelry and dinnerware, fine fabrics, luxury furnishing, and fine fragrances. Illustrating the pains and suffering of hell, and the pleasures of paradise, Sheikh Saleh drew this diverse group of women into a shared destiny. They might have come from different ethnic and religious backgrounds and had distinctive experiences, but they were now united in their religiosity, trajectories, and prospects in afterlife.

In March 2007 we turned to Belief and Life, and subsequently to Allah's mercifulness. One day, Sheikh Saleh talked about intentions, and how one should always reflect about one's intentions and behavior in everyday life. Ideally a person should constantly ask themselves "what can I do to improve myself?" If a person realized that they made a mistake it was crucial to reflect on and regret such wrongdoings. Thus a person became a "controlling institution" for their own acts. Special control should be reserved for the tongue, which often caused problems between people, and subsequently could easily get a person in trouble on judgment day. Individuals needed to control themselves both for the sake of those around them, but also with a view onto afterlife, as one ought not to pile up too many wrongdoings. If one asked a person for forgiveness, one not only did right by this person, but also took away from one's sins for afterlife. The Sheikh noted that one was thus "cleansing oneself" by asking for the forgiveness of others, and one was also lessening one's account in the next world (*ashan nikhaff al-hisab fi dunya akhira*). Good intentions and deeds, he continued, included relations and participation in society. He stressed that the pious needed to cooperate with Muslims and non-Muslims. It was paramount to understand the lives and practices of others, and to contribute to society. Like in his lectures of death, hell, and paradise when he had situated the women in an Islamic universe and its shared destiny, he now re-inserted them as Muslimas into society. This participation in society, however, had to be inspired by Islamic rationales and needed to include a clear vision onto the next world.

As we moved through the year, we discussed Ramadan and the *hajj*. When I started my second year in the group, some topics repeated themselves, which caused a few women to slow down their attendance. The core remained, as the group was their permanent and chosen space for discussion and socializing. When Sheikh Saleh explained aspects of heaven, hell, and paradise, he tied these abstract elements to this-worldly issues of gossip, intentions, social relations, and public participation. To accumulate good and pious deeds for the afterworld was not enough, he insisted, instead one had to live accordingly in this world, among Muslims and non-Muslims, the pious and non-believers. Sheikh Saleh frequently emphasized the importance of the headscarf or positively remarked on the fact that women who wore headscarves might encounter hardships in mainstream society. He assured the women that they would be rewarded for these hardships.

Mentioning the headscarf along with basic religious duties, points to efforts of localization and visible community construction in the Al-Nour Mosque. Sheikh Saleh and most community members agree that a *hijab* is a duty for pious women. Most women who regularly attend the mosque wear headscarves in the mosque and their everyday lives. Some, in particular younger women, are hesitant to wear a *hijab* for fear of discrimination in the job market. Others do not "yet" wear a headscarf, because they feel they are not ready for such a commitment. For converts to don the *hijab* is a particular challenge as they do not only face discrimination at work, but often also resentment if not rejection from their families. The Sheikh's gentle reminders about the *hijab* illustrate his focus on religious duties in Germany. Aware of the resentments that women with a headscarf face in the public sphere, he was adamant in applauding those who put their faith above such social limitations. The headscarf question has a political dimension as every woman with a headscarf in the public sphere symbolizes the presence of Islam (Yurdakul 2006; Oestreich 2004). Many Germans resent this symbolism, but for pious communities it signifies arrival and belonging. Women with headscarves in the urban public sphere also illustrate the growing civic engagements and professional achievements of pious Muslimas (e.g. Nökel 2002, 2004; Tarlo 2010).

Regardless of concrete topics and contents, it is important to understand that the broader purpose and implication of Sheik Saleh's teaching and the women's discussion are to draw group members into the Muslim tradition, and situate their lives and practices firmly within this tradition. Teaching factual knowledge, ways of reasoning and being in this world, Sheik Saleh guides these women in becoming and remaining pious Muslimas, but also points out ways to live as pious Muslimas in the city. In discussions among the women themselves (before and after the formal lesson), they negotiate often minute details of their daily lives (what food items do or might include miniscule quantities of *haram* substances?). While most of the lessons and debates are marked by a search for shared opinions and harmony, occasionally minor disagreements also occur.

Controversial Debates

Meetings of the women's Qur'an study group are lecture-based with a question and answer part at the end. Most sessions were characterized by eager agreement. On rare occasions when women found issues to be controversial, debates became livelier. One evening, the group was finishing the previous session's topic: marriage in Islam. Sheikh Saleh explained the concepts of "travel marriage" (*nikah misyar*), and marriage for a specified period of time (*nikah mut'ah*). He described the *nikah misyar*, its legal, social, and cultural context. He explained that it was practiced in Saudi Arabia and the Arab Gulf and legally recognized by Sunni Islam, if the following conditions were met: (1) Both spouses agreed on this marriage. (2) The woman renounced her right to live in her husband's house and her right to be supported by him. She remained in her own home and supported herself. The husband came for visits. (3) All the regular conditions for marriage were in place (witnesses, a representative of the woman was present, bridal money was paid). As Sheikh Saleh was explaining the context and occurrence for this marriage in Arabic and Zeinab translated in installments, the first questions emerged: Was this marriage practiced as a second marriage? Yes it was, he elaborated; often it was a marriage contracted by a man who frequently traveled to a particular place and took a second wife there. What about children, who would support them? The father would, he responded. With the translation time lag and some brief joking by the women who foresaw male abuse of such nuptial possibilities, the Sheikh's answers overlapped with ongoing smaller discussions around the table. Such an animated chaos rarely occurred in this otherwise quiet and disciplined group. At some moments there were two debates, one in German around the table, and a second in Arabic between the Sheikh and Zeinab. It was impossible to translate both sides in this context, and bits and pieces were lost in the shuffle. Group members were uncomfortable with the possibilities of secrecy and abuse that they foresaw in this type of marriage. Their discomfort was not with the legal possibility as such, but real life male behavior. One woman asked: "Are there *misyar* marriages practiced in Germany?" Zeinab translated, and the Sheikh responded in Egyptian Arabic, "*mish maugud henna*." (It does not exist here). Zeinab turned to him and quickly responded in Shami/Levantine Arabic: "*wallahi maujud!*" (For sure, they exist). The women in their German discussion had already moved on, and Zeinab did not translate the Sheikh's word or profess her disagreement with him any further.

Questions emerged about the forms and consequences of potential abuse of such marriages. Did a husband have to inform his first wife? What if the *misyar* wife became pregnant? What if all of a sudden she needed financial support? What if she or her child needed the husband when he was out of town? What if the husband already had four wives elsewhere, how could anybody know that he had taken an illegitimate fifth wife with a *nikah misyar*? What about the inheritance of the children if nobody at the husband's main residence knew about his travel marriage? Underlying their animated questions was not a disapproval of the rule, which the women accepted as divine law. They were concerned with what they felt was the very possible abuse by men. With considerable life and marital experience between them, this dozen of mostly middle-aged women felt that some men might abuse such a possibility. They felt that one had to be careful with men: Muslim and non-Muslim alike. The discussion proceeded based on shared assumptions that men were often weak, frequently acted to their own advantage, in particular with regard to marriage and women. The women worried about the everyday contexts in which such a marriage would exist with less-than-perfect individuals. This line of argumentation was alien to the Sheikh who preferred to lecture about abstract legal issues and stay away from messy real life circumstances and the actions of faulty individuals. He was most comfortable in the safe territory of abstract theology, seldom ventured into real life territories, and seldom engaged in controversial debates with the women who rarely challenged him.

Sheikh Saleh became progressively more uncomfortable and tried to end the debate, but the women would not let him. They wanted to hear some statement about the ills of social patriarchy, and how some men (that is all men, Muslims or not) were prone to abuse laws. But the Sheikh was unwilling to even concede that patriarchy existed, and in real life circumstances could indeed interfere with properly pious lifestyles. He was equally unwilling to acknowledge that some Muslim men might abuse Muslim law, or worse still might lie about their circumstances. One woman asked: "What if a man has a *misyar* marriage in a different country and then he dies? How will the wife and children receive their inheritance, if he never told anybody in his home country? That cannot be right then." Questions became trickier and aimed to produce a statement by the Sheikh that some men acted immorally and against the law. He either did not understand their concerns or, more likely, did not want to address them. Susanne-Samiha jumped in: "The question ultimately then is between Allah and the individual. If a man marries more women than he is supposed to, or does not tell one wife about the other, this is a question of his honesty and sincerity."

This intervention opened the space for the Sheikh to address male misbehavior and abuse of religious laws. Yet he remained unwilling to do so. Where the women saw a line between religious law and appropriate behavior, and individual male abuse and misbehavior, Sheikh Saleh did not see this line. For the women Muslim law and social patriarchy were two separate issues. The existence of social patriarchy did not discredit Islam. On the contrary, this discrepancy needed to be addressed for the sake of proper Islamic practices. To construct genuinely Islamic lifestyles, such practices needed to be examined and, if found to be un-Islamic, eliminated. The women's target of critic was neither the Sheikh, nor Muslim law, but male practices. The group wholeheartedly embraced the law, but rejected male misbehavior and dishonesty. For Sheikh Saleh the two—law and taken for granted ideal male behavior—seemed inseparable. In his view, there could be no gap between theological normativities and everyday practices. The women disagreed. Rarely, had I seen Sheikh Saleh so beleaguered by the women.

This discussion represents dynamic debates among many, often younger Muslims, who are unwilling to accept lessons or teachings without making sure that they are truly based in the Qur'an and *Sunna*. Believers strive to identify cultural practices that were conventionally claimed to be Islamic, but have little or no religious foundations. Piety to them does not mean to blindly accept traditions and time-honored practices, but involves an intellectual effort whereby ideas and practices are carefully analyzed with regard to their Qur'anic roots and justifications

(Deeb 2006; Jouili 2008; Klausing 2009). The lively exchange with the Sheikh was part of ongoing global debates about Muslim theology and religiosities in general, and women's rights, roles, and religiosities in particular, (see e.g. Barazangi 2004; Abou El Fadl 2001a, 2001b; Abou El Fadl et al. 2002; Barlas 2002; Wadud 1999, 2006; Al-Qaradawi 1989). Often such critical debates took place among women in the absence of the Sheikh or other males.

Another controversy unfolded in spring 2011 when the women's suite repeatedly remained locked during the day when women wanted to pray. Barred from prayer, some women went to the men's prayer room and prayed (at a distance) behind the men. This worked for a while until somebody put up a sign in the men's prayer room that told women not to pray there. Some women were outraged. In informal debates they complained about the lack of organization by the men who held the key to the women's suite, but failed at times to unlock the door. Some were angered when the men no longer allowed women to pray in the back, effectively barring them from prayer. Susanne-Samiha fumed: "That is the worst thing that one Muslim can do to another: to prevent them from praying. It is not our mistake that they keep forgetting to open the upstairs suite. Then, on top of that they prevent us from praying downstairs." Several women noted that they would continue to pray downstairs if they had to. Tension over the women's access to prayer spaces is not a unique problem of the Al-Nour Mosque. Kathrin Klausing (2009) complains about her own and other women's experiences of being denied access to prayer spaces, or being accused of disturbing or invalidating men's prayers when they discreetly lined up behind male worshippers.

Whether in group debates, or concrete issues like the sign in the men's prayer room, formal and informal discussions in the mosque illustrate a vibrant engagement with religiosity. Individuals challenge ideas, practices, and circumstance that they deem are not religiously "correct." What constitutes correct is in part a matter of personal interpretation. When one woman complained one day that her husband would not let her travel alone, another responded: "I have been flying to Lebanon alone for the last twenty years. I would have never gotten to see my family there if I had always waited for my husband to come along. I am sure the Prophet did not mean to impose hardships on women." Others agreed. Such small debates are crucial for individuals and the community to negotiate practices and to act as pious individuals outside the mosque.

The women's Qur'an study group is one of a few established groups that conduct their meetings in German, and subsequently functions as a gateway for new believers into Muslim religiosities and social worlds. Women learn the fundamentals of Islam and get to know others with similar trajectories. No question is too simple to be asked in this group. Questions range from grand theological questions (what is the way to paradise?), to how to pray correctly (is my prayer invalid if I picked up my child in the middle of the prayer?), to local cultural questions ("should my husband eat the non-*halal* meat at my mother's?"), to everyday issues (can women who do not cover their hair dye their hair?) and consumer questions (is the salami on the pizzas in Turkish restaurants really *halal*?).

In the course of formal lectures, question and answer sessions, and informal discussions after the meetings, women are socialized into piety and welcomed into a social community of Muslimas. Those who are willing slowly develop new pious subjectivities under the gentle guidance of their peers. Some women eventually leave this group for other groups, like a more intellectually minded group that meets in a civic center. Others take classes with the *Islamologische Institut*. Some circulate between groups. One woman joined a small regional association that debates issues of Islamic banking and is setting up their own banking experiment. Some women leave the group to settle into their Muslim lives and families and only return to the mosque for Friday prayers, holidays, and special events. Many remain in the orbit of the group and stay socially connected to core members.

Socializing Pious Selves

The Al-Nour Mosque has a communal ethos. While controversial issues exist, there are many agreed upon rules and practices. Most members try to abide by accepted regulations, refine some rules and communal practices, and help newcomers to understand and internalize these conventions. The mosque is an Islamic space and should be inhabited by its members and (most) visitors accordingly (Henkel 2007). Some rules are well established and beyond debate. Others are vague or handled variously by different individuals. Younger, newer, or less involved individuals occasionally make "mistakes" and are guided by others into understanding and following rules, especially those that differ from mainstream society. Gender segregation is an obvious difference. Men and women neither associate, nor shake hands in mosque facilities.[13] Since the mosque consists of three suites, gender segregation is logistically straightforward. For occasional events, especially those conducted beyond the confines of the mosque, like holiday celebrations (usually held in a school gym), these general rules are partially suspended.

Concerns about proper use, gender segregation, and the overall spatiality of the mosque illustrate how its spaces serve as experimental grounds for the negotiation of an Islamic spatiality and sociality. In contrast to secular urban spaces, over which the pious have little control, the community designs its own interior spatial universe and appropriate practices. As the pious enter the building, they leave public secular spaces and some of their rules behind. Girls who are past puberty and women should wear a *hijab*, and keep their distance from men and never encounter a member of the opposite sex alone. Once, Zeinab was expecting a man to deliver a bag when we were leaving the women's suite. She asked the last few women to stay until he came. When he arrived (the door was unlocked), he rang the bell, Zeinab quickly opened the door, took the bag, and the man disappeared within seconds. By asking the women to stay, Zeinab showed that she knew and respected the normativity of the mosque.

People's lives beyond the mosque are differently framed than those inside the mosque. Some women do not wear headscarves. For example, on Saturday morning when the teenage girls' group meets, some girls quickly put on their scarves outside the front door of the mosque building. Some women in the Qur'an study group put on their *hijab* in the bathroom of the women's suite. While there are friendly hints and occasional reminders about wearing a headscarf in the mosque, women make their own decision whether they wear the *hijab* outside the mosque. Reminders about practices like wearing the *hijab* inside the mosque are elements of a larger project to create and maintain Islamic spaces (Henkel 2007). For the pious, the mosque is their very own space. It accommodates modes of interaction and sociality that connect the mosque to other pious spaces and the global *ummah*. Since not everybody at the Al-Nour Mosque is equally familiar with the intricate details of religious practices and their resulting social and bodily practices, the mosque becomes a crucial site for embodied or habitual socialization. Because the Al-Nour Mosque attracts an ethnically diverse audience and numerous converts, these elements of habituation are more significant than in other mosques. Counting among its regulars and visitors a broad specter of Muslims, including those with limited knowledge about Islam, it is paramount for leaders and established community members to teach newcomers and fellow believers by way of constant engagement and guidance. Recent converts are assigned "partners" who support them in religious, personal, and social matters.

One Saturday morning as I was sitting and waiting in the women's prayer room, the teenage girls' group was starting their meeting in the far corner of the room. As more girls arrived, the group ran out of chairs. Amna, one of the older girls, got up and said she would bring chairs from a classroom. One minute later she returned, all out of breath, without a chair and reported to her friends: "Imagine, I ran into the classroom and there was a man in the room. So I quickly ran away without a chair." The group decided that it must have either been one of the men doing renovation work, or somebody involved in the administration of the children's Islamic study classes. A little later another girl went back, and as the man had left, she retrieved some chairs. Why would Amna, who went to public school and rode public transportation where she constantly encountered strange men, run away upon encountering a man in the mosque? Amna was aware that the mosque was different, and to be alone in a room with an unrelated male, even if only briefly, was against the ethos of the mosque. Thus she had to leave the room immediately, which she did. By reporting the incident to her group, Amna demonstrated that she respected the mosque's rules, and happily applied them. The framework in which she lived her everyday life at school and in the city did not coincide with the one that guided her behavior in the mosque. For Amna there was the added personal dimension, since as the child of a Spanish-Pakistani family where religion had never played much of a role, Amna had reverted to Islam about three year prior to this incident. With the help of this group, her friends, and some older women, Amna was internalizing a proper pious subjectivity.

On another Saturday I was standing in the hall. Suddenly a member of the same girls' group, who was supposed to pay the fee for a trip, came running into the hallway with a banknote in her hand. Laughingly she approached Sheikh Saleh wanting to shake his hand and pay her dues. He quickly withdrew his hand behind his back and gave her a questioning look that seemed to say, "Don't you know where you are?" While many community members do shake hands with members of the opposite sex outside the mosque ("it is odd not to do this in this society," one man remarked), this practice is not part of the internal behavioral grammar. Ideally such practices extend beyond the mosque. Individuals cannot avoid mixed-sex events, yet many try their best to stay true to their beliefs outside the mosque. One woman described her attendance at a class conference event in her daughter's school: "I make sure that I arrive early, so that I do not have to share a table with a man."

Within the mosque, believers challenge popular practices and try to replace them with Islamic ones. For instance, after Sophie professed the *shahada*, many women responded with cries of joy (*zaghrata*). However, Zeinab quickly called for *takbir* as a superior expression of pious joy. Similarly, most women wear socks for prayer as the Qur'an allowed only for a woman's face and hands to be exposed. Only a few older women, some newcomers, and visitors continue to pray without socks. Occasional visitors from Muslim majority countries are surprised by this custom and remark that "back home" women have always prayed barefoot.

For the pious to operate in the distinctly different social frameworks of dominant society and the mosque is neither hypocritical nor schizophrenic, but indicates the understanding that there are distinct spheres of life for which different rules apply. Believers understand the mosque as a special place where Islam informs all practices. They enjoy this space with its own sociability, and continue to refine individual and communal practices, mannerisms, and habits in this small Islamic utopia. Experiencing practices in an "Islamic ambiance" (Bowen 2010), individuals are expected to internalize them and act accordingly in other religiously defined spaces over which they have control, in particular, the home.

Global Links and Local Lives

On a rainy spring night in 2007 I walked with a few women from the Al-Nour Mosque to the train station. Zeinab and I were ahead of the others. In the group's session, Sheikh Saleh had suggested that we read *Erlaubtes und Verbotenes im Islam* (The Lawful and Prohibited in Islam; 1989) by Yusuf Al-Qaradawi. Zeinab and I talked about Sheikh Al-Qaradawi and she emphasized her great respect for him. She worried that there was nobody, even on the remote horizons, who would one day be able to take over his position. As for many in her circles, Sheikh Al-Qaradawi was *the* contemporary Muslim scholar for Zeinab. As an example of just how understanding of ordinary people Sheikh Al-Qaradawi was, Zeinab related how she had once wondered whether it was appropriate for her to wear pants and colorful outfits and scarves. She sent an email to Sheikh Al-Qaradawi and asked his advice. In his response, he noted that there was no reason why she could not wear these things. He stated that it was not only the question of what one wore, but also of how one wore it. To be safe, Zeinab posed the same question to Amr Khaled, the popular Egyptian TV preacher, who responded in a similar manner. To check one more voice, Zeinab sent the same question to a scholar in Saudi Arabia (she did not mention his name). He responded that women who wore pants or too many colors were thoroughly confused. Only dark colors and long loose-fitting dresses were permissible. Zeinab disregarded the response of the Saudi scholar. She noted that such thinkers had no idea about her everyday life and challenges in Germany. She went with Sheikh Al-Qaradawi and Amr Khaled's advice instead. She noted that their advice made sense, because after all she lived in Germany, and not in Saudi Arabia. She emphasized Sheikh Al-Qaradawi's better understanding of the circumstances of Muslims in minority contexts, whose challenge it was to be pious members of non-Muslim societies. Zeinab's search for appropriate clothes further illustrates how individuals are linked to and interact with global pious networks.

A few years ago, Andrea and her husband Mahmoud faced a similar question. They had lived in the same rental apartment for years, when the building went up for sale. As tenants, they had the chance to buy their apartment at a reasonable price. The deal was tempting and if they did not buy the apartment they would have to move. They wanted to buy the apartment, but worried whether it was permissible for them to use a bank loan to finance this purchase. Andrea and Mahmoud consulted several scholars and eventually settled for Yusuf Al-Qaradawi's ruling that it was permissible for Muslims in westerns context to buy one apartment/house for their own use with a bank loan (involving generally inadmissible interest payments). It was not allowed, the ruling continued, to buy a second unit for investment purposes. Al-Qaradawi's rationale, Andrea explained to me, was that Muslims would be disadvantaged versus their non-Muslim neighbors, as they would forever be paying rent and could not save up for their and their children's future.

Zeinab, Andrea, Mahmoud, and Susanne are involved in mosque affairs, and their respective professional and civic lives. They are also part of global networks of Islamic piety (Cooke and Lawrence 2005; Herrera and Bayat 2010; T. Ramadan 1998, 2003a, 2003b, 2004). They easily move between these circuits and successfully integrate them. Zeinab asked (global) scholars and a (global) popular preacher for advice. She accepted the opinions of Sheikh Al-Qaradawi and Amr Khaled as suitable for her life. Andrea and Mahmoud based their decision to buy their apartment on the ruling of Sheikh Al-Qaradawi. Whether individuals search for legal opinions or advice for their everyday lives; whether they listen to sermons or religious programming via satellite TV or on the Internet, listen to pious singers like Sami Yusuf, read theological books, or consume Islamic products, these increasingly globalized religious links and circuits weave them into the *ummah*. The Al-Nour Mosque, like many of its European counterparts constitutes a German-speaking "node in a complex and shifting global network of communication" (Bowen 2010: 45). As pious individuals follow Sheikh Al-Qaradawi's advice, listen to Amr Khaled's sermons, Hülya Kandemir, Ammar114, and Sami Yusuf's songs, or shop online for Islamic books, clothes, or food, everyday lifestyles, practices, and consumption patterns approximate those of other members of the *ummah*.

Even more than middle-aged individuals like Zeinab, Susanne, Andrea, and Mahmoud, younger people are drawn into global circuits of Islamic piety (An-nisa 2009; Boubekeur 2005; Bowen 2010: 149; Ghodsee 2010; Herrera and Bayat 2010; Pink 2009; Ali 2008). Many join mosques or participate in Muslim student or youth organizations that maintain global ties (Bowen 2010: 48; Bayoumi 2010; Saktanber 2010). In particular Arab mosques in university cities often include groups of young, educated, and single males, and a few females. With the growing awareness of individual membership in the *ummah*, for these younger people, ethnic and other social lines of division become secondary to religious identities rooted in the *ummah*. When looking for a spouse, young believers look for piety as an essential characteristic (Kandemir 2005; Backer 2009). Ethnicity and nationality become secondary. Educational achievements similarly often override ethnic and national considerations. When, for instance, in traditional Muslim socio-cultural contexts consideration of family, status, and social reputation played central roles with regard to marriage, in the "new" *ummah* and the context of "authenticated Islam" (Deeb 2006), religiosity is the most desired characteristic in a spouse. By the end of 2007, Amna (see above) decided that she was ready to get married. She spread the word in the mosque. Soon she was introduced to an Algerian student whom she married after a few (chaperoned) meetings. The couple married without dating and celebrated their wedding in a gender-segregated environment complying with the ethos of the mosque. They married ethnic others, social equals, and religious partners. They are "pioneers" of new lifestyles where religiosity supersedes other considerations. They distanced themselves from cultural traditions of Muslim majority countries and dominant German cultural norms. Their marriage and lives are locally rooted (Amna is a Stuttgarter), but also unfold in the physical (visits to Algeria) and spiritual (their engagements with theology and pious trends) context of the *ummah*.

Conclusion: Urban Religious Lifeworlds

In this chapter I examined the re-/making of pious selves and religiosities in the context of the Al-Nour Mosque. I illustrated how based on its associational context, smaller and more dispersed Arab community, larger number of student members and focus on converts, this mosque became a gateway to Islam for new Muslims or those interested in Islam, and a place to discuss and refine individual religiosities. With a diverse community and some members who know little about Islam, the Al-Nour Mosque has taken on the task of socializing newcomers into religious beliefs and practices and pious lifeworlds. The community integrates converts into the mosque and the *ummah*. In formal groups and informal conversations, special events like lectures or holiday celebrations, the mosque community provides its members and visitors with a multitude of settings where individuals can meet, discuss, learn about, and concretely practice their beliefs. The mosque is a home space for believers where they meet like-minded individuals, initiate friendship, create networks, experiment with and practice their religiosities, and most importantly search for answer for their religious questions. Individuals, groups, and events help the diverse faithful to articulate individual religiosities and live in society as pious Muslims. The manifold activities in the Al-Nour Mosque and public engagements of individual members or groups of members combine to a larger field in which the negotiation of individual pieties and pious lifestyles plays a central role. This larger field connects to global Islamic networks and circuits of theological debates, social activities, and consumer patterns (Pink 2009; Cesari 2010a; Kömeçoğlu 2004; Harb and Deeb 2011, 2013; Khosravi 2008).

In the sheltered and sheltering confines of the Al-Nour Mosque, the pious learn about and debate Islam, and strive to improve their religiosity They create a community that seeks to be a worthy part of the *ummah* and a creative part of urban society. Some community members carefully examine social and pious practices in the community. While rarely willing to openly voice criticism in the mosque, where dissent is seen as an offense against the communal ethos, they debate issues among themselves. They engage in debates about properly pious practices and vaguely circumscribe what is and is not permissible for the pious (Amir-Moazami 2010). They distinguish appropriately Islamic practices from cultural traditions, and very importantly for women, from social patriarchy (Wadud 2006). Similarly they identify lines between mainstream culture and local Islamic practices (e.g. with regard to dating or bank loans). In the process, believers create lifeworlds and practices that are both thoroughly local and deeply embedded in the *ummah*. While the mosque plays a central role in the lives of many members, most of them are also deeply involved in other social fields (Levitt 2008). For many their engagement with the mosque serves to articulate a way of participation in the urban public that is religiously acceptable and socially viable.

Post-Script: Settled

In 2007, seven years after her turn to Islam, and six years after her formal conversion, Susanne-Samiha was firmly settled in her life as a Muslima, the Al-Nour community, and the larger Muslim public sphere in Stuttgart. She was part of local and regional Islamic networks and had personal ties to believers in both Muslim majority and other minority contexts. She had acquired an impressive Islamic knowledge. She acted with ease as a Muslima in all spheres of life. Unlike earlier in her life, a man no longer decided her social life. She summarized her transformations:

> I finally have my own circle of friends and acquaintances of (more or less) similarly minded people . . . By way of my interest in Islam and my attendance of meetings in the mosque, I integrated into the mosque and became part of the community which initiated further contacts/relationships. I had, because Islam largely segregates the public lives of men and women, finally found entry to women's worlds, about which I had known nothing before/was not even conscious about previously. This was of incredible value (*Reichtum*) for me and important for my self-understanding as a woman . . . And finally I found (even if only a few) women/female friends with whom I can engage intellectually. In the past I did this mostly with men. Thus my life became more female which is closer to me and my personality. This is in part also related to Islamic dressing rules. Today I see the headscarf (for myself) as an irreducible part of my femininity. It is a protection for me, a sense of 'being respected' (*Respektiertwerden*) and a 'focus' [English in Susanne's original] for me, which again and again shows me the center of my life, my life for myself and with Allah . . . As a result I can encounter women who do not wear a headscarf, Muslimas or non-Muslimas, completely openly and freely.

After an initial period of learning and transformations (and a divorce), Susanne reached a way of life and religiosity that suited her. She is part of a mosque community, participates in other groups and events, and has a group of pious friends and acquaintances. She works with a headscarf. Occasionally she participates in public events having to do with Islam. She has become one of numerous pious Muslim Stuttgarters who participate in a myriad of public stages. I will introduce a number of such individuals in the next chapter.

Notes

1. The term *mulid* is used in colloquial Egyptian Arabic to denote a loud and chaotic situation or celebration.
2. See the small movement around the "Council of the Ex-Muslims" that was founded in 2007.
3. For an earlier account of conversion and subsequent theological work, see Muhammad Asad (1954, 1980).
4. The same term is used in pious Christian circles to describe similar people who once were consciously pious and then turned their backs to religion.
5. For another analysis of negotiation of religiosities in the Al-Nour Mosque, see Kuppinger 2014c.

6. The domina/SM studio keeps a low profile. Their clientele is surprisingly invisible. The fact that religious communities share premises with an SM studio is problematic and bespeaks their marginalized existence and overall neglect given to them by dominant urban society.
7. On its website the IGD notes that it "contributed in a considerable parts to the identity construction—(*Identitätsstiftung*) of Muslims, the creation of a German-speaking Muslim 'community' [English in the original], and to the accommodation of Muslim religious practices by way of the diverse activities" (http://www.igd-online.de/ueber-uns.html).
8. For years, the Munich mosque was the center of IGD activities. Ahmad von Denffer, who is an early convert and part of the inner circle of the Munich mosque, is a prolific writer and has published books and pamphlets about Islamic topics in German since 1977 (e.g. von Denffer 1983, 2000, 2003).
9. It is hard to say how many are German citizens. Anecdotal evidence suggests that numbers are growing.
10. Women who convert in the context of a marriage constitute a large group of converts (Baumann 2004: 8).
11. The controversial popular preacher Pierre Vogel routinely has mostly younger people convert at his public events. Many such conversions can be watched on http://www.youtube.com.
12. An institute based on Vienna (formerly in Frankfurt) that offers intellectually challenging seminars and programs about Islam. The seminars attract participants from Germany, Austria, and Switzerland and incidentally also serve to create broader networks among often highly educated and professional individuals, see also further below in this chapter.
13. For the symbolism of shaking hands, see Deeb (2006: 106).

CHAPTER 3

Public Lives

On a Sunday afternoon in November 2007, the "Women's Cultural Center Sarah" in Stuttgart held an event entitled "Conversation with Muslimas." Susanne-Samiha (see chapter 2) had met one of the organizing members of the center at a different occasion. The latter invited Susanne-Samiha to run an open debate at the center's café. Susanne-Samiha agreed and recruited Sibel, one of her friends who also occasionally participated in public events, to be her co-panelist. Founded in 1978, the Women's Cultural Center Sarah ("the Sarah") is the oldest center of its kind in Germany. Originating in the early women's movement of the 1970s, the Sarah offers a wide variety of social, cultural, political, artistic, professional, and spiritual activities and events. The Sarah accommodates debates, art exhibits, courses, and is a place (the café) for women to socialize, talk, engage, and support each other. The Sarah is a women's space, however, "occasionally, there are events to which male contemporaries are most welcome—they are marked in the program as such" (www.das-sarah.de).

When Elke (a friend from the Al-Nour Mosque), Tamima, Tala, and I arrived at the Sarah, only Susanne-Samiha, Sibel, and a few others were present. A table was set up in the front for the panelists facing rows of chairs, and tables with chairs in the back for the audience. The room eventually filled with about twenty-five women. A few women with headscarves sat on the left, mixed in with other women. On average the attending Muslimas were younger (largely in their twenties) than the rest of the audience (mostly in their forties and older). When the room had filled and the audience had supplied themselves with coffee and cake, Susanne-Samiha, Sibel, and the moderator took their seats at the panelists' table. The moderator introduced the topic and panelists. Susanne-Samiha prefaced her talk with a note that she and Sibel were representing their own opinions.

Susanne-Samiha started with an account of her conversion. She noted that it had taken her a year to convert, and that she had always been searching for spirituality. Once she started reading the Qur'an, she knew "that this was what I had been searching for." She related how she started to intensely read, talk to people, engage in debates, and attend meetings after this encounter with the Qur'an. "Then came the horrific 11th of September; but that was not my Islam and I wanted to make this understanding and my turn to Islam public." She converted soon after 9/11.[1] She explained features of Islam and her everyday life as a believer, including notes about praying and giving alms (*zakat*).

Next Sibel recounted that her parents had come from Turkey about forty years ago. The youngest among her siblings, she was born in Germany. Her father, in addition to his job, worked on weekends as an Imam in different mosque communities. Sibel explained that her family was religious and that she was raised a Muslim, "but without force." There were times in her teenage years when she struggled with religion, but then she consciously embraced Islam. A woman from the audience inquired what it meant to be raised a Muslim? Sibel responded, that she was taught rules of social conduct, every day practices (e.g. no pork), and concrete ritual practices (e.g. how to do ablutions and pray). She learned to recite the Qur'an, and was instructed how to deal with men, in particular those one could potentially marry. She stressed that her parents never controlled her, as they trusted her religiosity. At the age of twenty-three, she started to wear a headscarf.

Sibel noted that she was a trained industrial administrator and accountant (*Industriekauffrau* and *Bilanzbuchhalterin*) and worked part-time in her profession while studying toward an MBA at the University of Stuttgart. She outlined aspects of her religiosity and emphasized that for her, life was more than just "husband, children, and work." She explained how Islam had given her life an additional dimension and taught her to appreciate different facets of the world and creation. For example, her religiosity gave her an intense relationship with nature. Piety or pious practices structured her day and life in a timeframe that made explicit references to nature through the daily prayers and their scheduling according to the sun. "This gave me a different/new relationship to the world and time," she explained and added that, if one forgot a prayer one could not re-do it later, it was lost, which symbolized the irretrievable nature of time. The time given to a person was unique and precious. She related the "spiritual experiences" that came with "getting in touch with the Creator five times a day" and described the resulting calm and feeling of security (*Ruhe und Geborgenheit*). Ultimately, she insisted, the daily prayers gave her life a distinct frame. Susanne-Samiha added that the relation to the Creator was the principal feature of religiosity; it taught humans that there was an entirely different layer to their existence. Susanne-Samiha and Sibel continued to describe features of their spirituality. The audience posed questions, which the panelists answered in detail.

After a while, questions moved to the larger context of women and/in Islam. Quickly a predictable series of questions, starting with the supposed misogynist nature of Islam, were voiced. Susanne-Samiha responded: "I do not experience Islam as against women (*frauenfeindlich*), on the contrary, it raised my self-consciousness as a woman." A woman from the audience immediately countered:

"But there is the verse in the Qur'an about husbands beating their wives. You cannot discuss that away (*kann man nicht wegreden*)." A second woman added: "Would you let yourself be beaten?"

"Perhaps," Sibel humorously replied. The audience laughed and Sibel quickly returned the question: "But what is meant by beating here? Take the example of the Prophet Muhammad, he never beat his wives." Sibel insisted that this was a complex matter and needed to be analyzed in the context of the Qur'an and *Sunna*. She added that the Prophet had said to the faithful that "those among you are the best, who treat their wives the best."

She explained that Islam was a complicated theological and intellectual field (*komplexes Gedankengebäude*) and needed to be analyzed as such. With a brief hint to the complex history of Islam and Muslim theology, Sibel asserted that starting in the eleventh century women had been gradually pushed out of Muslim scholarship and the public sphere. Men started to dominate interpretations of the Qur'an and overall scholarship. Most women for most of Muslim history had been illiterate and had very limited theological knowledge, and knew little about their rights as women. These circumstances pointed to the imperative task for women to gain religious knowledge, as in fact the quest for knowledge was of fundamental importance for all Muslims. It was indispensable for men and women to seek knowledge. More questions from the audience followed: "What about the headscarf? Is it spiritual, political, or an issue of identity?" Sibel responded: "It is first and foremost a return to Islamic values (*Zurückbesinnung auf islamische Werte*), and a discovery of spirituality." Susanne-Samiha added, "The headscarf can only be worn in a spiritual manner." "One feels first and foremost like a human and not as a woman when one wears a headscarf," a Muslima from the audience elaborated.

This exchange engendered a debate about who should cover, and who was to blame for staring at women. Should women cover because men stared at them? Should men avert their gaze, and women should do as they please? Was it women's task to respond to and avoid male "misbehavior"? Or, should not men control themselves? Several non-Muslim women were passionate about this topic and unwilling to have their lifestyles circumscribed by male misbehavior. Male weakness, in their mind, should not limit female freedom. One woman was irritated: "But it should be possible for a woman to walk through the city at 2 A.M., even in a miniskirt. It is not she who is at fault, but those who look at her in the wrong way. It is the task of men to behave themselves."

Several women agreed that it was not for women to accommodate male misbehavior and have their freedom limited by male shortcomings and lust. The discussion became louder and a little more unruly. Soon, the moderator, for the first time, interfered: "Quite honestly, I find a discrepancy here. It takes some discipline for men to regularly pray five times a day. How can they not discipline themselves and turn their heads the other way when they see women who tempt them?"

She pondered how women on the one side were disciplined and worked hard to live by their faith, but then they gave men considerable leeway and did not hold them accountable for doing their part. She concluded: "Somehow we have a different sense of what freedom means (*Freiheitsbegriff*)." The discussion between the panelist and their Muslim and non-Muslim audience was lively and at times heated, but polite and respectful. The audience was genuinely curious about the Muslimas' lives, but made it clear that they would not consider this lifestyle for themselves. The debate lasted for over two hours. Judging by everybody's engagement and willingness to stay for more than two hours, the event was a success. While neither side "convinced" the other, they engaged each other, and the non-Muslim audience had the opportunity to get "insider" responses. While the positions of the interlocutors differed, they also shared some basic ideas and assumptions, albeit these were never mentioned as such. Coming from different starting points, both the Muslimas and the Sarah regulars understood that gender mixing was not (always) conducive to women's lives. Both recognized the strength of all-female spaces and socialities. These shared premises and the willingness to engage other women partially accounted for this successful event. The afternoon was a vital moment of cultural engagement and a building block for a more inclusive multi-religious urban public sphere.

In this chapter I introduce pious Muslims, their everyday lives, religiosities, and public engagements. Examining activities and pious trajectories, I maintain, that events like Susanne-Samiha and Sibel's panel, the small-scale activism of many people, and minute daily interactions are crucial for the construction of a multi-religious (and multi-ethnic) cityscape (Amiraux 2006: 41). I previously introduced Mr. Serdar, Mr. Ömer, Zeinab, and Sheikh Saleh who either moved in the public sphere, or mediated debates in mosques. The questions poses itself: Are these public figures unique individuals, or do they represent a much larger group of individuals who similarly produce the building blocks necessary for the construction of more inclusive cityscapes? What are the small encounters that produce cultural transformations? What types of activities unfold in urban spaces that further the localization of Islam, increase respect and recognition for Muslims, and mediate more inclusive urban cultures? Who are the local architects of a multi-religious cityscape? In what ways do ordinary individuals, often in invisible ways, participate in cultural processes?

(In-)Significant Citizens?

No person, moment, or space is too insignificant to contribute to cultural negotiations. Indeed "invisible" individuals are principal contributors and supporters of local dynamics and trends (de Certeau 1984; Holston 2008; Bayat 2010). Their daily acts and encounters further cement nascent urban cultural beginnings (Zukin 2010). Small and hidden incidents might over time produce new forms and practices (Amiraux 2006; Fadil 2006; Mitchell 2003). In the following I introduce six individuals of different genders, ages, ethnicities, classes, educational backgrounds, work situations, religiosities, and types of formal religious associations. These individuals' lives, religiosities, and choices illustrate the diversity and complexity of pious Muslim lifeworlds. Some of the individuals vaguely represent larger groups, others are more unique. With each person, I highlight different elements that influence the negotiation of Muslim lifeworlds, and illustrate modes of civic participation and cultural production. I provide background information about individuals' life histories to shed light on experiences that influenced their religiosities. These elements span decades and continents and are paramount for an understanding of the scope of these individuals' contemporary ideas and engagements. I knew all six interlocutors for about a year before I interviewed them. I had attended group discussions and formal events with some and had also socialized more or less intensely with others.

Pious Muslims are often accused of being disengaged from society. Like others, Muslims selectively create their civic participation. Their engagements reflect personal preferences (after all not everybody likes to play soccer, sing in a choir, or be part of a political party). Muslim lives—like those of most urbanites—reflect what Hajer and Reijndorp (2001: 84) have called "parochialism" whereby individuals largely move in and use a small number of urban spaces that best suit their interests and social and cultural preferences. Duplicating existing local/German patterns of a very associationally minded society (*Vereinsmeierei*) where many families' lives revolve around one central association (e.g. a church community, soccer club, tennis club, political party), pious Muslims' lives often center around, but are not limited to religiously inspired spaces, activities, and relationships, which might or might not be mosque based. Susanne-Samiha concluded her notes about her pious transformation: "The initial period of my Muslim life was marked by the consolidation of Islam in my life. Now that I feel strong in my belief, I feel that time has come for me to engage once more with other more worldly, societal things/problems, and also to participate as a Muslima in society. Being Muslim has now become a regular part (*Selbstverständlichkeit*) of my person, that I can now act as such in the world." In the face of public resentment, many believers feel the need to participate in public, especially in contexts where they can be instrumental in changing dominant ideas about Muslims (Fadil 2006: 67). Others conduct their everyday lives at work, in school, or the neighborhood as best as they can with the awareness that they represent Islam.

Public Spheres

Susanne-Samiha's embrace of Islam was a deeply personal experience. However, it becomes socially relevant in its public manifestations. Her momentary withdrawal from the public sphere during an initial period of intense learning and complex personal reconstruction was followed by a careful reinsertion of her new pious subjectivity into the Muslim public sphere and larger public sphere. Susanne-Samiha's engagements transcend her visible participation in public events, and include relatively hidden debates and compromises at her work place. Her public repositioning is best analyzed in the context of debates about the public sphere.

Jürgen Habermas (1990 [1962]) initiated debates about the public sphere.[2] He defined the (bourgeois) public sphere (*Öffentlichkeit*) as a site of rational exchange where citizens discussed issues as equals disregarding social, cultural, and economic differences. Habermas's public sphere is distinguished by equality and undisturbed by social exclusion, discrimination, and economic disadvantages. While frequently criticized, Habermas's concept remains crucial in debates about the public sphere. Oskar Negt and Alexander Kluge (1972) pointed to Habermas's oversight of economic inequalities that interfered with access to his idealized public sphere. They criticized the neglect of working-class cultures in the public sphere, and the devaluation of working-class cultural elements (e.g. linguistic forms). For Negt and Kluge, Habermas's public sphere was too narrowly defined. A more inclusive concept needed to account for working-class discourses and lifeworlds. Negt and Kluge insisted that theorists needed to analyze the interaction of the public sphere with capitalist production, question the role of the media as a tool of those in power, examine the nature of unequal access to the public sphere, and acknowledge the hegemony of bourgeois cultural forms and practices in this sphere.

Feminist scholars critically examined Habermas's public sphere and ensuing debates, and pointed to their relative gender blindness. Joan Landes (1988) examined the role of women in the French public sphere between 1750 and 1850 and insisted on Habermas's neglect of the role of women in the (historical) public sphere. She pointed to emerging bourgeois public spheres as parts of larger social and political configurations whose goal was to remake the role of women, relegate them to the domestic sphere, and silence their public/political voices. Women who remained in the public sphere (working-class or peasant women) were looked at with suspicion or contempt (E. Wilson 1992). Habermas's critics contend that the exclusive nature of the male bourgeois public sphere was a conscious construction and efficient tool for nineteenth-century elites to demarcate lines of political participation. These elites contested "old aristocratic and royal authorities" and excluded "popular/plebeian elements" (Eley 1992: 321). They had marked their own sphere of public interaction as *the* public sphere, and marked all others as irrelevant in the best and dangerous in the worst case.

Nancy Fraser identifies the bourgeois public sphere as "the prime institutional site for the construction of the consent that defines the new hegemonic mode of domination" in modern society (1992: 117). The public sphere is neither open nor equal. Rather, "subordinate groups sometimes cannot find the right voice or words to express their thought, and when they do, they discover they are not heard" (ibid.: 119). Fraser insists that "subordinated social groups—women, workers, peoples of color, and gays and lesbians have repeatedly found it advantageous to constitute alternative publics" (ibid.: 123). Using the example of the U.S. feminist counterpublic, Fraser illustrates that this public was created and maintained by an "variegated array of journals, bookstores, publishing companies, film and video distribution networks, lecture series, research centers, academic programs, conferences, conventions, festivals and local meetings" (ibid.). Subaltern counterpublics allow disenfranchised groups to experiment with and articulate ideas, find their voices, formulate demands, negotiate identities, and insert these in "the public at large" (ibid.: 124). Counterpublics accommodate "a widening of discursive contestation" (ibid.) as they allow small groups to challenge existing conventions, formulate agendas, and define mode of participation. As such they are essential ingredients of a democratic public sphere. Counterpublics at large, and small formal or informal groups vaguely located within their confines make hitherto hidden voices heard, and allow for emerging groups to formulate their positions and contributions. They constitute discursive beginnings, which can remake features and modes of public engagement. The public sphere in this perspective is not a coherent whole but becomes a "field of discursive connections" (Calhoun 1992a: 37). Craig Calhoun identifies "subsidiary public sphere[s]" as smaller groups (e.g. lawyers as a professional group) that might or might not be in conflict with the larger public sphere (ibid.: 37–38) as they express "sectional interests" (ibid.: 38).

Michael Warner (2002) examines public spheres as sites of participation, confrontation, and contestation whose debates are crucial elements of political life. These spheres and their concrete sites of engagement—large and small, visible or invisible—allow a critical public to challenge and restrain those in power. Counterpublics, "defined by their tension with a larger public" are essential for Warner (ibid.: 56). Debates in counterpublics are "understood to contravene the rules obtaining in the world at large, being structured by alternative dispositions or protocols, making different assumptions about what can be said and what goes without saying" (ibid.). Counterpublics accommodate and mediate the concerns of subordinate groups. They question and remake modes of feeling, expression, and participation. Referring to women's and gay and lesbian movements, Warner argues that they "can work to elaborate new worlds of culture and social relations" which facilitate diverse kinds of relations, vocabularies, "styles of embodiment" and "relations of care and pedagogy" (ibid.: 57). Warner's counterpublics are self-organized. They are frequently the results of pressing shared concerns (ibid.: 69) and linked to concrete times, circumstances, and spaces. A public brings together strangers who become associates in this public (ibid.: 74). Nobody automatically belongs to any public, and individuals can be part of multiple publics (ibid.: 70–71). The public sphere is not a pre-existing space or condition, but results from the contributions of participants and their contradictory opinions (Geulen 2004: 58). A genuine public allows for no exclusion (ibid.: 60).

The public sphere at large, counterpublics, and other public configurations are sites for the articulation and mediation of ideas, agendas, and identities. Constant engagement and controversy make diverse voices heard and creatively pit them against each other. New groups challenge dominant terms, modes of engagement and expressions, everyday practices, topics of debates, and broader social and cultural realities. If successful, hitherto silenced groups (e.g. women) or emerging groups (e.g. immigrants) constitute themselves as relevant voices in the dominant public sphere. Depending on broader political contexts, some efforts result in the configuration of subsidiary public spheres, while others remain counterpublics. Others alternately situate themselves in both spheres. Dynamics in the inclusive public sphere are open-ended and allow for emerging groups to leave their mark and transform this sphere. Groups like women, workers, people of color, gays and lesbians have challenged dominant European and North American public spheres and inserted new constituencies, topics of debate, vocabularies, sensitivities, and modes of engagement and confrontation. Until recently, these debates and conflicts unfolded on secular platforms using secular vocabularies.

Since the 1970s and gaining momentum in the 1980s, diverse Muslims, mosque communities, and Muslim associations have configured Muslim counterpublics and increasingly also subsidiary publics in Europe (Werbner 2002; Gerlach 2006; Jonker and Amiraux 2006; Göle and Ammann 2004; Lewis 1994, 2006)). Like Fraser described in the case of the feminist movement, these counterpublics center around an array of publications, publishers, meetings, films, lectures, cultural events, newspapers, newsletters, spaces, and Internet platforms (e.g. Bunt 2002, 2003, 2009; Kuppinger 2011a; Ammann 2004; Demiryürek 2007). They are accompanied by emerging consumer markets that offer specific products (e.g. modest Islamic fashion, *halal* foods; e.g. Fischer 2009). Commercial products might further define or mark individuals' relative position both within Muslim and broader social contexts (e.g. Haenni 2005; Boubekeur 2005; Tarlo 2010; Pink 2009; Kuppinger 2009). Islamic pamphlets and theological literature that early on had only been available in Turkish or Arabic are increasingly translated into German (e.g. Al-Qaradawi 1989; Khaled 2004, 2005a, 2005b, 2006; Gülen 2006; Karaman 2005; Maududi 2001; Said Nursi 2004; and the works of the controversial Harun Yahya e.g. 2003a, 2003b). These publications constitute crucial links for some believers to the *ummah*. Since about 2000 a nascent sphere of German theological and popular Islamic writing and debate emerged (Hofmann 1995; 1996; Reidegeld 2005; Zaidan 1999; von Denffer 2005; Wentzel 2004, Grimm 1995, 1999, 2000), including personal accounts of conversion or reversion and other inspirational texts (Kandemir 2005; Backer 2008, Uhlemayr 2010; Özelsel 2005). Publications of essays and commentary (Rieger 2007), manuals or self help literature (Demiryürek 2007), and children's and youth books (Aslan 1997; Yahya 2002) followed and proliferated. Websites (e.g. www.islam.de, or www.halal.de) accommodate cyber debates, and are central sites for the configuration of the Muslim German public sphere.

European Muslim counterpublics and subsidiary publics were initially ignored by dominant societies. Since 9/11, Muslims and the position of Islam in European public spheres moved center stage (Cesari 2010). In particular young and educated European Muslims participate in modern urban spaces, they use global communication networks, engage in public debates, follow consumption patterns of others, learn the rules of the market, live in secular time schemes, are familiar with values of individuation, professional worlds, and consumer society, and start to critically reflect about their own positions. (Göle 2004: 12–13). As citizens they ask for their legitimate rights and continue to spark passionate discussions and resentments (Amiraux 2006).

Debates among Muslims delineate emerging Muslim public spheres, which combine characteristics of counterpublics and subsidiary publics. These platforms facilitate the construction of pious subjectivities and public personae (Göle 2004: 21; Fadil 2006: 75). Emerging discourses and linguistic, bodily, verbal, material, and spatial practices further refine this sphere and progressively mark its participants and their growing engagement with the larger public sphere (Göle and Amman 2004; Jonker and Amiraux 2006; Tietze 2001; Jouili 2008; Schiffauer 2010). European Muslim public spheres are characterized by the tension between their position and self-definition as a counterpublic (and counterculture) and subsidiary public. National mosque associations have long understood themselves as a subsidiary public, but are often dealt with as either non-belonging or a dangerous counterculture. Only tiny groups, often self-identified *salafis*, insist on their roles as non-participants in the larger public sphere.

The simultaneous quest for sameness and difference characterizes the civic participation of many Muslims (Amiraux 2006: 43). The challenge is to be pious (i.e. respected members of the pious Muslim community), successful in dominant society, and heard in the dominant public sphere (Kuppinger 2011c). Sigrid Nökel summarizes this challenge for young women as "*Karriere plus Kopftuch*" (career plus headscarf; 2004: 285). The pious negotiate German and Islamic norms and construct bridges between them (Bowen 2010: 137). Individuals and groups reach specific compromises, which might spark controversy within Islamic circuits. This tension is creative and produces new practices that aim to be acceptable and successful on diverse stages (Nökel 2002; Gerlach 2006; Kandemir 2005; Spohr 1998; Uhlemayr 2010).

Acting in Public

Public engagement and debates are crucial features of pluralistic societies where citizenship transcends the ownership of a passport and voting in elections. Active citizenship implies individual participation in a web of social, cultural, and political interactions.³ Such citizenship necessitates diverse social links, and activities on urban, regional, or national platforms (Fadil 2006: 69). A prerequisite for individual and communal participation is the recognition of all as equal members of society (Modood 2005, 2007), which is linked to the visibility of individuals and groups (Jonker and Amiraux 2006; Göle and Ammann 2004). Pious actors strive to make religion/Islam "an integral element of citizenship" (Amir-Moazami 2010: 203). Tension marks dynamics of recognition, visibility, and equal participation of pious European Muslims (Modood 2005; Cesari 2004; Schiffauer 2008). Dominant society and media, often taken by surprise at what to them seem sudden demands of Muslims, only recently started to seriously engage Muslim concerns. The arrival of confident and eloquent pious Muslim actors continues to irritate segments of dominant society (Klausen 2005; Peter 2010; Shooman and Spielhaus 2010) who struggle with the idea that Muslims ask for their rights on equal footing as citizens (Bowen 2007, 2010; Amiraux 2006).

Complex everyday debates that underlie the slow but thorough construction of Muslim German discourses and platforms are rarely recognized and even less engaged by dominant society. They are quickly glossed over, or given negative labels such as "fundamentalist" or "extreme" (Schiffer 2005; Shooman and Spielhaus 2010; Bahners 2011). Yet, these efforts and debates form the basis of participation and citizenship. Whether observers approve of specific contents of ongoing debates is not the principal question; at stake is the existence of dynamic platforms and debates that are rooted in urban lifeworlds. Urban beginnings and national cultural and political transformations are initiated in small contexts, before they—already well-tested—reach the visible stages of public debates. It is the minute and unplanned everyday "footsteps" or "micro practices" (Göle 2004: 41) of ordinary people that launch larger debates. The acts of ordinary people in random places constitute the foundations of meaningful larger transformations (de Certeau 1984; Amiraux 2006: 35). In order to understand the minutiae of emerging publics and their debates it is paramount to search for the "elusive evidence of the ordinary" (Chauncey 1994:10), the small steps taken and words uttered in seemingly insignificant moments and spaces. I will now turn to six individuals and their diverse lifeworlds and public experiences.

Religiosity and Humanity

I met Emine Yıldız through school activities in the Park School in Nordbahnhof. We soon became friendly, and with some other women socialized occasionally over long breakfasts. For the interview, I invited Emine to my apartment. In a three-hour conversation Emine related aspects of her life history, shared thoughts about Islam, and explained what it meant be a practicing Muslima in

Stuttgart. In the following I draw on this interview and other shared experiences with Emine.

Emine was born in the mid-1960s in Turkey. Her father left for Germany the same year, leaving her mother and three children behind. He first worked in his learned craft in a small workshop not far from Stuttgart. He liked his work and boss. After some years he brought his wife to Germany for medical treatment, leaving the children with their grandmother. He had in the meanwhile taken a job with the railroad and moved into a railroad workers' apartment in Stuttgart-Nordbahnhof. Emine's mother's initial arrival started a long series of moves back and forth between Germany and Turkey, for all but the father. In the early 1970s, the parents brought Emine as the only child to Germany to keep her mother company. The parents lived in the same apartment that her father still has today. Emine attended Park School and loved school. She learned German quickly. "I watched plenty of German TV," Emine remembered, "and became all German." This worried her parents who sent her back to her grandmother in Turkey. In the meantime the parents had brought over Emine's older siblings who did some brief schooling and soon started to work. Emine now was the only child left in Turkey. She remembered: "I was looking at a picture of all my family wearing nice clothes and sitting on the couch in the apartment. They looked all so happy. But I was alone in Turkey and did not understand why." The next time she came on vacation to Germany, she fought with her father and insisted to stay with the rest of the family. He eventually gave in.

She went back to Park School and finished ninth grade. Then she started an apprenticeship as a hairdresser. Because of the low pay for hairdressers, she left the profession soon after she finished the three-year training, and started working in a factory. In the mid-1980s she married a man from Turkey who joined her in Stuttgart. Two years later her daughter was born. Emine continued working and left her child with her mother. Her husband eventually opened a small store where Emine later helped out. But Emine missed her daughter and wanted to work shorter hours and closer to home. Through connections she hooked up with the Häberle family who owned a local workshop. She started to clean first the office, later the residential part of the house, and eventually took over all sorts of tasks in the household. Emine emphasized that these were very decent people as they even registered her, which meant she received full health and retirement benefits.[4] She was well paid by the Häberles. Emine's family and the Häberle family became friendly and sometimes her sister also helped out with her employer. Her brother became an apprentice at the Häberle's workshop for a three-year professional training. Emine's mother and the elder Mrs. Häberle became friendly, and Mrs. Häberle sometimes came to Mrs. Yıldız's apartment and ate all sorts of Turkish food there. More recently, the workshop (like many similar small workshops) suffered a decline in contracts. Emine cut back her hours, and eventually only went there on special occasions. In 2011 she gave up working for the family and became a housewife, but always on the lookout for small jobs and social activities. In 2012 she participated in a three-month training as an occupational therapist/attendant for senior citizens. In early 2013 she took on a position in a senior citizens' residence. Emine's mother passed away in 2008 and her father now spends most of his time in Turkey.

When asked about her religious biography, Emine related how many years ago she went to a *Suleymanciye* (today's VIKZ) group to read the Qur'an. This group, she explained, later became the Takva Mosque. In the 1980s she stopped going and did not read the Qur'an for years. Years later with the emergence of new TV programs, Emine reconnected with religion. The first Turkish TV channels that were broadcast in Germany had no religious programs. Soon some channels added religious programs. While Emine had been praying and fasting before, it had been more of a habit for her, only now she started to more seriously think about religion. In 1993 she started to wear a headscarf as Islam had become more central and decisive in her life. Emine watched TV programs that included what she perceived as more sophisticated theologians who knew how to explain Islam and theological questions. Emine noted that she had never heard such debates before and was intrigued. By 1996, she remembered, with the advent of satellite TV, the religious programs become more frequent and better. There were lengthy Qur'an recitations during Ramadan, detailed interpretations of the Qur'an, or programs about the Prophet Muhammad. Many questions that she had were answered in these programs. With all the high-quality information and inspiration, Emine felt there was no need for her to go to a mosque. She said that "everybody has their own opinion" and ultimately needs to search for their own way of believing and practicing. Emine discusses pressing questions with her sisters, or sometimes with friends: "They support me in my belief and they help me research when I have a question." She also reminded me of the bookshelf in her living room with theological works. She noted that she reads the occasional theological book, but on the whole she preferred books about current people and politics, like for example the situation in Iraq and how people experienced these hardships.[5] For years mosques did not play a role in her life. This also holds for her husband who might only go to a mosque to get a haircut (many mosques have barbershops). In 2007 Emine noted once one joined a mosque, one acquired all sorts of obligations and she was not ready for that. Occasionally Emine attends events or lectures, like the *Islamwoche* (annual lecture series at University of Stuttgart). She is also an avid visitor of *kermes* (fairs for fundraising) events at local mosques. When I returned to Stuttgart after some months of absence June 2008, one of the first things that Emine told me were the numerous *kermes* events I had unfortunately missed.

Emine smiled when she remembered how she started to wear the headscarf and the Häberle grandmother "scolded" her for doing this. But, Emine added, the grandmother quickly changed her mind and praised her, recognizing the serious religious commitment, which she greatly respected. Having worked in this familiar environment, putting on the headscarf was not problematic for Emine. On the larger labor market, however, things are different. A while ago Emine went to the job center looking for a job. "With a headscarf this is a big problem," she noted. "Most jobs that deal with customers or the like are off for women with headscarves." She related how cleaning in a large hotel came up, but the employee at the job center noted, that even this would not work for her, because *"hohe Tiere"* (literally "high animals," i.e. the high and mighty) might pass by, as she would be pushing her cleaning cart through the halls. Emine was outraged by this remark. "Not even cleaning," she complained, "is open to women with headscarves. What difference does it make there?" She concluded that this is one more reason why her daughter, who at the time of our interview was studying for her final school exam (*Abitur*), should go to university, so that she can enter a profession where she will be free to wear a headscarf. Soon after her daughter started to study engineering at the University of Stuttgart.

Emine sees her faith as something that makes her happy and is foundational in her life. She is proud to be a believer. Faith, for her, is a commitment to divine principles that guide all aspects of life, and encounters with people, regardless of their religion or religiosity. Religion does not create boundaries for her but guides all human interactions. Emine told the story about when the Häberle grandmother, with whom "we had become family a long time ago, we have been close with them for thirty-five years now," died: "Of course we [Emine and her sister] attended the funeral, and of course we attended the church service. We have known and loved this woman for 35 years. How can we not go? She was a Christian, so we go to the Christian service. We went and sat with our headscarves in the church. At first people were surprised but then they knew who we were. Can you imagine not to attend the entire funeral of somebody whom who knew and loved for so long?"

Emine emphasized that human ties and respect are precisely what Islam fosters and as a pious Muslima it was her duty to show the utmost respect for those she loved, regardless of religion. She added another note with regard to showing interest in other religions and learning about them. She related how she went to Strasbourg with friends: "[O]f course, we entered the Cathedral. It is an important monument and also the house of God, why not visit it then? One of the group was an Muslim theologian and he went along to see the Cathedral. It was a beautiful and interesting place." Emine summed up her deeply religious relationship with people: "People are people (*Mensch ist Mensch*), I help people because they are people." Religiosity for Emine is not an end in itself or a way to exclusively achieve her own way to paradise. Islam for Emine means guidance in her relationship with the world. It also implies to work on the improvement of her pious self which she does by way of listening to TV preachers, consulting works of theology, and discussions with her female friends and relatives.

In November 2008 Emine went on the *hajj* to Mecca. As her husband did not want to accompany her, she signed up with a women's group at the Salam Mosque community. On this pilgrimage she connected with women from that mosque and has since become involved in some of their activities. She is less interested in the Qur'an study group ("they mostly read/recite the Qur'an, which I already know how to do") than in the women's social activities (they prepare food for sale, do handicrafts and sewing for the mosque's annual *kermes*, do women's breakfasts at the mosque). For the 2011 *kermes*, Emine spent several weeks sewing aprons, tablecloths, duvet covers, and other items in the mosque and at home. Emine and three or four other women were the core workers for this vast sewing project.

Emine is not involved in formal neighborhood activities, but some of her neighbors appreciate her knowledge of German and bureaucratic procedures. When a neighbor died, his family came to Emine to help arrange the transport of the body to Turkey for burial. The family had children who had grown up in the neighborhood, but they were at a loss of what to do and sent for her. She willingly obliged.

One of Emine's noteworthy deeds is her immense support for her younger sister. Emine who never had a chance for post-secondary education, vied to support her sister in her academic efforts. Whenever necessary she watched her nephews to give her sister time for her studies. Emine's support and investment in her sister's career remain invisible to outsiders but are paramount for her sister's professional success. At present Emine similarly supports her daughter who is a successful university student in the competitive, male-dominated field of engineering. Another contribution is her outspoken independence with regard to religious matters. She did not hesitate to participate in the pilgrimage to Mecca without her husband. Several women remarked about her courage to do so. In 2011 Emine proudly related how other women now considered such a step. Several women had already signed up (unaccompanied) for the pilgrimage in 2011.[6] When Emine was hired for her position as an occupational attendant at a senior residence in 2013 her headscarf was not an issue, as she had already done a short internship at the institution and the supervisors had greatly appreciated her work and especially her loving dedication to the elderly. She continues to work there with great enthusiasm. When an elderly woman made disparaging remarks about her wearing a headscarf, Emine noted: "these people are old, they don't know any better. I treat them with love regardless, and then they learn." She keeps telling me stories about how she "turned around" individual residents and how they came to like and appreciate her (and her headscarf) very much.

Emine is one of thousands of (invisible) individuals who by their daily acts design new ways for themselves and subsequently for others. She never lectures in public or participates in panel discussions, yet her contributions to urban culture form the foundations for trends and transformations, often long before the latter take shape. She lives her religion in the minutiae of her daily life and hopes to foster understanding for Islam on the one hand, and create meaningful encounters and relationship with diverse people on the other. Long before her sister became a successful professional, Emine helped prepare this success, as much as she helped by way of her sewing to contribute small building blocks to the success of a respected public institution like the Salam Mosque. Emine now continues her engagement in her work with the elderly.

Politics, Academia, and Religious Dialogue

In his early seventies, Dr. Karim Al-Mudarris exudes an air of intellectuality, elegance, cultural refinement, human wisdom, and sincere piety. Despite the fact that he spent most of his life in Iraq, he speaks impeccable German and in fact has a slight Swabian accent. Starting from Ramadan 2006, I met Dr. Al-Mudarris at events of the local Christian-Muslim dialogue association, and in a Qur'an study group for "Muslim and non-Muslim men and women" at the Al-Nour Mosque that I occasionally attended. Whenever it was Dr. Al-Mudarris's turn to do Qur'an interpretations, or presentations on other subjects, I was thoroughly intrigued by his analytical depth and profound insights into religious and other topics. Once he made a presentation about theatrical/stage elements in the Qur'an. Part of his presentation was dedicated to the interpretation of the Qur'anic scene of the men sleeping in a cave for several hundred years and their dog guarding them in the liminal space of the cave's entry. In fine detail Dr. Al-Mudarris illustrated what the complexity of this liminal position meant, and how it could define the respected, but also restricted, position of dogs in Muslim thought. On another occasion he summarized a rather vague discussion about a verse, and he noted that this verse clearly limited any sort of human judgment over other humans, as this was left to Allah. Regardless of the context or topic, one could always be assured that Dr. Al-Mudarris's remarks were profound and indeed their wisdom sometimes emerged only after another day of reflecting about their meaning. Based on his age and depth of knowledge, I thought that Dr. Al-Mudarris would be a great source of information on many issues. When I called him to ask for an interview including questions about the history of the Al-Nour Mosque, he told me that he might not be the best person as he had spent most of his career as a professor in Iraq. But he agreed to be interviewed nevertheless.

We set up an appointment for a Friday afternoon in the Al-Nour Mosque. Meeting a man there is difficult because of the fairly strict gender segregation. Arriving at the mosque, I stepped into the entrance area of the men's prayer room and asked the first man whether he had seen Dr. Al-Mudarris. It turned out that there was a lecture for men and women in the prayer room, so I went in. After briefly chatting with a waiting woman, Dr. Al-Mudarris and I went upstairs to the liminal (see chapter 2) third floor suite. We settled into a classroom, off the large communal room, that is used for children's instruction. Some children were playing in the large room while their mothers attended the event downstairs. We left the door to the classroom open. Dr. Al-Mudarris, being a well-prepared and dutiful colleague brought a typed biographical sketch to the interview that included important points and dates of his personal life and academic career. The following life history is based on this sketch, a two-and-a-half-hour conversation and notes from other shared encounters with Dr. Al-Mudarris.

Dr. Al-Mudarris was born in the late 1930s into an old family of Muslim scholars in Mosul, Iraq. His grandfather was known for his theological work and Dr. Al-Mudarris even brought one of his grandfather's books to the interview. Dr. Al-Mudarris described the cultural landscape of his childhood in Mosul as multi-ethnic and multi-religious. His grandfather who enjoyed much respect in the city acted as an informal referee or mediator in business disputes that involved Muslims, Christians, and Jews. Because of the great respect that the elder Al-Mudarris enjoyed, people accepted his judgments. One day a wool merchant had ordered a large quantity of wool from Baghdad. After ordering the wool, he decided that he did not want it any longer as he was afraid he would not be able to sell it. The merchant insisted that he take the wool as ordered. The elder Al-Mudarris was called to mediate between the quarreling parties. He maintained that one had to take what one had ordered as the other merchant had worked to deliver the materials. The local merchant accepted this ruling. In the end this worked in his favor as he easily sold the wool and indeed had to order a second shipment. Furthermore, Dr. Karim Al-Mudarris remembered how he frequently went to the bazaar with his father and how they were greeted with great respect. He emphasized the smooth co-existence of different ethnic and religious groups in the city. On Friday evening they would often hold Qur'an recitation and study sessions on the roof of somebody's house. On these official and formal occasions the Christian bishops would also attend and listen. When the bishops walked into the meeting everybody would get up to show respect. The stories that Dr. Al-Mudarris tells do not only serve to convey lessons related to the respective situations, but illustrate a multi-religious (and indeed multi-ethnic) urban culture and universe that constitutes a crucial point of reference for his own actions and interactions.

Dr. Al-Mudarris's father broke with the family tradition of religious scholarships and studied medicine and became a physician in Mosul. Planning to follow in his father's footsteps, he started to study biology at Baghdad University in 1954. He eventually moved into geology/paleontology. Upon finishing his B.Sc. he was given a stipend for graduate studies in Germany, where he arrived in 1960. After learning German he studied geology and in 1965 finished his diploma at the University of Tübingen. Dr. Al-Mudarris described his student years as both rich and personally difficult. "I have always been religious," he noted, but once he arrived in Germany, he no longer prayed as he felt he could never achieve ritual purity. Germany of the 1960s was very different from the Iraq of his childhood, and he thoroughly missed the respectful and easy co-existence of a diverse populations. During a stay in hospital, where he remembered being thoroughly lonely, the hospital chaplain came to talk to his roommate. The roommate cursed the chaplain and made it very clear that he had no use for religion. Dr. Al-Mudarris was appalled by the disrespect for the clergyman. After taking the abuse, the chaplain turned to him, and upon seeing his black hair and foreign features, he just looked at him and said "oh, but you are a Mohammedan," turned around and left. Dr. Al-Mudarris remembered, "I had been raised to have respect for all religions. I would have loved to talk to him, because I was lonely, but the chaplain could not recognize this need."

As a student Dr. Al-Mudarris was active in the student movement and in particular the struggle of African and Asian students. He was one of the founding members of the Afro-Asian Student Union at the University of Göttingen (before coming to Tübingen). In our telephone conversation before the interview, when I had asked him about how well he was informed about early Muslim activities in Germany, he had said: "In the 1960s I was more involved in student and leftist politics than with mosques." To underline his political involvement, he later stressed that he had participated in his first political demonstration against the partition of Palestine when he was in sixth grade in Mosul. Dr. Al-Mudarris noted that in the 1960s the focus of Muslim students and migrants was not on religion. He felt that it was the rejection that these groups experienced in Germany which led them to reconsider their religion. He identified two events that made him realize his marginal and difficult position in Germany.

During his first Ramadan in Germany, a few Muslim students organized to speak to the administration of the students' cafeteria to supply them with sandwiches for *suhur* (late night/early morning meal before the fast starts), so that the students could take their pre-dawn meals before the daily fast. The director of the cafeteria took days to organize this simple request. In the process the students had to listen to remarks like "what difference will the sandwiches make, Muhammad [the Prophet] won't let you into paradise, one way or the other." The director first produced some unrealistic suggestions on how to solve the problem. In response Muslim students signed a petition to underline their point. A Christian student from Mosul who belonged to the Jacobite sect and was very pious and had been active in his Church back home also joined for reasons of solidarity. He signed his name also making a point that—like his Muslim friends—he as a Jacobite did not eat pork. The petition came back with a vengeance and the director called Al-Mudarris to his office. The director was furious: "This really goes too far. First you oppress the Christians in Iraq and then you keep persecuting and forcing them to your side in Germany." He could not be convinced that the Christian Iraqi had signed out of his own free will and deep-felt solidarity with his Muslim compatriots. The director proceeded to physically push Al-Mudarris out of his office and told the faculty that the latter oppressed Christians. He proceeded to write a letter to the Iraqi embassy that Al-Mudarris was a troublemaker. This letter eventually was passed to relevant offices in Baghdad. Shortly after, in 1963, when the Baathists came to power, Al-Mudarris lost his stipend, based on this letter, which increased his troubles in Germany.

The second significant encounter happened on an excursion that Dr. Al-Mudarris took part in as a student. Staying in youth hostels, he faced the recurrent "pork question" where he had to explain why he did not eat pork. Worse, he had to listen to all sorts of remarks on the topic. One day on such an excursion, they started to debate European culture and history. Al-Mudarris participated and amazed others with his profound knowledge on the subject. One professor noted in astonishment: "why do you know so much about European culture and history and at the same time do not eat pork?" In the professor's mind the two were mutually exclusive. For Al-Mudarris this, of course, was not a contradiction. Instead it made him realize how much he had learned in school in Iraq about these subjects. "It dawned on me," he remembered, "just how European our education had been in a country where education had been designed by colonial powers. Education was all about the achievements (*Errungenschaften*) of Europeans. There was exactly a third of a page in one of the history books dedicated to Arab history." It was ironic that he had to come to Germany to finally learn more about Arab history when he started to take classes (on the side) in these subjects.

After a few interruptions Dr. Al-Mudarris finished in PhD in 1974. In 1975 he married a German woman and soon after the couple moved to Iraq where Dr. Al-Mudarris started teaching at a university. The couple had three children. In the summer of 1990, Mrs. Al-Mudarris took the children on a vacation to Germany. During that time Iraqi forces occupied Kuwait. "I immediately knew," Dr. Al-Mudarris remembered, "that this would end in a longer conflict and war. Therefore I told my wife to stay with the children in Germany." In his biographical sketch, Dr. Al-Mudarris noted for August 2, 1990: "Beginning of the separation from my family." He saw his family once more in Germany in 1991. After that he did not see them again until 2000, since as a professional he was no longer allowed to leave Iraq. About the years between 1991 and 2000, he wrote: "[Y]ears of deprivations (*Entbehrungen*), fears, the constant search for food and medication, and all basic necessities of life in an atmosphere of the terror of war of the US air force and the institutions (*Organe*) of the regime. According to WHO information about 2 million Iraqis died until the end of 1998. Of those 60 percent were children under the age of 5 years." This entry stands out in the biographical sketch because here Iraq and his personal biography merge. The separation from his family is minimized by the immense collective suffering (and dying) of the Iraqi nation. During that time, the time of the international embargo, Dr. Al-Mudarris recounted, it became next to impossible to teach. Even the most fundamental things were impossible. "As a geologist" he explained, "I needed to take my students to the field, that is, to the desert to collect materials." It would take weeks to apply for an appropriate vehicle for an excursion, and later even that was impossible. Being alone and with teaching becoming increasingly difficult, he started to study theology on the side.

In early 2000 he finished his studies and received his "license" as an *'alim* (religious scholar). In 1999 he applied to take early retirement, which was eventually granted. "Now I receive €38/month in retirement benefits in Iraq." A few weeks after he had received his theological license, he was allowed to leave Iraq and join his family in Germany. He left behind "a house with everything in it." In Germany he saw his wife and children for the first time in nine years. "When I had last seen my youngest daughter she had just started school, now she was taller than me."

In Germany he tried to get a job but everybody told him he was overqualified for what they wanted, until he eventually gave up. He started to join cultural, political, and religious circuits, attended public lectures and events, and participated in discussions. One day he ran into Moustafa Salama, the president of the Al-Nour Mosque who had noticed him on other occasions. Mr. Salama encouraged him and said "why don't you join us and participate in our activities?" At first he was hesitant but Mr. Salama encouraged him. Dr. Al-Mudarris liked the idea of remaining in touch with the mosque. He became more involved and eventually put his name up for election in the statewide *Zentralrat der Muslime* and was elected into their board of directors. He was also elected in his suburban town into the *Ausländerausschuss* (foreigners'/migrant committee), a body associated with the municipality that is consulted in migrant affairs. He is part of two Christian-Muslim Dialogue Associations and lectures occasionally about Islam and Iraq in various political and religious contexts.

Dr. Al-Mudarris's engagements in 2008 illustrate the complex combination of politics and religion that runs through his life, which points back to his childhood in multi-ethnic and multi-religious Mosul. Interfaith dialogue back then was not a political necessity, but a lived reality. It went without saying that Muslims stood up for respect of a bishop, and a Christian honored the ruling of a respected Muslim scholar. Respect for religions and religious tolerance pervades Dr. Al-Mudarris's life and politics. Their non-existence (e.g. the encounter with the hospital chaplain) is inexplicable to him. Equally fundamental are his left-leaning politics rooted in long history of anti-colonial, Third World and anti-neo-colonial engagements. From his youthful political experience of the 1948 demonstrations in support of the Palestinian cause, his 1960s involvement with African and Asian student organizations, his recollections of the 1967 trauma of Arab defeat, to his passionate involvement with the fate of Iraq, Dr. Al-Mudarris takes a critical political stance. Throughout our two-and-a-half-hour conversation, we kept slipping back into contemporary Iraqi politics. Contemporary Iraqi suffering and injustice deeply concern Dr. Al-Mudarris.

For most of his life, piety was important and indeed an inherent part of his activities, but only more recently, first with his theological studies and his turn to the Al-Nour Mosque and local Muslim politics, Islam and Muslim politics became more central concerns for Dr. Al-Mudarris. This was also fostered by the relative separation between political and religious public debates and activist circuits in

Stuttgart. Dr. Al-Mudarris participates in political discussions by way of his work in the foreigners' committee and his lecturing and occasional interviews to do with Iraq, Iraqi politics, and Middle Eastern affairs. His religious engagement unfolds on the different stage of the Christian-Muslim dialogue, and his engagement in Muslim affairs and politics by way of the *Zentralrat der Muslime*. The fact that these engagements are largely separate has less to do with Dr. Al-Mudarris, than with the segregation of the two themes/spheres in the urban public.

Dr. Al-Mudarris's "religious" activities are nonetheless political as religious dialogue and Muslim representative bodies are important platforms of urban interaction. Moving on different stages, Dr. Al-Mudarris serves as a link between constituencies. With his science background, religious education, refined knowledge, delicate mannerism, impeccable and eloquent German, and his age, he is a unique and highly respected person in religious and political circles. He brings a cosmopolitan outlook and profound tolerance to events and activities. Dr. Al-Mudarris is a visible participant in the urban public sphere. He is recognized as such and often invited to contribute to events.

Piety, Identity, and Belonging

I met Amna Gomez in the Al-Nour Mosque where she occasionally participated in the women's Qur'an study group. She also participated in one of the older teenage girls' groups and was part of an informal group of older girls who spent a lot of time together and in the mosque. Our paths crossed frequently as we attended the same events, lectures, and celebrations. Amna was born in the late 1980s and when I first met her she was attempting to finish her *Fachhochschulreife* (a degree that allows entry to professional universities). I had heard that Amna had a Pakistani father and a Spanish mother. Her dedication to the mosque and her unique background made me curious. When I asked her for an interview she immediately agreed. She told me that a journalist had only recently interviewed her and some friends for a short article. In December 2007, after we had known each other casually for about a year, I interviewed Amna in my apartment.

Amna was born and raised in Stuttgart. Her father was from Pakistan and had two children from a previous marriage with a German woman. Her older half-siblings grew up in Pakistan and only in their late teens returned to Germany. Amna's mother is from Spain and also had two children from a previous marriage with a German man. Unlike her husband, she brought her two children into the new marriage. Two more children were born in this marriage: Amna and her brother. Amna remarked that when she was growing up her father was not very religious. He did not pray; the only "Muslim thing" was that he did not eat pork. So her mother stopped cooking pork. Religion in general and Islam in particular did not play much of a role in the family. The family only celebrated Christian holidays.

Amna vaguely identified as Catholic. Her first deeper encounter with Islam was when she went to Pakistan with her family at the age of ten. There she learned more about Islam, but upon her return to Stuttgart this was of little consequence. When Amna was in her early teens her parents separated. Amna remembered that after the separation, her mother once more bought pork. In 2005 her father died.

Amna described her childhood as "very average." She grew up in a multi-ethnic neighborhood and went to a Christian preschool. German is her first language and she speaks neither Spanish nor Urdu. She always knew that she had some relation to Islam, but it did not mean much to her until her first trip to Pakistan. In her teenage years she started to increasingly reflect about her identity. She remembered how she often took great pride in her unusual identity and experimented with ways to describe herself and to surprise others. But she also increasingly asked herself the question of where she really belonged. She consciously researched aspects of her identity. Her father brought her to a Pakistani teacher for Qur'an and Urdu lessons. The lessons were boring and she did not last long with the teacher. She started to seek the company of other Muslims. A Turkish friend then gave her a prayer rug. Slowly she found her entry to Islam through friends and her own reflections. One day, when Amna was sixteen years old, she said the *shahada* alone at home. She entered a path of conscious piety and self-improvement. She connected to the Al Nour Mosque where she found a spiritual and social home. Soon much of her life and social activities were centered on the mosque and her group of girlfriends there.

Amna and her (half-)siblings (including one of Spanish-German parentage) illustrate a broad specter of Muslim (non)-religiosity. One of her half-brothers, Tobias, from her mother's first marriage who was born a Christian became vaguely interested in Islam by way of living with his non-practicing Muslim stepfather and even more so through his Turkish friends. Upon Amna's conversion/reversion to Islam, Tobias soon also converted. For Tobias this has been a long process of transformation and Amna notes that he has a very "Turkish touch" to him. Even though he converted, he does not pray much, she states with regret. Her two half-siblings who grew up in Pakistan, in contrast, have little to do with religion. One of them she describes as "being Muslim, but has become weak and no longer practices the religion." The other sibling does not practice at all and even cut all ties to the family. Her younger brother only recently started to show some interest in Islam and also started to pray. Her mother remains a Catholic who now celebrates both Christmas and *Eid*.

Having said the *shahada*, Amna entered on a quest of learning, achieving piety, and improving her Islamic practices. She started to pray, and read more about Islam. Soon she realized that she wanted to wear a *hijab* but her mother was opposed to this step. Living in a neighborhood where people know each other well, Mrs. Gomez was afraid of the neighbors and their talk and what this could do to Amna and the family. But Amna kept fighting and debating her mother who had grown up in a Catholic boarding school. There, Amna remarked, her mother had had "too much church" and no longer wanted to be very involved with religion. After two years of debate, Mrs. Gomez realized that this was not a youthful phase of Amna's, but she begged Amna to finish her *Mittlere Reife* (tenth-grade exam; prerequisite for professional training) before putting on the *hijab*. Amna felt she could no longer wait. One month before she finished tenth grade, at the age of eighteen, Amna started to wear a headscarf. On her first day in school with the headscarf nothing amazing happened, only the few remarks like "oh, now we will never again see your beautiful hair." Meanwhile, she happily related, her mother fully supports her (*sie steht hinter mir*). Even though Mrs. Gomez does not agree with the idea of the headscarf, she is proud of Amna and her strength. Mother and daughter are very close and Mrs. Gomez occasionally ventures into Amna's world in the mosque. Once, Mrs. Gomez accompanied Amna to a lecture at the Al-Nour Mosque where she sat with long open hair next to Amna with her headscarf.

When Amna reflected about the last few years of her life and her transformations, she was very happy and content with where she was today. She looked back to the often-tumultuous times of being a teenager, where one went through odd phases and was under constant pressure to be "cool." And still one did not understand what life was all about. "Now" she added, "I know why I live. I see many advantages for my life in Islam. Islam might not be the most beautiful religion, but it is the true religion." Being a pious Muslima gave Amna a framework for her life and a sense of belonging, especially after her father died. Her new visible piety unfolded smoothly and she never faced much rejection from non-Muslims, other than the occasional odd remarks.

Her parents, Amna explained, were "*Gastarbeiter*," meaning they were "foreign," and not very educated. They stood and were made to stand apart from mainstream German society of the 1970s and 1980s. Unlike her parents' generation, Amna explained that her generation needed to "completely integrate," and indeed they had become "normal Germans" (*normale Deutsche*) who were visible and did not want to hide. Amna saw her place in the middle of society, nothing set her apart and she would not let herself be put aside. Amna stressed it was an essential task for her generation of Muslims to educate society about their presence and lifestyles. Amna remarked on the frequent assumptions about her identity she triggered in people. As a woman with a headscarf, she is often thought of as foreign and uneducated. Once, when she and some of her pious girlfriends studied in a public library, a woman came up to them without knowing anything about them, and asked: "oh, are you learning/studying German?" Being perceived as foreign, Amna is frequently asked about her origins and nationality. When in the mood, she sometimes answers "I am Spanish" to puzzle people, but also to involve them in a debate about Islam, her piety, and participation in society.

In her first years as a pious Muslima, Amna spent much time with her friends from the girls' group and some younger married women in the mosque. At one point she helped run a group for younger girls and helped out in a homework tutoring program. She was active in the Stuttgart chapter of the Muslim Youth of Germany, which organizes various activities and also serves as a link to other local groups both in the region and nationally. In that context Amna was actively involved in organizing a larger regional meeting of youth groups from all over southern Germany in late 2007.

Elements of personal piety and improvement play a central role in Amna's life as she strives to become a better Muslima and to practice Islam correctly. But there is also the secondary quest for identity and belonging. Like Emine, she found herself pushed to the social margins as an immigrant child in a society that continues to draw harsh lines of exclusion. Unlike Emine, Amna could not fall back on an ethnic community as she spoke none of her parents' languages, and the respective communities, especially the Pakistani one, are rather small. Amna made it clear that she had no intention to hide, but wanted nothing short of being a respected member and participant in society. Her turn to pious Islam provided just that for her: self-confidence, a community, meaningful activities, and equal participation in a German-speaking context in the city. The Al-Nour Mosque became Amna's social and spiritual home, a home from which she proudly ventures into society. While dominant society would not describe places like the Al-Nour Mosque as its own institutions, it is without doubt part of this society, not least of all because of the increasingly dominant use of German in programs and among the pious, and the mosque's and its members' constant engagement with society. In the mosque, Amna and other regulars debate, articulate, and test aspects of their religiosity which they subsequently carry into their daily activities elsewhere.

For Amna, her conversion/reversion to Islam had far-reaching consequences. First and foremost it was a fundamentally important spiritual turn for her. But it also had comprehensive implications in her mundane social existence. By way of becoming a pious Muslima and socially positioning herself as such, she transcended the—in her case difficult—question of social and ethnic belonging. Whether she is Spanish, Pakistani, or German is no longer her most pressing concern. Instead she situated herself as a member of the local (and global) community of believers. She is German by way of citizenship, a Stuttgarter by way of her life history, and piously Muslim by choice. Her circle of friends understands her as many share similar biographies. One of her friends comes from a Lebanese-German family and is familiar with aspects of living in different cultural contexts and maneuvering complex families and identities. As a group these young women transcended nagging questions of "where do I belong?" or "who am I?" and self-consciously created lifestyles suitable for young pious Muslim Germans (see also Bayoumi 2010: 166). As a sheltered space, the mosque serves as an experimental and training stage for pious practices. While the mosque is centrally important for Amna and her friends, all of them have lives and social contexts apart from the mosque.

By the end of 2008 Amna married Tamer, a young man who had come from North Africa to study at the University of Stuttgart. The couple had been introduced at the Al-Nour Mosque. The mosque and the couple's peers served as mediators in this marriage arrangement. Amna and Tamer did not date before they married. Amna quit her schooling and started a professional training as a physician's assistant. The couple moved to a suburban town, but still attends the Al-Nour Mosque and remains part of its social circles. Amna is not a public figure, she neither lectures nor travels public circuits, but her everyday life, acts, and interactions produce noteworthy imprints which combined with those of others initiate and strengthen social trends and transformations. At a young age, Amna chose a religious lifestyle. This choice allowed her to create an appropriate identity, become part of a lively and supportive community and group of friends, and eventually find a suitable spouse. From a "searching" teenager, Amna evolved into a self-conscious young woman. By spring of 2011, Amna planned, upon completion of her physician's assistant training, to return to school to finish her *Fachhochschulreife* and later to study at the university. Amna's decisions and life, as one of the pioneers of a local pious lifestyle, are examples for others of her generation to consider and possibly follow. Three aspects are central here: (1) her decision not to date, and to have the mosque serve as a quasi-family in the quest to locate a suitable spouse. (2) Her continued pursuit of her education and independent lifestyle. (3) Her disregard for ethnicity (see also Bayoumi 2010: 160; Mazawi 2010: 186; Bowen 2010: 69). Amna and other younger individuals are paramount in the construction of local pious identities and lifestyles. These young adults are self-consciously local and piously Muslim. In their daily lives they negotiate and design local pious lifeworlds.

Spirituality and Intellectuality

I met Sibel Enver (see above) at the women's Qur'an studies group at the Al-Nour Mosque, which she irregularly attended. Sibel was part of a circle of younger largely professional women and students who met privately and attended events together. We watched movies together (usually to do with Islam, shown at alternative theaters), and at one point we were both on the apartment "search team" of a mutual friend. Sibel is very knowledgeable about the Stuttgart Muslim public sphere, and in addition to the Al-Nour Mosque group, she on and off attended other similar groups in mosques and elsewhere. She is active in the Stuttgart Muslim public sphere and occasionally lectures at events.

Sibel is the youngest of eight siblings. Her oldest five siblings were born in Turkey, the others in Germany. Her father has been in Germany for more than forty years, her mother just slightly less. Sibel was born in the late 1970s and grew up in a town outside Stuttgart. "Like most migrant children, I only went to the

Hauptschule. I was not the least challenged there," she remembered. "It is just that the teachers did not know what to do with foreign children and did not care too much either." Regardless, education was always central in her family and all of Sibel's siblings today are successful professionals. One of her older siblings, Sibel noted, "today is a dentist, something that was very hard for somebody who came here, without knowing German and went right to first or second grade." Among her siblings are a nurse, an architect, an industrial mechanic, and a business administrator. Sibel is an accountant. In 2008 she worked part-time and was enrolled in an MBA program. Sibel's father encouraged his children to take advantage of the opportunities they had and to work hard to achieve their goals. No matter where in the world you are, or end up, he insisted, education would always be good and open doors. Sibel mentioned that her father always was her role model. To illustrate his love for education, Sibel related that her father, now retired, is currently enrolled in a distance-learning program in economics at a Turkish university.

Sibel described herself as a pious Muslima by conscious choice. Her family had always been religious and prayed together, led by her father who taught her the basics of Islam. At the age of about thirteen or fourteen, Sibel went through a phase of doubt and wondered whether all these teachings were true. "Was there really a Prophet?" "Did God really exist?" were among the questions she contemplated. She intensively engaged with Islam and questions of faith, and eventually came to the realization (*Erkenntnis*) that "for me, this was the truth." She added, "[I]f one were to only live for oneself, for one's own set of goals, would that really be a goal? Would that really make sense?" Sibel resolved for herself, that it would not and that there was a larger truth with a higher goal to be found in religion, or more specifically in Islam. Her deliberate turn to Islam was certainly influenced by her religious upbringing, but ultimately it was her decision that she had reached through reflection and studying. Her decision was the beginning of an ongoing pious journey. To fully translate this belief into a lived reality took and continues to take time, immersion, and thought. When Sibel was nineteen years old, she started to pray regularly, four years later she started to wear a headscarf. Throughout she learned more about Islam, read the Qur'an, and improved her pious practices, like praying. When she first started to learn more about Islam, she sometimes read the religion pages in Turkish dailies, which helped both for her religious studies and to maintain her written Turkish. Today, she noted, these newspapers had become more secular and their religion pages contained less information.

With time Sibel accumulated a considerable theological knowledge and became involved in German language debates about Islam. She attended courses of the *Islamologische Institut* (see chapter 2). She remarked that these courses were the German language Islamic platform that operated on the most sophisticated academic level. Sibel was particularly impressed with the work of Amir Zaidan and Abdelrahman Reidegeld at the institute. Complex issues are debated at these seminars with the use of, what Sibel noted are correctly translated German concepts. Such concepts were important, Sibel explained, to accommodate German Muslim theologians and debates. Nevertheless, Sibel, added, it was best to leave some of the central terms like *wuduu* (ritual washing, ablutions) or *hadith* in Arabic to keep debates as precise as possible. Sharing these central terms connects believers and discussants across boundaries and ethnicities. The Islamology course was vital for Sibel, since it had endowed her with a scholarly approach to Islam and structured her theological knowledge. Once basic insights, concepts, and categories are in place, she explained, it was easy to add more information, and to profoundly analyze further questions. Sibel insisted that if people knew the basics of Islam in a systematic way, they would not easily fall prey to extremist thoughts. "Extremist thinking," she stated, "can only fall on fertile grounds where there is a certain ignorance." If in such a situation, "somebody with a certain aura or charisma comes along and tells passionate stories, then individuals might just be swept along (*schmeisst andere um*). If a person has enough fundamental information and understanding, they can critically challenge such rhetoric and not fall for it." A person will not follow what is not right, if they have sufficient knowledge, she concluded. With regard to politics and interests, Sibel remarked that the *Islamologische Institut* operated completely independently. They were not part of a mosque association or other Muslim associations. The institute financed itself by way its courses.[7] Sibel valued this independence from the politics of mosque associations. Sibel's thirst for knowledge about Islam guides her search for more sources of information. "Sometimes I just google particular terms which then also allows me to compare, for example, Turkish and other sources." She mentioned the writing of Gai Eaton who as a western Muslim particularly inspired her.[8] With more profound questions, she might send an e-mail to Abdelrahman Reidegeld, Amir Zaidan, or other individuals whom she respects and trusts.

Sibel is in touch and irregularly attend several Qur'an discussion groups. She prefers the diversity of the Al-Nour Mosque over some of the Turkish mosques ("many people would know my father"). She occasionally attends a Qur'an study group for female students or visits the German Qur'an study circle that meets in a public community center (*Bürgerhaus*). In early 2008 she was also involved in a newer independent discussion circle that had recently moved from a university location to a Moroccan mosque. Because of her involvement with several groups and contexts, Sibel is linked to a variety of public activities and debates. On occasion she is invited to speak about religious issues both in Muslim and non-Muslim contexts (see above).

Sibel situates herself as a pious Muslima first, and a German citizen of Turkish descent second. She is among a group of younger educated pious individuals who use several venues in the city to conduct their sophisticated debates about Muslim theology and lifestyles. Some of the venues are all female; others include men and women. Ethnicity plays no role in these circles, indeed their central marker is the exclusive use of the German language and the purposeful debate of local pious lifestyles and lifeworlds. Sibel and others in her circle, as students and professionals, are firmly rooted in mainstream society. Movie theaters and coffee shops are as much part of their lives as pious lectures or mosques are. Indeed, Sibel and her friends are wary of aspects of mosque associations and leadership that often reflect the lifeworlds and migrational experiences of an older (male) generation that they do not share. Mosques for them have lost the function as a sheltered social home where they can be among each other. Mosques have become places of debate from which they draw knowledge and inspiration for their public lives and engagements (Levitt 2008). Society is their home and their field of engagement and activities.

Sibel does not closely associate with any particular mosque. Over the years she picked groups and engagements that best fit her beliefs, social preferences, and intellectual interests. She and her loosely circumscribed group of younger intellectually minded friends frequent different groups, attend and organize particular events (e.g. the annual Islam Week at the local university), and meet in private spaces. She often traveled back to her suburban home alone late at night on public transportation ("not a problem, in the late trains you always ride in the first car close to the driver, then you are safe"). Like Dr. Al-Mudarris, she travels public circuits, but she speaks at smaller and less exposed events. Like Emine, Sibel picks her engagements carefully, and occasionally changes activities. She draws inspiration from different contexts at different times. Her trajectory reflects that of an educated largely thirty-something multi-ethnic constituency that intensely engages with Islam, leads consciously pious lives, but are not actively engaged in any specific mosque. In fact some of Sibel's peers see mosques as too tied up in (narrow) ethnic and political agendas. Their quest is for an Islam untainted by such politics and by the burden of traditional cultures and social patriarchal features. Sibel (and her peers) represent a new generation that smoothly combines religiosity and professional success (Göle 2004: 31; Tietze 2001). "Mosque-hoppers" like Sibel and her peers create ties between different mosques and ethnicities in the city, and by way of her involvement with the *Islamologische Institut* also across Germany, Austria, and Switzerland. In 2009 Sibel married a man of Turkish descent who lived a few towns over from where she grew up. Like Amna, Sibel did not date before marrying but being less involved in mosque communities, she chose the Internet as a suitable venue to find a spouse.

Family and Faith

I distinctly remember when I first heard Regina's voice. It was my first visit to the Al-Nour Mosque on the occasion of an *iftar* organized by the Christian-Muslim Dialogue Association in Ramadan of 2006. As I was talking to somebody, I heard a clear and loud voice behind me say in heavy Swabian dialect: "des hemmer dann älles selber ombaut," (we renovated all of this by ourselves). Struck by the mix of the pronoun "we" and the intensely Swabian accent, I turned around to find the speaker to be a woman in her forties wearing a long greenish *gallabeya* and a beige *hijab*. While I had met many converts before, to hear one speak in heavy Swabian dialect was new. Regina turned out to be one of the core members of the women's Qur'an study group at the Al-Nour Mosque. A year later, after many encounters and Swabian chats and conversations, I interviewed Regina in her dining room in a multi-ethnic working-class quarter of Stuttgart.

Regina was born in the early 1960s to family of Catholic migrants from the southern part of Baden-Württemberg. Her parents had come to Stuttgart in the 1950s in search of better jobs. Regina was raised in a Catholic environment where she participated in her first communion at the age of seven. "This," she remembered, "was much too young for such a religious event." She maintained a vague interest in religion, but struggled with some issues. "I kept thinking about some of the contradictions in the Catholic Church, like for example, that marriage is holy, but then the priest himself was not married." Some years later when she was supposed to be confirmed, Regina refused to go. She remembered that "the priest used to pull our hair or even knock our heads (*Kopfnuss*). I hated the man." Regina was never confirmed which produced trouble with the priest and embarrassment for her mother.

In the early 1980s she met Shukri, a Palestinian who had come to Germany to study. A year later they were married. Initially Shukri was not very religious. He prayed and fasted, but not regularly. To learn more about Islam, Regina joined a discussion groups that was the predecessor of the Muslim and non-Muslim discussion circle that still meets at the Al-Nour Mosque. In the 1980s, the group consisted of about twenty people, mostly younger to middle-aged couples (some of whom still constitute the core of this group today). Regina was impressed by the group (*die haben mir einfach imponiert*). Women and men sat together and had lively conversations. She learned a lot about Islam in the group and from its individual members. These encounters brought her closer to Islam. In 1988 she formally converted, started to pray and fast, and learn ever more about Islam, its beliefs, rules, and practices. Her conversion was not visible to the public. She kept her religiosity within her family. She did not wear a headscarf and continued wearing short sleeves in the summer. Regina eventually had four children whom she tries to raise as pious Muslims. Regina lives with her husband and children in the neighborhood where she has lived all her life and where her parents still reside. This made it difficult for her to make her conversion and growing piety visible, as her parents, neighbors, friends, and people whom she had known for all her life had to be confronted with these changes and their reactions had to be dealt with. Regina continued a life where she was her "old" self in public and her pious self in the limited contexts of her home, the discussion circle, her friends, and increasingly also the Al-Nour Mosque.

More than fifteen years after her conversion she became very ill. Regina in her humorous ways recounted, "I spent two weeks half-dead." During this illness she had plenty of time to think about her life. Again and again the question "why do you not cover your head?" came to her, until she finally said to herself: "That is it. I will cover my head from now on." Upon her recovery, she started to cover her hair. When she is out in her quarter she wears a hat or cap, depending on the season. "This way my hair is covered and people are confused as to whether this is a sort of fashion or some funny thing of mine. Like that I can avoid questions and strange stares." Those who knew her slowly got the point, yet there was never this very first moment where she would stand in a clearly identifiable *hijab* in front of those who had known her all her life. This quiet easing into her new identity nonetheless yielded long term results. "Many of the people I have known for all my life now only say 'hello' to me." There never were any direct comments, but they no longer really engage much with her. Some neighbors started to ignore her altogether. These changes did not escape her parents who were completely opposed to her decision. But there were also positive reactions. She remembered an Ethiopian mother whom she had met by way of her children's school. This woman reacted very positively when she heard that Regina was a Muslim. "For her this was not a problem, as in Ethiopia Christians and Muslim live peacefully with each other."

Over the years her piety has become the core of Regina's busy life. Raising four children, she also works full-time in the business that she and her husband started. In the complex lifescape of her family (nuclear and her parents), work, evolving piety, neighborhood culture, mosque involvement, traditional Palestinian culture, and moments of patriarchy, Regina fights multiple battles. Many compromises have been negotiated in the process. For example, on Christmas, she noted, the family gets together to eat and afterwards her children go to their grandparents to receive their gifts. "That way nobody gets insulted," she added. Then, there are such highly symbolic struggles about, for instance, overnight school trips or school camps (*Schullandheim*), which many Muslim parents do not allow, in particular, their daughters to attend. Several legal cases have been fought over this issue. Regina struggled with her husband and all her children attended these excursions. "This is part of school and I think it is important for them to go. If I raised them well, they will not go wild there, I would hope." The struggle over the headscarf is ironic in her family and says more about patriarchy than religion: "When I go to the mosque and wear a *hijab* on my way out, I have to be careful not to run into my father, as he gets angry when he sees that. In turn when my daughters [who do not wear the *hijab*] go out and wear tight clothes, they need to watch out not to be seen by my husband who does not like that. Men, I tell you. . . ." Over the years Regina managed to create many compromises that work, but sometimes they cost a lot of energy, and she remains caught between her parents, husband, and children trying to mediate and accommodate opposing ideas, practices, and lifestyles.

Over the course of two decades, Regina transitioned to a pious individual. She has no story of a dramatic conversion. Instead she eased her way into a religiosity that she feels very much at home in. As a down-to-earth and humorous Swabian, and deeply locally rooted person, it would not seem fitting for Regina to introduce social drama and shocking changes into her life. She is the member of a local family (with a background of regional migration) and community and spent years creating meaningful and workable compromises between her religiosity and the demands of being a local citizen, religious individual, part of a family, neighbor, and a mother. Regina's acts remain largely invisible. Regina never moved back and forth between countries and cultures. She has spent all life in the same quarter, in fact most of it in the same building. Her challenge and contribution is to show to those around her, that while her religion, spirituality, and her appearance might have changed, she is in many ways still the same person. Her humor and pronounced Swabian dialect bear witness to this. As such she illustrated that Islam is not only a German, but a thoroughly Swabian religion. She illustrated her ease of combining the various elements of her life at the Al-Nour Mosque's *Eid* (religious holiday) celebration in early January 2007. For the occasion she brought along home-baked local (Christmas) cookies. When she sat down with the other women at a long table in the school gym rented for the occasion, she placed her cookie containers in the middle of the table and repeated several times in the best local way "ässet no dia Käkks, ässet no!" (please eat these cookies; in heavy dialect). One of Regina's central contributions—in addition to swabianizing Islam—is her work of raising four children who will further negotiate local Muslim lifeworlds. Moreover, Regina's extremely careful and sensitive insertion of her transforming pious selves in her neighborhood probably served not only as a valuable lesson for some of her neighbors, but most likely also engendered numerous discussions among them about Islam in her life and the city at large.

Modesty and Love

The picture that sticks in my mind about Hassan Islamoğlu is him and the boys of the homework tutoring program at the Kulturhaus (social and cultural center in Nordbahnhof) playing soccer—regardless of the weather—on the *Bolzplatz* (activity field) next to the center. I was always impressed by his patience and energy to physically engage the many young, energetic, if not to say wild, boys in the program. Other than playing soccer, Hassan worked in the tutoring program and did various other jobs in the center. On occasions that involved guests or food, he ran the kitchen, prepared snacks, and supervised food-related activities. For months I had assumed that Hassan was a regular staff member, until one of the social workers told me that Hassan was unemployed and worked at the center as part of a publicly funded job-creation program (*1 Euro Job*), whereby unemployed individuals were hired with a pay of 1 Euro/hour (later 1.50 Euro) in the hope that employers would eventually create a real job for the person. Considering that Hassan worked for such a small amount of money, I was even more amazed at his sincere and serious involvement with the children and the institution. Hassan and I arranged an interview in the late afternoon, after the students from the tutoring program had left, in a classroom in the Kulturhaus. After I sat down, Hassan excused himself to perform his prayer. While not surprising in itself, it was unexpected as a multicultural crowd of secular, left-leaning social workers populated the center. Yet the center has a Muslim prayer facility that was administered by an Alevi group.

Hassan was born in Turkey in the 1970s. He grew up, studied, and worked as a primary school teacher in Turkey. In the mid-1990s he became engaged to a woman who was born and raised in Germany. Some time into their (long-distance) engagement his fiancée was diagnosed with cancer. While there would have been a possibility for Hassan to break the engagement, he never considered doing so. "If this was God's will, then it had to be that way," he remarked. In 2000, the couple married and Hassan moved, contrary to the original plan, to Germany. "The medical care and possibilities for treatment where just so much better for my wife here," he explained. "But ultimately I want to go back to Turkey." Two years after his arrival in Germany, the couple's only child was born. Hassan's teaching degree was not recognized in Germany, so he could not work in his field. He quickly learned German, but still could not find work. He said he would like to work anything in the larger field of education or social work. He asked the Job Center for any possibility of a 1 Euro Job, so long as it was in his field, including all sorts or social services. Eventually, through various twists, turns, and connections he received the offer of his current job program. First he worked at the cultural center for five months and eventually the job was continued several times, so by the end of 2007 he had worked there a total of twenty-two months at minimal pay.

Hassan loved his job and took it extremely serious. He came to the center in the late morning to help with the students' lunch program. In the afternoon he tutored the homework of primary school students. When the homework was done, he played soccer, basketball, catch, or whatever the children, that is, mostly the boys, wanted to do. On some days he did artwork with some children, or occasionally just sat outside with them and talked. He also served as a mediator and translator with some of the parents when they came to the center. On such occasions he would listen to all sorts of other issues that parents wanted to talk about or sought advice or help them fill out bureaucratic forms.

When I told Hassan that I admired his energy and patience seeing him run with hordes of little boys, he just said "Somebody has to be outside with them. This is very important for the boys. Soccer is important for them and it is good for them." Few of the other tutors (most of whom were younger women) ventured outside much, let alone played soccer. Hassan added: "When I see the boys outside, I just have to go outside." He remarked on the scarcity of males in the program. "It is so important to engage these boys, pay attention to them. You never know, many of the parents might not do much with them." For the most part Hassan really liked to be outside with the boys, it was simply fun, but then there were days when it was tiring, but Hassan made it very clear it was not just a job, but more of a moral duty that one cannot just put aside. Much of Hassan's engagement and activities are rooted in a deep felt religiosity, where, for example, to play soccer is not a mundane task, but part of Hassan's role in God's world.

Hassan grew up in a religious family. His father, in addition, to having a professional career was a *hoca* (imam, preacher) in his free time. Religion was always present in the family and Hassan learned the basics about Islam at home. While he had prayed as a child he prayed less during his teenage years. Like Sibel, Hassan developed an interest in Islam in his teenage years. His brothers, in contrast, showed little interest in religion as they grew older. Hassan started to read religious books and took a conscious decision to lead a pious life. Now he tried to do all his prayers and indeed also those he missed in the years when he only half-heartedly practiced. Hassan has a calendar where he records his prayers, and makes sure he makes up for the prayers he currently and in the past missed. "It is never too late to start praying. Better to start late than never. Allah is merciful with people," he noted. Islam, Hassan emphasized, was not only worship but encompassed every little aspect of life. His religiosity transcends personal piety and centrally involves social involvement and helping wherever it was needed. "Islam," he explained, "does not mean to live for oneself, or one's money, but to live for and with people." He elaborated: "Allah asks for your deeds, even the tiny or unimportant ones. When, for example, the light is on in one of the classrooms after the children leave or in any room that is not used, it is my duty to turn it off. This saves money, but more importantly also energy."

Energy much like anything else was Allah's resource and gift and therefore it was a duty to treat it with respect and not to waste it. Hassan added: "when I do *wuduu* for prayer, this can be done with two liters of water, there is no need to let the water run for a long time." Hassan saw his personal calling in his work with and for children. Hence his passionate soccer playing, while part of his vague job description, was much more the result of his recognition that this was a fundamentally important activity for the boys to manage their energy, to have fun, and also for him to bond with the boys to be able to gain their trust and talk to them about their lives and problems. Hassan explained that the foundations for his social involvement and his careful use of resources were all prescribed in the Qur'an and explained by the Prophet. One can learn how to be a good person and how to positively contribute to society from the Qur'an, and the Prophet will always be the model from which to learn details and practices.

I asked Hassan what it meant to be a pious Muslim in Germany. He responded it was both difficult and beautiful. It was difficult because many people had images of Muslims that were all about terrorists, images that had worsened after 9/11.

These images and the resulting mistrust and resentment in turn caused Muslims to be discontent. "People look at Muslims as dangerous, but none of this violence is written anywhere in the Qur'an." Hassan pointed to the role of the media in creating and maintaining such simplistic and negative images of Islam and Muslims. And in the end, both the media and the people remain ignorant of Islam and the Qur'an. In this unfortunate situation of misunderstandings, suspicion, and lack of trust, Hassan sees his task. "It is important for me to show, what is important for me, and to create positive sentiments. The task is to be useful/helpful to people and German society." The beautiful parts about being a pious Muslim in Germany for Hassan were the many and diverse mosques, where one can pray wherever and with whomever one chose. One could study the Qur'an in different mosques and contexts and was completely free in one's choices. One was free here to practice Islam the way one wanted to. This, he added, was not just the case in Germany, but he had noticed such freedom and diversity of mosques in Austria and the Netherlands where he had gone to visit relatives. "Nobody really ever asks one here, why one prays, and one can pray in many different places, for example, in a park." Hassan noted that he would only pray where it was appropriate and not too close to other people, "I always have a compass and a clean plastic bag with me, that way I can pray wherever I am."

Like many Muslim Stuttgarters, Hassan loves to go to the Salam Mosque to pray, shop, and socialize. "It is wonderful to pray there for the holidays, like *bayram* (holiday), one meets so many people there on such occasions." Also, he noted one could buy Turkish foods and household items, and one always ran into friends or acquaintances at this large complex. "But I do not only pray in that mosque, I might go anywhere, like to the nearby Takva Mosque."

Hassan's activities are framed by religiosity, which knows no boundaries of religion or ethnicity. He considers smallest steps and practices from the perspective of a pious Muslim. The waste of energy, resources, and most importantly a young life were challenges that he felt obliged to confront. Whether those he engages with are Muslims or not is no concern of his. They are God's beings and it is God's world, and the good needs to be done by believers. By early 2009 Hassan was lucky to get a "real" job in a similar institution in another part of the city. While not full-time it was a good start that hopefully one day converts into a full-time job. For Hassan religiosity implies a sense of being deeply rooted in this world and working hard on the tasks put in front of the believer. Whether he deals with Muslims or non-Muslims, or acts in a Muslim or non-Muslim context is irrelevant for him. Mosques do not play a central role in his religiosity. While he does go to various mosques to pray, he is not a member of any and attends no regular mosque groups or activities. Hassan neither lectures, preaches, nor travels public circuits, but leaves an imprint in his environment as a dedicated piously inspired social worker and social actor. His contributions help to localize Islam but most crucially aim to make the small spaces he travel better places for those he encounters.

134 | Faithfully Urban

Pious Participants

Emine, Dr. Al-Mudarris, Amna, Sibel, Regina, and Hassan differ in age, gender, ethnicity, work, education, family contexts, pious trajectories, and political agendas. Dr. Al-Mudarris stresses political activism and religious dialogue. He is an academic, lectures on Iraqi political concerns, contributes to religious debates and interfaith dialogue, participates in religious bodies like the Central Council of Muslims and secular platforms like the foreigners'/migrants' council of his town. Sibel combines spirituality, intellectuality, and civic engagement in a public sphere where she busily shuttles between work, study, Muslim debate groups, and Muslim, non-Muslims, or interfaith public events. In two decades of learning and struggle, Regina created a position for herself that is not perfect, but allows for a smooth everyday existence. She combines the teachings of Islam with the needs to be a dutiful daughter to her parents, a wife in her marriage, a mother, and a neighbor and citizen in her neighborhood. Hassan positioned himself in social work where he sees his calling not just in doing a job but as a religious duty. In the almost two years of the work at the Kulturhaus, people came to appreciate him, and he became a link for some parents to other contexts and institutions. Membership or regular participation in a mosque community is not important for Hassan ("I pray in very different mosques, depending on the time and where I am in the city"), as piety is deeply personal for him and lived in the worldly context of wherever he finds his task. Similarly, Emine sees her everyday life as a field where she contributes and fosters change as a pious Muslima without drawing much attention to herself and her deeds. She is involved with individuals in the neighborhood, or gives Qur'an lessons to her nieces. At one point she became more active in a local Muslim women's swimming club that she had been part of for some time. She sporadically attends activities of a women's group at the Salam Mosque, and helps her sister and other friends with their children. More recently she has dedicated much of her time, energy, and heart to her work at senior citizens' residence. Not too interested in the everyday activities of mosques, Emine lives and discusses her piety in the context of family, friends, and neighborhood. Amna, partly based on her young age and unique ethnic background, is engaged with issues of identity and belonging and how to best situate herself as a pious Muslima in society. Especially before she got married, she predominantly interacted with her friends in the mosque and regional Muslim youth association. Her marriage strengthened her ties to the mosque and its social universe. With this marriage she further configured local pious lifestyles and practices. Regina by way of her children, business, and mosque involvement is deeply embedded in local society. Many controversies to do with Islam directly reverberate in her life (e.g. the *hijab*). With plenty of patience and humor, she maneuvers them one at a time, like the school camps or family Christmas issues. Once she related the story how their business was searched in the security hype that swept the city in the months and years after 9/11, with a curious mix of annoyance and humor. "They said they came to look for illegal immigrant workers, but that was hard to believe. They searched every part of the business and even brought in dogs." In addition their business has been subject to several tax investigations always without any results. Regina just added: "Do you really think they take that much time for every single business in the city?"

With regard to their relationship to mosques, the six individuals differ considerably. Hassan was not involved with any mosque, but attended prayers at different mosques at his convenience. Dr. Al-Mudarris, Amna, Sibel and Regina had ties to the Al-Nour Mosque, but their relationships to the mosque varied. Regina, by way of her husband who was very active in the mosque, was most centrally and for the longest period of time involved in the mosque. More recently, since her children were getting older (they had attended Islamic instruction at the mosque), she was busy with the family business, and suffered from health problems, she had withdrawn from some activities. For Amna, as a young person searching for an identity, pious trajectory, and community, the mosque played the most important role among the six individuals. Before she married, Amna spent long hours in the mosque with her friends, especially on weekends. Sometimes members of the girls' group even slept there. Her mosque friends were her best friends. It was not surprising that she eventually married a young man from the mosque and that members of the mosque had been instrumental in the making of this marriage. Dr. Al-Mudarris's tie to the mosque—other than praying there—was the discussion group for Muslims and non-Muslims, which organizationally was not part of the mosque and only used the mosque's premises. Most of his involvements (regional Muslim affairs, Christian-Muslim dialogue, and local migrant politics) were centered on other localities. For Sibel, the Al-Nour Mosque was one stop among many others. Even though she once noted that she really enjoyed the Al-Nour Mosque because it was the most multicultural one in the city, this did not mean that she was in any way tied to this institution. In search of sophisticated debates and knowledge, and spaces for involvement and activism, Sibel had by 2009 shifted toward other groups and activities.

Analyzing the stories of these individuals, it is apparent the Muslim Stuttgart is a complex and multilayered field. Sibel illustrates possibilities of choosing from debates, activities, locations, and circles of friends to best suit one's own religiosity, and contributing to the urban Muslim and larger public spheres. She represents individuals who over the years shared in this trajectory or met as they were traveling similar paths. Despite diverse activities and sites of engagements, the local Muslim landscape is neither segregated nor fragmented. For example, the larger public context where Dr. Al-Mudarris and Sibel act includes a core group of active individuals who vaguely know each other. These circuits also involve locally more well-known Muslim and non-Muslim individuals like presidents of mosque associations or Christian-Muslim dialogue associations, and public officials. Emine represents women who are part of private debates about what it means to be a

Muslima or raise Muslim children. While membership and regular prayer in a mosque are not crucial for Emine, the larger Stuttgart mosque-scape is important for her. As a fan of *kermes* events, occasional shopper at mosque stores, and more recently through her pilgrimage, Emine is connected to the local and indeed regional mosque-scape, as she attends *kermes* events in regional towns like Ludwigsburg.

While an ethnic segregation remains in particular among the older generation, more recent arrivals (e.g. the Afghan community), and those who do not speak German, there is a convergence of ethnicities among younger individuals. I was not surprised when Emine's daughter told me that she had run into Amna at a henna party for a mutual friend. Muslim circuits intersect in diverse spaces. Groups transcend ethnic lines, and lines of religiosities. When the Muslim women's swimming club opened an exercise class and they were looking for participants, Emine gave me flyers to invite women at the Al-Nour Mosque.

Examining Amna's and Sibel's marriages it becomes apparent how complex forms and practices in Muslim Stuttgart are, and in what direction they might further evolve. Neither couple followed the cultural traditions prescribed by their distant places of origins. For Amna this was impossible considering her complex identity. Yet neither couple followed the local social customs or extensive dating and possible sharing of an apartment before marriage. Instead they found their spouses in their own ways employing local and contemporary procedures that reflect their complex lifeworlds. Amna decided for herself that it was time to get married and spread the word in the mosques, where friends then identified her husband as a possible choice. They met a few times in the context of the mosque and then decided to marry. Families played only a secondary role in this process. Her pious peers and her criteria that her future husband had to be a pious individual, regardless of ethnicity, guided her decision. For both Amna and Sibel piety was a central criterion in their searches. Both marriages depart from older forms of marriages arranged by families to unions arranged by individuals who value piety over ethnicity or family relations. They constitute new cultural forms as individuals search for their own spouses and engage in other social pursuit and activities but do so within the confines of pious local lifestyles (Bayat and Herrera 2010: 13).

The city is the stage for these individuals' lifeworlds and engagements. Piety never prevented them from participating in society. Instead piety creates new outlines and modes of participation. Individuals act as pious participants in homes, schools, work, and public spaces. They interact with others, discuss their ideas, articulate and strengthen trends, shape some cultural contexts and are shaped by others. Their involvements in mosques and other Muslim groups are integral parts of their lifeworlds and hence the cityscape. Some chose more exposed public platforms and visible engagement. Others operate on less conspicuous stages. Through their work, study, friendships and other relationships, worship, and ordinary daily interactions they are intricately woven into the urban public sphere.

Notes

1. I kept her account short as it duplicates details described in chapter 2.
2. An earlier version of this discussion of the public sphere was published in Kuppinger 2011c.
3. Scholars have used the term of "performing citizenship" (Macklin 2009: 284) or "public citizenship" to invoke such spheres of participation (Jackson 2009: 452).
4. Many domestic workers are unregistered which means they have no benefits.
5. Over the years Emine and I have exchanged notes about our readings, and shared books.
6. Women over forty or forty-five years are allowed to travel in groups without an individual *mahram* to Mecca.
7. The institute offers weekend seminars in different cities in Germany, Austria, and Switzerland. The courses end in exams and (informal) diplomas. There are several courses that ideally should be taken in sequence as they cover increasingly sophisticated texts and topics.
8. Gai Eaton (1921–2010) is a British convert to and scholar of Islam. See e.g. Eaton (1985).

CHAPTER 4

Resentment

Underground city train stations in Stuttgart are equipped with sizable screens that run advertisements, short news items, cartoons, and weather updates. Some items run for several days (advertisements), others (news) only for a day. On June 17, 2008, one such news update featured the story of an Imam or religious instructor at a mosque in the suburban town of Ditzingen who had struck a young student with a wooden stick. It is certainly a scandalous act for a teacher to beat a young child with a stick, but the fact that this news item was posted all over the city's train stations, by way of a media outlet that mixes news and entertainment, poses some serious questions. On the same day as the news update ran in the train stations, one of the local dailies, the *Stuttgarter Zeitung*, published an article about the same incident and recounted the curious sequence of events that led to its publication. The boy, described as a *Grundschüler* (primary school student; that is between six and ten years old), had already some time ago reported to his (public) school teacher that he had been beaten by his mosque teacher, including with a stick in his face (Wein 2008). The boy's mother confirmed these accusations and indeed the boy still had a scar in his face. The teacher went on to report this incident to the municipality. This beating without doubt posed questions, necessitated investigation, and possibly interference. A call to the mosque, conversation with the mosque association's president, a request for firing the teacher, or even an appeal to the child welfare agency (*Jugendamt*): there would have been many possibilities to address this accusation or incident. The *Stuttgarter Zeitung* article explained that the authorities of the neighboring town of Korntal-Münchingen (where the boy seemed to reside) had known about the incident for almost a year, but nobody reacted or took any action about this case. In the meanwhile a new mayor had taken office in Korntal-Münchingen. The new mayor, Joachim Wolf, heard about the case in December 2007 (ibid.). He proceeded to write an open letter which, Wein noted, he "spread widely" (*weit gestreut hat*; ibid.) in official places/offices. With this letter, Wolf "wanted to open the eyes of the responsible bodies/offices" (ibid.). For what exactly he wanted to open the officials' eyes, other than this one known case, is not clear. There is obviously no excuse for beating a young child with a wooden stick, but to automatically assume that this is a larger or even typical problem in mosques that needs to be announced to numerous offices (and subsequently to the public) is completely out of proportion with the incident. To widely publish this incident without further investigation or interaction with those involved and those in charge of the mosque and its instructional program is neither appropriate nor professional. The mayor of Ditzingen, where the mosque is located, was irritated that his colleague (from the neighboring community) had withheld such information and wondered why the case had not been addressed via regular channels and means a long time ago. In an interview the president of the mosque association noted that he had a hard time seeing the instructor in question as violent. He added that the respective instructor had only been at the mosque for a short time and had long since left the country.[1] One mother, who was also interviewed for the article, added that if the teacher indeed had been beating the children, the parents certainly would have interfered (ibid.). Whatever the details of this unfortunate case were, the fact that it was widely published in local train stations deserves further thought. Why is this brief news item so noteworthy? What makes it important or attractive? What are the sentiments that are addressed and possibly reinforced in readers? What sentiments are furthered with such an announcement? Why did some of the involved individuals/officials jump to the quick conclusion that this was a pervasive problem? What are some of the sentiments or resentments, and possibly prejudices that guide the thoughts and actions of individuals like Mayor Wolf? Where do they come from and how are they constructed? Why is this piece of news deemed appropriate to be spread by way of info-entertainment news media that by its very nature and location is centered on fast and flashy news items?

In this chapter I examine exemplary aspects of the landscape of popular ideas, sentiments, prejudices, and representations of Islam and Muslims in German media and public discourse. Newspaper articles, TV reports and talk shows, books, lectures, seminars, conference, exhibitions, and workshops frequently engage topics to do with Islam. In recent years, in particular since 9/11, there have been the almost predictable bi-monthly media hypes over topics related to Islam and Muslims. Honor killings, terrorism, Muslim women, Muslim loyalty to the constitution, the construction of individual mosques, or the growing number of mosques in the country at large, take turns with more global themes like the situation in Iraq and Afghanistan, the role of Islamist groups in the Arab uprising, or the problem of global terrorism and its possible threat to Germany. Conducted with more or less fervor and passion, these debates mediate public opinions with regard to local issues related to Islam and Muslims. Thus the violence of distant Muslim political regimes or militant groups mysteriously stands to explain very different contexts and incidents elsewhere, including in Germany. The fear of Islam,

Muslim militancy, or "oppression" of women are maintained and fostered in small incidents, larger discussions, or media hypes in an almost daily manner. Subtle and not so subtle images of violent acts and individuals, political oppression, and intolerance are routine features in the media and public debates. Such images can be easily mobilized at any moment for concrete (local) cases and circumstances. Subsequently one stick-wielding instructor in a local mosque can quickly be used to prove that an entire religion/culture is marked by excessive violence. Fed with constant (low-key) representations of supposed Muslim violence and intolerance, even the most minute instances of Muslim "misbehavior" can then be received with an all-knowing attitude of "I told you so."

In the following I examine the production and maintenance of fear and resentment of Islam in subtle and everyday manners. First I examine a publicly sponsored exhibit with the title "The Abused Religion: Islamists in Germany" (*Die missbrauchte Religion: Islamisten in Deutschland*) that was on display in Stuttgart in the fall of 2007. This exhibition aimed to present the dangers of "political Islamism," but I argue that it in fact helped to further strengthen existing stereotypes of Islam and Muslims. Describing the vaguely defined complex of "Islamism," the exhibition tried to illustrate Islamist trajectories, networks, and activities and warn about the dangers of militant Islamism. While the exhibition made ample efforts to absolve non-violent Muslims, the unmistakable subtext was that many Muslims could potentially to join militant Islamic groups, and indeed might be living with precisely such thoughts in Germany. My second example is a public event that accompanied this exhibition. This panel discussion illustrates aspects of Stuttgart's Islam debate circles and provides a glimpse at opinion making and exchanging processes. Finally, I analyze a controversial speech by the German President, Christian Wulff, in the fall of 2010, and the debates and responses that this speech triggered. In this speech President Wulff claimed that "Islam is part of Germany." This statement caused considerable debates in the days and weeks that followed his address. Opponents to the President's speech insisted on the foreign nature of Islam and reiterated predictable resentments along with arguments of why Muslims should remain outsiders and could never be trusted or become equal citizens. I also present exemplary contributions to this debate and illustrate how participants' conceptualizations of society and culture were surprisingly static and removed from existing urban cultures and experiences. Many discussants were either unable or unwilling to acknowledge ongoing local and global cultural and social transformations. Being stuck in the social, political, and cultural reality of the 1960s, commentators failed to understand existing multi-ethnic and multi-religious lifeworlds. The failure to comprehend processes of social and cultural transformation was rooted in widely shared notions of culture a fixed "entity" that is not prone to change easily, and if indeed it changed, its "purity" would be adulterated by "outside" influences.

Representing Islam

Much has been written in the last few decades about the representation of Islam and Muslims in Europe and North America. Edward Said's classic *Orientalism* (1979) followed by his inquiry into more contemporary political and journalistic representations in *Covering Islam* (1981) produced a flurry of works that challenged and criticized dominant images and representations of Islam and Muslims (and also Arabs as an ethnic group). In the years since *Orientalism* was first published, popular cultural representations of Islam and Muslims have been challenged by scholars, journalists, and other cultural critics, but surprisingly little has changed on both sides of the Atlantic with regard to the ongoing reproduction of underlying popular stereotypes and prejudices (Shaheen; 2008, 2009; for the case of Germany see e.g. Hippler and Lueg 2001; Schiffer 2005, 2008; Shooman and Spielhaus 2010). In fact, in some aspects, representations have become even more prejudiced and hostile to Muslims and Arabs in the aftermath of 9/11 (Shaheen 2008).

Regardless of critical scholarly and journalistic interventions, the end of the Cold War and collapse of the Soviet Union, the First and Second Gulf War, and finally the events of 9/11, ushered in an era of heightened anti-Muslim cultural sentiments. Islamophobia experienced a considerable renaissance, and popular culture embarked on a new wave of Islamophobic productions. Movies like *True Lies* (1994), *The Siege* (1998), *Three Kings* (1999), *Rules of Engagement* (2000), *Black Hawk Down* (2001), or *The Kingdom* (2007) were released in quick succession and globally distributed. These movies thrive on and perpetuate long-held stereotypes and prejudices, as they peddle an array of misrepresentations and gross biases about Arabs and Muslims including their allegedly violent nature, cowardice, mistreatment of women, and inability to efficiently and fairly run their affairs and countries (Shaheen 2008, 2009). Betty Mahmoody's book *Not Without My Daughter* (1989), which tells the story of a bitter divorce between an Iranian husband and an American wife, is similarly replete with stereotypes of violent, ignorant, insensitive, and "uncivilized" Iranians/Muslims. The book experienced intensive public attention in the wake of the first Iraq war and was quickly turned into a movie. Suddenly this book (and subsequently the movie) that told the story of one (American-Iranian) family gone sour, came to explain the essence of Arabs, Iranians, and Muslims. In the winter of 1990/91 the (translated) book was heavily marketed all over Germany and eventually sold a record-breaking four million copies in Germany.[2] The book and (to a lesser extent the movie) reinforced the existing "I told you so" attitudes about the violent and oppressive nature of Muslims and their countries.

The production of popular images and (subtle) resentments about Muslims starts at a very young age for many western consumers of popular culture. Disney's by-now classic children's movie *Aladdin* (1992) prepares the stage for anti-Muslim (and anti-Arab and anti-Middle Eastern) images at large. In the opening sequence of this film, a poem is read about the town the audience is about to enter, which says it "is barbaric, but it is home." In town the viewer first encounters a vendor at a market stall who sells a ludicrous instrument that can supposedly do impossible things, only to fall apart right after the vendor's demonstration. As we follow the predictably light-skinned hero, Aladdin, around the town of Agraba, we find miserably poor children who dig through garbage for food, not far from the splendid castle of the Sultan. Good-hearted Aladdin shares his only piece of bread with the children. Next we see (also good and light-skinned) Princess Jasmine going through the market, where some vendor threatens to cut her hand off for taking an apple. After Aladdin jumps to her rescue, he is hunted down through the entire town by the Sultan's army. Characterized by stupidity and ignorance, this army is not able to capture a young boy and his pet monkey. In these first fifteen minutes of the film, children are provided with an almost standard set of long-held prejudices about Islam and the Middle East: (1) the general assumption that somehow towns and lifestyles are "barbaric"; (2) their materials items are badly produced; (3) vendors (and others) use great rhetoric to cover up immense material flaws—in short, they cheat; (4) individuals and laws are excessively cruel; (5) the army (and officials) while materially well-equipped are ignorant and stupid, but can do much damage.

Once children have graduated from *Aladdin* and similar products, they are ready to consume more sophisticated, but similarly prejudiced popular cultural products and learn to subsequently approach more serious news in similar manners. Seen in the context of *Aladdin* and other popular culture productions, the story of the stick-wielding mosque instructor presented in the format of subway info-entertainment neatly fits in with pervasive images of excessively brutal Muslim individuals and their inappropriate disciplinary methods.

The Exhibition

In September 2007, a traveling exhibit designed by the *Bundesamt für Verfassungsschutz* (Agency for the Protection of the Constitution; Germany's State Security Agency) with the title "The Abused Religion: Islamists in Germany" (*Die missbrauchte Religion: Islamisten in Deutschland*) was on display in the basement of the impressive complex of the *Haus der Geschichte* (House of History) in Stuttgart. The exhibition was paralleled by a series of public events and lectures, and a final panel discussion.

I visited the Islamism exhibit on an early afternoon (after the morning shift of school classes had cleared out). The exhibition hall was quiet and there were about a dozen visitors, mostly middle-aged and older. I took ample time to take in details and take notes. Coincidentally, I happened to work my way through the exhibit at about the same speed as three older women (at least one of whom was a retired teacher as it later turned out). Without intending to, I overheard parts of their conversations and commentaries as I was taking notes. I started to include these in my notes and will weave them into my description. I include these ladies' commentaries (in italics in square brackets) as I introduce displayed posters, short texts, and images.

The exhibition was organized into six sections. Section 1 "Islam—A Great World Religion" provided basic information, data, and demographics of the Muslim world. It illustrated aspects of the extension and diversity of the Muslim world and noted the existence of several sects within Islam [*"this is just like with us"*]. On the next panel, it was asserted in large print that in the context of Germany "99% of the fellow Muslim citizens (*Mitbürger*) practice their religion peacefully and respect the values prescribed in the *Grundgesetz*." [*"This 1 percent is explosive"*]. The panel provided a detailed demographic breakdown of Muslims in Germany. It listed a total of 3.2 million Muslims, 1.75 million of whom were Turkish, 285,000 were Arab. Of the one million German Muslim citizens, 100,000 were ethnic Germans and the rest were mostly naturalized citizens of Turkish descent. Next was a large panel with the global distribution of Muslims. Muslim-majority countries were marked in bright red; orange was used for regions with sizable Muslim minorities. This use of colors made parts of Africa and Asia look like they were on fire, with the bright red centers that faded into orange (flammable?) peripheries.

Section 2 posed the question: "What is Islamism?" The first poster provided an immediate answer and definition: "Islamism is an extremist ideology that posits itself in opposition to western values and ordering/structuring ideas (*Ordnungsvorstellungen*)." "Islamism" was not defined by way of its contents/self-definition (if there is such a thing) but as an extremist, oppositional ideology. Internal characteristics, beliefs, tensions, and factions were conveniently glossed over. No mention was made of the vast diversity of religious, social, economic, cultural, and political activities that can possibly be included under the vague heading of (ill-defined) Islamism. Islamism became a monolithic movement. It was an (flammable) enemy that needed to be watched. Theological positions and contents were avoided in order to construct this enemy image. Next, the usual suspects were presented as part of a rather simplistic, monolithic, and unilinear intellectual history of a well-bounded ideology and movement. Rashid Rida (certainly a complex thinker, otherwise often discussed as a modernist), Abul Ala Maududi, Hassan al-Banna, and Sayid Qutb were referenced as the fathers of Islamism. "Islam is the solution" (a translation of the Muslim Brotherhood's slogan *islam huwa al-hal*) was presented as the motto of Islamism at large. Referring back to the German context, the next poster exclaimed that "altogether there are about 32 percent active Islamists," whose "methods range from the peaceful (*gewaltlos*) pursuit of Islamist goals to the support of the terrorist struggle." How the number of 32 percent was determined, or what precisely Islamist goals were remained unclear, even after the next poster spelled out that "the Islamist guiding thought (*Leitgedanke*) of a theocracy and the absolutist claims represented by Islamists are incompatible with the principle of liberal democratic foundational order (*freiheitlich demokratisch Grundordnung*)." The poster further explained that the Islamist ideology was based on a limited understanding of human rights. Clearly, in light of the recent arrest of a group of three young Muslims, two of whom had been ethnic Germans (the *Sauerlandgruppe* arrested in September 2007), who had allegedly stockpiled chemicals to be used as explosive for a terrorist attack, one of the ladies said: "how can Germans accept such thoughts?" The other responded that "the Ulmer Fritz [one of the men in question] probably joined such a group, because the Baader-Meinhof [reference to the 1977 RAF terrorist outfit] no longer existed."

"Legalist Islamists" was the theme of Section 3, which first introduced Iran-oriented Shi'a groups. Closer to home, the Islamic Community/Association Milli Görüş (*Islamische Gemeinschaft Milli Görüş e. V.*) was mentioned. The blurb provided the names (!!) of this association's current German leadership, and a membership figure of 26,500. Necmettin Erbakan, the Turkish politician, was mentioned as the association's spiritual leader. The *Islamische Gemeinschaft in Deutschland e. V.* (Islamic Community Germany; IDG) was the second group mentioned. The maintenance of a Muslim identity was listed as a goal of this community, which was described "as the largest cooperation in Germany of followers of the Egyptian Muslim Brotherhood (MB)." The poster furthermore explained that the "MB strives for the construction of an 'ideal Muslim state,' which would be solely based on the Sharia." The MB is described as working with a three-phase model: "(1) Spiritual Collection/Concentration; (2) Phase of Mission and Propaganda; (3) Realization [of their Model]." Concretely this would entail first the realization of a truly Muslim state in Egypt and subsequently the entire world. The posters stressed that neither Milli Görüş and nor IGD advocate or use violence to achieve their goals. Both associations are under the watch of German state security.

Section 4 was entitled "Islamist Organizations that Approve of the Use Violence: The Struggle for an Islamist Order" (*Gewaltbefürwortende islamistische Organisationen—Kampf für eine islamische Herrschaftsordnung*) and introduced organizations like Hizb at-Tahrir, HAMAS, Hizballah, Gamat al-Islamiya, GIA, GSPC (the last two are North African/Algerian movements), and the lesser known German phenomenon of the "Khalifatstaat" of the 1990s when a small group had seceded from the Milli Görüş community and announced the founding of a *Khalifat* (theocratic state) in Cologne. This panel listed these groups, but provided little further information about their history, configuration, activities, and goals. They were introduced as a vague, but serious threat.

By the time visitors reached Section 5, they had been taking a long left turn around the hall and were heading toward to the (back) wall. At a distance to the wall a room-like structure had been constructed with huge poster boards. The outside of this "room" was decorated with violent images of terrorist attacks (e.g.

the 1993 World Trade Center attack or the 2005 Bali attack). Through an opening/door, visitors could enter this structure. The interior walls were black. Four screens were mounted on the walls and displayed running images of terror, including clips of 9/11, Osama bin Laden, or an Islamic rapper with a gun whose face was covered by a mask/cloth. There was also an individual who held a Qur'an in one hand and a gun in the other, images of injured individuals, a gun pointed at the audience, a rapper dancing and soldiers marching in the background, or masked fighters. Guns pointed at the audience, helicopters, the destroyed Buddha statues in Afghanistan, the burning World Trade Center, soldiers and militants marched on the screens toward the audience, and some speakers seemed to yell at or address the audience with angry and fierce words. The room was equipped with headphones that visitors could use as they took in the visualized horrors. The sound consisted of a Muslim prayer followed by the sound of an explosion, the rhythmic and aggressive singing of a larger group, the sound of helicopters, nationalistic tunes, recitations from the Qur'an, and the sound of Osama bin Laden as a political speaker. The volume of the headphones was high and could not be adjusted [*"too loud for us, this is for people who go to discos"*]. Standing with the headphone in the room and watching the images moving across the screens produced a feeling of both fear and claustrophobia, as the viewer was caught in a small dark room where violent scenes and sound effects descended on them. Particularly disturbing was the mixing in of the call to prayer and Qur'an recitations with excessively violent and disturbing images and sounds.

Additional notes on the walls of this room, explained the role of "mujahedin" and their "homegrown" networks of unassociated individuals in Germany, referencing the attacks of Madrid in 2004 and London in 2005. The poster explained that these individuals were not part of organized groups, but formed small local violent outfits. "Today Mujahedin wage a global so-called 'holy war' (*jihad*)," the panel further noted. The atmosphere, coloring, images, and sounds of this room (or chamber of fear/horror?) were violent, oppressive, and scary as visitors somewhat unexpectedly found themselves in the middle of massive aggression, violence, militancy, and bloodshed. This room, designed as the core of the exhibit, channeled broad and vague movements into the concreteness of militant attacks, which in turn were promptly linked to the presence of hidden potential militants in Germany. Previous informational materials were translated into concrete fears as visitors entered not only the core of the exhibit, but the core of "Islamism." This core was dark, bloodthirsty, violent, and deeply threatening. It was not so much illustrated by words and explanations, but by drawing visitors into a horror chamber of bloodshed, fierce (not translated) rhetoric, threatening images and gesturing, and war sounds. As a next step, vague threats and fears were projected onto (invisible) individuals that potentially populated the everyday lives of visitors. The very real dangers of Islamism, the room suggested were not only somewhere out there in the world, but could indeed be hidden next door.

After the darkness, shock, and display of violence, visitors emerged to the brightly lit open area at the end of the hall that preceded the final section (lined along the wall that led back to the entrance). In this open area Islamist lifeworlds anchored in regional contexts were showcased and analyzed. Large posters were suspended from the ceiling that introduced elements of such lifeworlds (for visitors to be able to identify the hidden mujahedin in their neighborhood?) These posters had flashy titles like "Niqab am Neckar," "Dawa an der Donau," "Tauhid in Tübingen," or "Scharia in Stuttgart." These word plays with Muslims material items/markers (the *niqab* or face veil) and theological terms (*da'wa*, the call to Islam; *tawhid*, the unity of Allah, *sharia*, Muslim law) and the names of regional cities, towns, and rivers took up the sentiments from the dark room, indicating that dangers were indeed lurking just around the corner, or down the street in most familiar places. The respective posters listed an (odd) assortment of features and elements of supposed Islamist lifeworlds, many of which however were rather ordinary elements of pious Muslim lifeworlds that have nothing to do with militancy. The Saudi satellite TV channel *Iqra* was mentioned. Under the heading of "Scharia in Stuttgart," a poster explained that the younger generation "constitutes a core project in youth activities" (what's wrong with that?). Next, the poster quoted Fatima Grimm (an early convert, prolific writer and tireless lecturer about Islamic issues) who suggested to raise children as "true Muslims" (*wahre Muslime*) was a "real chance to produce an Islamic order in all spheres of life." The poster further explained under the heading of "worldview and life in Islam" that "daughters of conservative Muslim parents should get used early to a life under the veil by playing with the Muslim 'Fulla'-Barbie doll which can be bought at the Islam Week in Baden-Württemberg."[3] What indeed is dangerous about "conservative" or pious parents trying to raise their children within their respective lifeworlds (unless of course one assumes the a priori presence of violence and militancy in such households and environments)? What is wrong with giving one's daughter a Barbie-type doll that simply wears a headscarf and more clothes than the original Barbie? The poster next listed the creation of an *ummah* of "self-confident communities of believers" (wouldn't every church hope to have such a community?), and proceeded to quote Mustafa Islamoğlu who suggested that especially young people should not easily adapt to society (*passt euch nicht der Gesellschaft an*) but should instead remain true representatives of Islam (most pious Christian literature similarly warns against temptations and imitation of social mores and practices for the pious).[4]

The final part of the exhibition was entitled "The Federal Office for the Protection of the Constitution—In the Service of Freedom" (*Das Bundesamt für Verfassungsschutz—Im Auftrag der Freiheit*). Along the long wall leading back to the entrance, the exhibits included features and elements that illustrate both the tasks and concrete work of the State Security Agency (*Verfassungsschutz*). There was a computer screen on which the audience could watch a number of clips about roadside bombings in Iraq. Much like in a video game, this included a series of short clips where cars exploded (made and distributed by the perpetrators). If cars were not too visible in the clips a large red arrow indicated their presence. There were pictures of individuals wearing Palestinian *kafayas*, a *Hizballah* sign, and quotes that glorified past terrorist attacks (London and New York) and general violence and militancy. There were bookshelves filled with mostly Arabic books, journals, magazines, and pamphlets. These could impress most visitors more by the number of the items on display than by their actual contents, but might leave the vague association that all Arabic writing included terrorist contents. The last larger exhibit was a desk with a computer screen centrally placed on it. To its right, on a small wooden foldable stand (as are often used in mosques) was an open Qur'an, to the left were a small gun and a (rather curious) fan. Minus the gun, many Muslim students, clerks, or scholars might have a very similar basic set up on their desks. To put this work space on exhibit as a (dangerous) Islamist desk whose owner might scheme militant actions, once more suggests that any Muslim can quickly and easily turn into a terrorist by simply adding a gun to the mundane paraphernalia of their work space.

While the exhibit emphasizes in its early posters that 99 percent of the local Muslims are ordinary citizens, it suggests that the remaining 1 percent deserves heightened attention as they might already be scheming violent deeds. Moreover, the unsuspecting citizen is warned that their Muslim neighbors can quickly and easily be recruited into hidden global movements and could turn almost overnight into dangerous individuals. The Muslim student from next door might have— among his Arabic books—all sorts of dangerous "propaganda" literature. All he needs to do is add a (symbolic) gun to his desk in order to become a militant. Similarly, the pleasant Muslim family from down the street might buy their daughter a (dangerous?) Fulla doll that teaches the girl to be a good Muslima, and the girl might mysteriously turn into a "jihadist."

Debating Islam

The exhibition was scheduled for September 11 to 27, 2007, and coincided with the month of Ramadan. All the accompanying (evening) events further coincided with the local *iftar* time, which effectively prevented most pious Muslims from attending. When I asked one of the organizers at an event whether they had considered this unfortunate scheduling, he noted that it had been important for them to schedule the exhibit to coincide with the anniversary of 9/11. The inclusion of Muslims seemed secondary. One panel discussion included Yunus Demir, a Muslim interfaith activist (who later told me that he had been fasting on that day) and the organizers, seemingly unaware that he was fasting, did not even provide him with a snack or water to break his fast in the middle of the debate. The audience at the two events I attended represented Stuttgart's middle-aged to older *Bildungsbürgertum* (educated upper middle class).

On September 13, I attended a lecture by Dr. Rita Breuer, a representative of the *Verfassungsschutz*, entitled "Islamic Everyday Life between Integration and Parallel Society."[5] In her lecture Dr. Breuer illustrated largely normative aspects of Muslim life in Germany. She explained some of the problems that Muslims faced in a non-Muslim society (What foods to avoid? Where and how to bury the dead?). She explained the difference between *haram* and *halal* foods and how Muslims obtained detailed information about minute ingredients (e.g. gelatin or animal fats) in various foods or other products (e.g. alcohol in perfumes and toothpaste). She clarified aspects of *halal* slaughtering and their controversial nature in Germany. She proceeded to explain the details of (modest) Islamic clothes and dressing codes, and touched on the contentious issue of Muslim girls and swimming lessons in public schools (see chapter 6). She described the problems of professional women who wanted to combine career and headscarf. Moving through a standard list of foods, clothes, economic concerns (forbidden interest payments; questions of insurances), relationships with Christians, interfaith marriages, or funeral practices, Dr. Breuer listed rules and regulations but made only a few references to real life contexts or situations. Her elaborations remained detached from everyday lives. She concluded that overall "Muslims who regularly attended mosques did not want any regular contacts/relationships with Germans," as their rules and sentiments ultimately worked to set them apart from mainstream society. Indeed such pious individuals had "ever less common points of contact/engagement (*Berührungspunkte*) with mainstream society." Dr. Breuer noted that there were diverse Muslim lifeworlds in Germany and that individuals enjoyed a certain freedom in making their own choices about religious practices within a larger theological framework. She also pointed out that liberal Muslims were at times powerless in the face of conservative theologians.

After a brief intervention of the moderator, the floor was opened for a question and answer session. Individuals asked about details to do with *halal* slaughtering and Islamic banking. Somebody pointed to the profoundly anti-Semitic nature of Islamism and speculated about ties between Islamists and Neo-Nazi groups on that account. In this context, Dr. Breuer noted that Islamists rejected all ideas other than their own, and anti-Semitism was just one aspect of their ideology. Soon the debate moved to the recent surge of religiosity among Muslims. When and how did that happen? Dr. Breuer listed three central reasons: (1) as a reaction to discrimination; (2) as a result of Internet influences and "propaganda"; (3) as a reaction of (insecure) youths who searched for something to be proud of in the local society.

Another person in the audience wondered, "Why are we interested in Islam? Are Muslims also interested in us?" Dr. Breuer noted that there surely must be some respect taught in Muslim schools (in Muslim countries). She quickly added: "but if our school books were like theirs, then we would be in trouble" (*dann wäre was los*). From here the discussion moved in a direction where several members of the audience voiced their indignation about what they saw as inappropriate Muslim behaviors and demands. Somebody mentioned that Nadeem Elyas (a former president of the *Zentralrat der Muslime*, ZMD), when he had an audience with the Pope, gave the latter a Qur'an ("imagine if it was the reverse!"). Somebody quickly added "and there are many more such examples!" This statement produced instant applause. Another person related the story of when the Saudi national soccer team was in Germany for the 2006 World Cup. The speaker remembered that the team demanded that only Saudi TV channels could be played, no alcohol be served in the entire hotel, and all Bibles had to be removed from the rooms. The stories produced more passionate applause. Another person added that wearing a cross was a reason for arrest in Saudi Arabia. The audience seemed to compete for ever "better" stories of what Muslims demanded and what "we" gave to them and allowed them to do, which they would never reciprocate. Somebody summed up these sentiments: "Really, we are too naïve if we believe in the integration of Muslims in Deutschland." Another person added with regard to the 1 percent Islamists in Germany who are ready to use violence (the concrete number of 320 individuals was mentioned) "why are we not upset about this?" (*warum lässt uns das kalt?*). Another person bemoaned the appeasement of Muslims. Yet another complained that "we no longer appreciated our own values" (*was sind uns unsere Werte wert?*).

After Dr. Breuer had been trying—admittedly in a somewhat legalist and uninspiring manner—to explain the broad specter of Muslim lifeworlds and everyday issues, considerable parts of the question and answer period descended into an informed and educated Muslim bashing session where members of the audience told stories and news reports about inappropriate Muslim behavior and demands. While the topic of the evening had been Muslims in Germany, the audience happily indulged in debates about textbooks in the Muslim world, or the oddities of Saudi lifestyles and politics. Many Muslims would readily agree that these were problematic issues, but they had very little to do with the lives of German Muslims (none or few of whom were in the audience on this Ramadan evening). The audience exchanged their misgivings, fears, and resentments and bemoaned their own tolerance of things they really ought not to tolerate. Underlying was a clear sense that in some instances mainstream society was victimized by Muslim demands and persistence.

The President's Speech

At the official celebration of the twentieth anniversary of the German re-unification on October 3, 2010, the (then) President of Germany, Christian Wulff delivered a speech that recognized achievements of various constituencies, illustrated Germany's present challenges, and pointed to the country's future potentials. In a central part of his address, President Wulff pondered the continued meaning of the motto of the pre-unification freedom movement in East Germany: "We are the people." He pointed to the fact that Germany had become an immigrant nation and emphasized that, *who* the people were in the twenty-first century needed to be more comprehensively defined to include all those who lived in Germany and participated in the daily making and remaking of society. In the course of these deliberations, Wulff stated that, "Islam in the meanwhile has become part of Germany." Observers and commentators quickly picked up on this statement. The next day, Germany's most widely read tabloid, the *Bild Zeitung* (short: *Bild*) printed the President's statement in bold letters on its front page next to his picture (*Bild* 4.10. 2010). Other headlines and articles followed. The days and weeks after Wulff's speech witnessed lively and controversial debates about his statement about Islam in Germany, its justification, validity, and concrete social, cultural, and political implications. Some individuals and constituencies were taken by surprise at what they saw as an audacious assertion, others applauded Wulff's courage for making this long-overdue statement in an important public address, yet others voiced irritation about how stating the obvious could cause so much upheaval. Ensuing debates addressed questions like: How long would it take for any group and/or religion to become part of a nation? Could a nation even "absorb" new religious traditions? Could a "foreign" religion ever become a "local" religion? Could Islam ever be part of Germany? Could Islam be part of a culture that defined itself as "exclusively" Judeo-Christian? What defined a citizen? Countless individual observers, commentators, politicians, and different social, cultural, and religious constituencies joined this debate about the role and position of Islam and Muslims in Germany voicing their opinions in articles, commentaries, interviews, and cyberspace debates.

Because October 3, 2010, marked the twentieth anniversary of the German re-unification, President Wulff's speech was an address to the nation on an important national occasion.[6] It was also his first prominent address to the nation as President, since he had only been in office for about three months at the time. His speech was expected with some curiosity with regard to what topics he would give special attention. Titled "To Appreciate Diversity—To Foster Cohesion," the speech celebrated twenty years of effort and work to create one Germany out of two previously opposed and socially separated states. Wulff briefly reminded his audience in Bremen and those in front of their TV sets about how the re-unification had come about. He referred to the East German activists who had courageously demonstrated against the dictatorial East German regime in the time before the fall of the wall. He paid homage to the churches that had supported and sheltered many of these activists. Wulff explained that the East German freedom movement owed much to its predecessors, fellow activists, and noteworthy politicians in Poland, Russia, and Hungary. Having the East German freedom movement anchored in its wider Eastern European context, Wulff turned west to acknowledge the role of the United States and Germany's other western allies. The new Germany, he summarized, could only exist in the contexts of its neighbors and allies. He further recognized the work of German politicians between the 1950s and 1980s.

The next section of President Wulff's speech turned to the domestic affairs of the new Germany. "Our country has become more open," he started his reflections. Globalization had changed the economic, technological, and very importantly also the social and cultural composition of Germany. Cautiously he added, that in the process lifeworlds had been drifting apart, between old and young, rich and poor, the employed and unemployed, and those of different cultures and religions. The challenge for unity today, he stressed, was to bring these constituencies closer together to create a more inclusive (new) sentiment of "we are the people." The call of East German activists in 1989 "we are the people," foreshadowed a new self-consciousness in Germany and a new feeling of belonging that went along with a great responsibility that resulted from the German past. Along with this sentiment came a new sense of openness. Today, the call "we are the people," Wulff continued, had to be an invitation to all those who lived in Germany. A sense of "we" needed to be created that included both those who had been in the country for a long time and those who had arrived more recently. At this point Wulff departed from the more general mode of his deliberations and added a concrete example. He noted that sometimes he received letters from Muslims who wrote to him: "You are our President." To these letters, he emphasized, he "responded from the depth of my heart" (*dann antworte ich aus vollem Herzen*), "Yes, of course I am your President" (*Ja, natürlich bin ich Ihr Präsident*). He added that he had recently received a letter from a group of students of diverse backgrounds who stressed "we want to live here, we are Germany." Wulff underlined the importance of Germany embracing its newer citizens. Moving to the core of this section of his address, Wulff noted that "we" needed to discard three "foundational lies" (*Lebenslügen*): (1) Guest workers are transient residents; (2) Germany is not an immigrant country; (3) The illusionary nature of some debates about multiculturalism.

A better understanding of Germany's social and cultural reality and its challenges, however, can help to catch up with issues and problems that had long been ignored or neglected (e.g. language courses, Islamic religious instruction in schools). To produce meaningful transformations, President Wulff insisted, "First of all we need to take a clear position: an understanding of Germany that does not reduce belonging to a passport, a family history or a religion. Christianity without doubt is part of Germany. Judaism without doubt is part of Germany. This is our Christian-Jewish history. But Islam in the meantime has become part of Germany" (ibid.). After he established this fact, and underlined it with a quote from Goethe's *West-East Divan*, Wulff continued to stress that inclusion demanded participation and responsibility: "everybody should contribute their skills and ability to society."

After creating a discursive space for Muslims in German society, Wulff turned to issues of social inequality and society's responsibility for its poorest members. In an interesting rhetorical twist, he warned members of the elite not to withdraw into their upscale "parallel worlds." This expression is noteworthy as "parallel society" is frequently used to accuse Muslims of withdrawing into their own social worlds and not participating in society. Wulff concluded his address with a note that "this country belongs to all of us, whether from East or West, North or South, and regardless of origins."

The fact that the tabloid *Bild* chose Wulff's statement for its front page headline the day after the speech helped move the topic of Islam in Germany once more center stage for popular and public debates.[7] For many, including regular *Bild* readers, this statement was bold, if not to say outrageous. That a religion and its adherents would become part of a society after half a century of presence and participation is by no means a broadly accepted understanding. Instead, Islam for many ordinary citizens and politicians remains a "foreign" religion, located at a great distance to German culture and society. Islam is alien and indeed something to be feared for many and therefore one ought to be careful in one's dealings with the religion and its adherents. Many who joined in the debate quickly expressed these deep-seated (and well-maintained) resentments of Islam and Muslims. After the first three days of debate, *Bild* took a first brief look at the debate that it had helped initiate (*Bild Zeitung* 6.10.2010). The article's title "Warum hofieren Sie den Islam so, Herr Präsident? or "why are you courting Islam, Mister President?" speaks for itself. The choice of the term "courting" (*hofieren*) implies that Wulff is trying to appeal to Muslims from an inferior position. It is him who is asking Muslims for a favor and/or friendship. Courting is a matter of choice and not a necessity. Courting implies an unequal encounter where one party tries to gain the favor of another. The use of this term denies the possibility of a dialogue between partners. It further distorts the reality of Muslims as an established constituency in society. The article repeats popular sentiments about Muslims and immigrants at large: "Ever more citizens ask themselves: why do we talk so much about minorities—and so little about the majority? Do we have to pay more attention in the future to the values of Islam? Who, ever thinks of us?" (ibid.). These questions represent the claims of an "offended" majority that for too long has been "forced" to pay attention to minorities, somehow at the expense of its own needs. The sentiments of "how much more do they ask for?" or "do we have to give in to them?" frequently surface and imply that the majority is losing its culture and rights.

As much as Wulff tried to pull Muslims (and other immigrants) into a more comprehensive and inclusive German society, *Bild* seriously questions whether this is possible and desirable, and whether this in fact reflects the wishes of the "majority." The journalist in question (and the newspaper) does not want to see the framework of belonging extended in such a manner, and quotes an online survey the paper had commissioned on October 5 (no details are given about this survey, other than it was "representative"): 66 percent "of the Germans" said that Islam was not part of Germany, whereas only 24 percent agreed with Wulff (*Bild Zeitung* 6.10.2010). By cleverly using statistics that represent the ill-defined group of "the

Germans," *Bild* insists that ethnic Germans are the only ones whose voices count. Next the article quotes seven negative or critical entries into the President's online guest book, for example: "What do Muslims have to do with the re-unification? Did they tear down the wall?" or "Islam as an ideology is incompatible with Germany's culture, and societal order (*Gesellschaftsordnung*)." This is contrasted by only two positive remarks, one of which was made by Ali Kizilkaya, the president of Islamrat (Muslim umbrella organization associated with the Milli Görüş community). By many readers of *Bild*, as a Muslim, his voice might be considered "biased" and not be recognized as being as relevant as that on an ethnic German/non-Muslim.

With its initial headlines and follow-up articles, *Bild* positioned itself as the representative and indeed defender of the beleaguered majority that had somehow been betrayed by its President who favored becoming the "friend" of Muslims over standing up for the legitimate rights of his "real" German constituency. Politicians of the CDU's Bavarian sister CSU (Christian Social Union; *Christlich-Soziale Union*) immediately distanced themselves from Wulff's statement (*Frankfurter Allgemeine Zeitung* 5.10.2010). Hans-Peter Friedrich, the head of the CSU faction in the *Bundestag* (national parliament), spelled out his party's position: "To state in clarity: the *Leitkultur* in Germany is the Christian-Jewish occidental culture. This culture is not a Muslim one and will not be one in the future either "(ibid.). Friedrich added, "I will not sign on to the fact that Islam is part of our culture" (ibid.). Christian-Jewish culture, he insisted, was our *Leitkultur*, and everybody who wanted to live in Germany needed to integrate into this culture (ibid.).

Chancellor Angela Merkel tried to mediate between Wulff's statement and the CSU position. She insisted that even though Islam belonged to Germany, this did not automatically mean that it constituted a foundation of Germany's cultural understanding (*Frankfurter Allgemeine Zeitung* 5.10.2010). Friedrich added remarks about the limited "integrationability" (*Integrationsfähigkeit*) of some people/Muslims, but did not further substantiate this remark. He only mentioned the example of school classes that do not include any ethnic German children. His example, however, says more about the increasing class and ethnic segregation in cities, than about the "unwillingness" of some ill-defined groups to "integrate." Chancellor Merkel on a different occasion added that Islam was "of course welcome" in Germany within framework of freedom of religion. Islam (as a subject), she insisted, needed to feel committed to the values of the *Grundgesetz*, which were not negotiable (*Frankfurter Allgemeine Zeitung* 4.10.2010). There is, however, a significant difference between being welcome (as a guest?) and being a part or belonging to a place (Yeğenoğlu 2012; Balibar 2004; Derrida 1992).

Not surprisingly, Muslim groups and representatives welcomed the President's remarks. Ayman Mazyek, the president of the Central Council of Muslims (*Zentralrat der Muslime*; ZMD), voiced his hope that the statement would move things in Germany. He added that the speech was "a sign that Muslims are not second class citizens" (*Frankfurter Allgemeine Zeitung* 4.10.2010). Mazyek also expressed his fears that in the face of social and economic uncertainties, people might fall victim to "populists and charlatans" (ibid.). Politicians from the opposition, for example, Gregor Gysi from the Left Party, similarly welcomed and supported Wulff's remarks (ibid.). Politicians from the Green and Social Democrat opposition supported Wulff's statement, which remained controversial in Christian Democratic circles. The President of the German Protestant Church commented that Wulff simply had, in a rational manner, described the German reality (*Frankfurter Allgemeine Zeitung* 5.10.2010). Michel Friedman, a Jewish public intellectual and former vice-president of the Central Jewish Council (*Zentralrat der Juden*), similarly noted that Wulff's words merely reflected an existing German reality (*Frankfurter Allgemeine Zeitung* 4.10.2010).

Even though President Wulff's statement about Islam as part of Germany caused a significant public stir, it was neither unique nor unprecedented, even in conservative Christian Democratic circles.[8] High-ranking cabinet members had made similar remarks in recent years, but none had produced much noteworthy reaction. In 2006 the (then) Minister of the Interior, Wolfgang Schäuble (CDU), in the context of the first meeting of the official German Islam Conference (*Deutsche Islamkonferenz*; a government-sponsored dialogue series between government representatives and Muslim individuals and associations), had stated: "Islam is a part of Germany and Europe. Islam is part of our present and future" (*N-TV* 28.9.2006.) At the time few observers paid much attention to this statement as it was made with reference to the dialogue with Muslims, and thus was neither spoken at a prominent event nor to a large audience. Two years later, in an interview with the respected daily, *Frankfurter Allgemeine*, Wolfgang Schäuble repeated that "Islam is long since (*längst*) a part of our country" (*Frankfurter Allgemeine Zeitung* 1.3.2008). In this interview Schäuble responded to the sharp criticism of the writer and journalist, Ralph Giordano, who had accused Schäuble of being naïve in his dialogue with Muslims and of courting "bad (*üble*) representatives of political Islam" (ibid.). Again the remark was inconsequential. Two years later, in May 2010, in an interview about the first session of the second phase of the Islam Conference, Minister Schäuble reiterated his statement and emphasized once more that "Islam is presently part of German and Europe" (Prantl 2010). Again nobody picked up on the remark. Yet President Wulff's remarks in 2010 stirred such controversy, because they were made at a highly symbolic moment at a representative event. There, many observers concluded, they were utterly out of place.

Fear and Resentment: No End in Sight?

Mundane events and debates as illustrated above are deeply marked by a subtle and indeed sometimes not so subtle presence of Islamophobia, and irrational fears and resentments against Islam and Muslims. The exhibit of the "Islamist" desk with a computer, Qur'an, and gun best illustrates this. To put the Qur'an, which is dear to Muslims, right next to a gun on this desk creates wrong associations, and perpetuates existing irrational fears. The question and answer session that followed Dr. Breuer's lecture in part deteriorated into a venting session for stories about global Muslim misbehavior. Similarly, President Wulff's brief remark at a symbolic event caused public debates for weeks to come as numerous individuals and groups felt that his remark neither reflected the reality, nor was it in any way appropriate. These brief examples illustrate elements of a pervasive atmosphere of resentment, suspicion, and fear that many Muslims have to deal with on a daily level. Prejudices and resentment are ubiquitous and can be used and swiftly activated by small and subtle hints. They can further be wittingly or unwittingly elicited in diverse contexts for various purposes. For Muslims, these prejudices, fears, and resentments pose a constant threat and challenge in their individual and communal lives. It requires immense work and energy to constantly face and attempt to overcome their powerful and pervasive existence. I will turn to one rather successful example of such a struggle in the next chapter.

Notes

1. For lack of other teachers, some mosques occasionally bring in retirees from Turkey to teach.
2. http://www.bastei.de.
3. For details on the history, context, and marketing of Fulla and similar dolls, see Kuppinger (2009).
4. For details on the at times controversial thoughts of Mustafa Islamoğlu, see Islamoğlu (2009).
5. Much of the lecture was based on Dr. Breuer's book *Zwischen Ramadan und Reeperbahn* (2006).
6. For a full text of President Wulff's address, see *Frankfurter Allgemeine Zeitung*, "Christian Wulff: Vielfalt schätzen—Zusammenhalt fördern." 3 October.
7. Every day *Bild* has one short and bold front-page headline. Reading these headlines every day (they are all over newsstands and kiosks) provides a good insight into popular debates and sentiments. These headlines in a complex manner both reflect and construct ongoing debates. The paper's use of the Wulff quote as an October 4 headline helped initiate, foster, and support the ensuing public debate. The editors knew that many of their readers would object to this statement.
8. Christian Wulff was a member of the CDU before he became president. As a representative of the state, the German President is supposed to be above party politics.

CHAPTER 5

Our Mosque

June marks the beginning of the lively summer festival season in Stuttgart and Baden-Württemberg.[1] Organized by local authorities or civic associations, such occasions are important cultural and social events in villages, towns, and urban quarters. With increasing wealth and leisure time such festivals have proliferated since the 1970s. Local festivities are as much community-building events as they showcase local cultural topographies. Along parade routes, on fairgrounds, or patronizing the eateries of civic associations, diverse residents rub shoulders, recognize, renew, and remake communal ties. Demographic groups and organized associations represent their arrival or continued presence in the local public sphere. Neighborhood festivals illustrate social and cultural transformations and reflect—albeit with a significant time lag—long-term demographic changes and social and cultural transformations. Italian, Greek, Serbian, Portuguese, and secular Turkish associations regularly participate with folklore, dance, and music groups in parades or run food stalls at neighborhood festivals. The participation of mosque communities remains rare.

On a weekend in June 2007, the quarter of Stuttgart-Zuffenhausen celebrated its thirty-third Annual "Village" Festival (*Zuffenhäuser Fleckenfest*). Posters around the quarter promised "food and drink, music and a fun fair" for the entire weekend. The 2007 festival was also celebrating the 100th anniversary of Zuffenhausen being granted city rights. The fact that Zuffenhausen lost these rights after only twenty-four years, when it was annexed by the city of Stuttgart, did not detract from this reason for celebration. In honor of Zuffenhausen's brief moment of urban independence, the community council (*Bezirksbeirat*) organized a parade. Murat Serdar, the president of Zuffenhausen's Hussein Mosque informed me of this event and proudly related that for the first time community members would represent the mosque in a local parade. The mosque was also going to run a food stall on the fair grounds. On a hot Sunday, Tamima, Tala, and I stood at the bottom of Zuffenhausen's main street, the Unterländer Strasse, and watched floats and groups go by. After twenty minutes, in the middle of the typical parade fare of schools, sports and soccer clubs, music clubs and choirs, church groups, and the Red Cross, I recognized—coming down the hill—the Hussein Mosque group. Mr. Serdar walked in the front, dressed in a casual short-sleeve shirt, beige pants, and a colorful skullcap. Next to him was the Imam wearing a dark coat and white skullcap, and two young boys. More boys and young men followed; and women of different ages—all but one of whom wore headscarves. Some of the younger women and girls wore fashionable headscarves and outfits. One was dressed in a bright red skirt and matching red scarf combined with a white tight-fitting shirt; the colors of the Turkish flag. An older woman was dressed entirely in black. Another teenage girl wore the current fashion of tight black pants with a black miniskirt over the pants and a red shirt and scarf. At the end of the group two young men carried a banner that read: "The Muslim community greets all residents of Zuffenhausen and wishes happy feast days" (*Die Muslimische Gemeinde grüsst alle Zuffenhausener und wünscht frohe Festtage*). The group consisted of about twenty people. They threw no candies or other little gifts, like some other groups did.

The parade offered a glimpse at the cultural topography of Zuffenhausen. There were a choir (*Gesangverein*), a tractor lovers' association, carnival associations (*Faschingsvereine*), sports clubs from Zuffenhausen and beyond, groups of volunteer firefighters, a folklore association (*Trachtenverein*), mountain hikers or climbers (*Albverein*), a regional folklore and cultural association of ethnic Germans who had settled in Zuffenhausen as refugees after World War II (*Siebenbürgener Sachsen*), a German-Serbian sports and cultural association (Sloga e.V), a Russian association whose members carried a flag with Cyrillic writing on it, the Protestant church, the Catholic preschool (*Kindergarten*), the Red Cross, and others, reflecting a vibrant civic culture. The parade was dominated by ethnic German groups and associations, but with a visible migrant participation in some groups (schools, preschools, sport clubs). There were a few older migrant/refugee organizations like the *Siebenbürgener Sachsen* representing groups that had arrived in the middle of the last century, and slightly more recent arrivals, like the Serbian group. Considering that Zuffenhausen has a very diverse population, migrants and their descendants were underrepresented, indicating the time lag between the arrival of migrants, the formation of migrant organizations or the participation of migrants in existing groups, and their eventual visibility in the public sphere. The dominance of ethnic German groups points to the persistent self-representation of the community as ethnically German.

When the parade was over, we followed the crowd to the narrow streets of the old/original Zuffenhausen village at the eastern end of the main street, where the food stalls and fairground with children's rides had been set up. On the first street to the left after a grilled chicken stand, we found the Hussein Mosque's stall. There, Mr. Serdar, and several men and older boys were busy making and selling foods and drinks. They offered barbequed lamb and ground meat kebab, French fries, soft drinks, ice cream, and *baklava* (sweet and oily filo pastry). Their barbequing venture was operating at full capacity as the hungry and thirsty parade watchers all at once descended from the main street. On the one side of the stall, a 1970s popular hit *"Eine neue Liebe ist wie ein neues Leben"* (A new love is like a new life) was blasting. From the other side came the faint traces of a brass band playing German tunes. The mosque's two barbeques were packed with meat. The two boys who were doing the French fries could barely keep up with the demand. Behind the stall was a second tent separated from the front by a Turkish flag as a makeshift door. Behind the flag three women were preparing meat (no women worked up front). The "pillars" of the front tent were decorated with sheets of the Hussein Mosque's stationary, on which—printed in large letters—were verses from the Qur'an. Another sign said: "The Muslim community Zuffenhausen wishes all humans in this world, hand in hand, a just, free, democratic, humane, clean, merciful, peaceful, safe and tolerant world." Even with about ten people working, a line of customers formed at the stall. We patiently waited for our food, briefly chatted with Mr. Serdar, and with our food moved to the right of the stall and sat on some planters where we entered the soundscape of yet another loudspeaker that played *"Que sera, sera* . . . what will be, will be." Diagonally opposite the mosque's stand was a stall selling all sorts of pork products, and sausages, including the street fair favorite of barbequed *Schweinehals* (a pork specialty). Outlets for beer and wine were all over. Not too far away was a Greek stand selling gyros. Looking at the mosque stall's neighborhood, it was clear that Mr. Serdar and others had done initial convincing to get his community to participate in this event. To sell kebab and coke on a street fair in the immediate neighborhood or pork and alcohol was certainly new to many community members.

Participation in a parade, more than other forms of participation, symbolizes the local arrival and inclusion of the Hussein Mosque. Parades are important displays of urban public culture and serve to illustrate details of local cultural topographies for everybody to see (Zukin 1995: 21, 294). The inclusion of a mosque community in a neighborhood parade is still rare in German towns and cities as the public often remains oblivious or resentful of mosques. At the same time, not all mosque communities are ready or interested in participating in such events. The Hussein Mosque's participation in the Zuffenhausen parade signifies considerable involvement, discussion, respect, trust, and cooperation between the mosque and its urban quarter. The image of the Hussein Mosque representatives marching in the parade, sandwiched between local churches, sports clubs, brass bands, mountain hikers associations, voluntary fire fighter, and folk dance groups represents a crucial moment of civic arrival and inclusion. With its participation in the parade, the Hussein Mosque visibly positioned itself as a local association. This is remarkable if one remembers that when I first introduced Mr. Serdar (chapter 1), he was one of the VIKZ officials who came under considerable public attack in the Heslach mosque conflict that ended in the loss of a projected mosque facility in 2002, only five years before this parade. Back then, opponents had accused him and other mosque association board members of planning to build a center that might be radical, indoctrinate youths with fanatical ideas, and discriminate against women. A number of questions arise here: What had happened in the meanwhile to allow for the inclusion of the Hussein Mosque in this parade and the neighborhood at large? Is Zuffenhausen different from Heslach? Had the VIKZ dramatically changed in only a few years? Had the urban public experienced a dramatic change of mind? In short: what accounts for the relative local harmony and inclusion in Zuffenhausen in the summer of 2007, versus the prejudice and resentment experienced in Heslach only a few years earlier? What circumstances and dynamics account for the rather successful localization and inclusion of the Hussein Mosque?

In this chapter I examine aspects of the history, dynamics of inclusion, localization, participation, and everyday life of the Hussein Mosque in Stuttgart-Zuffenhausen. I chronicle moments in the history of Zuffenhausen and the Hussein Mosque community, and how their historical trajectories slowly merged in the last two decades. I outline events that produced respect, trust, and communication between different constituencies. The localization of a mosque community is a multilayered process that transcends the time and space of immediate encounters as both the neighborhood and the mosque community are the results of complex historical processes. Each has unique roots and experiences that influence their present existence and future trajectories. The quest is not for the mosque to "adjust" to a given cultural and social landscape. Rather the challenge is for the local community, the mosque, and other stakeholders to engage in shared transformative processes. I illustrate how Mr. Serdar, the mosque community, neighbors, the local quarter, its officials, and other institutions cooperated to include the Hussein Mosque in the local public sphere. Over time the Hussein Mosque became "our mosque" for many residents in Zuffenhausen.

Zuffenhausen is not noticeably different from Heslach. Both are former villages turned inner city multi-ethnic working-class quarters; both have a history of housing working-class newcomers to the city. But unlike the intense citywide and indeed statewide conflict that followed the VIKZ's purchase of a factory complex in Heslach in 1999, the same association's purchase of a smaller building in a largely residential area in Zuffenhausen had sparked little or no opposition in 1993. The initial absence of negative public attention never exposed the Hussein Mosque to broader political platforms and debates; no citizens' group formed to oppose the mosque. The subsequent emergence of the Hussein Mosque as a participant in the quarter's public sphere unfolded away from the spotlight of media attention and beyond the radar screen of xenophobic groups and right wing associations. The inclusion of the Hussein Mosque proceeded in small and unspectacular steps negotiated between individuals and small constituencies in contexts of increasing familiarity. Trust was built one step or one event/encounter at a time, as the mosque community, residents, local officials, and other civic associations, especially churches, became acquainted with each other.

The (peaceful) establishment of a mosque is the beginning of intricate processes of localization where religious, spatial, and cultural ideas, values, and specific historical and social experiences are mediated by diverse actors who have hitherto had little to do with each other, and are becoming familiar with each other along the way. Considering the complex nature of such encounters, it becomes apparent why the Heslach mosque project was doomed to fail, as little communication had existed prior to the mosque purchase between the mosque association, local residents and groups, and the local council. Strangers clashed, and ignorance and prejudice prevailed among considerable sections of the ethnic German population. With the much smaller size of the project in Zuffenhausen and little initial opposition, the mosque community was able to settle into its premises and subsequently carefully articulate its mode of civic interaction and participation. In particular after 1999 with the unfolding Heslach conflict, Mr. Serdar and other board members of the mosque association were acutely aware of possible misunderstandings and tensions. They quickly applied lessons learned in Heslach elsewhere in the city. The Hussein Mosque's success might reflect more favorable local circumstances in Zuffenhausen, but it is also rooted in mosque officials' keen understanding of how to present their cause in public, to formulate their engagement for the mosque, and voice their interest in cooperation with the local council and other civic institutions. In Zuffenhausen the latter were ready to reciprocate this engagement and interest.

Old and New Migrants, Old and New Religions

Popular media and commentators frequently depict post–World War II migration to northern Europe as a new phenomenon. Scholars have long refuted this perspective and illustrated much longer histories of population movements and migration within Europe and to Europe (Sassen 1999; Fenske 1980; Silverstein 2004; Castles and Davidson 2000; Lucassen 1987). Simultaneously, millions of Europeans left for the Americas starting in ever-larger numbers from the seventeenth century. Examining the "drama of people in motion in Europe," Saskia Sassen observes that "immigrant-receiving countries behave as though they were not parties to the process of immigration" (1999: xxiii, 1). The burden of adjustment and accommodation was to be single-handedly shouldered by incoming migrants. Taking the turn of the nineteenth century as a point of departure, Sassen illustrates how successive wars, religious tension and persecution, famines and other crises, but also economic booms and emerging prosperous regions accounted for considerable population shifts in Europe, which often followed or duplicated previous similar processes, or paths and circuits of migration (ibid.: 7). Sassen identifies routes and cycles of temporary migration, but also those that led to the permanent resettlement of individuals, families, or small communities. Well into the nineteenth century "receiving politics did not seek to restrain migratory and refugee inflows as they eventually would in the twentieth century" (ibid.: 11). Already in the late seventeenth century the Prussian king had invited French Protestants to work in his realm. A century later the Duke of Württemberg similarly allowed French Protestant refugees to settle and found their own villages on his lands (e.g. the villages of Perouse, Pinache, or Serres in the Stuttgart region). Many Europeans engaged in seasonal migration. Some ended up staying for good in their seasonal destinations. With the rapid transformations that accompanied Europe's industrialization, more individuals joined circuits of increasingly more permanent migration. The emergence of nation-states added new categories of "exiles" and "refugees" to this transient population (ibid.: 35). As rural and peasant economies disintegrated, former peasants were forced into industrializing cities in their own regions or elsewhere in Europe and beyond. Some resettled for good, others later returned to their former homes. Sassen reports that as many as a third of the immigrants to the United States in the first two decades of the twentieth century eventually returned to their homelands initiating patterns of circular migration (ibid.: 44).

By the turn of the twentieth century, Germany had become a destination for thousands of Polish and Italian workers. Emerging notions of (German) citizenship and national belonging marked these labor migrants as "foreigners," and they were treated and controlled as such. In 1913 Germany "legislated a strict conception of citizenship and nationhood embodied in jus sanguinis" (Sassen 1999: 61). The law determined descent as the basis of citizenship allowing Germans abroad to maintain their citizenship over generations while denying newcomers the right to belong. Simultaneously Germany established a "strict system of control over immigrant workers" (ibid.: 57). Work and residence permits circumscribed the movements and possibilities of migrants (ibid.). Wars, revolutions, ethnic strife, and economic crises in the decades to come swelled the ranks of those on the move. Forced labor, the horrors of the Holocaust, and the devastation of World War II put millions on the road.

When post–World War II labor migrants from the northern and southern shores of the Mediterranean arrived in Germany, they were just the latest group of newcomers following in the footsteps of older circuits and thousands of predecessors. How did these large-scale movements of workers, refugees, and displaced people unfold in concrete contexts? How did they settle and grow roots in their new localities? And most importantly, how did they become integral, recognized, and respected parts in their new localities, and creatively participate in local public spheres and urban cultures?

Topography of a Multi-Ethnic Working Class Quarter

Zuffenhausen is located north of downtown Stuttgart. The current administrational unit (*Bezirk*) of Zuffenhausen includes the old villages of Zuffenhausen and

Zazenhausen, the planned quarter of Neuwirtshaus (built in the 1930s), the post-World War II high-rise residential area of Rot, and a number of smaller residential extensions. Until its reconstruction into an underground line in 2011, the ride from downtown on the city train (U15) to Zuffenhausen provided a tour of the central parts of the quarter.[2] Entering from the south, the train passed the Hohenstein quarter (to the left or west) which is an early-twentieth-century residential neighborhood consisting of two- to four-story small privately owned apartment buildings arranged on a narrow grid of streets. Taking a peak at some backyards through entranceways or alleys, a lively landscape emerges. Backyards encompass an array of constructions and activities. There are small plots of vegetable gardens, fruit trees, decorative plants or shrubs, shacks, garages, small workshops, and even a few small factories. There are extensions to some buildings with additional residential spaces, garages with balconies on top, complete with clotheslines, makeshift balcony roofing, plants, and an assortment of seating and storage arrangements.

Continuing with the train toward the center of Zuffenhausen, one passed the town hall (*Bezirksamt*), a plain building on the right. Further ahead is the old village of Zuffenhausen where some of the small historic farmhouses have in recent years been converted to chic urban residences. Then the train took a sharp left turn and passed a 1970s strip mall/plaza with a Greek restaurant and an Italian ice cream parlor and coffee shop. Next, to the left, was the Protestant church. The train continued uphill on the quarter's main street, the Unterländer Strasse. To the right was Zuffenhausen-Mitte, which resembles the Hohenstein quarter. Hohenstein and Mitte only house about a third of Zuffenhausen's residents but form the geographical and social core of the community.[3] Leaving this core of Zuffenhausen, the train took a right turn, passed another residential neighborhood, and continued north toward Stammheim, its final destination.

The Unterländer Strasse and its environs provide a glimpse at the making of contemporary multi-ethnic working-class quarters. Most of Stuttgart's neighborhoods have at least one such main shopping venue. Types of stores and services reflect the respective neighborhood's socio-economic composition (Ceylan 2006; Yildiz 2009; Gliemann and Caesperlein 2009). The specter of possibilities extends from call and Internet shops, sports betting places, bars of various kinds, discount supermarkets on the lower economic end, to more upscale supermarkets, pricier specialty stores, boutiques, and organic supermarkets at the higher income end of the cityscape. In addition to the relative affordability of stores and services, neighborhood shopping venues also reflect ethnic mixes (Mattausch and Yildiz 2009). In more upscale neighborhoods, migrants and their descendants, if present, tend to provide services (shoe repair, tailoring services, locksmith services) and fast food, whereas in multi-ethnic working-class neighborhoods, they often also run grocery stores, clothes stores, call shops, or jewelry stores. The Unterländer Strasse features a regular (i.e. not a discount) supermarket, several bakeries (mostly belonging to larger chains), two (German) butcher stores (an indicator of relative wealth, and ethnicity), banks, chain drugstores, and an assortment of smaller specialty shops, bargain shops, two call shops, and several fast food outlets. There is a One Euro store that doubles as an Asia market, where cheap toys and household items are on shelves next to five-kilo bags of basmati rice, South Asian spices, alarm clocks that ring for Muslim prayer times, posters of Shahrukh Khan, and DVDs of Bollywood movies. In a prominent location, halfway up Unterländer Strasse, is a (Turkish) fashion and clothing store whose large windows are visible from afar. The store offers colorful, glittery, and shoulder-free evening gowns (a favorite for lavish wedding celebrations) next to modest Islamic fashion. There are floor-length skirts, long-sleeve blouses, pant and skirt suits, and accessories (pins; *bone,* a small head-covering worn under a headscarf) for women who wear headscarves, and there is a small selection of fashionable western-style women's clothes and shoes. Diagonally opposite from this store is Nuspl,[4] a curious but well-patronized department store. Nuspl has the making of a 1950s department store that sells almost everything in very cramped quarters. Most similar stores folded a long time ago under the onslaught of discount stores. The owners of Nuspl seemed to have understood the times and their customers and continued to cater perfectly to their increasingly multi-ethnic working-class customers for decades. Furthermore the street is home to two *Döner* outlets (Turkish fast food), a bakery/coffee shop, an Italian restaurant, a Chinese take-out, and several other smaller eateries (see also Freudenreich 2009). Turning right at the end of the ascent of the Unterländer Strasse, one enters a residential area that is interspersed with the remnants of a few smaller factories that bear witness to the mixed use of the area in the past. If one turns left and walks back down through the Hohenstein quarter, one can reach the suburban train (*S-Bahn*) station. This street and several of its side streets one passes through on the way to the station accommodate a mix of bars, betting places, a casino, curious small shops (like a cell phone "hospital"), and a sprinkling of leftover specialty stores (clothes etc.) that have the distinct flavor of by-gone days and whose days seem numbered, and a number of empty storefronts.

In 2011, Zuffenhausen had 35,585 inhabitants, of which 51.3 percent were migrants or individuals with migratory backgrounds, which is the highest percentage for any quarter in Stuttgart (Landeshauptstadt Stuttgart 2012/13: 21; at the opposite end was Degerloch with 26 percent, the city average was 39.9 percent).[5] Zuffenhausen is the first (and by 2011 still the only city quarter to cross the 50 percent mark with regard to residents with migratory roots (Zuffenhausen's figure for 2005 was 47.1 percent; Landeshauptstadt Stuttgart 2006: 304). Residents in Zuffenhausen have the smallest living spaces per person (34 square meters) in the city (average 39.3 square meters; Landeshauptstadt Stuttgart 2012/13: 23). Zuffenhausen has a higher (10.4 percent) than average (7.7 percent) rate of unemployment (ibid.: 25). In 2005, Zuffenhausen had a higher rate of households of families with children (21.1 percent) than the city average (18.1 percent; Landeshauptstadt

Stuttgart 2006: 26). Also in 2005, the average disposable household income in Zuffenhausen was €37,000 (Stuttgart €39,300) which is more than €10,000 less than in the wealthiest neighborhood of Sillenbuch (Landeshauptstadt Stuttgart 2006: 30). At the same time, 12.9 percent of Zuffanhausen's residents received welfare benefits, which was the highest figure in the city, compared to 8.9 percent citywide (ibid.: 30). Social differences between Stuttgart's neighborhoods are significant but not dramatic, and Zuffenhausen is clearly among the poorer and socially more disadvantaged quarters.

Regardless of its socioeconomic position, and precisely because of its multi-ethnic population, Zuffenhausen (and similar quarters) performs crucial tasks of everyday cultural negotiations. For example, in 2007, more than two-thirds of the quarter's preschool population had migratory roots, which at times makes for complex linguistic and cultural situations (Höfle and Raidt SZ 28.3.2007; by 2011 the figure was almost three-quarters, see Landeshauptstadt Stuttgart 2012/13: 300). Schools prepare diverse young populations for success in a competitive post-industrial economy. Not everybody succeeds and 70 percent of the special education students come from migrant families (Raidt SZ 21.11.2006). Individuals and institutions are faced with mundane questions like which compromises have to be designed to appropriately accommodate everybody and allow for a smooth co-existence. When one of the local public preschools celebrates its annual summer party a compromise was designed to allow for a festivity where everybody was comfortable. Two barbeques were set up, one for Muslims (no pork) and one for non-Muslims (including pork). One Muslim mother was put in charge of providing the meat for the largely Turkish and Bosnian Muslim families. "Then everybody eats," one of the teachers reported (ibid.).[6] A visit to the Hussein Mosque is part of this preschool's annual curriculum. In return the Muslim parents attend a Christmas service. Recently, the local Protestant preschool handed over its operation to the city. "How can we run a Christian preschool with only one or two Protestant children?" a Church official noted (ibid.). The Protestant community is in the process of downsizing its facilities while others religious groups, like the Hussein Mosque, a Romanian-Orthodox Church, and a Sikh community are growing deep roots in the quarter (ibid.). Surely there is tension in the community about new congregations, there are the predictable complaints about noise, parking problems, and too much traffic, but as the head of the local administration (*Bezirksvorsteher*) noted in 2006: "eventually, whatever the complaints, they always subside" (ibid.). He added, "Zuffenhausen has always attracted migrants. In the past people came from the Alb or from Hohenlohe, today they come from Turkey or Bosnia. In the past Catholics were the strangers (*Fremde*), today they are Muslims" (ibid.). He recounted the story of a Catholic blacksmith who remembered that when decades ago he had first moved to Zuffenhausen nobody did business with him, because he was Catholic (ibid.). But eventually people accepted him and used his services.

Zuffenhausen: Intersecting Roads, People, and Religions

In the Roman era a road ran from the castle in today's Bad Cannstatt past today's quarter of Zuffenhausen to Mainz and the Rhine Valley (Messerschmidt 1957: 24; Friedrich and Kull 2004: 52).[7] For centuries people and goods traveled through the area and left traces and influenced locals. The village of Zuffenhausen was first officially mentioned in a monastic document about land rights in 1204 (Messerschmidt 1957: 30; Ehmer 2004a: 70). By the end of the thirteenth century Zuffenhausen had its own Roman Catholic church district (*Pfarrei*) which denotes a more permanent and larger village (Ehmer 2004a: 68). The Johanneskirche (St. John's Church) was first mentioned in historical records in 1275 (Gühring 2004: 560). For most of the fourteenth century Zuffenhausen belonged to the Monastery of Bebenhausen (about 40 kilometers south of the village; Ehmer 2004a: 70). In the final years of the thirteenth century Stuttgart (about six kilometers south of the village) emerged as an urban center; a legal court and marketplace were mentioned there for the first time (Borst 1986: 36, 486). In 1287 Stuttgart was under siege by Rudolf von Habsburg as he attempted to reintegrate the region into his weak German Kingdom (ibid.: 43). After Stuttgart's capitulation to the German Emperor Heinrich VII (of the house of Luxembourg) in 1312, the city emerged as the center of the region. In 1321 the regional Count (*Graf*) Eberhard made Stuttgart his preferred residence. His domain of Württemberg consolidated as a political entity with Stuttgart as its nascent capital (ibid.: 42).

Located at a short distance north of this new seat of power, Zuffenhausen was pulled into the city's orbit, which often meant being drawn into struggles and warfare (Messerschmidt 1957: 34). In the fourteenth century a mayor (*Schultheiss*) was mentioned for Zuffenhausen. The mayor was the representative of the larger political body/legal system. He presided over the village court and pronounced judgments in small cases and personal disputes (Ehmer 2004a: 82). In the early fifteenth century when Count Eberhard IV consolidated his power and local rule, Zuffenhausen became part of the domain of Württemberg (versus being under monastic control; Messerschmidt 1957: 75; Ehmer 2004a: 89). After 1490 an imperial postal route that connected Brussels with Innsbruck and Venice passed by Zuffenhausen (using the old Roman road; Friedrich and Kull 2004: 61).[8] By the late fifteenth century, the Count of Württemberg drew considerable revenue from Zuffenhausen in money and kind (e.g. chickens, wheat, wine; Ehmer 2004a: 89).

The sixteenth century was marked by religious and political strive that accompanied the Protestant Reformation. The posting of Martin Luther's theses in 1517, had probably escaped the villagers in Zuffenhausen. At the time Württemberg was struggling with an oppressive ruler, Duke (*Herzog*) Ulrich (Gühring 2004a: 108), who was forced out of the country in 1519, when the Austrian Habsburg Dynasty took over his domain. In the upheaval of the Reformation and the ensuing political turmoil, peasants in southern Germany took this moment of instability to voice their demands to their landlords. Violent peasant revolts erupted. Political strive, peasant discontent, and religious issues intermingled in these revolts. The last local peasant uprising witnessed a devastating defeat in 1525 in Böblingen (twenty kilometers south of Zuffenhausen; Ehmer 2004b: 115). Political discontent increasingly collected under Protestant banners. On May 15, 1534, Duke Ulrich of Württemberg returned to Stuttgart (Borst 1986: 88). The next day he had a Protestant service performed in the central church, the *Stiftskirche*. Stuttgart's Protestant Reformation, which was tied to local political dynamics that unfolded in the context of peasant revolts and the (Catholic) Habsburg rule in Stuttgart, was formally completed (Borst 1986: 89). The footwork in the towns and village still lay ahead. To introduce and consolidate Protestant ways and order in his realm, Ulrich's son, Christoph, introduced the Church and School Order of 1559 to regulate Protestant life, preaching, and teaching. Catholic Zuffenhausen became Protestant Zuffenhausen. The Catholic *Johanneskirche* became the Protestant *Johanneskirche*. A basic school system was instituted (Messerschmidt 1957: 38) and in 1559 a "schoolmaster" (*Schulmeister*) was mentioned in Zuffenhausen. His tasks, beyond teaching, were to oversee the church building and activities (*Mesner*), and announce village news (*Büttel*; Ehmer 2004b: 126). The House of Württemberg and the associated Protestant Church slowly took control over considerable parts of the (landed) possessions of the older monasteries in the region (Ehmer 2004b: 127).

As long-distance trade and travel increased, Zuffenhausen's fate was increasingly interwoven with such movements. The old (Roman) north-south road that linked Holland by way of Frankfurt (with a crossroad to Strasbourg) to Cannstatt/Stuttgart, from where it continued to Venice (with crossroads to Nürnberg and Switzerland; Gühring 2004b: 147) connected the village to distant places. It was a blessing and a curse. In times of peace, journeymen and merchants, much appreciated by local innkeepers, traveled the roads. In times of war armies marched through, often leaving trails of looting and devastation. Throughout, the village had to shoulder some of the road's maintenance costs (largely in labor; ibid.). In 1550 the Emperor of Germany took a breakfast stop in the village. He was accompanied by a huge entourage that included "bears, elephants, and other curiosities" (Messerschmidt 1957: 38). By the turn of the seventeenth century Duke Friedrich II, hard-pressed by expenses for a luxurious lifestyle, hired miners to search for coal. One small mine was outside Zuffenhausen (Gühring 2004b: 143). Miners from distant regions like Mömpelgard/Monbéliard (France, at the time associated with Württemberg), Saxony, and Hessen (ibid.: 144) were brought to work this mine.

In 1620 Zuffenhausen had 500 residents of whom 109 where citizens (*Bürger*).[9] The village consisted of 160 buildings (Messerschmidt 1957: 40). In 1634, during the War of Thirty Years, Zuffenhausen and eight surrounding villages were largely destroyed when Spanish troops set them on fire. Surviving villagers escaped to (walled) Cannstatt, where some stayed for several years. To make matters worse, the plague hit the region and more people died (Gühring 2004c: 195). By 1639 some surviving villagers returned to their devastated homes (ibid.: 198). Only about a third of the villagers rebuilt their houses (Messerschmidt 1957: 40).[10] The coming years witnessed more armies marching through and more looting (Gühring 2004c: 198). In the seventeenth century, armies, individual soldiers, and families of soldiers came through Zuffenhausen, some stayed for a while, children were born, and sick or older travelers died (ibid.: 203). A French Protestant was housed in the poor house, and the son of a Swedish officer died in the village (ibid.: 203-4). A few Calvinists and Catholics were counted among the villagers in 1654 (ibid.: 212). Wars and the plague repeatedly robbed the village of workers, including craftspeople, but migrants, especially from Switzerland, replenished the work force. Some were journeymen who married local women (ibid.: 217). War refugees and economically motivated migrants (e.g. Swiss who left their less-fertile mountain villages) helped rebuild devastated villages in Württemberg (ibid.: 222). Zuffenhausen church books mention a Polish man who married a local woman. Another man originated in the Salzburg area (ibid.).

In 1652 the village introduced the institution of a church assembly (*Kirchenkonvent*). Once a month, either in the church or the village hall (*Rathaus*), a meeting was held which played the role of a church, school, moral, and police supervisory board. The assembly debated and also punished minor offenses, including marital disputes, disorderly conduct, screaming on the street, staying out past curfew, or skipping school. The assembly was also in charge of hiring the village midwife, gravedigger, police, and day and night watchmen. This assembly functioned well into the nineteenth century (Gühring 2004c).

The War of the Spanish Succession (1701-1713/14) brought more turmoil to the Stuttgart region when French and Bavarians troops fought the Austrian, English, and Dutch armies. More looting soldiers descended onto villagers (Gühring 2004c: 213). The trans-European nature of this turmoil, and how small villages were woven into these nets of relations (or animosities) is best illustrated by the baptism of a boy, Peter Lorenz, in Zuffenhausen in 1746. His father, Pierre Lorend, was a French soldier who had deserted his troops. He had last been fighting with a Swiss regiment that was in the service of Sardinia (Gühring 2004d: 232).

In 1717 Duke Eberhard Ludwig built a hunting lodge outside Zuffenhausen (the "Schlotwiesen"). In 1806 Emperor Napoleon stayed there for a hunting expedition organized in his honor by the King of Württemberg (Binder 2004: 274). In the early nineteenth century Zuffenhausen (with a population of just over 1,000) was a rural village. Many residents were poor and worked as day laborers. With the ascent of Stuttgart as a royal residence (and the Kingdom of Württemberg as part of the consolidating German nation-state) and aspiring modern industrial capital city, Zuffenhausen's links to the city intensified. The opening of the first railroad in 1846 from Stuttgart to Ludwigsburg, which ran past Zuffenhausen, and the industrialization of Stuttgart, triggered economic and social transformations in Zuffenhausen. Duke Eberhard Ludwig's Schlotwiesen hunting lodge illustrates these transformations. In 1818 the original lodge was demolished and only the groundskeeper's residence remained. In 1828 the premises were used by a Pietist Brother Community as an Institution to Save Children (*Rettungsanstalt für Kinder*), which offered instructional courses for female early childhood educators (*Kleinkindpflegerin*). The institution soon moved to a neighboring village. The building and real estate were sold to two industrialists who started a "cottonvelvet and Manchester" production as the premises were located close to the new railroad (Messerschmidt 1957: 43–44). This factory, which employed sixteen workers on twenty-five mechanic steam-powered weaving machines, was Zuffenhausen's first industrial plant (ibid.: 58).

By 1859 Zuffenhausen's economy comprised five inns (*Wirtschaften*; two had their own breweries), two merchants, a small storekeeper (*Krämer*), a mill, and a few craftsmen. Most residents still worked in agriculture. Four carpenters sold some of their products at exhibitions or to furniture stores in Stuttgart (Messerschmidt 1957: 52–53). Day laborers worked in the royal gardens, road construction, quarries, railways, or a sugar factory in Stuttgart. Industrialization and new transportation brought new institutions and residents to Zuffenhausen. In 1821 an "industrial" school opened, where girls between the ages of eleven and fourteen were taught needlepoint and other crafts twice a week in the afternoon (ibid.: 56). By 1853 the village school expanded to include four large classrooms (*Schulsäle*), one master teacher, two assistant teachers, and one teacher's aid (together they taught 420 children). Rapid social change was accompanied by social tension and misbehavior. The church convent of May 24, 1824, noted: "Such great disorder has started to occur on Sundays that often a horrible screaming and shouting happens in the streets that causes public annoyances, that the church convent has stipulated that whoever in the future on Sundays displays such immoral behavior will be punished to pay 1 *Pfund Heller*" (Messerschmidt 1957: 57).

Zuffenhausen's industrialization gained momentum in the mid-1860s. In 1864 a glass factory opened, followed in rapid succession by a factory for volcanic elements in 1865 (*vulkanische Bausteine*), a tar factory in 1873, and a factory for agricultural machines in 1875 (Messerschmidt 1957: 60). More followed, among them a large metal processing plant in 1880 (ibid.). The establishment of larger industries triggered the additional growth of smaller workshops and production sites in the village. By 1880 the village economy included 286 independent workshops and companies. This number increased to 322 by 1890 and more than 400 in 1895 (ibid.). Especially successful were furniture producers who expanded their existing ties to Stuttgart and did contract piecework for urban stores.

New factories, the easy commute to Stuttgart, and affordable housing led to the influx of more labor migrants in the 1880s (Messerschmidt 1957: 61). Zuffenhausen transformed from a peasant village to an urban workers' quarter. Between 1870 and 1895 residents more than doubled from 2,513 to 5,727 (ibid.). The village had to adjust its infrastructure: schools needed extensions, and new streets had to be built. The author of the 1957 local history accused village leaders of inappropriate and self-centered politics at this significant transitional moment: "Because of the opposing interests of various wealthy families, the absence of a mayor who understood the significance of the situation and developments, and the resisting attitude of many long-time residents toward the newcomers (*Reingeschmeckte*), the extension of industrial and residential quarters in Zuffenhausen was—in contrast to Feuerbach—not separated. One simply let things go their way, which was decisive for the transition to a workers' quarter." Also, "nobody understood, in the interest of a smooth (*gedeihliches*) communal life, to bring old and new Zuffenhausen residents in a cultural context closer together" (Messerschmidt 1957: 61).

By the turn of the twentieth century this caused a precarious situation in Zuffenhausen, which had never made a decision as to its future, either as a residential or an industrial quarter. The quarter had patches of both in close proximity or even interwoven with each other. The decision for a more comprehensive plan for the community's future became paramount after 1895 when Stuttgart's industries, cramped into the central valley, ran out of space and new legal codes banished noxious industries from central locations. Yet the Zuffenhausen village council engaged in petty fighting (*kleinlicher Rathauskrieg*), where personal gain from real estate transactions took precedence over long-term planning (Messerschmidt 1957: 63). These "unhappy real estate and property politics" led to the cutting up of areas and mixing of uses, as zoning, unlike in neighboring communities, was non-existent (ibid.).

The years before World War I brought more growth, rapid transformations, and increasing numbers of incoming rural migrants. More, mostly smaller, factories settled in Zuffenhausen, which in 1907 received city rights (i.e. had more than 10,000 residents). New streets were built to accommodate residential buildings. Zuffenhausen's authorities built a sewage system, installed streets lights, connected the town to the electricity system, extended existing schools, and opened new ones such as a trade school and a middle school (*Realschule*). In 1909 Zuffenhausen was connected to Stuttgart by a tram line (today's U15; Messerschmidt 1957: 66–67). A year later the tram ran every twelve minutes to Stuttgart. In 1910 Zuffenhausen had 12,752 inhabitants (ibid.: 64; a 400 percent increase in thirty-five years). With the new arrivals came more diversity. In 1859 Protestant Zuffenhausen had been home to only three Catholics. The new industries brought in more Catholic workers (Messerschmidt 1957: 69), and by 1900 the Catholic community included 572 individuals. For years they had gone to neighboring Feuerbach to attend services until in 1898 services started to be held in the Catholic school in Zuffenhausen (ibid.: 70). Attempts were made by some locals to accommodate the newcomers. Once, the Protestant minister had the Protestant church bells ring for a couple who married at the Catholic school and had asked for wedding bells (ibid.). In 1902, a Catholic church was built (ibid.).

Among the new residents in nineteenth-century Zuffenhausen were a small number of Jews, most prominently Moritz Moses Horkheimer who in 1885, together with his brother Richard, founded a company for sorting/processing cotton and wool rags in Stuttgart. In 1898 they opened a plant, which soon employed 150 workers, in Zuffenhausen (Gühring 2004e: 402). Horkheimer's son Max, the philosopher and sociologist, was born in Zuffenhausen in 1895 (ibid.). In 1918 the elder Horkheimer was made an honorary citizen of Zuffenhausen (*Ehrenbürger*). The otherwise detailed history of Zuffenhausen (Gühring 2004) remains curiously silent about the fate of the Horkheimer family, their company, and the fates of other Jews in Zuffenhausen.[11] Roland Müller briefly notes that the Moritz Moses Horkheimer at the age of eight-one, together with his wife, "had to immigrate to Switzerland in 1939" (2004: 442).

World War I brought Zuffenhausen's rapid development to a halt. After the war, local planning departed from the fragmented ways of the turn-of-the-century years. Zuffenhausen faced an acute housing crisis and proceeded to add much-needed housing. A nonprofit communal housing cooperation (*Gemeinnützige Baugenossenschaft Zuffenhausen*) constructed apartment buildings (Messerschmidt 1957: 71).[12] In the 1920s Zuffenhausen experienced considerable financial problems, which were partially due to the fact that the town's industrial basis/area was too small, as it had never delineated a sizable industrial zone (like neighboring Feuerbach had done). As the situation became precarious, "there was only one way out: to join a wealthier neighboring community" (ibid.: 74). Zuffenhausen chose to go with Stuttgart and became a city quarter in 1931. This move brought quick improvements with regard to electricity, telephone, and schools, as the town hooked into larger urban networks and services. The future of Zuffenhausen was now negotiated in Stuttgart. In the early 1930s Zuffenhausen laid out its first larger industrial zone. Industries boomed—some of them already in the unfortunate preparation for World War II. Zuffenhausen kept growing and had 21,500 residents in 1939 (Messerschmidt 1957: 79). Two new residential areas were opened in addition to the planned settlement of Neuwirtshaus where 307 families found homes in 1935 (ibid.).

During World War II, as most local men were drafted, industrial and especially war production was kept up with women and increasingly with forced labor. Zuffenhausen housed numerous forced laborers (mostly from the Soviet Union and Eastern Europe; Schäfer 2001). Forced laborers were kept in camps, assigned to private households, or other special accommodations. The former hunting lodge at the Schlotwiese was turned into a forced labor camp. Inmates were not allowed to freely move in the community. They only left the camps for "work." Initially companies that used forced laborers had constructed huts or shacks on their premises, but soon these were no longer enough. By 1942, about 16,000 forced laborers were held captive in Stuttgart. In 1943 the number had doubled (Müller 2004: 442). To accommodate these forced laborers, the city built additional barracks on the fields of the Zuffenhausen sports club and rented them to the companies who used forced labor. The city of Stuttgart maintained a labor camp with 400 people (including women, children, and elderly individuals) in Zuffenhausen. Western European forced laborers (French, Belgian, or Italian) were assigned to live in private households in the community (Messerschmidt 1957: 79).

In several large allied bombardments of Stuttgart between July and December 1944, Zuffenhausen was seriously hit.[13] Because of their makeshift accommodation, forced laborers died in disproportionally large numbers in the bombardments (Müller 2004: 444). On April 21, 1945, the Nazi-era came to an end in Zuffenhausen when French troops took over the quarter (ibid.: 450). Intensive movements of individuals in various directions characterized the immediate postwar period. Forced laborers were repatriated. As soon as they left their accommodation, returning evacuees replaced them. They were joined by 1,250 individuals of German descent from Yugoslavia, expelled Germans from various eastern territories, and other refugees. In addition to the old hunting lodge compound, the municipality assigned people to emergency shelters in Zuffenhausen (Messerschmidt 1957: 81).

Soon Zuffenhausen, like the rest of Stuttgart, started a period of rapid reconstruction. In 1949 the settlement of Rot was started. By 1956, 16,500 individuals found new homes in its high-rise apartment buildings (Messerschmidt: 82). At the time Rot was considered "the most modern neighborhood in West Germany" (Landeshauptstadt Stuttgart 2006: 301). Numerous expelled Germans (*Heimatvertriebene*) settled in the community. Some started to open small businesses (Messerschmidt 1957: 84). Construction and infrastructural projects proceeded at top speed: new bus lines, tram lines, schools, childcare, and new churches (a Catholic and Protestant one in Rot) were rapidly built. In 1948 industries started to rebuild. Older industrial areas consolidated and new zones opened. In the 1950s, Zuffenhausen had seventy companies that employed a total of 11,000 people. Only ten of them had more than 200 employees (ibid.: 86). Zuffenhausen's rapid post–World War II industrial expansion quickly absorbed refugees and others. By the mid-1950s newcomers from southern Europe joined this previous wave of arrivals. Soon Italians, Greeks, Turks, Moroccan, Yugoslavians, and others settled in the quarter.

In 1938 a small automotive construction and development company under the leadership of Ferdinand Porsche, that had been founded a few years earlier, settled in Zuffenhausen. The company produced plans and designs for different types of vehicles for other producers, among others for the Volkswagen Beetle. After a brief postwar stint in Austria where the Porsche prototype 356 was developed, the company returned to Zuffenhausen in 1949. In April 1950 the first 356 was built in Zuffenhausen (Bogen *SN* 24.3.2010). Over the next decades the company and its increasingly global reputation grew dramatically. In 2010 Porsche had 5000 employees in Zuffenhausen (*Stuttgarter Zeitung* 21.7.2010). In 2009 the spectacularly designed Porsche Museum opened on the edge of the vast

Porsche terrain in Zuffenhausen. In addition to Porsche as its crown jewel, contemporary Zuffenhausen is home to an array of companies that operate, among others, in the fields of communication technologies, software development; employer personnel services, or logistics.

Tragedy and Transformations

Zuffenhausen transformed from a predominantly Protestant peasant village to a Protestant and Catholic urban working-class quarter when it entered into the orbit of Stuttgart's industrialization starting in the late nineteenth century. For some decades in the late nineteenth and early twentieth century Zuffenhausen was the home of a small number of Jewish families. During the Holocaust these families either escaped, or were chased out of their homes, or quietly taken away and murdered. Their possessions were taken over by individuals or the public. The experiences and tragedies of Zuffenhausen's Jews are not well documented (see note 11). During World War II, Zuffenhausen became a site of forced labor. Roland Müller includes a brief testimony of a former forced laborer who said that on a lucky day, he would leave the laborer's camp and even go to see a movie (2004: 443). This, however, does not seem to represent the experiences of most others who fared much worse (Herbert 1990, 1999).

After World War II, Zuffenhausen absorbed thousands of displaced people and refugees. Starting in the mid-1950s, the arrival of Italian, Spanish, and Portuguese Catholics, and Greek and Serbian Orthodox Christians added to the existing ethnic and religious mix. The arrival of Turkish, Moroccan, Bosnian, or Tunisian Muslims in the 1960s added yet other ethnic and religious groups to the community. Like their predecessors, diverse Muslims went to work in local factories. Some stayed for a few years and then returned to their homeland, others stayed and raised their families in Zuffenhausen. Like among earlier migrants, some of the more entrepreneurially minded new arrivals, after some factory work, set up their own businesses to serve the needs of their own, but soon also the community at large. Some opened food places, or grocery and produce stores, others entered services (e.g. shoe repair, locksmith service, tailoring), others bought existing businesses and reworked them to fit their purposes (e.g. jewelry).

In an article about Zuffenhausen, Josef-Otto Freudenreich, one of Stuttgart's most critical observers (e.g. 2008) described the conundrum of the quarter as "two worlds that do not come together" (Freudenreich *SZ* 26.1.2009). There are the wealthy who come to Zuffenhausen from all over the world to pick up their latest model Porsche, and Porsche's well-paid managerial and engineering class, but this does not translate into a wealthy urban environment. Freudenreich adds that the latter "race home on the *Autobahn*" to their suburban hometowns (ibid.).[14] Zuffenhausen, its material environment and social context, benefits relatively little from this wealth.

The Hussein Mosque

The Hussein Mosque is located in a largely residential part of Zuffenhausen. The mosque's modest building looks like a typical 1950s two-story residential building. To reach the building one crosses a small yard, and then climbs some steep stairs up to the entrance. The glass door and small adjacent glass front sometimes have signs and information on display. For instance, before the *Eid Al-Adha* (Feast of Sacrifice) there was a sign about where to buy appropriate animals for own consumption or as a donation. Depending on the time of the day and day of the week, one can hear sociable voices or lively and loud children's voices from inside the building as one climbs the stairs. Upon entering the building, there is a carpeted area. Long low shelves along the wall in the hallway indicate that one is to take off one's shoes upon entering the building. Immediately to the right is the prayer room. Decorated with tiles in white, blue, and green, there are verses from the Qur'an running along the walls, and artfully framed calligraphic renderings of the names of the first four *khalif*s (first leaders of Muslims after the death of the Prophet; i.e. Abu Bakr, Omar, Osman, Ali) and the name of one of the Prophet's grandsons, Hussein. Diagonally opposite the door is the high wooden *minbar*. To the left is a smaller pulpit just large enough to contain a chair for the preacher to sit in. This pulpit opens from the front and a small staircase can be pulled out to climb in. Pushed to the side along one wall are low tables and a few chairs for children's Qur'an studies. As the largest space in this facility, this room accommodates prayers and religious instruction, lectures for the community, interfaith dialogue, or other public events. The Hussein Mosque's prayer room is among the most intricately decorated ones in Stuttgart. Its details bespeak its members' dedication and investment of time and money.

Further down the hall (past the prayer room) is a small suite that includes a reception room and an office. This suite looks more like a residential apartment (it was one in the past) with a private office, than the administration of an institution. The first (large) room is furnished with a couch set and also contains a TV. It looks and feels like a living room. The windows on the left side open onto a backyard that includes a small wooden structure to sit in (*Laube*). This garden view enhances the sense of a comfortable home setting. The second room is Mr. Serdar's office, which can only be entered through the quasi-living room. The office contains a desk and a set of couches that accommodate about half a dozen people. The building's (lower) floor contains two more small rooms. The upper floor accommodates a small student dormitory, complete with kitchen, bedrooms, and living spaces. With its relative small premises, well-renovated and comfortably furnished rooms, the Hussein Mosque communicates a sense of home and familiarity. In part based on spatial limitations, the Hussein Mosque does not offer many activities for women. No formal space is set aside for their prayer or dedicated to their activities.

The VIKZ bought this building in 1993. Until then the community only had the limited facilities of the Takva Mosque located closer to downtown. Worshippers from Zuffenhausen and northern city quarters attended prayers and activities in the Takva Mosque. With the growing number of community members in these northern neighborhoods, "we decided," Mr. Serdar remembered, "to have a mosque in this community." The VIKZ bought the premises from a small Christian community, which closed for lack of members. Building codes stipulate that in case of a change of use of a building (*Nutzungsänderung*), all neighbors need to be informed and heard about the anticipated changes. If the mode of use (here as a religious facility) is continued, a transaction requires no hearing. No public uproar followed this real estate transaction. After some renovations the community settled into its new premises. Being aware of general public sentiments with regard to mosques, the community made sure to prevent problems with neighbors. Mr. Serdar emphasized that the mosque has always tried to be on the very best terms with its immediate neighbors and the Zuffenhausen community. Aware of the ever-present complains by the public about excessive noise, too many cars, and general parking problems, Mr. Serdar noted that from the beginning he told community members not to block streets or driveways. He furthermore stressed that the congregation always made efforts to invite visitors, and to participate in local events and activities.

In 2007 the Hussein Mosque had about 100 dues-paying members. "This means that the actual community is larger," Mr. Serdar noted, as only the heads of households are registered members, "but most have families who also attend the mosque and its activities." About seventy men regularly attend Friday prayers and more come for holiday prayers. The mosque has a large program of religious instruction for children and youths. On weekends the premises are full with children. "It is important for us to teach the young, and start with the children when they are small," Mr. Serdar explained, "because once they reach their teenage years, in particular the boys, many stop coming and get busy with other things. If they come here for a few years, then at least they know the basics. Many then come back once they get older, are married, and have their own children." In order to understand the localization of the Hussein Mosque it is helpful to look at the larger historical and organizational context of this small community.

The Associations of Islamic Cultural Centers

The Hussein Mosque traces its local ancestry to the Islamic Union that emerged in a small downtown location (Immenhofer Strasse) in 1968. It is among the oldest, if not the oldest such organized group in Stuttgart. Initially the group had no formal Imam. Some men who had worked as imams in Turkey took turns leading prayers. Occupying limited facilities, the community rented larger premises for holidays to accommodate prayers and celebrations. This group's first facility had been rented and organized by an informal group of men. The Islamic Union eventually emerged as an association that provided a broader organizational framework. In September 1973 the "Islamic Cultural Center" was founded and incorporated in Cologne as a legal association, which became the center of similarly minded associations in Germany.[15] The association absorbed or was joined by smaller local groups. As a growing umbrella organization, the Cologne association provided help and guidance for local groups among them the Islamic Union in Stuttgart. In 1980, a number of such small associations once more united as the Association of Islamic Cultural Associations (*Verband Islamischer Kulturzentren e.V.*; VIKZ) to create "a legally tangible and central capable (*handlungsfähige*) representation" on a national level (ibid.). Cologne remained the national headquarters (ibid.).[16] In 1980 the Stuttgarter community moved to a larger (rented) defunct industrial facility north of downtown, which became the Takva Mosque.

After several organizational transformations, individual VIKZ mosques today are independent legal associations (*Verein*), which operate under the national umbrella of the VIKZ and the regional LVIKZ (Regional Association of Islamic Cultural Centers). The Hussein and Takva Mosques each are such associations. Beyond the national level, the VIKZ is loosely tied to a global organization that maintains branches (run by Turkish immigrants) as far away as Australia and the United States (Jonker 2002). In 1979 the Islamic Cultural Center, which at the time was the leading Muslim association in Germany (Jonker 2002: 123), applied for the status of a public legal association (*Körperschaft des öffentlichen Rechts*). This is the status that the Protestant and Catholic Churches and the Central Jewish Council have, that allows close cooperation with the state and comes with benefits, like religious taxes (*Kirchensteuer*) being collected by the state and passed on to the religious organization (Fetzer and Soper 2005). In 1979 the Islamic Cultural Center maintained 150 communities in West Germany (ibid.: 91). A rather unfortunate campaign started by the Association of German Unions (*Deutscher Gewerkschaftsbund*) prevented a positive response to this application and created a hostile tone for decades to come.[17] In the process the Islamic Cultural Centers were labeled as reactionary. They were accused of indoctrinating children with outdated pedagogical methods. The association contested these claims, yet the accusations continued. The organization issued statements and corrections of its public image, but the community struggled with this damage to its reputation for years to come. The association was accused of being secretive and even militant. Yet none of these accusations were found to be true (Jonker 2002: 105).

Starting in the 1990s the VIKZ Cologne headquarters advised local communities to acquire properties instead of renting premises as many families had permanently settled in Germany (Jonker 2002: 125). In 1999 internal restructuring resulted in the creation of eleven regional associations (LVIKZ) that would be better in tune with individual communities than the distant Cologne headquarters.

Younger individuals were chosen as regional representatives who were well-suited for public appearances and capable of constructing a better social infrastructure for their communities (ibid.: 132). Internal (among them a change in national leadership) and external dynamics provoked the withdrawal of the VIKZ from public affairs in 2000. At the same time the association left the Central Council of Muslims (*Zentralrat der Muslime* ZMD). The national association's withdrawal was only temporary and the VIKZ has since resurfaced in public bodies. Many mosque communities continued their local involvements unabated. In 2007, the VIKZ was one of the founding members of the Muslim Coordination Council (*Koordinationsrat der Muslime*, KRM), a national association that brings together four larger Muslims associations (DİTİB; VIKZ; *Islamrat für die Bundesrepublik Deutschland*, IR; *Zentralrat der Muslime*, ZMD).

In 2002 the VIKZ had 315 mosques/centers in Germany and 135 in other western European countries (Jonker 2002: 127). These centers "exclusively focus[es] on Turkish speaking populations around the world" (ibid.: 128). Jonker calls them a "fundamentally Turkish phenomenon" (ibid.). In recent years, women have become increasingly involved in VIKZ communities and developed their own spheres and activities in congregations (Jonker 2002: 147). The association insists on equality in the religious sphere, yet the national administration remains a male domain (ibid.: 150; see also www.vikz.de). The core activity of the association and individual mosques remains the instruction of children, which is seen as a service to the larger Muslim community. The association carries the cost of this instruction (ibid.: 184). The age group of the ten- to thirteen-year-olds is the special target of these efforts, as it is increasingly hard to keep teenage boys in particular involved in mosque activities ("after they are fifteen it is very hard to keep most boys" as Mr. Serdar noted). Instructors hope to implant the seed of Islamic learning in these children, which might bear fruit later, or bring some individuals back to the mosque once they have children of their own.

Communities of Believers

Elements of today's VIKZ are rooted in fourteenth-century Bukhara (in today's Uzbekistan) where Sheikh Baha-uddin Naqshband by way of a dream/vision initiated a *sufi* (mystic) order with a new form of meditation: the silent *dhikr*. A religious "virtuosity" lived by way of "self discipline, inner strength and restraint" (Jonker 2002: 27) marked the emerging Naqshbandi Order. The imitation of the life of the Prophet Muhammad took a central position in the new order (ibid.: 30). Everyday piety was paramount for its (male) members. The teacher or sheikh played a crucial role for individuals in the process of initiation to a new lifestyle and religious experience. "Students initially were caught up in the love for their teacher. Only this experience could guide them on their way to God" (ibid.: 36).

The teacher transcended the role of instructor and became a living link to a chain that connected the individual believer back to the first believers, and ultimately to the Prophet Muhammad (ibid.: 268). Over the centuries the order developed a wide network of spiritual centers/lodges in the Ottoman Empire, India, and other places. Some lodges were places where politically and economically influential men withdrew to, and met. Women were absent from these activities (ibid.: 37). The radical politics of the young Turkish Republic in the 1920s put an abrupt end to these lodges, their activities and influence, and repositioned them as illegal or oppositional groups.

Suleyman Hilmi Tunahan (1888–1959) was born in the Balkans in the borderlands of today's Romania and Bulgaria. His early life was marked by the decline and disintegration of the Ottoman Empire, war, and refugee movements as Turks were pushed out of formerly Ottoman territories. His father provided the best possible Islamic education for young Suleyman and after years of struggle Suleyman studied theology at the Fatih Medrese in late Ottoman Istanbul. His studies included the prestigious training to be a judge (Jonker 2002: 51). Eventually he became a teacher/professor. The founding of the Turkish Republic in 1923 put a sudden end to Suleyman's career and world of classic Muslim learning. In 1924 the new government closed all institutions of Muslim learning in an attempt to undermine Ottoman-Islamic scholarship and power (ibid.: 56). The Naqshbandi Order was outlawed and its convents closed. All mosques were brought under government control and the religious bureaucracy was fired. Suleyman was robbed of his job, professional future, and spiritual/Sufi trajectory (ibid.: 57).

Public Istanbul in the 1920s was marked by rapid modernization and western lifestyles. There was little room for religion, and even less for religious scholars and Sufi mystics in the new republic. These changes, however, did not necessarily extend to the poorer urban quarters and even less to rural areas. Modernization and the creation of a laicist order ultimately resulted in a long-term "societal division which produced the emergence of a laicist and a religious camp" (Jonker 2002: 61). Suleyman was solidly rooted in the second. His position in the initial years of the republic was marginal. His expertise was not sought after; indeed it was seen as a threat. He withdrew and held onto his beliefs. Unlike others, Suleyman did not join political or resistance movements but turned his back to worldly affairs. Gerdien Jonker notes that he tended toward "praying for the world instead of acting in it" (ibid.: 63).

In 1928 religion and its practice were put under the control of a government agency. While operating in opposition to the state and its laicist principles, Suleyman—so the VIKZ self-portrait emphasizes—always remained within the "framework of the current constitution and the laws of the Turkish state" (www.vikz.de). Several legal cases were issued against him, but they either yielded no results or he was acquitted (ibid.). While the new government, elite, and part of the emerging middle class were favoring a western European social and political model,

Suleyman held on to a different model, that of the classic Sufi order, whose centerpiece was the teacher/master–student relationship. Faced with intense opposition to religion and religious learning, Suleyman increasingly saw it as his task to preserve and pass on precisely this knowledge, and the lifestyle and social order that went along with it. Suleyman started to develop a method of teaching and learning that allowed him to pass on this cherished knowledge, and to work toward the continuity of Muslim learning, often in the absence of any texts. Such teaching could only be done in the context of very personal (male) teacher-student relationships which remained deeply rooted in a religious-social environment where among others things, gender relations were clearly regulated and not much influenced by the policies of the new republic. Suleyman became a wandering teacher/preacher who traversed the country—predominantly the countryside—to teach whoever was willing to learn (Jonker 2002: 64). He spent over thirty years on the road. Just to carry religious books was at times a dangerous undertaking. In response Suleyman refined his method to quickly teach people—even the illiterate—to read Arabic and thus to read the Qur'an. Faced with adverse conditions and the lack of time on the part of his students, he created a selection of Naqshbandi learning based on "texts of eight centuries which he perceived as necessary to acquire knowledge about the tradition" (ibid.: 67). Many of Suleyman's students ended up preaching and teaching in their villages. His method and message flourished, relatively unnoticed by the government, in the countryside.

Suleyman Tunahan had two daughters whom, in the absence of sons, he began to instruct in Muslim theology. This default solution marked a break with the tradition of male students and teachers, and initiated the "tradition of female learning" (Jonker 2002: 69) which was to allow women a role in the community. By way of his activities Suleyman helped to create a female model that stood in contrast to the republican one. He fostered the vision of "an intelligent, indeed learned woman, who is well versed in Islamic sciences" (ibid.: 70). In the course of several decades of dedicated teaching Suleyman created a sizable network of students and followers: "By way of simple concentration and being a role model, Suleyman enabled [his students] to create a spiritual bond, without necessitating a mediator. Thus the centerpiece of the order was ready for transformation. And indeed the order did not dissolve, but took on the form of a lay community" (*Laiengemeinschaft*; ibid.: 75).

After years of hidden teaching, the religious situation eased in Turkey. Suleyman, who died in 1959, however, did live to see these more far-reaching changes. In 1959, the government instituted a course of study for teachers of religion. Yet expressions of religion continued to be marked as backward, and potentially dangerous for the state. After Suleyman's death, under the leadership of his son-in-law, the lay community grew and spread (Jonker 2002: 77). Their situation remained precarious, as the republic did not "recognize the loyalty to Islamic practices" as a rightful element of the public sphere. Instead authorities understood such practices "exclusively as an anti-republican attitude, which was sooner or later to lead to political subversion" (ibid.: 83). Regardless, members of the lay community continued Suleyman's work and taught and preached (mostly in remote places). Through the ups and downs of the turbulent 1970s and the military dictatorship in the 1980s, the lay community attracted more believers. The community paid special attention to the young and their religious instruction in midst of state enforced laicism. By 1986 "the Suleyman community took care of 100,000 youths in 450 centers in Turkey, the state in contrast reached only 62,000 youths" (ibid.: 90). Because Suleyman's influence was most profound in the countryside and most labor migrants came from rural villages, it is not surprising, that in the absence of a hostile state, dedicated individuals soon founded communities in Germany.

Connecting Fates and Histories

The histories of Zuffenhausen, Naqshbandi Sufism, and the lay community initiated by Suleyman Tunahan unfolded in different locations. For a long time, they were only very remotely connected by way of large-scale political encounters and possibly elite travel and trade. The lives of peasants in Zuffenhausen and those in Anatolian villages unfolded at a distance to one another, until more recent processes of globalization brought them together. When followers of Suleyman Tunahan bought the defunct premises of a small Christian community, individuals who had hitherto known little about the respective other constituency started to interact, slowly got to know each other, and reluctantly started to negotiate a vaguely shared future.

Like in many other new mosque communities, the Hussein Mosque's initial years were spent renovating premises and consolidating the community, its internal organization, activities, and groups. In this period the mosque's board established good neighborly relations in its immediate vicinity. Once the community had settled into its premises and routine communal life, it started to look beyond its confines and sought out possibilities of local participation (Schmid, Akça, and Barwig 2008: 98). Mr. Serdar repeatedly emphasized how important good neighborliness, participation in local affairs, and cooperation with local authorities have always been for the Hussein Mosque. He and others understood that it was essential for the mosque's local recognition, participation, and inclusion to create a visible presence, work against prejudices and stereotypes, construct a role for the mosque in the community, and become a regular local player.

With a smile, Mr. Serdar recounted the initial surprise of some officials when several years ago he asked to participate in a municipal Christmas celebration. Nobody had expected that a mosque community would be interested in such an event. After he stated his interest, Mr. Serdar was invited and attended the event. Other invitations followed. With his tireless efforts and many instances of successful cooperation, Mr. Serdar and the Hussein Mosque slowly entered public circuits and became increasingly well-known as a local institution with a keen interest in public affairs and civic cooperation. Mr. Serdar's and the mosque's names became permanent entries in the phone lists of local authorities, churches, and civic associations. Numerous small steps and minute engagements fostered this inclusion.

Open Mosque

In the late 1990s mosque associations introduced the annual Day of the Open Mosque when mosques open their doors to the public and offer events for their neighbors and the interested public. National mosque associations decided to schedule this day on October 3 (German national holiday that marks the reunification) to symbolize the inclusion of Muslims into the new Germany. The significance of the Day of the Open Mosque was dramatically altered after 9/11, and ever more mosques participated in the event. Suddenly, after decades of public disinterest and neglect, mosques had moved center stage. They were scrutinized as potential threats to state security, and accused of harboring radical preachers, oppressing women, and indoctrinating children with unsuitable ideas. It was up to mosques to prove otherwise to the often-resentful local and national public (Schmid, Akça, and Barwig 2008: 100).

On October 3, 2006, I called Mr. Serdar at the Hussein Mosque. I had previously met him at an event and he had agreed to further cooperation. He explained that his mosque did not participate in this year's Open Day because they had had their own open house (*kermes*) in spring (see also below). Nevertheless he invited me to the mosque because he had work to do and had time to talk about my project. On this rainy afternoon I went to the Hussein Mosque for the first time. Standing in the hall, somewhat lost and waiting for Mr. Serdar, a man offered to find Mr. Serdar. Soon Mr. Serdar arrived. In his forties, wearing shirt, tie and a dress jacket, Mr. Serdar looked formal, but immediately impressed me with his friendly, kind, open, and sociable personality. First, we briefly sat in a small front office next to the prayer room. After about ten minutes we moved to his office in the back. We talked informally about my project, the mosque, community, and larger VIKZ organization. Several times men entered the office to ask Mr. Serdar questions or to pick up items. Mr. Serdar explained things to me, answered the men's questions, and handed out requested materials. It was apparent that Mr. Serdar was in charge, and that he was a gentle, well-liked, and respected person.

We had talked less than half an hour when a young man brought in a middle-aged ethnic German visitor. The newcomer reported that he had found the mosque's address on a list of "open" mosques on the Internet. Mr. Serdar invited the visitor to join our conversation. The visitor introduced himself as a teacher in a middle school (*Realschule*), and started asking questions. We moved from questions about the community to those about the meaning of Ramadan (it was Ramadan) and soon arrived at the ubiquitous headscarf debate. For this teacher the headscarf was something non-/pre-modern that did not fit into our contemporary world. When Mr. Serdar related how many educated or "modern" women wore headscarves and participated in all sorts of activities, the teacher objected: "but aren't there also many modern women in Muslim countries?" Mr. Serdar responded "but this has nothing to do with modern or not. There is no such contrast or difference." It was hard for the teacher to move the image of a woman with a headscarf into his modern secular universe. It was equally hard for him to understand that the divine could play such a role for somebody who was "modern." In the middle of the headscarf debate, a younger couple arrived, also for the Open Day. From then on every five or ten minutes somebody else arrived. The young helpers brought in extra chairs. Soon, two people had to stand by the door, as about a dozen visitors squeezed into the small office. Mr. Serdar, even though he had earlier announced that he had to leave, moved the whole group to the prayer room. There he explained the mosque facility and answered more questions. An older man who had been walking along with the group offered to pray one *raka* (unit of the prayer) for the guests. More visitors arrived. Eventually the first group, including myself, started to leave and Mr. Serdar handed everybody a small booklet with further information. Then he guided a second tour. Mr. Serdar's patient and flexible handling of this (unplanned) Open Day reflects his broader public engagement and the mosque's involvement in the quarter's public sphere.

Ramadan and the Long Night of Culture

The ongoing search of villages, towns, and urban quarters for new festivals, events, and entertainment has started to encroach onto the night. Long nights of museums and culture are recent additions to urban festive landscapes. In September 2007 Zuffenhausen had its *1. Zuffenhäuser Kulturnacht* (1st Zuffenhausen Night of Culture). The numbering of the event hints at the invention of a new tradition. For this inaugural night, twenty local institutions and associations held open houses, staged performances and shows, and many shops remained open until 11 P.M.[18] The Hussein Mosque participated with an open house. Starting in the later afternoon, young men gave mosque tours to the interested public. As the long night occurred in the month of Ramadan, Mr. Serdar conveniently combined the open door and long culture night with the VIKZ's annual turn in the Christian-Muslim dialogue organization's (*Gesellschaft für Christlich-islamische Begegnung und Zusammenarbeit*; CIBZ) *iftar* cycle. Because of the limited space in the mosque, Mr. Serdar rented a school gym and invited the mosque community, official guests, and friends of the mosque from Zuffenhausen and beyond.

When I arrived at the gym over half hour before sunset (fast-breaking time), the place was still empty. There were long rows of tables neatly set up for the meal. Young men were busy running back and forth, bringing in the last few items, arranging and rearranging things here and there. Mr. Serdar, as the host, was helping and greeting guests. The tables were set up in two sections. A front section of several tables closer to the stage was reserved for invited guests. A similar-sized section to the back was for community members. As no guests were seated yet, I walked through the invitee section to read the name cards, which included a broad selection of local and city representatives. Mr. Serdar and his colleagues had cast their net wide and wisely. The invited guests included, among others, representatives of local churches; the head of the local council (*Bezirksvorsteher*); the city's representative for migration; representatives of several other mosque associations; a Turkish-German social democrat city councilman; and one of the presidents of the city's other Christian-Muslim interfaith initiative (*Koordinationsrat des Christlich-Islamischen Dialogs*; KCID), who is a widely sought-after figure in public debates. While not everybody showed up, many invitees did come.

Because this event was new in this context (gym), and the guests (entire community, invited Muslim and non-Muslim guests) had never met in this formation, spatial arrangements needed to be negotiated as the event unfolded. Soon after I arrived, the Muslim president of the interfaith dialogue association, Mr. Mamdouh, and his wife, whom I knew from other occasions, arrived. We started to chat and Mr. Serdar soon came over to offer chairs. There was initial confusion about where men and women should sit. Mr. Serdar first said that men and women would sit separately, as was the custom of the community. Mrs. Mamdouh and I went to a table in the second (community) section where women would be seated. As more of the non-Muslim invitees arrived, couples started to sit together. Mr. Serdar became uncomfortable with our assigned seats, came over and said Mrs. Mamdouh and I could sit in the invitee section. He apologized and noted that the community women were not used to sitting with men. There were a few more such back and forth moves when, for instance, a young female German convert sat in the community's women section and then moved to the invitee section.

The uncertain seating arrangements and their ongoing negotiation symbolize larger processes of localization. Community members were used to sit in gender-segregated arrangements whereas many invitees (Muslim and non-Muslim) preferred to sit together as couples or in mixed-gender arrangements. In the end the entire hall was vaguely separated between the community (in the back) and the invitees (in the front), but some individuals moved back and forth between the quarters. A look at the invitee section disclosed additional patterns and compromises. Some representatives of other mosque associations who would at events in their own mosques sit in gender-segregated arrangements, sat as couples among the non-Muslim guests. Muslim and non-Muslim couples (of various ethnicities) shared tables, and a number of Turkish and/or Muslim men of different religiosities who had come without their wives occupied another table. This male contingent included an assortment of representatives of the Milli Görüş community, left-leaning social workers, and social democratic politicians that are rarely seen together. In the end it seemed that everybody was comfortable with their place and company.

The event, which included short greetings and speeches, was a success. While some community members and guests stayed with their own groups, they shared the hall, listened to the same speakers, witnessed other guests, and found an agreeable mode of sitting and socializing. The initial back and forth and insecurity about seating arrangements symbolizes negotiations about larger "social seating arrangements." What events can best bring people together? Who should compromise their ways in what manner? What are the ways and arrangements that make such events acceptable and indeed enjoyable for everybody involved? Mr. Serdar's initial moving around of guests is best understood as his flexible managements of needs and sensitivities. A *modus vivendi* was quickly found. The seating arrangement allowed for different groups to encounter each other from a distance, but also, if they were ready, from nearby. Many guests moved places in the course of the evening.

The Night of Culture was an especially suitable event for the Hussein Mosque to participate because it constituted the establishment of a new festive tradition. Unlike in the parade, where the mosque had joined an existing event, here they were part, as founding participants, of the introduction of a new form or emerging tradition. Mr. Serdar's innovative idea of the large *iftar* (by invitation only for non-community members) was a success and a cultural building block in which individual labor, creative social imagination, local cooperation, and respect produce a more inclusive cityscape.

Socializing: The *Kermes*

The Hussein Mosque not only participates in neighborhood activities and celebrations, but also invites others to its premises. For years the community has been organizing an annual *kermes* or small fair to which they invite members, neighbors, the local community, and all those interested. Annual *kermes* events, which usually take place in late spring to early summer, are a mainstay of the urban (and regional) mosque-scape and serve multiple purposes. They accommodate community building and socializing. At the same time they are fundraisers where the women cook and bake fantastic amounts of food, which is sold for the community's benefit. At some events handmade crafts like embroidered pillowcases or crocheted tablecloths are sold. At a *kermes* one can also buy religious literature and religiously inspired products (e.g. headscarves and other accessories). Some individuals (see Emine, chapter 3) take the *kermes* season as a chance to visit other mosques and strengthen ties of friendship with people and places. It is increasingly expected for mosque representatives to pay visits to other mosques' *kermes*. Emine noticed for the Salam Mosque's *kermes* in 2011 that representatives from all other Turkish mosques had come. Framed by the season of popular festivals and street and neighborhood fairs, the Hussein Mosque *kermes* employs established models and pulls them into the context and service of the mosque. Set up in good weather in the mosque's front and back yards, the *kermes* attracts Muslims and non-Muslims who in this casual atmosphere can enjoy relaxed conversations, socialize, and eat good food.

The Hussein *kermes* in April 2007[19] included "traditional" tents complete with carpets, golden teacups, water-pipes, cushions, decorations, and crafts hung from the walls. On Mr. Serdar's pictures, mosque officials had their photographs taken with each other and with non-Muslim visitors in these tents. More space was provided in large "regular" tents. Seated on the standard festival benches (*Bierbänke*), individuals and families (men and women), insiders and outsiders enjoyed food and conversation. In the mosque's small backyard, behind Mr. Serdar's office, some women, seated on the ground in front of low tables, were preparing Turkish bread for visitors to watch and eat. In the prayer room there were clothes and books on display for sale. Other than the plentiful women with headscarves and the breadbaking activities, the event looked like many other urban summer celebrations. Favored by the location in a residential neighborhood and ownership of a front yard, this outdoor event carries the mosque to the outside and eases visitors' way in. Visible for neighbors and passers-by, the fair minimizes barriers of entrance. Visitors can take a look from the street at this familiar festivity with food, drink (other than alcohol), and socializing, before entering. Unlike an open house at a mosque, the *kermes* provides an entry to the community without an obligation to engage with religious features.

Social Work

The VIKZ runs student dormitories in Germany and elsewhere.[20] Their goal is to support students who visit public schools and provide them with Islamic instruction. The students (most are between twelve and eighteen years old) reside in the dormitories and attend local schools and occasionally also universities. The dormitory provides room and board, tutoring services, Islamic instruction based on Suleyman Tunahan's model, and social and cultural activities. Students pay a monthly fee of about €150, the association covers the rest of the cost (Markert *SN* 29.5.2008; Ackermann et al. 2006). During the week the students live in the dormitory. They spend part of the weekend at home with their families, but return to the mosque for more religious instruction. The dormitories are based on older Turkish models where in towns or cities students from the countryside took up residence in dormitories if they had no relatives to stay with. These institutions provided a home away from home and often included possibilities to further Islamic instruction for young men as they learned other professions. In the German context, the idea of providing boys (and girls) with profound Islamic instruction and socializing them into properly Islamic lifestyle has remained largely the same. The reasons for running or joining a dormitory have, however, changed. In a social context where many immigrant youths, in particular Turkish boys, struggle with school and are more likely than others to drop out, and fall victim to the temptations of street culture, and even worse petty crime and street violence, student dormitories take on another function. They provide a sheltered space that is characterized by strict rules that prevent boys from aimlessly hanging out in the streets. Instead, the rather rigid schedule and close supervision foster more thorough engagement with school and provide academic support for those whose parents cannot provide it.

The Hussein Mosque includes an upper floor with residential facilities. In the late 1990s these facilities were used for occasional weekend activities for girls. A girls' student dormitory (*Schülerwohnheim*) was planned on this floor in 2001.[21] These plans were controversial among the board of directors. Some older board members figured it would be easy to set up a dormitory modeled on experiences in Turkey. Student dormitories worked in Turkey and had been established elsewhere in Germany (some were licensed and others were not; see Ackermann et al. 2006). Why then, the elders' argument, should this not work in Zuffenhausen? Why would the local community care much about these plans? The older men's attitude bespeaks on the one side their distance to the local social and legal reality, and on the other side is the result of having been ignored for decades by dominant society. They did not conceive of the new institution as being part of local society. Instead it belonged to a different Turkish reality. Whether the dormitory was in tune with the legal framework of youth welfare agencies (*Jugendamt*) was not their concern. Some younger board members were hesitant and warned against the trouble such an endeavor could produce. In the meanwhile the younger faction contacted the *Jugendamt*, which eventually noted that because of the limited size of the facility the planned dormitory could only accommodate ten students. Internally, the older faction prevailed and a girls' dormitory was set up in August 2001 before the necessary license was granted. Some girls were registered in the addresses of local community members. Reflecting about this girls' dormitory, Mr. Serdar noted: "Mr. Ömer [see chapter 1] and I had warned about starting this project without a license, but some of the other board members thought that it would just be like in Turkey and things would just work out. At the same time we were trying to apply for a license."

Things quickly unfolded in the fall of 2001. Authorities soon realized that the (unlicensed) dormitory was operating. At the same time, the heated controversy over the VIKZ's purchase of a factory complex in Stuttgart-Heslach was at its height (see chapter 1) and 9/11 fundamentally changed the political landscape. The dormitory conflict escalated. Local police and state security took over and contacted Mr. Serdar. Only because of Mr. Serdar's excellent local connections and his ability to explain intentions, there was no immediate police raid of the dormitory. Instead, he explained, "The three of us, the local head of police, the state security officer, and I went to the mosque, all in plain clothes, to avoid a scandal in the neighborhood. The two officials looked at the dormitory and we immediately folded its operation and the girls were sent home. A week later, nonetheless, several police cars and police officers in uniform showed up to close the dormitory, but nobody was there any longer. Of course all the neighbors saw the police entering the building."

The case of the short-lived girls' dormitory illustrates the generational conflict within the association's board of directors where older members were not too concerned about local legal issues and looked to establish an institution based on Turkish models. They were not ready to listen to the younger members' doubts, as the German legal frame appeared distant to their reasoning. Years of neglect from the side of dominant society had taught them to quietly proceed with their plans. But times had changed and 9/11 had refueled dominant society's fears and resentment of Islam and Muslim activities. Disregard was replaced by resentment, fear, and suspicion. *Jugendamt* regulations stipulate a clear framework for running a dormitory. To close down an unlicensed facility is a routine administrational procedure initiated by the *Jugendamt*. The presence in this case of the head of police and state security for a standard social welfare procedure indicates much larger tension and fear.

In the political climate of December 2001, the closure of a small girls' dormitory in a mosque was no longer a simple intervention to correct violations of youth welfare laws, but became a political case. At this historical moment of political hype and overreaction, an unlicensed dormitory evoked (irrational) fears of militant training camps or radical mosque schools in distant lands. The mosque elders' once neglected or even shunned world moved center stage for political authorities and members of dominant society. The violation of administrative regulations now constituted a threat to state security.

After the dormitory was shut down, the mosque's board of directors applied for a license—this time for a boys' dormitory—which was eventually temporarily granted for the period between 2003 and 2005. After 2005 the dormitory received an unlimited license. In 2007 this small institution accommodated ten school-age boys who attended public schools and lived in the upstairs quarters of the mosque. Two outside homework tutors who come several afternoons a week provide academic support to residents. They further receive Islamic religious instruction and practice their faith together. A young teacher and educator, Mr. Arslan, lives with the boys in the mosque and oversees aspects of their religious instruction and coordinates social and cultural activities.

In 2007 two students explained about their lives in the dormitory, that they were here for the better grades that this way of life provided for them. It was the outside world, or concretely success in mainstream society, that guided their decision to live in the mosque. When I asked them about their professional trajectories, they mentioned engineering and other university studies. Mr. Arslan mentioned past success stories of those who finished their *Abitur*[22] and moved on to university studies. Another resident noted that he was going to finish his *Mittlere Reife*[23] this summer and then leave: "Things worked well here for me, but now it is time to move on." While religious instruction and practices play a central role in the dormitory, success in mainstream society is frequently mentioned as a motivation to join such an institution. Fear of male street culture and its detrimental effects on teenage boys is an important aspect for some parents. The mother of one boy explained her rationale for sending her son: "I want him to succeed in school and not to hang around on the street. Too much happens out there. One of my son's old friends already fathered a child. I want something different for my son. They help here with his schoolwork and they closely watch him. I appreciate that."

The boys similarly valued the help with schoolwork, but also commented on the support and friendship in the group. The timetable keeps them focused and allows for an intense communal experience. This strict plan and supervision provide structure and rules when some parents fear losing control over sons, as the mother of an eight-year-old boy (who lived at home) said, "I am not looking forward to him being fifteen. What if he starts hanging out with those boys in the streets? What are they doing there? They don't work or do anything. They just get into trouble."

Talking to some older boys in the dormitory, it was obvious that they had their eyes on academic success. They saw the dormitory as an excellent way to pursue this goal. The success of some of their predecessors who now attended universities further motivated them. None of the few boys that I talked to mentioned a religious career as a possibility. In a different context an older community member remarked on career choices: "Once a boy has his *Abitur* and can study engineering or computers, nobody thinks about becoming a *hoca* [preacher or imam] any longer. It pays nothing compared to what they can make with a good university degree."

Dormitories like the Hussein Mosque's are often accused to fostering a withdrawal into separate worlds, yet a closer look at the dormitory shows that the teenagers are motivated by the hope for success in the world beyond the mosque. Parents and elders in the mosque are aware of the dangers of street life and hope to provide these boys with an alternative. The dormitory is not a space of escape from society, but a sheltered space that prepares boys for success in society.

On a typical day, the boys' lives are structured by to a relatively fixed schedule. At 6:15 A.M. they get up and ready for school. Those who have no afternoon lessons at school return for lunch. Between 1 P.M. and 2:30 P.M. they can play, do sports, or watch TV. From 2:30 until 5:00 P.M. the tutors come to supervise and help with homework. Those with afternoon lessons return from school later. Between 5 and 6:30 P.M. the boys can play computers or read. Then they eat dinner together. Between 7:30 and 8:30 P.M. there is religious instruction. After 8:30 P.M. there is more quiet or reading time. By 9:15 P.M. the boys go to sleep. The boys perform their daily prayers together which adds a second, however, always changing structure to their lives. In the winter, their shared evening prayer roughly marks the end of their afternoon tutoring session. They perform their night prayer around dinnertime. In June and July when the days are long and the evening, night, and morning prayers all occur during their sleep hours, the boys go to sleep later to perform the evening prayer. "Then," one of the older boys explained, "We go to sleep and set the alarm clock for a rather late night prayer. Then we perform the night prayer just after 1 A.M. After that we wait for about ten minutes and go right ahead with the morning prayer. That way we do not have to get up twice in the night." In the winter all the prayers fall into the boys' regular waking hours. The Imam, Mr. Arslan, and other occasional teachers, teach daily religious instruction and lessons. All religious instruction is in Turkish. The students learn the basics of their faith by way of the VIKZ manual *Ilmihal* and other theological texts. On weekends they join their peers who only attend weekend instruction.

In addition to their academic and religious studies, the boys participate in the upkeep and cleaning of the mosque. They help serving meals and keeping their rooms (two boys share a room) and shared bathroom facilities clean. Mr. Arslan noted that this fosters responsibility in particular for those who are used to their mothers doing all the work for them. When asked why, in addition to academic ambitions, they preferred life in the dormitory, one teenager noted, that the boys in the dormitory were "more decent" than those on the street, they used better language and were more focused. "We do not go out like others in the evening," he added, "and that keeps us out of a lot of trouble."

When I asked Mr. Arslan what exactly the role of religion was for him in the context of his work and instruction of the boys, he explained: "Religion is everything. Religion is practiced by way of cleanliness, hard and dedicated work. It is practiced in school and at work. Success in that way also is part of religion. Religion, life, and good deeds, they are all one. This is part of what makes my work so interesting, but also very challenging. Education is never easy. But with courage and love, education can succeed." Apart from the regular academic and religious activities, there are occasional social and cultural activities like trips in the region (e.g. museums, fun/activity parks). The boys play ping pong, soccer, or go to the public pool. The dormitory invites occasional outside speakers for seminars about topics such as drugs, alcohol, or professional orientation. They invite professionals (e.g. a lawyer) to inform the teenagers about their work.

Our Mosque

The list of the Hussein Mosque's activities is long. For instance, I attended lectures for women about Internet use by children and teenagers, and a drug prevention series organized by the local police. The first such event was slow. The second one, for which the officer brought huge show cases of drugs and drug paraphernalia, sparked considerable debate, and the women asked many questions. While the organizational context of the events was imbalanced, as one woman noted: "it was more that the police wanted to come and make contacts," this second session was a success as most of the women actively engaged in the debate. When the organizers handed out feedback sheets asking the women how useful the event had been, I sat with a group of women who started to discuss what exactly counted for addiction. One woman related the story of her neighbor who was very worried about her husband who habitually took painkillers, but claimed that this was no problem. "But my neighbor thinks he takes way too much and too regularly. Isn't that addiction, too?" This sparked a debate among four women about the limits of the "regular" use of medication.

Participating in activities and bringing outsiders to the mosque are crucial issues for Mr. Serdar and others in the community. Toward the end of the *iftar* at the local gym (see above), I talked to Mr. Serdar about the event and the open house at the mosque (which neither he nor I had attended). He called over two young men who had served as guides in the mosque. They proudly reported that there had been more than seventy visitors. Mr. Serdar was surprised, as he noted he had only bought ten of the entrance bracelets for the event that visitors could buy at any participating place for all other places. When I chatted with Mr. Serdar about the mosque's participation in the Open Night of Culture, I asked whether the head of the local council indeed called him now for every public event or celebration, just like he called the churches and other associations.

"Yes," Mr. Serdar responded, and quickly added, "and that's how it should be!" He smiled and I agreed with him. The Hussein Mosque is an increasingly recognized and respected part of the local public sphere. Since the original formation of a migrant workers' prayer room in the 1960s, the Hussein Mosque and the LVIKZ have come a long way. The mosque transformed from an all male to a more family-centered institution. It moved from "invisible" rented facilities to visible own premises. Today the mosque includes a vibrant program of Islamic instruction for children and youth, and runs a successful licensed student dormitory. The mosque is seen by many, in particular the local council, as "our" mosque and is included in activities that warrant the participation of local constituencies. The quarter of Zuffenhausen and the Hussein Mosque community have worked hard to get to know each other. In the process the sense of the "other" side has increasingly given way to a partnership that is marked by belonging and participation.

In the initial months of my research I had marveled at the exemplary cooperation of the Hussein Mosque and Zuffenhausen's local council and administration. While this is, to use Mr. Serdar's words "how it should be," it is still far from the reality for most mosque communities. I wondered whether there was a unique element that had facilitated this cooperation. One day in a conversation with Mr. Serdar's daughter, we came to talk about this unique cooperation, and in particular the close relationship between her father and the head of the local council. She laughed and said, "well, we have known him [head of the local council] quite well for a long time, as I went to school with his children." While this certainly does not explain the whole extend of this successful cooperation, it points to an important element of personal familiarity, respect, and trust that had developed between the two men over the years of knowing each other, not only as municipal administrator and mosque president, but also as fathers and private individuals. This relationship helped nurture the success and position of the Hussein Mosque in Zuffenhausen and indicates how important personal relationships of respect are in process of successful localization. It is less the large-scale programs, discussions, and conferences that create viable new communities and cultural landscapes that accommodate the needs of all stakeholders, but the everyday steps and hard work of dedicated individuals. The Hussein Mosque has come a long way toward becoming "our mosque," and considerable work remains to be done for other mosques to become similarly ordinary and undisputed parts of the city.

Representing Zuffenhausen

The Hussein Mosque is visible and present at many local events, yet remains invisible and unaccounted for in larger discourses and representations. Immigrants are rarely acknowledged as crucial makers and shapers of German urban cultures. When Zuffenhausen celebrates its dramatic post–World War II reconstruction, industrial growth, and cultural achievements, immigrants deserve as much credit for their labor as do locals and ethnic German war refugees. Some timid advances have been made, like the inclusion in the parade, yet blatant blind spots and misrepresentations remain.

The detailed 600-page history of Zuffenhausen (Gühring 2004), for instance, does not mention any Muslim presence. The book includes a thorough overview of contemporary churches and secular associations (ibid.: 559–84) but does not introduce the Hussein Mosque (or other Muslim congregations).[24] In the two chapters dedicated to the post–World War II era (Beer 2004; Meyle 2004), there are only two brief mentions of southern European labor migrants, specifically Italians in the context of the housing shortage in the 1950s (Beer 2004: 515, 516). Zuffenhausen's image as drawn by Albrecht Gühring and his collaborators reflects only one (limited) perspective on the community's recent history. Other groups and actors are neither recognized nor described. This perspective is not surprising when one looks at the picture of the members of the local history association (Meyle 2004: 548), which includes only middle-aged to older ethnic German males. Zuffenhausen's local council in 2003 was an all-ethnic German assembly (ibid.: 544). Gühring's book, like other similar ones (e.g. Jürgen Hagel on Bad Cannstatt, 2002) constitute accounts of quarters that are populated and shaped by ethnic Germans (see also Faltin and Lorenz 2011). With the power of urban discourse and image making still vested in dominant German political bodies, texts, and civic associations, it is not surprising that the presence of Muslims is often ignored or becomes a matter of public controversy. The stunning silence about the contributions of multi-ethnic urban constituencies is particularly ironic and painful in a community like Zuffenhausen, where as of 2011 more than half of the residents have migratory roots.

The Hussein Mosque's local inclusion is a laudable achievement for all involved, but unfortunately it is far from the norm, and remains restricted to its immediate quarter. The processes of Islam becoming a recognized local religion and Muslims becoming participants and shapers of urban cultures are still in their early stages. If organized Muslim communities continue to face such a steep uphill battle, the question emerges of how do individuals pious Muslims fare in their everyday lives and neighborhoods. I will examine such individual lives and experiences in a multi-ethnic urban quarter with a large Muslim population in the next chapter.

Notes

1. School vacations start by the end of July, hence many people have to stay put in June and July.
2. This description of Zuffenhausen and the Unterländer Strasse is based on notes from 2009. There is a fluctuation of stores on this street. On the U15, see also *Der 15er* (2011).
3. The postwar satellite of Rot, an assortment of smaller apartment blocks and high rises houses about 10,000 residents (Landeshauptstadt Stuttgart 2012/13: 307).
4. Nuspl is the real name of this store.
5. This comparative figure is for administrational units. There are smaller units that have higher percentages.
6. Setting up two barbeques is becoming a standard procedure for festivities in multi-ethnic quarters.
7. Friedrich and Kull report about two *Urwege* (pre-Roman roads) crossing at Zuffenhausen. One east-west path came from Pforzheim, it crossed with a less important north-south path (2004: 58).
8. The route was run by Thurn and Taxis. The headquarters of Porsche are located on this old postal route (Friedrich and Kull 2004: 61).
9. To become a *Bürger* (town/village citizen with full civic rights) depended on the ownership of property.
10. In 1621 Zuffenhausen had 514 inhabitants, by 1641 there were only 98 left (Gühring 2004c: 222).

11. For accounts of the fates of Stuttgarter Jews during the Holocaust, see e.g. Marx (2004) and Uhlmann (1992). See also http://www.stolpersteine-stuttgart.de. This website provides biographical sketches for at least four murdered Jews from Zuffenhausen (Julius Beikert, Franziska and Siegfried Sander, Pauline Schneider).
12. Until 1931, 38 buildings with 227 apartments were finished (Messerschmidt 1957: 71).
13. By the end of the war of a total of 3,205 residential buildings, 313 were completely destroyed, 247 were seriously damaged, 468 were damaged, and 1,171 were slightly damaged (Messerschmidt 1957: 80).
14. Freudenreich estimated in the same article that about 40 percent of the quarter's population was Muslim (*SZ* 26.1.2009). This estimate seems rather high.
15. http://www.vikz.de.
16. Cologne is the head quarter of several national mosque associations.
17. Jonker (2002: 91) provides an account of this affair that illustrates a curious mix of German and Turkish political camps, and irrational fears that were to frame debates for years to come.
18. Since Germany has laws regulating opening hours for stores, these are unusually long hours.
19. I did not attend this event. My description is based on pictures and Mr. Serdar's account.
20. In 2008, the VIKZ ran sixteen boys' and three girls' dormitories in Germany (Markert *SZ* 29.5.2008). Mr. Serdar reported about new dormitories in countries like Malaysia, Japan, and South Africa.
21. The following account is based on a conversation with Mr. Serdar on July 21, 2008.
22. School diploma (twelfth or thirteenth grade) that is a prerequisite for university studies.
23. School diploma (tenth grade) that is a prerequisite for most white-collar apprenticeships (e.g. banking, insurances, nursing etc.).
24. Similarly, the book provides only a brief passage about the fate of local Jews, where in the case of Moritz Moses Horkheimer, it is not even mentioned that the family was Jewish. The book simply notes that the Horkheimers were forced into exile (Müller 2004: 402).

CHAPTER 6

In the Neighborhood

Dzamila had invited Ulrike, Amra, and me with our children for coffee and playing on one of the first days of the school summer vacation in 2007. Eleven children ran around the apartment, which was almost empty because Dzamila and her family were moving and had packed most of their belongings. The (former) living room, where we sat, contained only some mattresses on which Dzamila and her three children had slept the last few nights. Dzamila served coffee and cookies on a shaky small table around which we sat on the floor. The children enjoyed the spaciousness of the empty apartment. Dzamila and Amra are from Bosnia and Ulrike is a German convert to Islam. All lived in Stuttgart-Nordbahnhof, and had children in the Park School which is how we met. On this summer morning, the mood was relaxed. As the children played, we started talking about some recent problems with the Islamic religious instruction class at the school.[1] In an act of messy planning, the Islamic studies teacher had scheduled a trip to an out-of-town mosque for first graders on the same day as these children went to a theater production on the Killesberg which involved a forty-five minute hike each way. On the day in question, I had chaperoned the theater trip and was surprised that some of these six and seven years olds would have to go on a second trip which included a half-hour train ride. The children had looked exhausted after the theater trip. It turned out that once we arrived back at the school, the Islamic studies teacher had cancelled the trip after she had learned about the theater excursion. At Dzamila's coffee hour, Ulrike vented her anger at this incident on several accounts. First, she noted that the planning had been a mess. How could the teacher plan a trip when there already was another major outing on the same day? Dzamila and Amra agreed, but added to the teacher's defense that she was not from the Park School and only came for the Islamic religious instruction, thus she was out of touch with the everyday flow of things at the school. Ulrike further complained that to call off a trip at such short notice was irresponsible as parents had planned accordingly. She noted that one of her friends had scheduled a doctor's appointment for that afternoon knowing that her son would be away for the afternoon.

If it had not been for Ulrike who took the boy home, he would have been left on the street for the entire afternoon. How could the teacher not think of this when calling off a trip? Why had she not kept the children for a regular lesson instead? And to top it all, Ulrike reported, the teacher had collected €5 per child for the trip. The money had never been returned to Ulrike's daughter. As Ulrike gained momentum with her anger, she said: "First thing next school year, I will go to the principal and complain about this and demand my €5 back. It is my right to have this money returned, even if I have to make a fuss. I will not remain quiet about this mess. And the organizational issues need to be addressed as well. If I cannot rely on the instruction taking place when it is supposed to, this does not work!"

She talked fast and continued to vent her anger. Dzamila eventually looked at her and very calmly said: "Ulrike, you need to practice *sabr* [patience; Arabic], you are a Muslim." Amra added: "*Sabr* is important. Things go wrong and people make mistakes. Just ask for your money and leave it at that." Ulrike responded, "Patience is good, but I just cannot put up quietly with this woman's mess. I need to voice my points for these things to change." The conversation went back and forth on this topic for a while longer, but soon turned to the issue of Dzamila's pending move, what was left to do, and how we would all miss her.

In May 2007 Stuttgart's soccer team, the VfB Stuttgart, won the national championship (*Bundesliga*). On the Saturday afternoon toward the end of the decisive match, I was walking with friends down the main street of the Nordbahnhof neighborhood. We passed one of the many bars on the street where about a dozen young boys were watching the final minutes of the game through a window standing outside on the sidewalk. The very moment as we passed the boys, one could hear the referee blowing the whistle—the game was over. The multi-ethnic group of young boys, among whom I recognized some of the local Afghan boys, immediately broke out in screams: "STUTTGART! STUTTGART! STUTTGART! VFB! VFB! "STUTTGART! VFB!" The boys yelled at the top of their lungs as they hugged each other and jumped up and down the sidewalk. Stuttgart was national champion. A few more screams could be heard from surrounding apartments. Only seconds later, firecrackers went off further down the street. Stuttgart's success, which would end in a super-size public celebration attended by almost 100,000 fans on the downtown Schlossplatz (Castle Square) and elsewhere in the city for most of the night, was already loudly celebrated in this working-class immigrant neighborhood.

The women's coffee hour, and the boys' noisy soccer celebration have little in common, other than that they took place in the same neighborhood, Nordbahnhof, and both included diverse participants. The scenes illustrate elements of cultural interactions and ongoing transformations in small urban spaces where ordinary people casually debate religion, negotiate identities, produce culture and everyday practices, and partake in broader cultural transformations. In the process they continuously change the neighborhood as much as neighborhood culture changes aspects of their lives. By way of participating in the neighborhood, they become part of the city, negotiate what it means to be a Stuttgarter, and remake the city to accommodate their presence and reflect their cultural contributions, production, and creativity.

Stuttgart-Nordbahnhof is a multi-ethnic working-class neighborhood located close to downtown and the city's main train station. The quarter is a bordered on all sides by railways, former railway facilities, a large cemetery, and a vast park. Central parts of neighborhood were built in the closing years of the nineteenth century as railroad workers' housing. Initially populated by migrants from the southern German countryside, the neighborhood has for over a century accommodated diverse migrants who came from increasingly more distant locations and brought with them ever more cultural, ethnic, religious, and linguistic diversity. Successive generations of new Stuttgarters were raised in Nordbahnhof by their migrant parents. The multi-ethnic street celebration of Stuttgart's soccer victory demonstrates the integrative function of the neighborhood (and also soccer). Some of the participating Afghan boys' families had only arrived in Stuttgart in the last decade and a half. The (younger) boys were born in Stuttgart. Most of their mothers spoke no German, but the boys are enthusiastic participants in the local urban culture. The multi-ethnic composition of the group bears further witness to the everyday cultural encounters that have always been at the center of this neighborhood. The women's coffee hour illustrates how diverse individuals meet, socialize, and discuss their concerns in the neighborhood. More specifically the women's gathering illustrates how diverse Muslims encounter each other in the neighborhood, and how they discuss religious issues across ethnic borders and varying religiosities.

In this chapter I examine moments, spaces, and interactions involving diverse individuals in the Nordbahnhof quarter. I introduce a number of (past and present) residents, and examine their life histories and experiences in the neighborhood. I analyze the negotiation and configuration of local lifeworlds where neighbors and friends daily interact with each other. They share spaces and institutions, sometimes discuss everyday matters, argue, and celebrate with each other. Individuals routinely interact in their buildings, (large) backyards, streets, local stores, playgrounds, the local school, cultural center, civic associations, and on public transportation. They chat in stairways and hallways, at local city train stations, and outside the supermarket, bakery, or school gate. In the summer, residents share public benches along the quarter's main street and on a quiet pedestrian side street. Those who are willing to participate in a multitude of minute neighborly encounters are often drawn into local social networks, loosely configured neighborly ties, or closer ties of neighborliness and friendship. Even the most reclusive individuals on occasion walk the neighborhood streets or wait for the city train, and thus at least minimally encounter their neighbors. Families with children are tied into the social orbit of preschools, schools, parks, playgrounds, or after-school programs. Most residents shop in the neighborhood discount supermarkets and a small number of other stores. Some frequent local bars and cafés. Elderly residents often socialize on the benches on pedestrian streets. Some elderly women for a while even brought their dining room chairs outside on summer evenings to supplement the benches outside their front door, which only accommodated four individuals. They maintained an "open house" where the core group was Turkish, but they also had "visitors" of other ethnicities. Other elderly women regularly congregate in a small playground in the mornings when there are no children. A Turkish-German family regularly had their "open" house in the playground on summer evenings where the Turkish wife supplied tea or coffee and snacks for her girlfriends and their children. Her German husband followed the conversation from the next bench. As the women chatted in Turkish (which he obviously understood), he threw in his commentaries in German. Shared spaces and fleeting social encounters create a vague sense of belonging and community. Residents recognize each other; many greet each other or sometimes stop in public spaces to chat. Many elderly men know each other from decades of shared work on the railways. Newcomers can grow roots in the neighborhood and by extension in the city. Many develop a considerable sense of pride in the neighborhood. With their participation individuals and groups appropriate and remake neighborhood spaces and practices. As individuals and groups, residents challenge and reinvent local cultural forms and practices. They articulate new identities and ways of belonging. But how do such processes unfold in concrete contexts? How do they manifest themselves in the lives of individual residents? How have they worked and changed over the last century? How do young Afghan boys turn into ardent supporters of the local soccer team? How do women of different ethnicities, religions, and religiosities come to sit together and debate theological issues over a cup of coffee? What implications does this have for the neighborhood and city? Do cultural transformations remain local and thus irrelevant for the city? Or, do neighborhood cultural negotiations result in more far-reaching transformations beyond the neighborhood? What is the role of a multi-ethnic and multi-religious neighborhood like Nordbahnhof in the city at large? What do small neighborhood encounters contribute to the localization of Islam and Muslim in the city? How do such interactions figure in larger transformations of the urban cultural and religious geography?

To be sure: not all encounters in Nordbahnhof are happy, friendly, culturally creative, and marked by mutual respect and tolerance. There are arguments, sometimes loudly carried out on the street. Rowdy and loud teenage boys occasionally occupy specific benches or public spaces. In summer, some boys play loud rounds of soccer until late into the night on the two local small soccer fields (*Bolzplatz*). Insignificant conflicts, like over wrongly parked cars sometimes turn into loud and aggressive shouting matches where participants are quick to insult each other using offensive slurs with regard to, especially, ethnicity and age. Younger kids and teenagers occasionally engage in minor acts of vandalism (e.g. kicking light posts, throwing garbage in the back windows of local stores), and political groups spray buildings (there is one notorious leftist Kurdish sprayer). Some kids have been caught shoplifting in local stores. Visitors to one of the local bars notoriously park illegally around the bar and often take off at high speed endangering the lives of those who pass by. Visitors of bars are frequently loud at night and occasional fights break out among them. Many residents insist that patrons of one bar (illegally) gamble behind closed doors. Unemployment runs high in particular among male youths who did not finish school at all or only finished the mandatory nine years of the *Hauptschule*. Some residents of two homeless shelters located at the southern and northern ends of the neighborhood use the discount supermarket to supply themselves with cheap alcohol. A few of these men make the benches along the main street into their living room. They sit all day, consume several bottles of beer and return to their shelter in the evening after their "shift." Walter, one of these residents has been a neighborhood fixture for years. He usually takes his position in front of the supermarket (other than the times when he mysteriously disappears for some weeks). Everybody knows him by name. He either talks to himself or others, but never ventures too far from the supermarket. On some days he seems angry. On good days he occasionally sings at the top of his lungs, and is indeed quite a good singer. Another man, Fritz, used to occupy one particular bench for several years. He looked like he had seen much better days, but withered away on his bench. Some local kids would make fun of him and call him names. He died in the winter of 2010/11. While the neighborhood has had a series of social issues, neighborly quarrels, and conflicts, I will in this chapter focus on the neighborhood's largely neglected but crucial role as a site of urban cultural production, and analyze culturally creative and constructive scenes and situations.

Creative Neighborhood Cultures

In the following I introduce individuals and examine moments of engagement to illustrate cultural creativity and transformations. I explore how individuals' experiences contribute to the neighborhood and urban culture. I demonstrate how change unfolds as the result of both cultural tension and minute ordinary interactions and conversations between residents. I describe how newcomers settle and how the neighborhood reflects their arrival by way of small and smallest accommodations. Over time newcomers become long-term residents and decisive participants in local cultural negotiations. Previous newcomers turn into tomorrow's old-timers who perpetuate shared practices and facilitate transformations initiated by the next cohort of arrivals.

Quarters like Nordbahnhof are central to contemporary German urban cultures as they are at the forefront of urban transformations and accommodate the localization of new arrivals. Recent migrants, established migrants, and long-term residents, partly forced by residential proximity, but also guided by curiosity and neighborliness, formulate ways of living that reflect vastly different ideas, practices, beliefs, and lifestyles. The new forms and practices they articulate are cultural "beginnings," that—if successful—might prove to become models for other quarters and the city at large. Sharon Zukin illustrates how today's "urban beginnings" are the groundwork for tomorrow's cultural transformations, new forms, and practices (2010). Today's cultural production in multi-ethnic working-class quarters constitutes tomorrow's urban authenticity, in particular, in the face of powerful global processes of corporate homogenization, gentrification, and consumer culture which often dominate contemporary cities, their commercial centers, cultural production, and spectacular architectural projects. Birgit Mattausch and Erol Yildiz argue that multi-ethnic working-class quarters have long constituted the cultural wealth of German cities (2009; see also Schiffauer 1997; Bukow et al. 2011). In an era of global homogenization of downtown areas, shopping venues, and the creation of seemingly generic megaprojects or "non-places," such as consumer arenas, transportation hubs, and leisure spaces (Altshuler and Luberoff 2003; Flyvbjerg et al. 2003; Augé 1995), the cultural creativity and innovation of inner city multi-ethnic quarters becomes a crucial element of urban cultures (Sassen 2000; Chappell 2010; Holston 2008; Sieber et al. 2012; Jonuz and Schulze 2011). Many older multi-ethnic working-class neighborhoods (especially in U.S. cities) have in recent decades attracted the eye of investors who seek to develop and commercialize the "cozy" or "exotic" feel of these quarters. In the process of ensuing gentrification neighborhoods change dramatically (e.g. Abu-Lughod 1994; Mele 2000; Modan 2007). Similar processes are underway in Germany, with Berlin's Prenzlauer Berg and Kreuzberg being the most prominent examples.

To insist on the creative role and contributions of multi-ethnic working-class neighborhoods does not mean that other quarters are not creative or "authentic" spaces, or that they are any less "real." While a gentrified space or neighborhood might duplicate other similar spatialities and processes in other cities, they nonetheless constitute concrete local compromises and configurations. My point here is to describe and analyze neighborhood spaces and cultures that are often overlooked, or even cast aside as irrelevant or not representative.

In the 1970s and 1980s many migrants to German cities settled in partly deserted or undesirable neighborhoods as they were excluded from other quarters. In some cities they revived these neighborhoods and remade aspects of public life to accommodate their social, cultural, and economic needs. Vibrant public and commercial spaces and cultures emerged (Ceylan 2006; Mattausch and Yildiz 2009; Bukow et al. 2011). Initially largely patronized by migrants from other parts of the city, some such quarters or their main shopping venues also attracted individuals who sought to consume their "exotic" flair (Yildiz 2009; Jonuz and Schulze 2011), or simply came for inexpensive merchandise (Kuppinger 2010a, 2011b).

Multi-ethnic neighborhoods and small urban spaces constitute one element of the increasingly rare creative expressions of local culture in the face of globalized spaces and consumer cultures (Zukin 2010: 170; Gliemann and Caesperlein 2009; Peraldi 2009). Such local cultural production is often controversial as it challenges cultural hegemonies. Zukin insists that participation in local cultural production is a right. New beginnings are an urban necessity: "Authentic is a social right, it's also poor, ethnic and democratic. Authenticity speaks for the right of a city, and a neighborhood, to offer residents, workers, store owners and street vendors the opportunity to put down roots—to represent, paradoxically both origins and new beginnings" (2010: 26). This, I argue includes the rights of diverse groups to continue their religious traditions and create local beginnings for the latter (Stephen and Wittner 1998; Stepick et al. 2009a; Numrich 2000).

Inner-city multi-ethnic neighborhoods are frequently depicted as problematic spaces (*sozialer Brennpunkt*). While these quarters do harbor problems, which reflect social, economic, educational, and employment inequalities, they also include dynamic cultural processes. Scholars of urban cultures (Gans 1962; Katznelson 1982; Mele 2000; Lin 1998; Zukin 2010) and religions (Orsi 1999; Sciorra 1999; Livezey 2000; Rey and Stepick 2009) have long pointed out the (overlooked) creative cultural powers of multi-ethnic and multi-religious working-class quarters. Ira Katznelson aptly noted, that for local residents "their neighborhoods are theirs alone" (1982: 1), as elites and municipal budgets do not invest vast sums in their cultural activities. Neither are they deemed central for urban cultural representations (Walley 2013). Sharon Zukin demonstrates that away from downtown, in neighborhoods, individual and communal identities have been negotiated by successive generations of new arrivals (1995: pp.187). Urban cultures are remade in these neighborhoods, one step and one small conversation at a time.

Zukin states that in the United States well into the 1960s, downtowns—dominated by modern institutions, department stores, and narrowly defined cultural and ideological universes—remained the dream and goal of most residents of working-class and immigrant quarters. Suburban malls later supplemented downtown dreamscapes. Yet beyond the dreamscape of "downtown shopping districts and suburban malls," Zukin insists, there always existed "ethnic shopping streets" and diverse ethnic cultures in neighborhoods (ibid.: 190; see Walley 2013). On streets and public spaces, immigrant residents engage in the task of becoming local, constructing local identities, and re-/formulating urban cultures and topographies. Once these are accepted by local constituencies they can be inserted into broader urban cultures. They become the foundation of future authenticities. Zukin identifies shopping streets in multi-ethnic quarters as both lifelines and central stages of local public cultures and cultural production. She argues: "I am convinced that the ordinary shopping districts frequented by ordinary people are important sites for the negotiating the street level practices of urban public culture in all large cities" (1995: 191).

Zukin's analysis of "ethnic shopping streets" needs to be supplemented by an examination of other public or semi-public spaces such as schools, cultural centers, or work places as central spaces for minute cultural negotiation and production (see Hajer and Reijndorp 2001). Public schools are also important here, as beliefs and lifestyles more immediately come to meet and possibly conflict in the confined spaces or classrooms and intense everyday interaction. Public spaces in urban quarters often serve as testing grounds for individuals, groups, and institutions where they experiment with forms and practices.

Religion in the Neighborhood

For a long time, much of the urban studies literature assumed a secular city where needs were formulated and conflicts debated in mutually agreed upon secular terms. A number of recent studies, however, has turned to examine the role of public religion (Casanova 1994), religion in the public sphere (Salvatore 2007), and increasingly also the role of urban religion (Winston 1999), or religion in the city (Orsi 1999; Bielo 2009, 2011a, 2011b; Elisha 2010, 2011; Eade 2010; Gale 2005; David 2102). Scholars increasingly analyze religion not only as being practiced in the city, but more importantly as being *of* the city. They insist that religion, religiosities, and religious congregations are crucially affected and indeed reflect urban transformations (Livezey 2000), and in turn are vital actors and elements in such processes and the articulation of changing urban cultures (Orsi 1985).

At a historical moment when some scholars talk about the advent of the postsecular city (Baker and Beaumont 2011; Cloke and Beaumont 2012; Kong 2001), it is paramount to examine the role of religion in urban cultural transformations (Peach and Gale 2003; Astor 2012; Levitt 2008; Hervieu-Léger 2002; AlSayyad and Massoumi 2010). How do cities accommodate religious individuals and groups? How do cities facilitate the religious needs of new arrivals? Can religious elements be easily inserted into urban lifeworlds and public cultures? How does everyday life in neighborhoods deal with religious differences? What role does or can religion play in everyday lives and cultures? How does neighborhood culture articulate new identities and modes of participation for religiously diverse newcomers? Can such neighborhood solutions become models for the city at large?

One cannot understand (religious) lifeworlds exclusively from the perspective of houses of worship or religious communities. Churches, mosques, synagogues, or temples might be central nodes in the lives of some believers, but they are not for others. Even those who spend much time in such religious spaces among likeminded people, live most of their lives outside such sheltered spaces. While mosques are often at the center of public debates about Islam, they are not the only places where pious Muslim lives unfold (AlSayyad 2002: 17; Henkel 2007; Tarlo 2010; Kepel 1987). Many Muslims rarely or never enter mosques. Some go to mosques to pray, but do not participate in other activities there. Some, in particular, women almost never go to mosques yet take religion seriously and practice/pray at home. Women, like Dzamila, Amra, and Ulrike often debate religious issues with their female friends and relatives at home, read books, or consult Internet resources.

Religiosity plays a central role for many individuals, yet their beliefs and practices are not communicated in all contexts in which they interact. The pious might be known to their friends and neighbors as harboring specific beliefs, but these do not transpire in all everyday encounters. Sometimes ethnicity plays a more decisive role than religiosity, or Islam/religiosity is tied to nationalities and ethnicities like Turkish, Kurdish, Bosnian, Afghan, or Iraqi. At one moment individuals might perceive of themselves as first and foremost Turkish, while in the next encounter they might emphasize their Muslim identity. Cultural negotiations about the role of Islam/Muslims in the neighborhood are complexly interwoven with ethnic issues.

Nordbahnhof

In the mid nineteenth century the area north of downtown Stuttgart was largely agricultural, dotted with a few residential houses. Starting from the 1850s, one of the first local railway lines, connecting Stuttgart with the town of Ludwigsburg, cut through this area. As the railroad expanded, its vicinity was slowly taken over by more railways and railroad facilities. In the 1870s when this district was still outside the (built) city, a large cemetery, the Pragfriedhof, was established west of the railroad tracks. In the final two decades of the nineteenth century the railroad and its facilities rapidly expanded on the northern outskirts of the city. With this fast growth, the city's northern fringes lost their attraction for single-family homes. Instead numerous transportation companies and industrial plants (e.g. a large brewery) settled along the railroad. Immediately north of the railroad tracks and the new industrial plants a small neighborhood of privately owned apartment buildings emerged in the 1880s. In March 1894, in response to a pressing housing shortage in Stuttgart, the Royal Railroad Building section submitted a plan to the municipal planning authorities proposing the construction "of new family apartments for lower employees (*Unterbedienstete*)" on land surrounded by the railroad tracks, cemetery, and expanding industrial facilities (Baurechtsamt D4701). The project covered ten small city blocks. (ibid.). Construction quickly started and most buildings were finished by 1896. This old railroad workers' settlement, today still lovingly called by older urban dwellers the "little railroad workers' village" (*Eisenbahnerdörfle*) is the core of Nordbahnhof.[2] Until the 1990s, residence in these buildings was limited to railroad workers.

The railroad workers' apartment buildings are uniform three and four floor brick buildings. Corner units on the quarter's main street, the Nordbahnhofstrasse (from now N-Street), include small corner stores, only one of which is currently used as such. Until World War II the central parts of the neighborhood consisted of uniform red and white brick buildings. In the war several buildings were destroyed when the neighborhood, because of its proximity to the main train station and other central railroad facilities, was the target of several large air raids. The destroyed buildings were replaced in the 1950s by aesthetically less attractive structures. In addition to the old railroad workers housing, the quarter includes on its northeastern edges apartment buildings for postal workers that were constructed in the 1920s and 1930s. The northernmost part of the neighborhood is a cooperative settlement that was built in the 1950s to alleviate the housing shortage after World War II.

N-Street forms the spine of the quarter. Running north-south, it houses most local businesses. Once a busy road connecting Stuttgart to the town of Ludwigsburg, N-Street was the site of numerous accidents and cost several local lives. After a particularly tragic accident when a mother and her child were killed in 1984, the city decided to reroute traffic and turn N-Street into a pedestrian area. Today only local traffic and the city train, which connects the quarter to downtown, run on this street. The train has three stops on N-Street: one is at the northern end of the street (next to the suburban train station), one in the center, and a third at the southern end. Along the west side of N-Street is one row of privately owned residential and commercial buildings. Behind these buildings are defunct railroad facilities. Private individuals do not own any of the buildings on the east side of the street.

The neighborhood has a school (Park School), an intercultural community center (Kulturhaus), a Protestant church (united with three other congregations for lack of members), a vocational school that serves students from the city and the region, a new day care and after-school facility, and Protestant and Catholic preschools. A Catholic church and a mosque are at walking distance (two stops on the train) outside the community. At the southern end of N-Street is a homeless shelter for men, which houses transitional clients and a number of mostly older permanent residents. Another homeless shelter for mostly immigrant men is at the far northern edge of the neighborhood. Also in the southern part of the community is a group home for single mothers and their children. In 2007, the National Agency for Work moved into new large premises on the southern section of N-Street. Diagonal across the street from this agency is an artists' colony/studios in an old factory yard (slated for removal in 2014). A large cinema complex lies on the southeastern edge of the quarter. In 2008 the state health department moved into a new building on the northern part of N-Street. In 2012 an educational facility of the Protestant Church opened in a newly constructed building next to the health department.

The area to the west of N-Street includes remnants of former railroad facilities. Surrounding these facilities is a large wasteland once occupied by railways and railroad facilities, and a number of defunct industrial facilities. A huge metal scrap and junkyard is one of the last working leftovers from the area's industrial and railroad past. On the western edge of the wasteland are vast old railroad repair facilities (*Wagenhallen*) that currently serve as a performance venue and accommodate artists' residences. Depending on the season and the artists in residence, the wasteland/yard that surrounds the *Wagenhallen* has for years been an adventurous landscape dotted with pieces of art and all sorts of discarded items. For years the facilities also included a coffee shop with outdoor seating in the summer.

Until recently a number of artists lived in old train cars sitting on small stretches of defunct rail on the eastern edge of the wasteland. A Kurdish artist turned his car into an elaborate piece of art complete with a high freestanding platform that included a "throne" and other large and fancy pieces of furniture. Being situated adjacent to a bridge, this artist had the clever idea of installing a "hose" from the railroad bridge (that ran above his car and included a pedestrian sidewalk) to his car where one can insert "donations" for his art. Next to the hose on the bridge was a short introduction to the artist and his work. Throwing money in the hose was a children's favorite for the sound of the traveling money. The last artist inhabitants were forced out of their train car residences in 2011 in preparation for the hugely controversial mega-train station project *Stuttgart 21* that foresees the replacement of the current main train station with a subterranean one and a comprehensive remake of other defunct railroad facilities. Moving the train station underground, enormous stretches of the current railscape could then be turned into valuable downtown real estate. The project has been the object of an ongoing heated controversy in the city as many see it as a gigantic waste of money to replace a functioning train station with a new one whose efficiency is doubted by numerous experts. Others predict serious damage to the city's mineral water springs (the second largest in Europe, after Budapest). Construction of the mega-project started in 2010 in midst of controversy and massive protest, but has come to numerous intermittent halts for political and technical reasons (see e.g. Schorlau 2012; Lösch et al. 2010; Ostertag 2008). Nordbahnhof is located at the northern edge of the core project area and will be dramatically affected, regardless of the final outlines of the project. Many residents in Nordbahnhof fearfully anticipate the results of *Stuttgart 21*. Since 2012/13 the neighborhood suffers from the dramatically increased traffic of trucks that transport soil/dirt from the downtown construction sites (on a street on the eastern outskirt of the community).

At the southern end of the old railways wasteland, just north of the cemetery is an old urban garden colony (*Schrebergärten*). Slightly set back from the street is the entrance to the gardens that are administered by an association of urban gardeners (*Kleingärtnerverein*). Hidden from the outside by large trees, the colony is a green oasis. Once a year, during the association's annual Radish Festival, the colony is open for visitors. Neatly arranged garden plots contain flowers and vegetables. Each plot includes a tiny wooden house. The beautiful garden arrangements, national (German and Italian) and regional flags (Bavarian), and the ubiquitous German garden dwarves (*Gartenzwerg*), old wagon wheels, and other decorations bespeak the love and care of owners who spend long evening and weekend hours in their gardens.

In the 1990s, the railroad workers' apartments were opened to the public. Residents with other jobs and employers moved in. But until the present many railroad employees and railroad retirees live in the neighborhood.[3] In recent years individuals of German descent from the former Soviet Union; war refugees from Bosnia, Macedonia, Afghanistan, and Iraq; and immigrants from Eastern European and East Germany (the former GDR) moved to the neighborhood. At the dawn of the twenty-first century, Nordbahnhof accommodates vastly diverse residents. Turkish, Turkish-Kurdish, German, Portuguese, Italian, Spanish, Greek, Bosnian, Iraqi-Kurdish, Iraqi, Iranian, Czech, Hungarian, Serbian, Russian, Croatian, Sinti, Macedonian, Afghan, Egyptian, Ghanaian, Nigerian, Kenyan, Cameroonian, Tunisian, Moroccan, Palestinian, Algerian, Vietnamese, Chinese, Ethiopian, Eritrean, Somali, American, Sri Lankan, Venezuelan, Honduran, and other individuals and families reside in the quarter. Numerous intercultural families, like for example German-Portuguese, German-Turkish, German-Egyptian, German-Italian, German-Algerian, Czech-Greek, Tunisian-Italian, Algerian-Turkish, Turkish-Italian, Serbian-Bosnian, or Russian-Italian, live in the neighborhood.

Muslims account for about a third of the quarter's population. There is no official count, but helpful indicators. In 2007 of about sixty first graders in the local school just under half were Muslims (or of Muslim descent). Almost half of the population of the larger quarter (46.9 percent) is listed as either without religion, or with a religion other than Protestant or Catholic (Landeshauptstadt Stuttgart 2013: 49). While it is difficult to identify those without religious affiliations or those who are Muslims, this figure is higher than in wealthier quarters (e.g. Degerloch 40.1 percent; ibid.: 133).[4]

The quarter is officially called "Auf der Prag" (no relation to the Czech capital), but is popularly known as Nordbahnhof.[5] The quarter is part of the administrative quarter (*Bezirk*) of Stuttgart-Nord, which also includes the upscale hillside quarter of Killesberg. Statistics that represent the Stuttgart-Nord area are difficult to interpret, as they reflect an average of one of the city's poorest and one of the richest neighborhoods. The disparity between the units that form Stuttgart-Nord is, for example, illustrated by the percentages of German citizens. 51.1 percent of the Auf der Prag residents have German citizenship (which includes a considerable number of naturalized citizens), in Killesberg the figure is 94.4 percent (Landeshauptstadt Stuttgart 2006: 59). The majority of (the local minority of) ethnic German residents in Nordbahnhof are railroad retirees who have lived here for decades. There are only very few younger ethnic German families with children in the neighborhood as most ethnic Germans are wary of living in a immigrant quarter and even more so of sending their children to a school where more than

80 percent of the students have a background of migration. Italians and even more so Greeks display similar patterns with more older and less young individuals in the neighborhood. The Turkish community is probably demographically the most evenly distributed in particular in the winter months as many retirees spend their summers in Turkey and winters in Germany. A few large Afghan families constitute their own local subculture as almost none of the women speak German. African migrants are almost exclusively younger individuals and families. Most of them reside in a number of newer buildings on the southern edge of the quarter.

Becoming Part of the City

From its inception, Nordbahnhof was a migrant neighborhood where railroad workers were provided with rentals by their employer. The first cohort of migrants/residents at the turn of the twentieth century was largely of regional origin. Many were Catholics from economically disadvantaged southern parts of the state/kingdom (Oberschwaben), or a similar region about sixty miles northeast of Stuttgart (Hohenlohe). For Protestant Stuttgart, these Catholic arrivals initially constituted strangers or outsiders (Köhler 1990). A century ago, the identity of a "Catholic Stuttgarter" seemed impossible to "old" Stuttgarters. Protestant-Catholic marriages, which in the early years of the twentieth century were often considered family disasters, are no longer a topic of conversation. Catholic Stuttgarters became normalized decades ago.

After World War II tens of thousands of German war refugees, and refugees from Soviet-occupied East Germany arrived in the city. Some who found work with the railroad settled in Nordbahnhof. In the early 1950s, pressed for labor, the railroad and postal administrations brought in workers from regional areas and (Catholic) Bavaria. With the rapid postwar economic growth, starting from the mid-1950s, migrant workers from Italy, Spain, Portugal, Greece, Turkey, Tunisia, Morocco, or Yugoslavia arrived in Stuttgart. For many railroad workers, Nordbahnhof was their first family home in Germany (many men had lived in workers' dormitories before they brought their families; Kurz 1995).

Whether for Catholics from Hohenlohe, Catholics from Portugal, Muslims from Turkey, Bosnia, or Afghanistan, Nordbahnhof has for more than 100 years been a place of entry to Stuttgart. While parent generations often remain tied to their home regions, their children develop new identities. They become Stuttgarters and often strongly identify with the neighborhood and the city. In the past the children of migrants turned into Catholic Stuttgarters of Hohenlohe descent, today they become Muslim Stuttgarters of Turkish, Iraqi, or Macedonian descent. In the process they make local urban cultures and identities more inclusive. Regardless of this considerable communal cultural work, much of Nordbahnhof's contributions to the city and urban culture remain invisible. Urban elites continue to overlook these transformations that started to gain momentum, in particular, in the 1950s and 1960s (Bukow et al. 2011). Neighborhood cultural innovations are often relegated to the status of the "exotic" at best, or in the worst case as "unacceptable." Cultural compromises as articulated in multi-ethnic neighborhoods are defined as "alien" to "German" culture, when in reality they are dynamic urban popular cultures with deep local roots.[6] The lack of understanding of such sites of intense cultural negotiation constitutes a serious impediment to the recognition of immigrants as crucial urban actors.

A Catholic Stuttgarter: The 1940s and 1950s

Mr. Werner Friedrich and I had arranged to meet on the corner of N-Street and a side street on what turned out to be a beautiful sunny Monday morning in May 2007. Mr. Friedrich is a tall man in his late sixties. The interview took the form of a long walk through neighborhood streets where Mr. Friedrich showed me places and narrated his childhood memories. We first walked toward the postal workers' housing. There we entered a large rectangular yard that is between four buildings that front different streets. The residents of about sixty apartments share the yard. As we entered the yard, Mr. Friedrich started our trip back to the 1940s (he was born in 1940), World War II, and the postwar period. First he pointed out the apartment where he grew up, and where his mother lived until her death a few years ago: "It is only a small two bed-room apartment and we were eight children, but back then it all worked, somehow. We never felt that this was not big enough." Mr. Friedrich parents' had come from Hohenlohe and were Catholics. With a smile he added, "We were special with the eight children. Everybody knew us. The butcher's wife even sometimes packed up an extra sausage knowing how many we were." Mr. Friedrich's father had come to Stuttgart in search of work and a better future. He worked as a postal worker for most of his life. Mr. Friedrich took a look around the large yard, which today is planted with grass and has a few places to hang laundry. Since it was morning there were no children, but in the afternoons the local yards are often full with playing children. Looking from the northern end over the yard, Mr. Friedrich reminisced: "All this was very different in the past. In the middle there was the fire pond and around it were the vegetable gardens of the residents, which were very important in the war and postwar years. The janitor (*Hausmeister*) of the complex always made sure that nobody went swimming in the pond or walked in the vegetable plots. Some children did swim in the pond, if the janitor saw them, he was furious."

Pointing toward the northeastern corner of the complex, Mr. Friedrich explained: "Over there were the shared laundry facilities (*Waschhaus*). Every family would get to use the facility every six weeks on an assigned day. This was hard labor for my mother, as she had to wash huge piles of laundry. She would spend an entire day toiling away soaking, boiling, rinsing and wringing heavy pieces of laundry. On those days she would not even cook."

From laundry we moved to bathing. Mr. Friedrich recollected: "Back then, none of the apartments had a bathroom. We went to the public bath." Located next to today's little playground at the southern end of the neighborhood, the old bathhouse still stands. It functioned as a bathhouse until the 1970s—when all the old apartments finally had bathrooms installed. Today the bathhouse contains apartments, after it served as an office for the public health administration for some years. Mr. Friedrich explained: "The bathhouse was a railroad facility. They could use it for free. We, as postal people, had to pay to use it. But we got reduced rates. We paid 20 Pfennig for half an hour. And then we had to make sure to clean the tub and not leave any dirt behind. We had our own bathhouse in the city in the Kronenstrasse. We had an ID card to get in there. But it was further away in the city and more inconvenient."

He added that the bathhouse also included a small grocery store. Looking through the open gateway toward the new daycare facilities east of the yard, Mr. Friedrich continued: "Over there were the postal sorting facilities. Many women worked there, many did nightshifts, sorting packages. There was also a large repair workshop for postal vehicles. Beyond that—where the two school complexes are today—there were a few unused patches of land and beyond that were *Schrebergärten* (small urban garden colonies). The empty spaces next to the post facilities were parts of our childhood 'playground'. Neighborhood children spent a lot of time there. Thinking back, it is amazing to think how few accidents or injuries happened in this wilderness." The urban garden plots that Mr. Friedrich mentioned were crucial for many families in the postwar years; they planted fruits and vegetables and kept chickens and rabbits there.

Looking around the yard once more, Mr. Friedrich reflected about his family. Sometime in the late 1920s or early 1930s his parents had moved from rural Hohenlohe to Stuttgart. His father found work with the postal services and received housing for his family in the newly constructed postal workers' apartments. While the family kept in touch with their rural relatives, and their Catholic faith, the children increasingly identified with the city, in particular their neighborhood and neighborhood peers.

Born in 1940, Mr. Friedrich does not remember much about World War II. In the last weeks of the war, in the spring of 1945, he and many other children were evacuated to the countryside (he stayed with his grandparents). The quarter's location—close to the railways and railway facilities—made it a prime target for Allied bombing. In several large air raids in 1944 and 1945 the neighborhood was heavily hit and numerous apartment buildings were destroyed. As soon as the war was over, Mr. Friedrich and his siblings returned to Stuttgart, as their building had not been hit.

When I returned in 1945 many buildings were in ruins. This rubble was now our playground. I still remember exactly which buildings had been destroyed and what some of the rubble mounds looked like. Looking back, this all seems dangerous, but we did not think that way back then. That was our life. We went around the neighborhood with groups of children, and there were plenty of us. This is when there also were many "latch key children" who were out all day long. Their fathers had died in the war and their mothers had to work. Those mothers who were lucky got jobs in the postal sorting facilities by the end of the street.

Mr. Friedrich explained that there was one shift that ran from 8 P.M. to midnight and another that ran from 11 P.M. to 6 A.M.: "Working these shifts, the women would be home during the day. In the summer, during school vacations, by about 8:30 A.M. all the children were out playing for the whole day. The older ones took care of the younger ones and surprisingly little happened. Times were different, and there were only two cars on the entire street that fronted our building in these early postwar years." We continued toward the small pedestrian side street (just off N-Street) at the center of the quarter which is lined with benches in the shade of large trees. These benches are the preferred seating of many elderly residents. About halfway up the street, Mr. Friedrich stopped and pointed to a building and the sidewalk in front of it: "Look, this building was completely destroyed, it was all rubble. And here, were the sidewalk is, there was a mount on stones and rubble which remained for quite some time. There was so much to be cleaned up. It could not all be done at once."

Mr. Friedrich reminisced about a childhood largely spent outside with groups of neighborhood children where the older ones watched out for the little ones. With the postwar economic recovery, however, some of the neighborhood calm and safety vanished, as N-Street, which had always been part of the regional road network connecting Stuttgart to Ludwigsburg, turned into a busy thoroughfare. Trucks raced through the street and accidents happened. Mr. Friedrich remembered several people being killed in the postwar years, among them one of his friends who had been riding his bicycle and was hit by a truck.

Before World War II the southern part of the neighborhood was home to a large brewery (with a restaurant, and beer garden overlooking the railroad and main train station). This expansive compound was completely destroyed in the war and remained a ruin for years. "We went onto the old brewery yard and played with the rubble and pieces of glass and all sorts of bottle caps that were plentiful all over," Mr. Friedrich remembered. The last remaining tiny corner of this expansive factory complex and vibrant leisure compound remained until 2012 when it was torn down for the *Stuttgart 21* project. There was an old piece of wrought iron fence (with old trees growing through the fence) at the southern tip of these premises which looked like the only leftover of the once famous "English Garden" (*Englischer Garten*; the beer garden).

As Mr. Friedrich and I settled on a tree-shaded bench, Mr. Friedrich recalled more childhood memories. In fall of 1946 he started school, at a time when the city was struggling to provide schooling. He went to the Hill School, south of the neighborhood, which had been seriously damaged in the war bombardments.[7] For lack of classrooms, classes were taught in two daily shifts. Materials were scarce. Mr. Friedrich remembered: "To start school each student had to bring four large pieces of coal (*Bricket*), and a stack of newspapers to heat the classroom in the winter. We were sixty-two children in my first grade. There was one class with all boys and one with all girls. The third class was mixed."

When Mr. Friedrich started school, Stuttgart witnessed the arrival of tens of thousands of war refugees from parts of the Soviet Union, Poland, and other Eastern European countries. "There were refugees in a temporary building (*Baracke*) at the southern end of the neighborhood, others were in the Park," Mr. Friedrich recounted. Those, who were lucky to obtain employment with the railroad or postal services and to receive housing as the reconstruction of destroyed buildings gained speed, were able to permanently settle in the neighborhood.

When talking about religion and the Protestant-Catholic relationships in the neighborhood, Mr. Friedrich proudly related: "There was never a problem between Catholics and Protestant here. We were all friends and grew up together. In fact, we practiced *Ökumene* (Christian dialogue) before everybody started talking about it. It was part of our religious instruction that in seventh or eighth grade we went to visit the instruction and church of the other denomination. Nobody did such things back then, but we did. That is how we learned about each other's religion."

The postwar years in Stuttgart were marked by a construction frenzy because almost 60 percent of Stuttgart's built environment had been destroyed. The urban garden plots in the northern part of Nordbahnhof were turned into a small neighborhood of apartment buildings. The Park School was opened in 1953 to alleviate the pressure on the overcrowded Hill School. The construction of new apartments and the influx of refugees increased the neighborhood population. Destroyed industries were rebuilt and new ones added, as Germany embarked on its postwar *Wirtschaftswunder* (economic miracle). As the postwar economy boomed, more workers were recruited, among them individuals from less industrialized areas in Bavaria. Mr. Friedrich remembered: "The railroad and post office were recruiting in the *Bayerischer Wald*. First only men came." Many stayed and either married locally or brought their wives from Bavaria. Soon war refugees and workers from other parts of Germany could no longer fill the demand for labor and Germany started a program to recruit foreign labor. Mr. Friedrich recounted: "In 1954 the first Italians arrived in Nordbahnhof. That was new and exciting." The facilities at the southern end of the neighborhood that had earlier housed war refugees were turned into a residence for "guest workers" who were on short term contracts and hence without their families. Soon, the men whose contracts with the railroad kept being renewed started to bring their wives and children. A few married local women. Nordbahnhof became a destination, in particular, for a group of men from the Italian town of Accettura. Over the decades a lively back and forth developed between Nordbahnhof and Accettura. These ties are still held up today. Mr. Friedrich left the neighborhood in the mid-1950s and thus only witnessed the first group of arriving migrants. Soon more workers came from Spain, Portugal, Greece, former Yugoslavia, Turkey, Tunisia, and Morocco.

Railroad work (and to a lesser extent postal work), its hierarchies and related associations dominated life in Nordbahnhof and provided a frame that transcended cultural and religious differences. The shared work experiences of men (and some women) provided a larger frame of reference for local lives.[8] Postal workers and their activities took a backseat to the railroad workers' culture. Everybody, including the children, knew the type of work and rank of local men. At the top of the hierarchy were those who drove the locomotive engines (*Lokführer*). Unlike all others, who were wage laborers, *Lokführer* were tenured state employees (*Beamte*). Mr. Friedrich explained:

> They [*Lokführer*] would go to work wearing their white gloves for everybody to see. They socialized among themselves and even had some of their own social associations. Next in the hierarchy were those who oversaw the trains (*Zugführer*) and then came the conductors (*Schaffner*). Then there were plenty of other manual workers, some of whom also had rather dangerous jobs, like the *Rangierer* (those who park and assemble the trains). I remember when a *Rangierer* was killed one day, really close by. There was a difference between the railroad and postal families. All the railroad children got free train tickets and could go on trips with their parents. The postal children had none of this.

In their free time individuals and families socialized in work related associations like the railroad sports club, or choir, or they worked garden plots in the surrounding colonies. The postal workers also had their own sports club. Others joined the local sports club, the SV Prag, which in its best years in the 1950s even produced a national boxing champion. Then, as today, there were several bars/simple restaurants along N-Street. Mr. Friedrich commented: "Most people could not afford to eat out. One might go there for a very special occasion like a wedding or so. Or children would be sent there with an earthenware container (*Krug*) to fetch some beer for a special guest at home." Two of today's bars have been marked on city maps as bar/restaurants for the last 100 years.

Mr. Friedrich and I ended our interview and neighborhood tour over coffee in the outside seating area of one of the oldest local bars and restaurants, which today serves "Greek-German" cuisine. Catching up further on notes and searching for other interesting stories, Mr. Friedrich related a story about how the children after the war outwitted U.S. army truck drivers who transported coal, so that pieces of coal would fall off trucks for the children to take home. Like many of

Mr. Friedrich's recollections, it is not the story itself that is of relevance, but more importantly the sense of "we" and community that it conveys. Granting even a certain nostalgia about his childhood and childhood home, Mr. Friedrich's memories are communal stories. He did not relate individual experiences of going places in the city with, for example, his mother or father. Central actors were the children, who in groups played or roamed the neighborhood, who were squeezed in large numbers into a classroom, and watched out for each other. Largely on their own without much adult supervision, they engaged with each other, formed friendships, negotiated differences, and in the process became local and proud of their neighborhood. Regional origins and religion took a backseat in their identities. Work-related hierarchies dominated differences. There were the children of the (white-gloved) employees versus workers' children; there were the privileged railway families (with free access to the local bath house and free railroad tickets) versus the postal worker families. Relations of production, or what Zygmunt Bauman (2007) called the "society of producers" marked social differences and neutralized other markers of identity. Together, the children of local Protestants, regional Catholics, Bavarian Catholics, Catholic and Protestant ethnic German war refugees from various Eastern European regions and Soviet-occupied East Germany, and from the mid-1950s also Italian, Spanish, Portuguese, and other children negotiated new identities that were largely framed in class terms. The quarter spatially framed their activities and identities. Much of the lives of Mr. Friedrich and his peers unfolded in public and communal contexts where the children of migrants learned city ways and survival, and very importantly tolerance and understanding of others by way of intense everyday encounters. Mr. Friedrich's parents in their hearts remained *Hohenloher*. "But we were Stuttgarters," he emphasized with a sense of pride and achievement.

Migrant Experiences: Arriving in the Early 1950s

I first met Mr. and Mrs. Haller at the International Summer Festival of the Kulturhaus in 2007. A week later I ran into them again at the "Radish Festival" of the local urban gardeners' association. When I asked the couple whether they wanted to participate in my research and be interviewed, they immediately agreed. A week later on a Monday morning, Mr. and Mrs. Haller came to my apartment. We chatted some and very casually conducted the interview. Mr. Haller was born in 1923, and his wife is a few years his junior. At a young age he was drafted to fight in World War II. He was lucky to be wounded in 1942 on the way to Stalingrad, as very few of those who went on to Stalingrad returned alive. Later he was moved to France, and eventually ended up a prisoner of war with the French. Between 1945 and 1948 he was working in a French prison camp. In 1948 he returned to his native Hohenlohe where he worked in a metal workshop for some time. For lack of good jobs and because of the low wages in the region, Mr. Haller moved to Stuttgart in January 1951. His dream was to drive a locomotive. However, because of his war injury, he was not allowed to start this career. Nonetheless he remained in Stuttgart: "Back home I made fifty-eight Pfennig an hour, doing qualified metal piece work. Here in Stuttgart I made DM 1.05 for doing unskilled labor with the railways. So I stayed. Work was hard and many could not keep up, but I stayed."

He lived in a sublet room in a larger apartment. Within the year he met and married his wife, who was from Stuttgart. Mrs. Haller smiled when he recounted this and added proudly, "I am a real "Stuttgarter fruit" (*Stuttgarter Früchtle*) and a "stair slider" (*Stäffelesrutscher;* due its hilly location, Stuttgart has many long and steep public stairs)." Soon a child was born. Initially the three lived in one room, as housing was still scarce. After some moves, the young family ended up in Nordbahnhof in the apartment where the couple still lived in 2007.

Mr. Haller is a railroad man through and through. His speech is full of railroad terms, insider speech, and abbreviations. Again and again, I had to ask for clarification as he listed technical details, or issues of work organization and hierarchies. In great detail, Mr. Haller recounted the weekly cleaning of steam engines, which ran well into the 1960s. He listed steam and diesel locomotives in rapid succession with their model and type numbers, and years of production and service. With great ease he explained the railroad workers and clerical workers' hierarchies that set the parameters for work and private lives. The powerful structure of railroad work and related social hierarchies accommodated a smooth start for newcomers into the local social world (and hierarchy). It was not so much places of origins or religious affiliations that accounted for local positions, social status, and involvement, but a worker's rank in the railroad's hierarchical universe. Like Mr. Friedrich, Mr. Haller commented on the special position and pride of locomotive drivers "with their white gloves." They formed the top of the local hierarchy and largely socialized among themselves. He remembered that everybody was acutely aware of these men's standing with the railroads. They had their own social associations and functions. Working with the railroad and living in a railroad workers' quarter, the family's life was firmly rooted in the railroad world. While the Hallers never much participated in the various associations, they were regulars at one of the railroad choir's frequent concerts.

The Hallers recounted how the neighborhood had many small shops where one could buy almost everything and chat with other residents. There was Mrs. Schmid who for a long time had a houseware store on N-Street in one of the oldest (private) buildings in the quarter. She sold pots, pans, silverware, and similar items. The store has long since closed and the storefront is now empty. There were two local family-owned bakeries and a butcher store, none of which still exist. There was a small drugstore, a dentist, and at least two *Wirtschaften* (old type bar that also served food), where some of the men went to drink. Weddings, communions, confirmations, and other larger family celebrations were held in these locales. The Hallers bemoan the fact that this cohesive social life, framed by the shared context and social references of railroad and postal workers, no longer exists. Families met in the past, and there was chatting on the stairs and in the halls. Now, Mrs. Haller complained, people no longer cared. But then again, she added, "there are many differences. The Croatian and Pakistani families in the building occasionally bring up a piece of cake. In contrast some of the young Germans cannot open their mouths to greet people."

Living close to the Kulturhaus, the Hallers complain about the considerable noise level there. In particular, the nightly soccer playing in the summer until 10 or 11 P.M. is often unbearably loud. "It is day until after 10 P.M.," Mr. Haller explains, "and then they still get plenty of light from the nearby street lights that they can continue even after dark. This is hard for us older people." Still, the Hallers never considered moving somewhere else.

Unlike Mr. Friedrich who had spent his childhood in the neighborhood and shared the fate of many children who had to leave if they started to work elsewhere (and hence had no access to local apartments) and only came back to visit and still harbored great love for the quarter, the Hallers have spent half a century in the neighborhood. The lifeworld they had known and were part of in the first few decades slowly changed along with the residents of the neighborhood. The fact that those who did not follow in their parents' occupational footsteps had to leave the neighborhood contributed to the fluctuation among residents over the decades (until the 1990s). The effect was two-sided. Younger generations were forced out of the cozy and somewhat sheltered migrant and railroad/postal community. Those who stayed in the neighborhood, as they stepped into their parents' occupational footsteps, encountered the next generation of newcomers; each wave came from a geographically more distant location as the twentieth and later the twenty-first centuries unfolded.

Mr. Haller died in November 2011 in a senior citizen residence in a Hohenlohe town. Like many of his Italian, Spanish, or Turkish neighbors and colleagues he had chosen to spend his last days in his old home. His obituary (*Traueranzeige*) in the *Stuttgarter Zeitung* made reference to decades spent in Nordbahnhof. His daughter remains in Stuttgart.

A Muslim Stuttgarter: The 1970s to the Present

I met Lale Öztürk through the neighborhood school. I came to know her more closely when we were involved in the organization of a school celebration. We also chaperoned school trips together. With some neighborhood friends, we soon organized irregular and informal revolving shared breakfasts. When I asked Lale for an interview, she readily agreed, as she was in a similar situation writing her thesis for her degree in social work, which also involved interviews. Lale and I became close friends. We have cooperated in school affairs, and also participated in public events and discussions together. Lale has long since finished her degree and embarked on a very successful career as a social worker.

Lale was born in Nordbahnhof in the mid-1970s, the youngest child of a Turkish family. She is the only one of her siblings born in Germany. She noted that, unlike her siblings, she entered a new and different multicultural world. "The midwife who assisted in my birth was Greek," she noted and laughed. Lale's father had come to Germany in the 1960s. In the early 1970s he brought first his wife and then one of the older children to Stuttgart. Lale's older siblings lived back and forth between Germany and Turkey in those years. She, in contrast, grew up entirely in Germany. Lale spent her childhood with her parents and siblings in a one-bedroom apartment. "We lived a very simple, almost poor life, as my father sent a lot of money back to Turkey." Lale's father worked with the railroad and lived the life and dreams of most first-generation migrants: to save most of his income and return to Turkey. In 2008 more than forty years after his arrival, he divided his time between Germany and Turkey. In 2012 Lale's oldest sister retired with her husband in Turkey. Her other siblings are in Germany.

When Lale was a child, her parents knew little about the German educational system. Only when somebody told them about preschool did they sent Lale there. When she started first grade her German was weak and she initially was behind in school, because of language problems. But she soon caught up. In fourth grade Lale had the grades to transfer to the *Realschule*, but nevertheless remained in the *Hauptschule*. Later she transferred to a *Wirtschaftsschule* finished her *Mittlere Reife*, then went to a *Wirtschaftsgymnasium* and finally did her *Abitur*. Lale remembered: "It was my sister, who greatly supported me through all of this. She insisted on my right to achieve things she had been denied because she was older and had missed out on similar opportunities. She kept saying to me: 'you can do this, you have to do this.'" After she finished school Lale married and moved to Turkey. There she studied German and German language teaching at the university. Back then she did not yet have a German passport and had to travel back and forth between Germany and Turkey every six months in order not to lose her permanent residency in Germany, and to be with her family in Stuttgart. "This was all fine and nice, but once I had the first child it became increasingly tedious." But most of all she missed her family. After five years in Turkey, Lale and her husband, who knew no German, came back to Germany. Her husband had a rough start. He cleaned buildings and waited tables but eventually found a suitable clerical job in a Turkish company. In Turkey he had been very involved in sports and obtained a referee license for basketball. Today he spends much of his free time and weekends as a referee in Germany's national basketball league.

Lale recounted that growing up, her father had been very religious. He always did his prayers. Her mother was less involved with religion, but wore a traditional headscarf. "You know" Lale explained, "the kind where the hair sticks out. And she wore short sleeves with it." Lale's father never forced religion on his children, her brother even drank alcohol occasionally, and her father knew about it. As a child, Lale went to Qur'an lessons at a mosque. "But I did not really pray and also did not always fast. I lived my youth. When I was about sixteen or seventeen years old I started to think more about life and death. I started to read simple books about religion." Things dramatically changed when her first child was born prematurely with some health problems. The baby struggled to survive. In that situation Lale turned to religion and found strength in faith. "I received strength through prayer. Prayer was a time of quiet and provided new strength in this situation. I felt prayer was the time where I could put everything aside." In this stressful situation Lale understood the importance of prayer. "This was not for the sake of tradition, but for myself. I am not a person to practice in groups, but by myself." Having faced the struggle and survival of her baby, and having drawn so much strength from prayer in this period, Lale felt the need to put on the *hijab* to complete her newfound religiosity.

Before the daughter started school, the family moved back to Germany. Lale was happy to be close to her family. She and her husband found an apartment in Nordbahnhof. Lale enjoys the multicultural aspects of Stuttgart. "Ultimately," she noted, "it is easier to be accepted here. Even Istanbul has some way to go to become a really multicultural city." Lale felt that in Turkey people defined each other more by way of their possessions than in Germany. Appearances played a big role there, she complained. "Here," she added, "you can say whatever you want." This of course does not mean that everything is nice and easy in Germany, she added.

Lale's professional struggles and trajectory unfold beyond the neighborhood, but are nevertheless relevant, as she carries experiences and lessons back to the neighborhood, in particular to the context of the local school where Lale was very active while her children were in primary school. After her return to Germany, her sister insisted that she needed a profession, since teaching German as a foreign language was not a great career field. Lale decided to become a school teacher. In fall of 2001 she entered university, which turned out rather nightmarish. In the immediate post-9/11 weeks and months, Lale remembered that the atmosphere at the university was tense. Nobody would sit next to her—the student with the *hijab*. Nobody talked to her. Only one student, the daughter of traveling entertainers (*Schausteller*) would ever sit next to her. If she missed a lecture, nobody shared their notes. Once a professor declared in a lecture "my life has changed since September 11" and directly looked Lale in the eyes. Lale was amazed and hurt, but too shy to say anything and only thought to herself "mine, too!" After four semesters she could no longer bear this atmosphere. A friend of hers who studied social work suggested she transfer to that field. Lale followed the advice and transferred to the smaller setting of a social work college (*Fachhochschule*): "Now I am really happy and my studies are fun! As a person I have really greatly benefitted, I have grown personally, philosophically, and ethically. There is almost nothing negative in this program."

After the painful experiences in her first course of study, Lale decided to exchange what she called the "large" headscarf (the scarf that falls over the shoulders) for the "small" headscarf (tied behind the head, leaving the neck uncovered). "It is amazing how differently people react to this small difference. I am not sure what it is. Are they less afraid of this headscarf? Some people might also think of this as just a fashionable thing." The "small" headscarf appears to symbolize what Lale called "an opening of the person. It gave me room to breathe again, all this discrimination really made it hard to breathe (*nimmt die Luft weg*)."

Soon Lale faced the next hurdle. For her studies she had to do two internships. Even the "small" headscarf is a major obstacle for professional engagement in Germany. In her first internship, Lale was lucky to receive the job with her headscarf. As an intern she was hired without the director of the institution ever having met her. Once she started working, this director refused to greet her. Only much later, he asked her "Why do you wear a headscarf, because of religion or fashion?" Being tired of such question she just responded "for fashion." For her second internship she decided to not attach the obligatory picture to her application. In the job interview the predictable question about the headscarf and why exactly she was wearing was asked. This time she said that she was wearing it for religious reasons, but was also willing to work without. Initially the program director said Lale could work with the headscarf, but then the director presented the issue to the respective work team which caused a lengthy debate. The director eventually sent Lale a long letter about this discussion and the reactions of the colleagues in which she explained that there were strong opinions among the social workers that the headscarf was a symbol of oppression and that it would be hard for some of them to deal with this symbol. Nonetheless, they grudgingly agreed that they would give it a try and Lale could do her internship wearing a headscarf. At that point Lale decided that she would take her headscarf off at work. "I simply did not have the strength to continue fighting." In the end these debates caused an odd atmosphere for Lale, but she did her best at work regardless, because she was interested in this social agency's work. Lale appreciated the way the director had always been very respectful of her and her beliefs throughout this encounter. Relationships with some colleagues were marked by (their) insecurity and odd questions. One colleague eventually confronted Lale and said: "I know you are a pious Muslima, I am a lesbian, do you have a problem with that (*macht dir das was aus?*)." Lale was surprised by this question, and just responded "everyone in their own ways." To avoid further debates and tension, Lale decided not to pray at work during this internship.

This internship involved public encounters and involvement with her clients. Lale rode public transportation and visited a variety of places (without a headscarf), which gave her two distinct sets of experiences in/of the city: one with and one without a headscarf. She noted a dramatic difference. People treated her very differently in the two contexts. For many people the headscarf creates invisible barriers and social distance. Wearing or not wearing a headscarf, Lale moved between being perceived by many as an insider and outsider of local society. Lale sees her headscarf encounters in the professional world as ironic. On the one side, people point to the headscarf as a symbol for oppression, but then when a Muslima with a headscarf wants to work, especially as a professional, she is prevented from doing so. This is a major contradiction that Lale and many others repeatedly pointed out.

In addition to her studies and later professional career, Lale is very involved with her children and their school work. Whether as a student, intern, professional, or mother, Lale participates in public contexts as a pious Muslima. Participation and discussion are paramount to her and she is willing to make certain compromises as ultimately this might foster more positive long-term changes. She patiently answers repetitive, sometimes ignorant, or even offensive questions as a way to initiate and maintain constructive debates. "In the end," she figures, "I do more for Islam than many of the women who more completely cover up but do not venture into society or who fight more single-minded struggles. Or, think about Mrs. Ludin! What did she change in the end? Did she really improve things for the rest of us? Or did she make things worse by creating a problem for everybody?"[9]

At the *Laternenlauf* on St. Martin's day[10] as the younger Park School children happily walked through the dark park with their friends and lanterns, Lale and I had a conversation about the meaning of Islam and piety in her life. Walking through the dark park only faintly lit by the children's lanterns, Lale explained that being second-generation Turkish, Turkishness was important to her, but not all-decisive like for her parents. She liked Turkey but did not want to move there at present. Germany was her home. This is where she has spent most of her life and where she engages in debates, observes social developments, and participates in civic life. Turkishness, of course, was relevant for her, but ultimately she spoke, thought, and interacted in a multicultural German universe as a person of Turkish descent. Islam, in contrast to Turkishness, was less in collision with her participation in society. Somehow it was Islam or being a pious Muslima that accommodated her full-fledged participation. As a pious Muslima she confidently entered the social, cultural, and political realm. She carried something from her origins into her current life. In 2008 Lale explained why she rarely went to mosques: "I do not fit the standard image of the Muslima. Only in Istanbul I sometimes go to the big and beautiful mosques. But then again in Istanbul everybody does as they please. Women wear or do not wear a headscarf in their daily lives. Some wear it only to pray."

Here she hinted at the soft pressure exerted by some mosque communities on pious women. Lale felt that mosques often exerted too much social control over their members, where "everybody searched for the one hair sticking out from the headscarf." In the end, she noted mosques were not that important for women. On a different occasion, Lale noted that she and her husband had been thinking about sending the children to a mosque for instruction as they felt that the children needed better instruction than they as parents could provide. They opted for a relative to teach the children. Sometime later, one daughter joined lessons at her best friend's mosque.

Lale's story is marked by a quest for belonging and participation. While she was living in Turkey, she realized that she wanted to be in Germany with her family. Returning to Germany she looked for a meaningful job as a way for constructive participation in society. Throughout the struggle to belong and participate, Nordbahnhof was an undisputed home space. After her stay in Turkey, Lale settled once more in Nordbahnhof close to her family. While her studies and later career unfolded outside the quarter, she remained rooted in the quarter.

In her first course of study Lale endured considerable adversity. She only gave up when she had a feasible alternative path lined up. Participation, to Lale means compromise, but from all sides. She never wanted to take off her headscarf to work, but at one point in her career this made life easier. Since Lale finished her degree, she has worked in two different settings wearing her headscarf. As an established professional she is no longer willing to accept a position where she would have to remove the headscarf. Being a Muslima in Germany for Lale is a matter of inner strength and conviction and has less to do with the drawing of boundaries. Indeed, it is precisely her full-fledged engagement with society that is rooted in her Muslim faith and identity. Her search for Islam and becoming a better Muslim is tightly linked to her participation in society. Questions about what compromises to make, only emerge in non-Muslim contexts. She is committed to Islam but also sees life as something that needs to have *nafs* (Arabic, spirit, but also used in Turkish), in the sense of joy, warmth, liveliness, and happiness. Religiosity for Lale is not the blind following of laws but implies a certain freedom to compromise on smaller issues. "What would be wrong," she noted one day, "if I dance at a wedding in an all women's setting? That cannot be sin. I call that *nafs*."

It is important for Lale to bring lessons learned in different contexts back to the neighborhood and creatively insert them in local contexts. For example, in the pre-Christmas season a debate emerged among some Muslim mothers whether it was allowed for Muslim children to participate in the crafts sessions at school where the children worked on Christmas decorations. One woman was opposed, as this was a distinctly Christian activity. Lale eventually convinced this woman to allow her child to attend the sessions. "Let them have fun making things together," Lale told her friend. "And they can just do snowmen and the like. They don't even need to cut out Santa Clauses. They are just kids." Her friend obliged and let her child participate under the condition that she would produce snowmen instead of Santa Clauses. The teacher readily agreed. As a parent representative at the school, Lale quickly established a reputation with the principal and administration for her willingness and ability to talk, mediate, and formulate compromises that respect the ideas and sensitivities of different constituencies.

Upon finishing her degree, Lale briefly worked as a caseworker with Turkish families. "There is plenty to do, and I am well-situated to do the job, speaking

Turkish and knowing the culture." She worked with a headscarf. Within a few months she moved to a career job in the field of migration and integration, which was what she had hoped for. Besides her professional work, Lale with increasing frequency lectures at mosques about issues of social work and education. While she earlier on had little to do with mosques, Lale has gradually been drawn into the orbit of (Turkish) mosques largely because of her social work expertise. Mosques in general and women groups in particular approach Lale to lecture and give advice on issues of social work, child welfare, and related topics. Lale quickly recognized the social work "void" in mosques, and provides help as much as her schedule allows her. Lale sees great potential in this sphere for future professional work for her. Lale quickly established a reputation for herself in mosques and easily fills meeting rooms with women eager to hear her advice. I accompanied her once for such a lecture. Lale spoke without notes (in Turkish) and quickly pulled her audience in. Within twenty minutes Lale established an atmosphere where women asked what seemed to be all the questions about the German social/child welfare system they had always wanted to ask. Lale could barely keep up answering the many questions and concerns. At times Lale has a list of mosques (of different associations) that are in line for lectures and events. In 2011 Lale took on a new job as the director of an independent project in the broader field of migration/integration social affairs and politics.

Within only a few years, Lale has become an actor in the urban and political sphere of Stuttgart and closely cooperates with central political figures in this field. She continues to live in Nordbahnhof. Once, Lale almost solemnly pronounced in a semi-public context: "I am practicing German and a Stuttgarter with all my heart" (*Ich bin praktizierende Deutsche und mit ganzem Herzen Stuttgarterin*).

Migrant Experiences: The 2000s

Like Lale, I met Ulrike Meier-Mahmoudi through the Park School. Ulrike was part of the minority of ethnic German parents in the school. Wearing a dark colored *himar*, Ulrike (a convert to Islam) was visibly different from both her German compatriots in the school yard and the women of Turkish or Bosnian background who wore *hijab*s and colorful outfits. Ulrike was part of the group of friends that also included Lale and which organized rotating breakfasts in 2007. After some brief encounters, Ulrike and I set up an interview, which marked the beginning of a friendship and more time spent together. Ulrike is a very lively person. She is humorous and a great storyteller. I remember one day in her living room when Lale, Emine, and myself were sitting together and Ulrike told stories about her *umra* (minor pilgrimage) and how she managed on the various stages to deal with the overwhelming crowd. We could not stop laughing about her stories. On a different occasion another friend remarked about Ulrike, "isn't it amazing how many words she can squeeze into one minute?" Ulrike has three children and is always doing things for school, preparing children's programs for her mosque, baby-sitting friends' children, or teaching Arabic to her Afghan neighbors' children. Ulrike is highly visible with her *himar* when she moves—always at a very fast pace—through the neighborhood. Running in large strides across the schoolyard chasing after her youngest with flying robes is a most characteristic image of Ulrike.

Ulrike was born in the late 1970s in the former GDR. She grew up in a large city in an era when religion was shunned. Children who went to religious instruction in school were discriminated against in subtle ways. She nevertheless went. She vaguely identified as a Christian. The question of who she was or what her way or goal in life was, early on occupied Ulrike. Her mother was an atheist and thus not very helpful in spiritual matters. Ulrike remembers praying to God when she was afraid as a child. She said, "I had my own little religion. It was childlike, an image of God on a cloud or so." Nature simply could not be all a coincidence, she decided in her child's mind. At the time of the collapse of the GDR, Ulrike was on the verge becoming a teenager. Issues of religions, ethics, and Christianity were now freely debated in school. Christianity, however, remained distant to Ulrike. The Christian image of God was too personified for her. God almost seemed like a human being in her perception. Jesus and the idea of trinity seemed too human to her.

When she was in eighth grade one of her girlfriends befriended an Iraqi woman who ran a food stall by the train station in their city. The woman started to tell the girls about Islam, and at the age of fifteen years, Ulrike's friend converted. This friend started to bring books and pamphlets to Ulrike who eagerly read the materials which spoke to some of her innermost questions. It was in particular the concept of *tawhid* (unity of God) that appealed to Ulrike. Allah in these books was unique and all-encompassing. There was no sense in even trying to imagine anything about Allah. From the age of fifteen, Ulrike remembered, she started to do Muslim prayers, but only irregularly. When I asked her when she had actually said the *shahada*, Ulrike responded that this was never of central importance to her. Her turn to Islam had been a long and gradual process. She read books, tried to learn and understand Islam and incrementally articulated her religiosity, following the Qur'an and *Sunna*. With regard to the "official" *shahada*, she noted that she never did that even years after she had started to practice more seriously. "I only did that when I had to, because I wanted to do the *umra* and I needed official papers about being a Muslim for the visa to Saudi-Arabia."

Becoming a pious Muslima for Ulrike is a lifelong process of learning. The bookshelves in her living room testify to that, as they hold volumes of *tafsir*, *hadith*s collections, and other theological works. She contrasts her trajectory to that of born, or as she says "traditional" Muslims who just pray and fast out of habit. In search of spirituality and a community of like-minded women, she joined one of the early Muslim communities in eastern Germany and became a founding member of its women's chapter. In this community she met an Algerian, Salim, whom she married in 1996. When I asked her whether she had consciously sought out a Muslim husband, she said it just so happened because of the circles in which she moved. Salim was religious, but, she noted, had no profound knowledge of Islam. He had never formally studied his religion. Ulrike and Salim embarked on a spiritual journey and started improving their practices together. In the meanwhile Ulrike had finished school and started to train as a legal assistant in a lawyer's office.

In December 1998 Ulrike performed her *umra*. Mecca was an overpowering experience for her. She felt that she was removed from all worldly affairs. As she stood in front of the *Kaaba* all she could repeat again and again was "*subhan-Allah*" (Allah is glorious, Glory belongs to Allah) from the depth of her heart. It became clear to her that "the only thing that was important was Allah, nothing else, not our environment or work or anything." She returned from Mecca with a different sense of life. Before the *umra* Ulrike had worn a headscarf, but not at work. Upon her return she decided that she could not continue that way. Her mother and grandmother with whom Ulrike had always been very close knew about her conversion and, while not thrilled, supported her decision. Work, however, was different. Her boss made it clear from the beginning that he did not want a worker with a headscarf. Tired of what she called her "double life" (*Doppelleben*) she quit her job. "You have to know that when I first started to wear the *hijab*, I only wore a headscarf, not *himar*, and I wore it with jeans and such types of clothes." She figured that she would either find another job or study social work. She applied to two law firms. One rejected her and the second hired her without any reservations. A few weeks after her return from Saudi-Arabia, she started in the office of a very pious Christian lawyer. "He was very serious about his religion, he fasted. Occasionally he would even sent female employees back home if they showed up in extremely short skirts." He explained that he preferred "too much religion over too little." Ulrike's experience with this employer was fundamentally positive. It frequently happened, however, that clients upon arriving looked helplessly around the office searching for a clerical assistant, thinking that Ulrike in her *hijab* and later *himar* was the cleaning lady. She humorously dealt with these situations. Her boss never debated her decision to start wearing a dark *himar*. Ulrike embarked on a successful career as a legal assistant and soon became the office manager. Salim however, had a hard time finding permanent work in a situation of notorious unemployment in eastern Germany. In the early years of the twenty-first century the couple had their first two children.

Salim eventually started looking for work in Stuttgart where he had a brother and job prospects were better than in the East. He found an industrial job. Ulrike, however, had a well-paying job ("they paid me by western standards") and knew that it would be next to impossible to get any job, let alone an office manager position, wearing a *himar*. She stayed behind with the children who went to day care and spent time with Ulrike's parents. Salim commuted on the weekends. While life in the East was not easy for a Muslima, Ulrike preferred staying because of the immense support of the friends/sisters in her mosque who formed a tight network. Ulrike frequently talks about "her sisters" and still spends much of the school vacations with them, and her parents in the East. Remembering everyday life in the East, Ulrike has unpleasant memories: "As far as Islam is concerned, this is really new territory (*Neuland*). On a few occasions people were spitting at me or my husband. On others they just call us 'murderer', 'terrorist', or 'animal abuser' [because of the controversy over *halal* butchering, PK] on the street." After one such experience, Ulrike's daughter asked her, "Mami, what did we do that these people are so angry with us?" Ulrike added that many Arab women are afraid to go out on the streets, as the resentments are too overwhelming for them. Some simple could not bear it and left.[11]

In 2006 Ulrike had her third child and her oldest daughter, Karima, had to start school. Ulrike and Salim decided that they no longer wanted to live apart. With three children, Ulrike also wanted to stay home for some time. After giving birth to Ibrahim in the East ("I wanted to be with the sisters"), Ulrike moved to Stuttgart. In a competitive and discriminatory rental situation, the family had a hard time finding an apartment "people just stare at us when they see us together," Ulrike noted. Salim has a long beard and (often) wears *salafi* clothes, that is—among other things—baggy distinctly above angle length pants. In his free time he sometimes wears a long white cloak with a skull cap. Ulrike and Salim ended up in Nordbahnhof in a building that also houses some large Afghan families. "And even for this apartment," Ulrike explained, "there were 50 applicants. It was sheer luck that we got it. It happened that the administrator at the agency was from my city and after we had talked on the phone a few times, she decided to give us the apartment." Being German and speaking with a distinct regional dialect tremendously helped Ulrike in this case. She enjoys the Nordbahnhof neighborhood for its density of Muslims. "Finally, the children can have many Muslim friends." Omar, her second oldest, takes advantage of this situation and frequently takes off with the numerous Afghan boys in the building and surrounding. "You turn around and he is gone," Ulrike notes. "But I don't always like it that much, because when they are inside these boys watch way too much TV."

Having Muslim neighbors and friends, Ulrike explains, makes life easier because of shared interests, practices, and taboos. Living in non-Muslim contexts, tensions will invariably emerge for children as worldviews and lifestyles might clash. "Take, for example dancing, or kissing boys. This is out of the question for me." In a thoroughly non-Muslim environment, she feels it was hard for Karima to develop as a Muslima. Here in Nordbahnhof where Muslims are an established social and cultural group, things are easier. Back in East Germany they had lived in two separate worlds: the public sphere and the (invisible) Muslim sphere. In Nordbahnhof things are more integrated. Here, Karima can do her prayers with a friend from school.

Once Karima started school, Ulrike was elected to be the representative of Karima's first grade class to the school's parents' assembly. While the students at the school are largely of immigrant descent, the parents' assembly included a disproportionate number of ethnic Germans. This had less to do with them being pushy, but more with the fears of many parents of running for even such an insignificant office. Not shy and somewhat familiar with the system (not completely as she had partly grown up under the GDR regime), this was no challenge for Ulrike.

"But don't think," Ulrike noted in the middle of heaping praise on the neighborhood, "that Stuttgart as a whole is dramatically more tolerant than the East. Outside the confines of Nordbahnhof things are different." Least of all people stare at Ulrike. Remarks on the street are more subtle but in the end equally painful. One of the more frequent ones can best be summed up with the sigh "poor women" that Ulrike occasionally overhears. One day she arrived at my house all out of breath and said "quick, give me a piece of paper, I have to write something." After I handed her the paper she scribbled an email address and then explained: "I was just walking down N-Street when this driver of a van stuck his head out of his car and shouted 'what is this? Why are you wearing this thing here?' and got all angry about my clothes. This is not the first time this happened, but since the van had the company's website on it, I will send them an e-mail and complain. Once a similar thing happened back home and the company apologized and we even got a free city tour."

One day when she was out with her children somebody said, "Why don't you just have two kids. Why have so many and then be a burden on the state (*dem Staat auf der Tasche liegen*)." Ulrike wondered why anybody would say this without knowing her family situation. The remark indicates a sense of "their" versus "our" children. Ulrike's children for this commentator cannot be "ours." Her husband faces similar problems at work. His boss told him: "So long as you have this beard, you won't get anywhere with me" (*sind Sie bei mir unten durch*).

Regardless, Ulrike insists that she can practice Islam most freely in Germany. Algeria just does not feel like home to her, she is "too German" for that, she noted. It is not the religion there but social and cultural life at large. In her usual funny way she recounted some of her experiences there: "There is garbage all over, they do not care about the environment, which they should as good Muslims. One day we walked down the street with my niece and she was drinking a bottle of Orangina. Upon finishing the bottle, she just threw it on the sidewalk. I got upset and made her pick up the bottle and carry it to a garbage can. I tell you, when we landed in Berlin and I saw all the clean and green spaces I was really glad to be home." Ulrike also does not share ideas about women's work and position in Algeria: "One day I spent long hours with my sisters-in-law cleaning and processing a huge mountain of tiny fish. It was tedious and boring. I don't want to live and work like that. I'd rather cook simple things and read a book instead."

Ulrike has no use for social patriarchy. She explains that the Qur'an and *Sunna* do not proscribe long hours of tedious housework, but instead encourage studying and engagement with people—which she does with great joy. Returning from a vacation in Algeria in 2008 she complained: "I wanted to go to the mosque there, but some of the men said I should not go and that it was inappropriate for a woman to go. I quoted them a *hadith* that supported my opinion but they were not convinced and I did not go in the end."

Since Ulrike moved to Stuttgart, she has been very active in the Al-Yassin Mosque. She and her children spend two afternoons a week teaching and studying there. Ulrike is one of three women there who run a large children's program that accommodates about 100 children. She puts much energy and thought in her work, but complains about the lack of help from other women: "It is amazing how three women are left with so much work, when there are so many women! Of course I will continue my work there but we need to get more women to participate. We cannot shoulder all this responsibility." Ulrike is also a leader/teacher in a women's Qur'an study group.

Within two years Ulrike found a home, friends, and activities in the neighborhood and beyond. She is content in Nordbahnhof:

> This works really well for me, better than moving to Algeria as my husband sometimes suggests. Islamically speaking, I would not gain by moving to Algeria. As I said, they would not even let me pray in a mosque. There is so much about their religious practices that is not really in the Qur'an. And the way they treat women is also not very Islamic. The men make them work hard and help very little. The public schools are not very good and there are no good Islamic schools. I am much better off here, and so is Karima. I want her to get a good education.

Ulrike quickly established a reputation at the local school for being willing to help and discuss issues. Therefore other Muslim parents sometimes approach her to voice concerns at the school. As a recent migrant to the neighborhood and Muslim German, Ulrike insists on inserting her religious sensitivities into the everyday life of the neighborhood and school. Her outspoken and visible presence both challenges and reinforces elements of the quarter's culture. As an ethnic German Ulrike is part of a local minority, as a recent migrant to the neighborhood she is part of a long chain of arrivals, and as a Muslim she is part of the largest religious group in the neighborhood. As a pious Muslima she connects to local Muslim lifestyles and social circles.

Negotiating Neighborhood Culture: Swimming Lessons

With her professional experience, sensitive personality, and reflective nature, Lale became an important interlocutor about Muslim affairs for the principal of the Park School.[12] She frequently cooperated with Ulrike in school affairs. Whether or not Muslim girls should attend swimming lessons in public schools is a controversial topic of debate in Germany (Schiffauer, 2010: 303; Ewing 2008: 190). Often articulated as a strictly either/or matter, shades and possibilities in between are overlooked. The Park School's administration and the school system at large prescribe swimming in the curriculum. Ms. Bauer, the principal, noted that "swimming can be a life-saving skill and therefore is important for everybody and needs to be taught." Some Muslim parents felt differently about swimming lessons. Pious Muslim sentiments about the integrity of the body, and religious rules that prohibit displaying one's body in front of members of the opposite sex conflict with the school curriculum. A compromise needed to be found. The task at hand was not to show that either side was right or wrong. The challenge was to find ways to accommodate both. In a conversation about swimming lessons, Ms. Bauer explained that swimming is usually in the curriculum for sixth or seventh graders.[13] At this point, around puberty, it is unacceptable for many Muslims to have their daughters (and also their sons) attend swimming lessons. Understanding these sensitivities, Ms. Bauer noted that the school decided a while ago to move the swimming lessons to grade three when children are still young enough to swim together in a public pool.[14] For most parents this was an acceptable compromise and they sent their children to the lessons. Some pious parents, who agreed with the general idea of swimming as a necessary skill, decided to have their girls swim in outfits that covered their shoulder and knees. With the availability of various modest Islamic swimsuits, it was no problem for savvy parents to find appropriate outfits that covered girls' bodies but did become see-through or too heavy in the water. Nobody objected to these swimsuits. The school appreciated these parents' efforts. Only a few families objected to swimming lessons altogether. Yet they did not voice their disagreement out loud. A girl might simply not show up for swimming or for some weeks pretend to be sick on the day of swimming lessons. These cases remained rare over the years. Teachers and the principal try to speak with parents and devise compromises to assure that a girl can learn to swim.

Recently an Afghan family did not send their daughter to the swimming lesson, without saying that they were opposed to swimming. Most Afghans are recent arrivals in the city and few participate in school and neighborhood activities. They have little experience in civic participation and tend to voice their disagreement with withdrawal.[15] The girl in question started to "coincidentally" miss swimming or "forget" her swimsuit. When contacted, the family responded that they would comply and send their daughter. This back and forth could have gone on for a few more weeks, but Ms. Bauer decided that the school was losing valuable time. She contacted Lale and Ulrike whose daughters wore tight knee length swim shorts and short-sleeved swim shirts for the lessons. Ms. Bauer asked them where they had purchased these outfits and whether there was any possibility to acquire an outfit for the girl who was avoiding swimming lessons. Lale had a long-sleeved swimming top with a hood (bought in Turkey) at home, which she then donated to the school. Moreover, she purchased (long) swim pants in a local store using funds that has been donated to the school. After the combined efforts of Lale, Ulrike, and Ms. Bauer, the girl's father continued to make excuses for his daughter's "coincidental" absences. Regardless of this disappointment, Ms. Bauer kept the swimming outfit and it soon found other users. The outfit is now school property, which girls can borrow. Once their swimming lessons are over they are supposed to return the outfit, which can then be given to the next girl.[16]

Negotiating Neighborhood Culture: Celebrating *Eid*

A few days before the end of Ramadan in 2007, Tamima and Tala received an invitation, decorated with the image of a mosque and children's stickers of Nemo, for Karima's *Eid* celebration on a Sunday afternoon. When we arrived in their apartment, all the guests of this girls' party were there: Lale's daughters, and Aziza and her baby sister Hadia who were from Afghanistan and lived in the building. The only boy was Karima's younger brother. Ulrike's husband and baby son were at the mosque. The kitchen and living room were decorated with colorful paper mosques, palm trees, and crescents hung from strings across the rooms. The kitchen table was set with snacks. A white cake decorated with colorful sprinkles was on the counter. After some playing, Ulrike called the children to explain the games of the day. "We are playing a day in Ramadan," she announced. "We will start early in the morning and then do games for every part of the day. We will start in the living room with the *suhur*."

We moved to the living room, where she had prepared a cotton bag filled with small food items. Every child took something to start their *suhur* and grabbed into the bag and felt items and guessed what it was before they could take it. The children played two rounds of guessing. Next was the real *suhur* which was the cake and juice set up in the kitchen. After that everybody was ready for the fast and various tasks. Ulrike explained: "Ramadan is the time when one is supposed to do good deeds. That means for children that they should help their mothers. So, next we do two household games to help our mothers. First, we need to hang laundry, and second to sweep the floor." Three children were given piles of the baby's clothes and clothespins and had to hang them on a laundry rack. The other three children had to sweep three wooden beads across the living room and the children's room with a broom. The mood was great and everybody was cheering for the contestants. After each game the winner received six gifts which they had to share—in true Ramadan spirit—with everybody. "Next," Ulrike explained, "we have to get ready for the *Eid el Fitr*. That means we have to bake and decorate cookies." We moved back to the kitchen where she held up two large boxes with simple homemade cookies in different shapes, and decoration materials, like sprinkles. With powdered sugar and lemon juice she quickly produced white frosting. "The task is to make these really beautiful for the *Eid*," she told the children as she prepared the workspace. Everybody was excited and ready to work. Ulrike looked over to me and looking at the cookies, she said and smiled "Christmas cookies." "I figured," I replied looking at this familiar type of baked goods. "Why not?" she smiled. "Precisely," I responded, but nobody paid attention to us as frosting, glazing, and colorful decorating were under way at the table. As our Ramadan day was nearing its end, Ulrike explained the next step: "The evening prayer and breaking of the fast are approaching. Now everybody needs to go to the mosque for their prayers. We will go out together, and everybody will run from the back door to the playground, up to the slide, call *Allahu Akbar* and then run back over to the swing, run around it and return to the starting point."

The children got dressed. The girls all wore headscarves for this activity and they ran downstairs, raced to the playground and came back. While we stayed downstairs for a few minutes, Ulrike's husband who had returned from the mosque started cooking the dinner, or really, the *iftar* for the guests. Soon the kids sat around the kitchen table and ate pasta. But Ramadan was not over yet. After dinner, a last task awaited the guests. In the living room, Ulrike explained the last game: "Before Ramadan is over, you have to give your *zakat* to the mosque." Holding up a card board mosque, wrapped in blue glossy paper with two minarets made of kitchen towel rolls and a yellow crescent on top, Ulrike opened the front "door" of the mosques, and noted that the *zakat* needed to be deposited inside the mosque. Three one Euro coins were the *zakat* which she put on the coffee table. These coins had to be carried one by one on a slippery plastic fork to the mosque which she set up in the hall. Time was taken with a cell phone. The children ran, the coins dropped, the audience cheered and yelled, and everybody had a great time. Four hours of the party were over in no time and nobody was ready to go home. The children dispersed in groups, Omar and one girl who were both great dinosaur fans retreated to his dinosaur collection. The other girls sat on Karima's loft bed, read, drew, and did girls' talk. Little Hadia had left a while ago, only Ibrahim wandered from room to room as the older children sent him along to prevent him from interfering in their games and talk.

Ulrike's children's *Eid* celebration offers a glimpse at a religious lifeworld which is rooted in and inspired by both Islamic and German cultural contexts. Indeed, this little party neatly symbolizes the emerging German Muslim cultural milieu. Ulrike does not celebrate her children's birthdays with parties. Yet she does not want to deprive them of the possibility to invite friends and have fun parties. Therefore each *Eid*, either Karima or Omar can invite their friends (Ibrahim is still too young to be integrated in this program). Drawing on the genre of the German children's birthday with cake, decoration, plenty of games (the burden of preparation, materials, and organization is on the mother), and dinner all held in the home, Ulrike has re-crafted this tradition to fit her purpose and beliefs. In addition to offering fun games (most are standard birthday fare), Ulrike has integrated these games in a larger educational narrative of Ramadan, its mundane activities, moral teachings, and religious obligations. Ulrike has cleverly woven the two traditions together to produce an event that smoothly fits in both contexts and reflects its dual ancestry. She took an available German model and pulled it into a Muslim context. She dressed the fun parts and games of conventional birthday parties in a Muslim and educational garb to produce an effect that suits her ideal children's lifeworld. The result is a party that is as Islamic as it is German.

Negotiating Neighborhood Culture: Aynur's Hair Salon

Hairdressers, the world over, are notorious for their communicative realities and potentials. Aynur's Hair Salon in Nordbahnhof is no exception.[17] Not only is this location a great communicative platform, it is a veritable stage of cultural cooperation, negotiation, and production. In the limited spatiality of this medium-size neighborhood hair salon, cultural worlds are negotiated, made, and remade in daily multi-ethnic encounters. The physical proximity of cutting hair and doing nails combined with the trust involved in letting others work on one's body adds to the density of the salon's sociality. By crossing habitual lines of how close one gets to others, a hair salon allows for a social permeability and quality of exchange that is rare elsewhere. Random encounters in the nonetheless predictable framework of a hair salon allow for exchanges between people who would not necessarily meet, and they allow for the possibility to listen to and participate in the semi-public conversations of hairstylists and clients.

Over the years I became a regular at Aynur's. One day in November 2007 I went for a haircut at the salon. I walked to Aynur's to check whether she had time the same day. Many of Aynur's clients arrange their appointment this way, just dropping by on neighborhood errands. Largely a women's salon, this business serves men, but in smaller numbers. Aynur Mesut, the owner, told me to come back in an hour, which I did. When I returned, a young woman had her nails done, an older woman was waiting for her hair to be blow dried, and a third woman had her hair straightened. Ms. Mesut and her three assistants were busy. Ms. Mesut, who was in her forties, is of Turkish Alevi descent. One of the younger stylists, Mira, is Albanian. Sarah, the assistant who straightened an African woman's hair is Eritrean and specializes in African hair.[18] People come here especially for her services. Conversations were carried on across the salon.

After a while, a cashier of the local discount grocery, a middle-aged Turkish woman who is very sociable and never short of words and jokes, entered the store. She spiced up conversation which continued to be carried on largely in German. It is clear that Ms. Mesut prefers for such semi-public conversations to be carried out in German so that (almost) everybody in the store is included. The younger assistant jokingly kept calling the new arrival "Ms. Discounter." Ms. Discounter turned to the Albanian stylists and asked about her pending wedding and whether she would be invited. The assistant responded that it was going to be in Albania, otherwise she could of course come. "I'll go to Albania, no problem," Ms. Discounter replied. Ms. Discounter and Mira exchanged notes about the specificities Turkish and Albanian weddings, a veritable lesson in comparative cultural studies for everybody else to absorb.

After a while conversation moved to various bodily aches and pains to hair colors, and the fact that the national lottery's jackpot had increased to 25 million Euro for the weekend. Everybody agreed, they would win this sum. Ms. Discounter added that even if she won she would continue to have her hair done at Aynur's. Meanwhile places were shifted and Ms. Discounter moved to the hair washing seat and kept chatting from this more distant space. Aynur was cutting my hair and Sarah had finished her customer and moved to the back to add some color to her own hair. Mira got coloring ready for Ms. Discounter. They were talking about totally rejuvenating the woman by hair color and make up. In the middle of this conversation an elderly woman came running in the store crossed to the back and quickly said: "You know why I am here." "Sure any time," Ms. Mesut replied, as the hurried woman disappeared in the bathroom. When the woman re-emerged from the bathroom, she tried to explain and apologize, Ms. Mesut said, that we all knew what it was like and the woman was welcome any time. The hurried visitor said her thanks and disappeared. Ms. Discounter started to philosophize about the correct temperature for washing hair. "Ideally," she pontificated, "one should always wash one's hair with fairly cold water. I just saw an expert hairdresser talk about this on TV." Sarah who had entered the talking stage again from the backroom overheard this last piece of expert information and turned to Ms. Discounter: "That might work for your European hair, but African hair certainly needs hot water. What do you guys know!" The respective temperature and water needs of hair were briefly debated, when another elderly German woman came in, walked straight up to Ms. Mesut and said in a low voice: "Did you know, Mrs. Bergmann has already been buried." "Oh, is that so," Ms. Mesut replied, "that was very fast." "Such is life," replied the woman and continued to ask whether she could come by the next day for a haircut. "Sure, come early at 9:30," Ms. Mesut responded without looking at her appointment book.

Conversations at Aynur's vary with the presence of customers and the changing younger hairstylists. Regardless of who is present, there is always a minimum of four to five ethnicities and women of different generations. Hair, health, TV programs, family relations, marriages, weddings, and sometimes deaths are central topics of conversation. Some customers are lively discussants like Ms. Discounter, while others only listen. Frequently such discussions are lessons on comparative cultures as stylists and customers exchange notes about weddings, family issues and problems, conflicts with in-laws, family gift giving expectations, and the like. Occasionally some of the elderly women will volunteer stories about the "old days" in Nordbahnhof. Rarely have I left Aynur's without having heard interesting accounts and stories that furthered my understanding of the quarter, its residents, and past and present cultural diversity.

Negotiating Neighborhood Culture: Public Celebrations

The Nordbahnhof is a lively stage for summer festivals. The first and largest such celebration is the International Neighborhood Festival, which takes place on a Saturday in late June/early July at the Kulturhaus. In the past tables and benches were set up on the center's soccer and play field. Starting in 2011 the event was moved to the adjacent street which was closed off for the day. The set-up of this event includes a sizable stage with speakers and spaces for presentations and numerous food stalls run by international groups and neighborhood associations that regularly met at the Kulturhaus. At the 2007 International Festival a Turkish dance group offered pop corn and waffles, the Portuguese folklore group barbequed fish and shrimps, and had cakes and coffee on their list. The urban gardeners' association sold sausages (*Rote Wurst*), French fries, soft drinks, and beer. A Turkish classical music band offered a broad selection of Turkish appetizers, stuffed pita bread and tea. An Italian group baked pizza.

The afternoon officially started with the folklore and music groups. A recently founded (April 2007) Portuguese fanfare group marched into the yard with rhythmic loud drumming. Their beat captivated the audience as they almost in slow motion moved from the entrance of the yard to the stage area. The benches were crowded with people of diverse backgrounds. There were national, ethnic, and age clusters. The northwestern corner, close to the popcorn stand, was German and older, as were the few rows of tables right next to the stall of the small gardeners' association. Looking at this cluster from the slightly elevated vantage of the entrance to the yard, they seemed marginal by ethnicity and age. There were clusters of Turkish women who wore headscarves, clusters of those without, and groups that included both. Next to me sat three women in their forties in headscarves sipping coffee and smoking cigarettes. Closer to the stage, there was an elderly couple who presides over a large established local Kurdish family. Two of their young grandchildren were with them and crawled over and under the benches and tables. One table over Mr. and Mrs. Haller sat, each with a glass of beer in front of them (this was the occasion I first met them). They did not sit in the German retiree block, but in the multicultural section closer to the stage. Then there were the truly multicultural tables of teenagers. No ethnic or age groups, however, dominated the scenery.

To be sure, there are moments of tension and resentment, but these are part of the complex task of negotiating neighborhood culture. For instance, there was the elderly male who walked behind me as I entered the yard, and who under his breath mumbled to his wife: "But there are only Turks here." I did not hear the rest of their conversation. However his statement had not been an angry one, but one uttered with a sense of accommodating a disappointment. It did not make the man turn around and leave. Instead I watched him walk in, search for a space and enjoy the festival. His remark indicated his sense of a less than perfect but nonetheless acceptable situation. Things had taken a turn that he was not completely happy with, but it did not change anything in his attendance of the event. At least superficially he accepted the multi-ethnic scene and became part of it.

The performance of the Turkish folklore group pulled members of the audience in, some joined the dancers. Little girls danced in front of the performers. Some people clapped along. Portuguese and Spanish dance groups followed and also moved the audience with their rhythms. Later the Portuguese Fanfare group marched in a second time with their loud drumming. By 7 P.M., some people started to leave. The remaining audience, well-fed and entertained sat happily and peacefully together. By 8:30 P.M. (it was still light out on this summer evening) a Turkish band started to play. Some younger girls danced in front of the stage. Soon the band only made their announcements in Turkish. None of the young dancers seemed to care. At this hour the event had become a teenager party where dancing mattered most and words were secondary for the multi-ethnic dancers. Whether the music was announced in Turkish, Italian or German made little difference to them, so long as it were danceable rhythms.

The 2010 International Festival included a food stall run by an African cultural association that reflected the growing presence of Africans in the quarter. The stall has since become a permanent fixture. The 2012 Festival included both a cake stall and lengthy performance of a Kosovo-Albanian cultural group. Relative newcomers (at least in larger numbers), Kosovo-Albanians thus both introduced and situated themselves as a permanent local constituency. Watching the Kosovo-Albanians from a table in the front row was a multi-ethnic table of sixth, seventh, and eighth graders from the local school. Among this dozen teenagers I counted nine national/ethnic origins (Turkish, Portuguese, German, Italian, Macedonian, Afghan, Kurdish, Serbian, and Russian).

Every year the International Festival is followed by other celebrations in the neighborhood like the school's International Summer Festival (an irregular event), the annual street fair (*Hocketse*) of the northern half of the community, and the annual Radish Festival (*Rettichfest*) in the urban garden colony at the southwestern fringes of the community. The International Festival is by far the most diverse of these celebrations.

Producing Culture

Nordbahnhof, like other similar urban quarters, has for more than a century shouldered the fundamentally important task of negotiating urban cultures and identities. This railroad and later also postal workers' neighborhood has accommodated successive generations of migrants to the city. Generations of migrant children grew up together in this quarter. While their parents remained often tied to their old homes, the children made Nordbahnhof (and Stuttgart) their homes. Backyard and street culture mark these children's stories. Multi-ethnic and intergenerational neighborhood celebrations, shared spaces like Aynur's hair salon, encounters at the local school, and spaces of daily meetings and interactions are of paramount importance in the construction of the neighborhood's multi-ethnic and multi-religious culture. Transformations and innovations designed by individuals, and the footsteps taken by groups remake the community they collectively inhabit. With time these innovations become normalized and can spill over to other urban contexts. New forms and practices are slowly woven into the fabric of local lifeworlds and radiate outward into the city by way of individuals' participation in other spaces, contexts, and institutions. Some aspects become known like, for example, Muslims' avoidance of pork and alcohol, and become part of the neighborhood and eventually also urban cultural grammar. For instance, the use of two barbeque fixtures (pork and non-pork) has become standard practice in school and other celebrations in multi-ethnic neighborhoods.

When I talked to an elderly man at the street fair of the northern part of the neighborhood about the relative absence of in particular Turkish neighbors, he noted: "I don't quite understand this, as we made sure that we have beef dishes, coffee, and soft drinks for them." This statement indicates that this man/the organizers saw the absence of their Turkish/Muslim neighbors as a void. They made sure to address their respective dietary requirements. This attention to Muslim needs indicates that (unlike in many other German contexts) Muslims are important, respected, and sought after local partners. Indeed, this man bemoaned their absence.

The International Festival at the Kulturhaus provides a glimpse at neighborhood encounters. Diverse residents of the neighborhood enjoy each other's cultural performances, food, and company. Muslim lifeworlds are vaguely woven into this cultural complexity. The food stall of the (more secularly minded Turkish folklore group) served neither alcohol nor pork. Other stalls also included non-pork options. The presence of a considerable number of women with headscarves marked the existence of local pious lifeworlds. These women and their less visible (pious) spouses and children saw no contradiction between their religiosity and being at this festival. The festival and other activities at the Kulturhaus are integral parts of local pious lifeworlds. In neighborhoods like Nordbahnhof (and Zuffenhausen), Islam and Muslim practices are established elements of local cultures. It is impossible to miss Ramadan in the neighborhood. It is taken for granted that the week-long all day school summer camp for the Park School's third graders includes a non-pork lunch option. The localization of Muslim (and of course other ethnic and religious) practices is an ongoing process, as new issues and details are debated (e.g. how many days should students take off for Muslim holidays?). In the everyday friction, but also excitement of such negotiations, new forms and compromises constantly emerge (e.g. the annual "secular" *iftar* at the Kulturhaus) that slowly enter the social imaginaries of the neighborhood. They become normalized and are no longer noteworthy for local residents. Not all residents directly participate in cultural negotiations, nor do all residents share in all practices and compromises. Yet there is a broader neighborhood ethos, which for many constitutes the foundation of the sentimental attachment and pride they harbor for the neighborhood. The man who briefly "complained" about the presence of too many Turks at the International Festival can be understood as being involved in his own negotiations, when he, regardless of his remark, attended the festivities. He joined and allowed the festival atmosphere to possibly convince him that this diversity worked well for everybody.

Living in close proximity with each other and engaging with neighbors results in personal ties and cultural understandings that are of crucial importance for future urban cultures. Mr. and Mrs. Haller drank their beer in the middle of a multi-ethnic and multi-religious crowd. They appreciate the politeness of their Pakistani/Muslim neighbors, and harbor no fear of Islam or Muslims in their everyday lives. While screaming soccer-playing youngsters annoy the couple, they enjoy most other features of Nordbahnhof, their home of half a century.

The everyday experiences and cultural negotiations of individuals like Mr. Friedrich, Mr. and Mrs, Haller, Ms. Bauer, Lale, Ulrike, Ms. Mesut, her employees and clients, and many others are central ingredients of present and future urban cultures. Framed by institutions like schools, cultural centers, mosques, churches, but also as individual encounters in streets, playgrounds, stores, and homes, these instances of cultural dialogue or more precisely multilogue are rarely recognized by dominant societies as immensely valuable contributions to German cities. The neglect of the cultural dynamics of multi-ethnic working-class quarters is not new. Since the nineteenth century, migrants to the industrializing cities of Europe and the United States have been demonized and accused of undermining established (bourgeois) urban cultures. Rarely were their cultural potentials and work recognized or appreciated. Examining a quarter like Nordbahnhof, it becomes apparent that its residents engage in the crucial daily work of cultural negotiation. As urban and national elites debate abstract and ideologically charged topics like honor killings and forced marriage, individuals in multi-ethnic and multi-religious working-class quarters expand their energy in finding practical and respectful solutions to issues that are meaningful to themselves, their neighbors, and quarters. In Nordbahnhof, residents have performed such paramount cultural labor for more than a century. Catholics from Hohenlohe became Stuttgarters in the past and Muslim Turks have become Stuttgarters more recently. Individuals interact in the neighborhood on a more equal basis than they could on larger urban, let alone national platforms. The wealth of cultural work and resources available in Nordbahnhof is an overlooked and untapped resource in the making of more egalitarian urban cultures. The current emphasis on the national (middle-class and ethnic German) public sphere as a space for cultural and religious negotiations misses out on the strength and long experience of multi-ethnic working-class quarters in the creation of future urban cultures and identities.

Conclusion: At Home

Mr. Friedrich and Lale never met. Yet they have much in common as they both are typical Nordbahnhof "children" despite differences in gender, generation, ethnicity, and religion. Mr. Friedrich made it very clear in our neighborhood walk, that he felt a strong sense of belonging to his old neighborhood and the city. He contrasted himself and his peers to their parents' generation and emphasized: "We were Stuttgarters." They were Catholic Stuttgarters in the 1950s when this was not yet a normalized identity. Lale made the almost identical statement: "I am . . . a Stuttgarter with all my heart" (*Ich bin . . . mit ganzem Herzen Stuttgarterin*). In the early twenty-first century, Lale represents the first generation of Muslim Stuttgarters.

Notes

1. The Park School was one of twelve schools in the state that was part of a project in 2006 offering Islamic religious instruction in addition to Protestant and Catholic instruction.
2. The name refers back to the *Postdörfle*, an earlier similar development for postal workers developed by Eduard Pfeiffer, a local Jewish philanthropist, in the 1860s and 1870s.
3. Railroad workers still have preferential access to the apartments.
4. Figures for Nordbahnhof are notoriously hard to work with, as the quarter is part of the urban district of "Nord" which also includes one Stuttgart's wealthiest quarters, the hillside community Killesberg. Since Killesberg comprises over a third of the district, it can safely be assumed that the non-Protestant and non-Catholic population is even larger in the remaining parts of the district.
5. The administrative unit of Nordbahnhof includes the north train station and housing situated west of N-Street. The unit "Am Pragfriedhof" forms the southern outskirts of the area. I worked in the central "Auf der Prag" area.
6. Beauregard and Bounds speak about the "thick" relationships that characterize neighborhood life and concrete urban civic participation. These form a foundation of "urban citizenship" (2000: 243).
7. Peer-Uli Faerber neatly chronicles prewar life at this school in his novel *Der Stadtinspektor* (1988).
8. Christine Walley describes a similar phenomenon for a steel workers' neighborhood in Chicago (2013: 156).
9. The reference is to Fereshte Ludin who fought a long and tedious struggle about becoming a public school teacher wearing a headscarf. The case went all the way to the constitutional court and was rejected. See Eakin (2003); Landler (2003).

10. This is an event usually on or around November 9, when children walk around in neighborhoods with paper lanterns. While based on the religious story of St. Martin, it has long turned into popular culture.
11. See also the murder of Marwa Al-Sherbini in Dresden in 2009.
12. A shorter version of this encounter was published in Kuppinger 2014a.
13. The Park School is a *Grund- und Hauptschule* that provides a general elementary program for all neighborhood children in grades one to four (*Grundschule*). In grades five to nine the school provides instruction for those who aim for skilled blue-collar jobs. In the hierarchical German school system *Hauptschule* is the "lowest" in a three-tiered system. In practice this means, that children who did not "make it" into higher tiered schools, remain in the Hauptschule. In recent years this system has been the topic of debate and target of criticism. As of 2013 the school offers an enlarged program that includes a tenth grade.
14. Public pools are tricky as most include large window fronts, where even if the school children swim in sex-segregated groups, there are passers-by to reckon with.
15. One local middle-aged pious Muslim woman of Turkish decent noted about the relative isolation and strict focus onto Afghan culture and tradition, "we were like this, years ago, but this will change with time."
16. Lale related the solution of a *Gymnasium* (fifth to twelfth grade) where swimming lessons for girls take place between 7 and 9 A.M. before the official hours of a (public) pool. Pious girls swim there in regular swimsuits, as the view from outside is completely blocked by huge bushes, and only the female teacher and students are present.
17. For another account of Aynur's Hair Salon, see Kuppinger 2014d.
18. Over the years there has been fluctuation among the younger hairstylists. Regardless, the hairstylists always represent local diversity.

Conclusion

In the fall of 2007 when I was working as a homework tutor at the Kulturhaus, I helped Adnan, an eighth-grader, with his English homework. We started talking about the ongoing month of Ramadan and how he was keeping the fast, and what other practices made this month special for him. Adnan proudly noted that he easily managed to fast and do his schoolwork. Adnan, a Kurd from Turkey who came to Germany as a young child, also related how on most Ramadan evenings he went with one of his Afghan friends to an Afghan mosque to pray. When I asked him why he chose an Afghan mosque when there were so many Turkish mosques in Stuttgart, he explained that they went to this mosque because his friend felt more comfortable there. "For me this makes no difference. The prayers are all the same."

Adnan and individuals like Dr. Al-Mudarris, Sibel, Susanne-Samiha, or Hassan whom we met in earlier chapters are mobile urban citizens who navigate the city not only for their everyday work, social activities, or entertainment, but also in search of spiritual opportunities and religious engagements. Their "mosque-hopping" and related movements across the cityscape are not isolated acts of personal preference, but reflect broader patterns of urban mobilities, which are crucial to the construction of Muslim material, social, and spiritual geographies. Individual urban mobilities are crucial elements in the articulation of local Muslim subjectivities, and foundational features of the construction of Muslim spiritual and cultural topographies.

Individual urban mobility and movements are often the result of long-term and long-distance mobilities (e.g. labor migration, voluntary mobility of international students, involuntary movements of refugees). Long-distance mobility brought Muslims to German cities. Everyday individual urban mobilities create and intensify emerging religious and cultural topographies (Kuppinger 2014b, 2014f). Small-scale individual mobilities bring large-scale mobilities full circle and create concrete urban cultural and religious geographies which become integral parts of the urban public sphere, and regional and global Muslim circuits and networks. In this book I examined Muslim localization, participation, and inclusion in a German city. I illustrated how Islam is well on the way to becoming an established urban religion. In this conclusion I introduce one final element in the creation of local Muslim lives and geographies: individual mobilities. I take a look at mobilities in the configuration of Stuttgart's material and spiritual Muslim topography. I illustrate how especially in the past two decades mostly younger individuals by way of their mobilities created multilayered connections, moments of cooperation, and shared platforms that intensified and consolidated nascent urban Muslim cultures as part of national and global Muslim networks, and broader urban religious and cultural topographies. Emerging dynamic Muslim social, cultural, and religious topographies are the result of complex interactions between mosque communities and their members and their respective ethnic contexts, individual lifeworlds and mobilities, urban spatial politics, popular resentment, and global Islamic trends. Pious individuals use their knowledge of the city, modes of communication, and high degrees of urban mobility to weave their lives, pieties, and spatial circuits into a much tighter spiritual web than was the case with earlier generations of Muslims. Moreover they firmly situate their activities in the web of urban dynamics. Their religiosity is *of* the city.

Mobilities, Spatial Nodes, and Networks

Circuits of mobility engendered by the post–World War II economic boom ushered in the first phase of large-scale arrival of Muslims in Germany in the early 1960s building on vague foundations of earlier Muslim presence and activities. The first generation of Turkish, Moroccan, Tunisian, or Bosnian migrants left their home countries in search of better jobs. Their mobility was limited to moving back and forth between these two places as they hoped to quickly return to their countries of origin. Mobility for these predominantly male migrants was more of a necessity than an opportunity. Many of this first generation of migrants remained rather immobile in their German contexts, where they often only moved between a limited number of spaces (home/workers' dormitories, work places, soon prayer spaces, emerging ethnic bars and cultural associations, train stations as public meeting points). For instance, Lale (chapter 6) remembered the advice her father gave her as a child not to venture too far into "German" spaces, as one never knew what awaited one there and whether one was welcome. Fear of the unknown, but also the fear of rejection and resentment frequently characterized the early migrants' movements in and relationship to the city. Feeling, or in fact very much made to feel like strangers, many first-generation migrants rarely freely moved around, explored, and even less claimed or remade urban spaces. Their footsteps followed a given path and hardly ever challenged or renegotiated existing spatialities (de Certeau 1984). They remained "strangers in the city" (Schiffauer 1997); isolated and invisible, not only because of their relative immobility, but even more so because dominant society ignored, shunned, often resented, and closely circumscribed their presence. In the 1960s migrants were present in the city, but were excluded from creative participation.

Starting from the 1970s migrants and their families became more established. As their numbers grew, in particular, Turkish migrants started to slowly create ethnic enclaves mostly in places that had been partially deserted or given up by German residents (Kaya 2001; Ewing 2008b; Tietze 2001; Ceylan 2006; Jenkner 2008). Ignored by dominant society, individuals and groups created commercial, social, and religious spaces, where they felt at home (Mandel 1990, 1996, 2008; Mattausch and Yildiz 2009). Such quarters (e.g. Nordbahnhof), commercial streets (e.g. N-Street), or mosque complexes (e.g. the Salam Mosque; see also Kuppinger 2010a, 2011b) often became central nodes for urban and regional communities where individuals and families met to shop, socialize, pray, or celebrate. These emerging spaces expanded and intensified urban and regional circuits of mobility, sociality, and exchange (Gliemann and Caesperlein 2008; Yildiz 2009; Jenkner 2008; Kuppinger 2010a, 2011b). In this early phase of localization additional small nodes were continuously added to the still limited urban ethnic and/or religious circuits. They had, however, little impact on the cityscape at large. The increased number of nodes and their growing attraction among insiders represented a quantitative change with regard to the Muslim presence in German cities, but did not yet translate into qualitative urban transformations or effective civic participation. Until the turn of the twenty-first century dominant society on the one hand largely ignored these spaces and on the other had actively limited or fought their expansion (see chapter 1).

Starting in the 1980s, the second and soon third generations of Turkish and other Muslims were born, raised, or came of age in Germany. They did not restrict their mobility patterns and movements to the limited number of nodes and small urban circuits of their (grand-) parents. Socialized in local schools, places, and institutions, these younger individuals did not share their (grand-) parents' inhibitions about the city. Not only did they become visible, but more importantly they wanted to be visible and recognized. They claimed access to spaces and participation in the city (Jonker and Amiraux 2006; Göle and Ammann 2004; Tarlo 2010). It was no longer a matter of adding new nodes to existing (invisible) religious and ethnic circuits, but to insert relevant Muslim forms, practices, and demands into the cityscape (e.g. the addition of the Imam to the school celebration). The point was no longer that Muslims and their communities would be (very unwillingly) accommodated in the city, but that the city was to "naturally" and inherently reflect the presence of its Muslim citizens.

Starting from the 1990s, the growth, localization, and consolidation of mosque communities resulted in the purchase of larger and better premises for many communities (e.g the expansion of the Al-Nour Mosque). Communities had outgrown their backyard facilities and wished to acquire better and larger facilities that they could permanently inhabit. In the course of the 1990s and even more acutely after 9/11, individuals and communities wanted to show to the public that they had long since arrived and become ordinary urban constituencies (e.g. by way of intensified participation in interfaith activities). At ease in the city, individuals moved across spaces, creating new and intensifying existing Muslim links and networks. They inserted religious practices (e.g. praying in the park, the quest for prayer spaces in work spaces), asked for reasonable accommodations (e.g. change of work shifts during Ramadan), introduced religious symbols (e.g. the headscarf), and created new food markets and products (e.g. *halal* products). The public presence and participation of pious Muslims incrementally changed aspects of urban spaces and culture to accommodate their needs. Their visibility, movements, and mobility, as pious individuals consolidated into the configuration of a Muslim spiritual geography as an integral and inseparable part of the city. In order for comprehensive Muslim spiritual geographies to emerge, well-established individual mosque communities were paramount. A member of one mosque's board of directors explained: "first you have to get settled and renovate your own house, before you can reach out and invite guests." Established spatial nodes or home spaces are the prerequisite for further urban mobility and the creation of complex links, participation, and cooperation in the city.

Mosque Hoppers: Pious Trajectories and Relations

In the early years of the twenty-first century pious Muslims and their communities were firmly established in Stuttgart. Even if dominant society was/is unaware or struggling with this fact, Muslims belong to the city as much as the city belongs to them. At home in the city, some communities, and even more so pious individuals, started to create links and cooperate with diverse other groups and associations. They organized events and activities together with other Muslim, Christian, Jewish, or secular organizations and institutions. In short: today pious Muslims are active urban citizens and cultural producers. Mr. Serdar recounted how when he first asked the local council to be included in its Christmas celebrations: "They were very surprised but then invited us. Now we are invited every year." In the twenty-first century individuals and groups are no longer satisfied with the isolated nodes of the past, where Muslims largely met Muslims, Turks met Turks, or Arabs met Arabs. Many move into and claim spaces in mainstream society as pious Muslims. Younger individuals with deep roots in the city confidently formulate their demands and do the necessary footwork. The city is theirs, and they navigate and negotiate its spaces as ordinary urbanites.

The events of 9/11 changed the mainstream perception and treatment of Muslims in Germany. First identified as *Gastarbeiter*, later as Turks or Moroccans, then foreign fellow residents/citizens (*ausländische Mitbürger*) and migrants, almost overnight they became "Muslims." Turks, Moroccans, Afghans, Iranians, Bosnians, or Iraqis, women and men, old and young, wealthy and poor, fourth generation or recent arrival—they were indiscriminately described as Muslims and subsequently as suspicious. This blanket suspicion indirectly encouraged some Muslims to strengthen links and relationships among local pious groups and communities.

Many younger pious Muslims are increasingly less concerned about ethnic "home" aspects when looking for a mosque or pious group, but they hope to meet and engage people who share their religiosities, pious practices, and lifeworlds. For many individuals the ethnicity and language of their (grand-) parents becomes secondary. Growing numbers of pious individuals marry pious spouses across ethnic boundaries (e.g. Ulrike and Salim, or Amna and Tamer). Encouraged by shared experiences in schools, workplaces, and neighborhoods, their intimate knowledge of the city, native use of the German language, urban mobility, and an interest in varying ethnic customs and religious practices, some believers accompany their peers to different mosques. For the purpose of Qur'an study and partially for social aspects, others similarly traverse the urban mosque-scape in search of the most suitable group and instruction. Sibel, for instance, attended the German language Qur'an study group at the Al-Nour Mosque for some time. She enjoyed the instruction and company at this group, but also noted: "My father is very involved in the Turkish Muslim circles, and in many such places people know me. When I go to the Arab mosques this does not happen." Simultaneously she attended a Qur'an study/discussion group at the local university. This group later moved to a local Moroccan mosque. Sibel moreover occasionally attended the German Muslim Association's Qur'an study group (for men and women) that meets in a civic center (*Bürgerhaus*). For years Sibel has been trying to educate herself in Muslim theology, using such local resources, but also tapping into wider networks like the Internet, and the courses of the *Islamologische Institut*. As a result of her intensive studying, Sibel is occasionally approached to participate in events as a speaker or discussant. For example, at a regional meeting of the Muslim Youth of Germany (organizationally close to the umbrella organization of the Al-Nour Mosque) that was held in a gym in Stuttgart, she talked to the youngsters about her experiences as a pious Muslima in everyday life. The event at "the Sarah" that Sibel and Susanne-Samiha conducted was a well-attended and successful public lecture and discussion about women and Islam (see chapter 3).

Mr. Serdar, perhaps more than many others, represents Muslim Stuttgart in both Muslim and non-Muslim circuits. He tirelessly travels the city in the service of the Muslim cause. As the president of the Hussein Mosque, he has weathered earlier battles about mosque constructions (the Heslach case), made a name for himself and gained immense respect in the process, and was later called into a commission to design the curriculum for a state-wide pilot project in Islamic religious education in public schools. Mr. Serdar is invited to numerous local events, panel discussions, and conferences to do with Islam and interfaith dialogue. Whether at an *iftar* at the Bosnian or Al-Nour Mosques, the conference center of the Catholic diocese, events sponsored by Christian-Muslim dialogue associations, or the municipality, Mr. Serdar is a frequent and valued guest, speaker, and discussant. In 2010/11 together with the Protestant church in Zuffenhausen, Mr. Serdar organized an ambitious year-long series with the title "To Approach One Another" that included thirty-three events at different venues in the quarter. In the fall of 2011 Mr. Serdar was invited as the only Muslim representative at the New Year's reception of the city's Jewish community. In addition to being available as a Muslim representative and speaker, Mr. Serdar also fosters movement into the Hussein Mosque when the community (like many others) invites members, friends, neighbors, and the interested public to events like the annual *kermes* or the day of the open mosque on the German national holiday (see chapter 5). In September 2007 the Hussein Mosque participated in Zuffenhausen's first Open Night event, which brought dozens of interested visitors to the mosque.

A plethora of even minute movements and activities of individuals and mosque communities have in the past few decades established a vibrant Muslim public and spiritual geography where the pious can pick and choose between different spaces, activities, events, and programs. This geography is complexly linked to diverse and overlapping circuits of larger urban religious, ethnic, cultural, and social landscapes. Individual footsteps (e.g. praying in the park; designing a Muslim children's party), group activities (e.g. a stall on a flea market run by a Muslim girls' group), and communal involvement (e.g. participation in a quarter's Open Night) over time connect diverse networks of Muslim participation and cultural production. I will briefly look at a few crucial nodes in these circuits that have not been discussed in the previous chapters.

The Islam Week

For individuals' steps and movements to converge into larger circuits and spatialities, it is paramount that people periodically encounter each other and experience the cohesion of the networks and topographies they produced over time. One such event has in recent years been the *Islamwoche* (Islam Week) organized by the Muslim Student Union at the University of Stuttgart. One of the oldest (if not the oldest) events of its type in Germany, the *Islamwoche* offers a week of lectures by nationally known Muslim thinkers, activists, and theologians. Some are known for their writing or preaching and others for their organizational and political engagement on behalf of pious Muslims and their communities. Conceptualized in part as an outreach to non-Muslims, the event attracts a predominantly Muslim audience. The lecture series serves as a meeting space for individuals and a community-constructing platform for mobile individuals. Visitors come to listen to the prominent speakers who represent the emerging national Muslim public sphere and to meet and connect with their urban and regional pious peers.

On a sunny evening in June 2008 I walked up a hill toward an auditorium of the University of Stuttgart not far from the city center. As I approached my destination it was apparent by the density of women with headscarves and a few young men with beards that I was going to attend a Muslim event. Groups of mostly younger people stood chatting at the entrance and in the lobby of the building. Many of them appeared to be students. I headed upstairs toward the auditorium where I ran into Susanne-Samiha who was running the bookstall (see chapters 2 and 3). Susanne-Samiha is not a university student, but nevertheless was very involved with the planning and running of the event. We chatted a little as I looked over the books on display. Eventually I entered the auditorium, which could hold about 300 people. I sat down in the middle block. As I looked around I noticed a few younger people who I knew by sight from the Al-Nour Mosque. About 120 people had come on this evening to listen to Abdelrahman Reidegeld, a well-known theologian and author (Reidegeld 2005). I had heard a lot about him from Susanne-Samiha and others who had attended courses of the *Islamologische Institut* where he was a central organizer and lecturer. Mr. Reidegeld, who is a trained anthropologist and Muslim theologian, has accumulated a small following in particular among ethnic German converts to Islam. Tonight he addressed the theme of the week's events: time ruptures. More specifically, he discussed theories and conceptions of time. He touched on aspects of the temporality/historicity of the Qur'an and its eternal features/message. Mr. Reidegeld, who is in his early forties, is a charismatic and eloquent speaker. He neatly connected abstract theological expertise with political topics, and everyday concerns and practices. He combined notes about environmental problems ("we really should not ruin Allah's creation with cars") with remarks about the necessity to reflect about how Islamic our everyday practices really were ("do we base our lives too much on myths that we ourselves have constructed?"), and the quest for a holistic Muslim lifestyle ("we need to revisit, but not blindly copy the time of the Prophet"). In his fast and sharp elaborations, Reidegeld quoted the Prophet, referred to Salah Ad-Din, quoted Machiavelli, reflected on the viability of delinking oneself as an individual from circuits of (bank) interest, and encouraged Muslims to become more self-critical. The lecture was followed by a lively question-and-answer session. Somebody asked whether it would be better for Muslims to ask to be given their salaries in cash in order to avoid banks and systems of interest. Mr. Reidegeld responded that this might be a beginning, but at present not really a comprehensive solution. Later he gave advice about what literature was best for beginning believers. Somebody asked him how to recognize the elements of the Qur'an that are eternal and those that are expression of their specific (human) time? Throughout the lecture and question and answer session, Mr. Reidegeld remained at a relatively sophisticated and abstract level. Looking around the audience one could notice that some listeners were entirely absorbed in his elaboration, but that he had also lost some others. Children were playing, several cell phones rang, and a small but consistent amount of traffic shuffled in and out of the auditorium.

Overall, however, the event was a success judging from the sizable crowd which remained until the end of the lengthy question-and-answer session. Some lined up afterward to individually talk to Mr. Reidegeld.

On my way out I stopped at the table of the Islamic Social Services and Information Center, an independent institution that offers German language Islamic instruction for children and publishes Islamic teaching materials and other religious texts (e.g. Aslan 1997). Crossing the downstairs lobby I encountered Yunis Demir, one of the central activists of the local interfaith coalition (who sat through the discussion about Islamism during Ramadan in a public venue, without being given food or drink for his *iftar*, see chapter 4), and the Imam of the Al-Nour Mosque. This mixing and mingling of different pious Muslims at the *Islamwoche* reflects formal (the Muslim Student Union) and informal circuits of participation and cooperation. Many mosque youth groups or Qur'an study groups suspend their weekly meetings in order to (collectively) attend the events of the *Islamwoche*. Deliberations about which speakers to listen to (before the events), and debates about the quality of lectures (afterward) provide much material for discussions for many believers. Whether an individual is of Turkish, Egyptian, Moroccan, or Bosnian descent or is an ethnic German convert to Islam plays no role in the context of the Islam Week. In fact attending this week-long event is almost a "must" for many. It reflects interest in more sophisticated theology, as well as awareness of and participation in larger circuits or preaching and writing. More than any other local event, the Islam Week unites and makes visible younger and mobile pious Muslims in Stuttgart.

Larger Circuits of Pious Travel and Mobility

As hinted at with the example of the Islam Week, many younger locally rooted and involved individuals seek to connect and participate in larger circuits of Muslim religiosities. The courses of the *Islamologische Institut* that bring younger, more independent (because of the weekend commitment), and more academically inclined individuals together from different parts of Germany, Austria, and Switzerland are one platform on which believers connect beyond the city. National and regional mosque association meetings have similar effects. Moreover, a growing number of activities and small organizations draw in people from different locations. On the one hand there are a few Sufi (Islamic mystics) lodges and meeting places (Özelsel 2005). On the other hand there are a number of traveling preachers and lecturers who attract considerable crowds (and occasional controversy) for their scheduled events.

In 2008 a small group of individuals started to meet in Karlsruhe (about one hour west of Stuttgart) to discuss issues of interest-free savings and loans, and to eventually organize an interest-free savings and loans association. Consisting largely of thirty- and forty-something middle-class individuals, the group theoretically and theologically reflected on existing interest systems and feasible alternative systems. In monthly meetings they developed a plan to create their own interest-free savings and loan association. In the meanwhile they became a registered civic association. They arranged with a bank for an interest-free account into which members deposited monthly sums. Registered members are eligible for contractually regulated loans from the shared account if need arises.

Layered and Shifting Mobilities

Other regional and national circuits and networks of mobilities allow for cooperation and contacts between similarly minded individuals. Rahma, a Moroccan engineering student at the University of Stuttgart, joined a nationally organized trip for pious Muslims to Andalusia where the group would visit the remnants of Muslim Andalusia. On this trip she met Hakan, a pious man of Turkish descent who was a medical student from another German city. Within a few months after the trip, Rahma and Hakan married in the Al-Nour Mosque in Stuttgart (see also Kuppinger 2014c). Weddings in Morocco and Turkey followed. In the meanwhile the new couple settled in Stuttgart, where Rahma works as an engineer and Hakan as a physician. The experiences of Rahma and Hakan illustrate complexly layered and interwoven mobilities that constitute and shape individual lives, and outline future urban German Muslim lifestyles and lifeworlds. A few years earlier Rahma had come to Stuttgart to study at the university. Hakan is a second-generation Turkish-German reflecting earlier cycles of labor migration. Both were rooted in local pious communities but also moved in national pious circuits. They met each other in the context of religiously inspired tourism. Their three weddings symbolize the larger circuits and networks (Germany, Morocco, and Turkey) in which they live. As highly qualified professionals Rahma and Hakan currently live in Stuttgart.

Muslim Stuttgart

When the first generation of labor migrants arrived in German cities, they often remained locked into a small number of spaces. Dominant society denied the new arrivals the right to participate and creatively engage with urban spaces and cultures. The migrants themselves initially planned for their speedy return to their homeland and showed little interest in urban participation. They remained "immobile" and isolated urban dwellers. Some soon rented modest prayer rooms, often hidden away in backyards and out-of-the-way locations. Even when more sizable mosques replaced these earlier smaller facilities, they remained largely invisible and isolated as their members and visitors moved between a few spaces in the city. By the 1990s the immobility and isolation of the first generation gave way to the increased mobility and participation of their children and grandchildren. At home in Stuttgart, members of the second and third generation knew the city, belonged to the city, moved across the cityscape, claimed spaces, created new spaces, remade others by their presence, and inserted new practices and uses into existing spaces. They had roots in the city and saw themselves as ordinary citizens. Local mobilities completed global mobilities as younger pious Muslims crisscrossed the cityscape. They claim their share of civic participation, cultural production, and spatial ownership. These individuals' links, trajectories and connections slowly merged into a more coherent Muslim cultural and public sphere, which today is an inherent part of urban culture and the public sphere at large.

The challenge for pious Muslims was not only to create meaningful urban networks and a local Muslim culture, but to connect these to emerging regional and national religious circuits. In the process pious Muslims in Stuttgart have become integral and creative parts of the cityscape. They normalized Muslim life in the city (e.g. praying in the park, wearing a headscarf to school or work) by their presence in and movement across the city. Mosque-hoppers like Adnan or Hassan, Muslim representatives and officials like Mr. Serdar, and dedicated learners and public speakers like Sibel are central cultural actors and producers as they link mosques, provide necessary information, participate on civic platforms, and claim spaces and practices for Muslim communities. To be successful such individuals need to be at ease in the city and its plethora of public spaces and stages. Without these local mobilities, global mobilities do not come to a conclusion and cannot connect to existing and historical local and global circuits. On a more personal level, these individuals can further foster local religious and cultural contexts. Amna and Tamer (chapters 2 and 3) recently had a daughter, Noura, who is part of a new and solidly rooted generation of Muslim Stuttgarters. We can only hope that Noura will face fewer obstacles than Muslims of previous generations. The city is hers as much as anybody else's.

Glossary

(A) denotes Arab terms; (G) German terms; and (T) Turkish terms.

Terms

Abayah (A)	Gulf-style Islamic dress.
Abitur (G)	twelve (or thirteen) year school diploma that allows for university studies.
Ausländer (G)	foreigner (often used in an exclusionary or even derogatory way)
Bayram (T)	holiday.
Bezirk (G)	urban district, administrational unit.
Bezirksamt (G)	local council.
Bezirksrat (G)	local representative.
Bezirksbeirat (G)	local council
Bezirkvorsteher (G)	head of the local council. Head neighborhood administrator.
Bürgerhaus (G)	civic center where civic associations can meet.
Da'wa (A)	call to Islam.
Dhikr (A)	"remembrance of Allah," mystic practice, can involve the recitation of the name of Allah or other invocations.
Döner (T)	type of meat/kebab. The most favorite/common street food in Germany.
Eid (A)	(religious) holiday, festivity.
Eid al-Adha (A)	holiday/feast of the sacrifice.
Eid al-Fitr (A)	holiday das marks the end of Ramadan.
Fachhochschule (G)	professional university
Fachhochschulreife (G)	twelve-year school diploma that allows entry to a professional university.
Fatiha (A)	the opening chapter of the Qur'an.
Gallabeya (A)	Egyptian-style Islamic dress.
Gastarbeiter (G)	guest worker.

248 | Glossary

Gemeinderat (G)	city/town/village council. In most cities this body is called "Stadtrat" (city council). Stuttgart uses the term *Gemeinderat*, which is used in communities of all sizes, even the smallest villages.
Grundgesetz (G)	the German Constitution.
Grundschule (G)	primary school (grades 1–4).
Hadith (A)	an account of a saying/statement or act of the Prophet Muhammad.
Hajj (A)	pilgrimage to Mecca.
Halal (A)	allowed according to Islamic law
Halal food	allowed foods, including ritually slaughtered meat.
Hauptschule (G)	school that includes grades 5–9 and prepares students for apprenticeships in craft. Considerable controversies arose over this school form in recent years. The *Hauptschule* is slowly replaced by a 5–10th grade *Werkrealschule*. Other possible forms are under debate.
Hijab (A)	headscarf.
Himar (A)	Islamic women's dress that includes a wide dress/skirt and a head covering that falls loosely over the shoulders and covers the upper body.
Hinterhofmoschee (G)	backyard mosque.
Hoca (T)	imam, preacher.
Ibadat (A)	Islamic practices broadly related to matters of belief and worship.
Iman (A)	faith.
Islamologisches Institut (G)	an institute based in Vienna (formerly based in Frankfurt) that holds rather sophisticated courses/course sequences about Islam.
Islamwoche (G)	(largely) annual events at the University of Stuttgart that bring well-known Muslim speakers to town and attract a larger and diverse number of mostly younger local believers. In recent years many other cities/universities have started such programs.
Jugendamt (G)	Public/city agency for youth welfare.
Kermes (T)	communal get-together and fundraising event, mostly held in the spring.
Kindergarten (G)	preschool, for children between the ages of three and six years.
Kopftuch (G)	headscarf.

Leitkultur (G)	"guiding culture" a term volunteered by a conservative politician in 2000. The term caused widespread public debates. It was willingly adopted by some and adamantly and sarcastically rejected by others. In leftist circles it became the butt of much joking.
Mihrab (A)	recess/niche that indicates the direction of prayer in a mosque.
Minbar (A)	pulpit in a mosque.
Mittlere Reife (G)	ten-year school diploma that prepares for entry into white-collar professional training/apprenticeships. It also allows for entry to a *Wirtschaftsgymnasium* and similar secondary schools that lead to the *Abitur*.
Mu'amalat (A)	Muslim practices related to everyday life and social practices.
Mulid (A)	celebration of the birthday of a saint or also the Prophet Muhammad. Popularly the term is also sometimes used to denote a somewhat chaotic/disorganized situation.
Niqab (A)	face veil.
Parallelgesellschaft (G)	a recent term used to accuse (largely Muslims) immigrants of disappearing or hiding in rather disconnected "parallel societies."
Realschule (G)	school that includes grade 5–10 and ends in the *Mittlere Reife* diploma.
Salafi (A)	individual dedicated to imitating the life/lifestyle of the Prophet Muhammad down to the most minute details.
S-Bahn (G)	suburban train.
Shahada (A)	profession of Muslim faith/being/becoming a Muslim. The shahada states that there is only one God and Muhammad is his Prophet.
Shalwar-qamis	South Asian–style dress/pants combination.
Sharia (A)	Muslim law/legal code or framework. Includes a broad variety of religious, moral, economic, social, and other aspects.
Sufi (A)	Islamic mystic, mysticism.
Suhur (A)	late night/early morning meal before starting to fast in Ramadan.
Sunna (A)	framework or rules/wisdom for Muslims based on the saying, teachings, and acts of the Prophet Muhammad.
Tafsir (A)	interpretation of the Qur'an.
Takbir (A)	call to praise Allah.
Tawhid (A)	the unity of Allah.

250 | Glossary

U-Bahn (G) city train.
Ummah (A) the (global) community of Muslims/believers.
Umra (A) the lesser pilgrimage to Mecca.
Verein (G) legally registered civic association or club.
Wirtschaftsgymnasium (G) secondary school (grades 9–12, or 13) that allows students who finished the *Mittlere Reife* to reach the university entrance diploma (*Abitur*).
Zakat (A) alms.

Abbreviations

CIBZ   Gesellschaft für Christlich-Islamische Begegnung und Zusammenarbeit Stuttgart e.V.
CIG   Christlich-Islamische Gesellschaft (dissolved in 2013)
DİTİB Diyanet İşleri Türk İslam Birliği; Islamisch-Türkische Union der Anstalt für Religion e.V.
IGD   Islamische Gemeinschaft in Deutschland e.V.
IR   Islamrat für die Bundesrepublik Deutschland e.V.
KCID   Koordinationsrat der christlich-islamischen Dialogs e.V.
KRM   Koordinationsrat der Muslime
MJD   Muslimische Jugend Deutschland
MSU   Muslimische Studenten Union Stuttgart
LVIKZ Landesverband der Islamischen Kulturzentren e. V.
VIKZ   Verband der Islamischen Kulturzentren e.V.
ZDJ   Zentralat der Juden in Deutschland e.V.
ZMD   Zentralrat der Muslime in Deutschland e.V.

Bibliography

Abaza, Mona. 2001. "Shopping Malls, Consumer Culture and the Reshaping of Public Space in Egypt." *Theory, Culture and Society* 18: 97–122.
———. 2006. *Changing Consumer Cultures in Modern Egypt*. Cairo: American University in Cairo Press.
———. 2011. "Critical Commentary. Cairo's Downtown Imagined: Dubaisation or Nostalgia?" *Urban Studies* 48(6): 1075–1085.
Abbas, Tahir. 2005. *Muslim Britain: Communities under Pressure*. London: Zed Press.
Abdullah, Muhammad Salim. 1974. *Moslems unter uns: Situation, Herausforderung, Gespräch*. Stuttgart: Quell Verlag.
———. 1981. *Geschichte des Islams in Deutschland*. Graz: Styria Verlag.
———. 1993. *Was will der Islam in Deutschland?* Gütersloh: Gütersloher Verlagshaus.
———. 2002. *Islam*. Düsseldorf: Patmos.
Abou El Fadl, Khaled. 2001a. *Speaking in God's Name: Islamic Law, Authority, and Women*. Oxford: Oneworld Publications.
———. 2001b. *And God Knows the Soldiers: The Authoritative and the Authoritarian in Islamic Discourse*. Washington, DC: University Press of America.
Abou El Fadl, Khaled, Tariq Ali, Milton Viorst, John Esposito, et al. 2002. *The Place of Tolerance in Islam*. Boston: Beacon Press.
Abu-Lughod, Janet. 1994. *From Urban Village to East Village*. Cambridge: Blackwell.
Abu-Lughod, Lila. 1986. *Veiled Sentiments: Honor and Poetry in a Bedouin Society*. Berkeley: University of California Press.
———. 1990. "Romance of Resistance: Tracing Transformations of Power through Bedouin Women." *American Ethnologist* 17(1): 41–55.
———. 2013. *Do Muslim Women Need Saving?* Cambridge, MA: Harvard University Press.
Ackermann, Lutz, Jürgen Dahlkamp, and Markus Verbeet. 2006. "Und nachts der Koran." *Der Spiegel* No. 46, 13 November.
Akgün, Lale. 2008. *Tante Semra im Leberkäseland*. Frankfurt: Fischer Verlag.
Al-Hamarneh, Ala, and Jörn Thielmann. 2008. *Islam and Muslims in Germany*. Leiden: Brill.
Alim, H. Samy. 2005. "A New Research Agenda: Exploring the Translocal Hip Hop *Umma*." In *Muslim Networks: From Hajj to Hip Hop*, edited by Miriam Cooke and Bruce Lawrence, 264–274. Chapel Hill: University of North Carolina Press.
Allievi, Stefano. 2005. "How the Immigrant Became Muslim." *Revue Européenne des Migration Internationales* 21(2): 2–21.
AlSayyad, Nezar, ed. 2001. *Hybrid Urbanism: On the Identity Discourse and the Built Environment*. Westport, CT: Praeger.
———. 2002. "Muslim Europe and Euro-Islam: On the Discourses of Identity and Culture." In AlSayyad and Castells 2002, 9–30.

AlSayyad, Nezar, and Manuel Castells, eds. 2002. *Muslim Europe or Euro-Islam: Politics, Culture and Citizenship in the Age of Globalization*. Lanham, MD: Lexington Books.
AlSayyad, Nezar, and Mejgan Massoumi, eds. 2010. *The Fundamentalist City? Religiosity and the Remaking of Urban Space*. Abingdon, UK: Routledge.
Al-Qaradawi, Jusuf. 1989. *Erlaubtes und Verbotenes im Islam*. Munich: SDK Bavaria Verlag.
Altshuler, Alan, and David Luberoff. 2003. *Mega-Projects: The Challenging Politics of Urban Public Investment*. Washington, DC: The Brookings Institution.
Amiraux, Valérie. 2006. "Speaking as a Muslim: Avoiding Religion in French Public Space." In Jonker and Amiraux 2006, 21–52.
Amir-Moazami, Schirin. 2010. "Avoiding 'Youthfulness?' Young Muslims Negotiating Gender." In Herrera and Bayat 2010, 189–206.
Amirpur, Katajun, and Ludwig Ammann, eds. 2006. *Der Islam am Wendepunkt*. Freiburg: Herder.
Ammann, Ludwig. 2004. *Cola und Koran: Das Wagnis einer islamischen Renaissance*. Freiburg: Herder.
Amouroux, Christa. 2009. "Normalizing Christiania." *City and Society* 21(1): 108–132.
Andreasch, Robert. 2008. "PRO-Aktivitäten in Berlin und Brandenburg." In Häusler 2008, 104–114.
Annisa, Firly. 2009. "Representation of Fashions as Muslima Identity in *Paras* Magazine." In Pink 2009, 259–266.
Appadurai, Arjun. 1996. *Modernity at Large*. Minneapolis: University of Minnesota Press.
Arab, Pooyan Tamimi. 2013. "The Biggest Mosque in Europe!" In *Religious Architecture*, edited by Oskar Verkaaik, 47-62. Amsterdam: University of Amsterdam Press.
Arikan, Hasan. 2002. *Der kurzgefasste Ilmihal*. Cologne: Verband der Islamischen Kulturzentren.
Asad, Muhammad. 1954. *The Road to Mecca*. New York: Simon and Schuster.
———. 1980. *The Message of Qur'an*. East Grinstead: New Era Publications.
Asad, Talal. 1986. *The Idea of an Anthropology of Islam*. Washington, DC: Georgetown University Press, Occasional Papers Series, Center for Contemporary Arab Studies.
———. 1993. *Genealogies of Religion: Discipline and Reasons of Power in Christianity and Islam*. Baltimore: Johns Hopkins University Press.
———. 1999. "Religion, Nation-State and Secularism." In *Nation and Religion*, edited by Peter van der Veer, 178–196. Princeton, NJ: Princeton University Press.
———. 2003. *Formations of the Secular: Christianity, Islam, Modernity*. Stanford, CA: Stanford University Press.
Aslan, Nida Anette. 1997. *Ali liebt Fatima*. Stuttgart: Islamisches Sozialdienst- und Informationszentrum.
Astor, Avi. 2012. "Memory, Community, and Opposition to Mosques: The Case of Badalona." *Theory and Society* 41(4): 325–349.
Augé, Marc. 1995. *Non-Places*. London: Verso.
Backer, Kristiane. 2009. *Von MTV nach Mekka*. Berlin: List/Ullstein.
Bade, Klaus, ed. 1992. *Deutsche im Ausland. Fremde in Deutschland*. Munich: Beck.
Baden-Württemberg, Staatsministerium. 2005. *Muslime in Baden-Württemberg*. Stuttgart. Bericht für den Ministerrat.
Badillo, David. 2006. *Latinos and the New Immigrant Church*. Baltimore, MD: Johns Hopkins University Press.
Bahners, Patrick. 2011. *Die Panikmacher: Die deutsche Angst vor dem Islam*. Munich: Beck.
Bahr, Ulrich. 2006. "Moscheebau in Kreuzberg." In *Islamisches Gemeindeleben in Berlin*, edited by Riem Spielhaus and Alexa Färber, 80–84. Berlin: Der Beauftragte des Senats für Integration und Migration.

Balibar, Etienne. 2004. *We, the People of Europe?* Princeton, NJ: Princeton University Press.
Barazangi, Nimat Hafez. 2004. *Women's Identity and the Qur'an: A New Reading.* Gainesville: University Press of Florida.
———. 2005. "Silent Revolution of a Muslim Arab American Scholar Activist." In *Muslim Activist Women in North America*, edited by Katherine Bullock, 1–18. Austin: University of Texas Press.
Barlas, Asma. 2002. *"Believing Women" in Islam: Unreading Patriarchal Interpretations of the Qur'an.* Austin: University of Texas Press.
Bauknecht, Bernd. 2001. *Muslime in Deutschland von 1920 bis 1945.* Cologne: Teiresias Verlag.
Bauer, Joe, and Lutz Schelhorn. 2008. "Unsere kleine Stadt der Welt." *Stuttgarter Nachrichten*, 28 March.
Bauman, Zygmunt. 1998. *Globalization.* New York: Columbia University Press.
———. 2004. *Wasted Lives: Modernity and its Outcasts.* Cambridge: Polity Press.
———. 2007. *Liquid Times.* Cambridge: Polity Press.
———. 2008. *Consuming Life.* Cambridge: Polity Press.
Baumann, Maria. 2004. *Katharina heisst jetzt Ayşe.* Regensburg: Scriptorium.
Bayat, Asef. 1997. *Street Politics.* New York: Columbia University Press.
———. 2007. *Making Islam Democratic.* Stanford, CA: Stanford University Press.
———. 2010. *Life as Politics.* Stanford, CA: Stanford University Press.
Bayat, Asef, and Linda Herrera. 2010. "Introduction: Being Young and Muslim in Neoliberal Times." In Herrera and Bayat 2010, 3–26.
Bayoumi, Moustafa. 2010. "Being Young, Muslim and American in Brooklyn." In Herrera and Bayat 2010, 161–174.
Beaumont, Justin and Christopher Baker. 2011a. *Postsecular Cities.* London: Continuum.
———. 2011b. "Postcolonialism and Religion: New Spaces of 'Belonging and Becoming' in the Postsecular City." In *Postsecular Cities*, edited by Justin Beaumont and Christopher Baker, 33–49. London: Continuum.
Beauregard, Robert A., and Anna Bounds. 2000. "Urban Citizenship." In Isin 2000, 243–256.
Beer, Mathias. 2004. "Zuffenhausen in der Zeit nach dem Zweiten Weltkrieg." In Gühring 2004a, 477–528.
Beinhauer-Köhler, Bärbel, and Claus Leggewie. 2009. *Moscheen in Deutschland.* Munich: Beck.
Belz, Walter, and Andreas Brunold. 1997. *Stuttgart: Stadt im Wandel: vom 19. ins 21. Jahrhundert.* Tübingen: Silberburg Verlag.
Benhabib, Seyla, and Judith Resnik, eds. 2009. *Migrations and Mobilities: Citizenship, Borders and Gender.* New York: New York University Press.
Berman, Marshall. 1988. *All That Is Solid Melts into Air.* New York: Penguin Books.
Bielo, James. 2009. *Words upon the Word: An Ethnography of Evangelical Bible Study.* New York: New York University Press.
———. 2011a. "Purity, Danger, and Redemption: Notes on Urban Missional Evangelicals." *American Ethnologist* 38(2): 267–280.
———. 2011b. "City of Man, City of God: The Re-Urbanization of American Evangelicals." *City and Society* 23(S1): 2–23.
Bienzle, Bruno. 2000. "Moschee: Stadt bemüht sich um Schadensbegrenzung." *Stuttgarter Nachrichten*, 12 February.
Bild Zeitung. 2010. "Warum hofieren Sie den Islam so, Herr Präsident?" 6 October. Accessed 12 October 2012. http://www.bild.de.
Bilmen, Ömer Nasuhi. n.d. *Feinheiten islamischen Glaubens: Islamischer Katechismus.* N.p.: Astec Verlag.

Binder, Petra. 2004. "Vom Herzogtum zum Königreich 1762-1870." In Gühring 2004a, 272–338.
Body-Gendrot, Sophie, and Marco Martiniello. 2000. *Minorities in European Cities: The Dynamics of Social Integration and Social Exclusion at the Neighborhood Level.* New York: St. Martin's Press.
Bölsche, Jochen. 2008. "Die Lanzen der Eroberer." *Spiegel Spezial* No. 2 (Allah im Abendland): 72–79.
Boender, Welmoet. 2006. "From Migrant to Citizen: The Role of the Islamic University of Rotterdam in the Formulation of Dutch Citizenship." In Jonker and Amiraux 2006, 103–122.
Bogen, Uwe. 2010. "Wo das Herz von Porsche schlägt." *Stuttgarter Nachrichten*, 24 March.
Borgmann, Thomas. 2001. "Niederlage für Muslime." *Stuttgarter Zeitung*, 15 December.
———. 2008. "Die schwäbische Sparpolitik hat sich ausgezahlt." *Stuttgarter Zeitung*, 28 June.
Borris, Maria. 1973. *Ausländische Arbeiter in einer Grossstadt.* Frankfurt: Europäische Verlagsanstalt.
Borst, Otto. 1986. *Stuttgart: Die Geschichte einer Stadt.* Stuttgart: Theiss Verlag.
BouAkar, Hiba. 2012. "Contesting Beirut's Frontier." *City and Society* 24(2): 150–172.
Boubekeur, Amel. 2005. "Cool and Competitive: Muslim Culture in the West." *ISIM Review* 16: 12–13.
Bourdieu, Pierre. 1984. *Distinction.* Cambridge, MA: Harvard University Press.
Bowen, John. 2005. "Beyond Migration: Islam as a Transnational Public Space." *Journal of Ethnic and Migration Research* 30(5): 879–894.
———. 2007. *Why the French Don't Like the Headscarf.* Princeton, NJ: Princeton University Press.
———. 2010. *Can Islam Be French?* Princeton, NJ: Princeton University Press.
Bozay, Kemal. 2008. "Kulturkampf von rechts—Das Dilemma der Kölner Moscheedebatte." In Häusler 2008, 198–212.
Brand, Jochen. 2008. "Neue Moschee im Gewerbegebiet Wangen-Hedelfingen." *Stuttgarter Zeitung*, 22 October.
Brand, Jürgen, and Michael Heller. 2007. "Porsche baut neue Lackiererei in Zuffenhausen." *Stuttgarter Zeitung*, 5 December.
Brandt, Andrea, and Cordula Meyer. 2006. "Und nachts der Koran." *Der Spiegel* No. 46, November 13.
Breuer, Rita. 2006. *Zwischen Ramadan und Reeperbahn.* Freiburg: Herder.
Brown, Karen McCarthy. 1999. "Staying Grounded in a High-Rise Building: Ecological Dissonance and Ritual Accommodation in Haitian Vodou." In Orsi 1999, 79–102.
Brubaker, Rogers. 2012. "Categories of Analysis and Categories of Practice: A Note on the Study of Muslims in European Countries of Immigration." *Ethnic and Racial Studies* 36(1): 1–8.
Buchmeier, Frank. 2006. "Minarette im schwäbischen Abendland." *Stuttgarter Zeitung*, 12 December.
Buggenhagen, Beth. 2012. "Fashioning Piety: Women's Dress, Money and Faith Among Senegalese Muslims in New York City." *City and Society* 24(1): 84–104.
Bukow, Wolf-Dietrich, Gerda Heck, Erika Schulze, and Erol Yildiz, eds. 2011. *Neue Vielfalt in der urbanen Stadtgesellschaft.* Wiesbaden: Verlag für Sozialwissenschaften.
Bullock, Katherine, ed. 2005. *Muslim Activist Women in North America.* Austin: University of Texas Press.
Bunt, Gary. 2002 *Virtually Islamic.* Cardiff: University of Wales Press.

———. 2003. *Islam in the Digital Age*. London: Pluto Press.
———. 2009. *iMuslim. Rewiring the House of Islam*. Chapel Hill: University of North Carolina Press.
Bury, Mathias. 2008. "Porsche liebäugelt mit Niederlassung auf dem Pragsattel." *Stuttgarter Zeitung*, 5 June.
Caglar, Ayşe. 2004. "Mediascapes, Advertisement Industries and Cosmopolitan Transformations: German Turks in Germany." *New German Critique* 92: 39–61.
Cahill, Caitlin. 2007. "Negotiating Grit and Glamour: Young Women of Color and the Gentrification of the Lower East Side." *City and Society* 19(2): 202–231.
Caldeira, Teresa. 2000. *City of Walls: Crime, Segregation, and Citizenship in Sao Paolo*. Berkeley: University of California Press.
Calhoun, Craig, ed. 1992a. "Introduction: Habermas and the Public Sphere." In *Habermas and the Public Sphere*, edited by Craig Calhoun, 1–48. Cambridge, MA: MIT Press.
———. 1992b. *Habermas and the Public Sphere*. Cambridge, MA: MIT Press.
Calhoun, Craig, Mark Juergensmeyer, and Jonathan VanAntwerpen, eds. 2011. *Rethinking Secularism*. Oxford: Oxford University Press.
Casanova, José. 1994. *Public Religion in the Modern World*. Chicago: University of Chicago Press.
Castles, Stephen, and Alastair Davidson. 2000. *Citizenship and Migration: Globalization and the Politics of Belonging*. London: Macmillan.
Cesari, Jocelyn. 2004. *When Islam and Democracy Meet: Muslims in Europe and the United States*. New York: Palgrave.
———. 2005a. "Mosque Conflict in European Cities: Introduction." *Journal of Ethnic and Migration Studies* 31(6): 1015–1024.
———. 2005b. "Mosques in French Cities: Toward the End of a Conflict?" *Journal of Ethnic and Migration Studies* 31(6): 1025–1043.
———, ed. 2010a. *Muslims in the West After 9/11*. London: Routledge.
———. 2010b. "The Securitization of Islam in Europe." In Cesari 2010a, 9–27.
———. 2013. *Why the West Fears Islam*. New York: Palgrave MacMillan.
Ceylan, Rauf. 2006. *Ethnische Kolonien*. Wiesbaden: VS Verlag für Sozialwissenschaften.
Chammah, Maurice. 2010. "Cosmopolitan Islamism and Its Critics." *Arab Media and Society* 10 Spring. http://www.arabmediasociety.com/?article=731.
Chappell, Ben. 2010. "Custom Contestations: Lowriders and Urban Space." *City and Society* 22(1): 25–48.
Chauncey, George. 1994. *Gay New York*. New York: Basic Books.
Cloke, Paul, and Justin Beaumont. 2012. "Geographies of Postsecular Rapprochement in the City." *Progress in Human Geography* 37(1): 27–51.
Cohn-Bendit, Daniel, and Thomas Schmid. 1992. *Heimat Babylon*. Hamburg: Hoffman und Campe.
Cooke, Miriam, and Bruce Lawrence. 2005. *Muslim Networks: From Hajj to Hip Hop*. Chapel Hill: University of North Carolina Press.
Costabel, Gabriella. 2009. *Gemeinden anderer Sprachen und Herkunft in Württemberg*. Stuttgart: Evangelischer Oberkirchenrat. http://www.elk-wue.de/fileadmin/mediapool/elk-wue/dokumente/Gemeinden_anderer-Sprachen-Herkunft_Wuertt-April09.pdf.
Crolly, Hannelore. 2010. "Das Saarland hat seinen eigenen Minarett-Streit." *Welt Online*, 14 February. Accessed 26 April 2011. http://www.welt.de/politik/deutschland/article6382184.
Cumming-Bruce, Nick, and Steven Erlanger. 2009. "Swiss Ban Building of Minarets on Mosques." *New York Times*, 29 November.

Cziesche, Dominik, Dietmar Hipp, Felix Kurz, Barbara Schmitt, Matthias Schreiber, Martin Sümering, Silvia Tyburski, and Andreas Ulrich. 2003. "Das Kreuz mit dem Koran." *Der Spiegel* No. 40, 29 March.
David, Ann. 2012. "Sacralising the City: Sound, Space and Performance in Hindu Ritual Practice in London." *Culture and Religion* 13(4): 449–467.
Davis, Mike. 1992. *City of Quartz*. New York: Vintage Books.
Deeb, Lara. 2006. *An Enchanted Modern: Gender and Public Piety in Shi'i Lebanon*. Princeton, NJ: Princeton University Press.
Deeb, Lara, and Mona Harb. 2013. *Leisurely Islam: Negotiating Geography and Morality in Shi'ite South Beirut*. Princeton, NJ: Princeton University Press.
De Certeau, Michel. 1984. *The Practice of Everyday Life*. Berkeley: University of California Press.
Demiryürek, Murat. 2007. *Jung und Muslim*. Berlin: Green Palace.
Delanty, Gerard. 2000. "The Resurgence of the City in Europe? The Spaces of European Citizenship." In Isin 2000, 79–92.
Der 15er: Stuttgarts letzte Strassenbahn (n.a.). 2011. Stuttgart: Stammheimer Bürgerverein.
Derrida, Jacques. 1992. *The Other Heading*. Bloomington: Indiana University Press.
Desplat, Patrick, and Dorothea Schulz, eds. 2012. *Prayer in the City*. Bielefeld: Transscript.
Diakonie Württemberg. 2010. "50 Jahre Diakonie und Griechen." 25 February. Accesssed 2 July 2011. http://www.diakonie-wuerttemberg.de.
Doomernik, Jeroen. 1995. "The Institutionalization of Turkish Islam in Germany and the Netherlands: A Comparison." *Ethnic and Racial Studies* 18(1): 46–63.
Dror, Rachel, Alfred Hagemann, and Joachim Hahn. 2006. *Jüdisches Leben in Stuttgart-Bad Cannstatt*. Essen: Klartext Verlagsgesellschaft.
Duneier, Mitchell. 2000. *Sidewalk*. New York: Farrar, Straus and Giroux.
Dwyer, Claire, David Gilbert, and Bindi Shah. 2012. "Faith and Suburbia: Secularisation, Modernity and the Changing Geographies or Religion in London's Suburbs." *Transactions of the Institute of British Geographers* 38(3): 403–419.
Eade, John. 2010. "Excluding and Including the 'Other' in the Global City: Religious Missionaries Among Muslim and Catholic Migrants in London." In AlSayyad and Massoumi 2010, 235–256.
———. 2012. "Religion, Home-Making and Migration Across a Globalising City: Responding to Mobility in London." *Culture and Religion* 13(4): 469–483.
Eakin, Hugh. 2003. "German Cause Célèbre: A Teacher's Headscarf." *New York Times*, 30 June.
Eaton, Charles le Gai. 1985. *Islam and the Destiny of Man*. Albany, NY: SUNY Press.
Ebaugh, Helen Rose, and Janet Saltzman Chafetz. 2000. *Religion and the New Immigrants*. Walnut Creek, CA: Altamira Press.
Ehmer, Hermann. 2004a. "Zuffenhausen im Mittelalter." In Gühring 2004a, 67–92.
———. 2004b. "Zuffenhausen in der Reformationszeit." In Gühring 2004a, 67–92.
Eickelman, Dale, and James Piscatori. 1996. *Muslim Politics*. Princeton, NJ: Princeton University Press.
Eley, Geoff. 1992. "Nations, Publics, and Political Cultures: Placing Habermas in the Nineteenth Century." In *Habermas and the Public Sphere*, edited by Craig Calhoun, 289–339. Cambridge, MA: MIT Press.
El-Guindi, Fadwa. 1999. *Veil: Modesty, Privacy and Resistance*. Oxford: Berg.
Elisha, Omri. 2010. "Taking the (Inner) City for God: Ambiguities in Urban Social Engagement among Conservative White Evangelicals." In AlSayyad and Massoumi 2010, 235–256.
———. 2011. *Moral Ambition: Moblization and Social Outreach in Evangelical Megachurches*. Berkeley: University of California Press.

Ellin, Nan, ed. 1997. *Architecture of Fear*. New York: Princeton Architectural Press.
El-Nawawy, Mohammed, and Adel Iskandar. 2003. *Al-Jazeera*. Cambridge, MA: Westview Press.
Escudier, Alexandre, and Brigitte Sauzay. 2003. *Der Islam in Europa: der Umgang mit dem Islam in Frankreich und Deutschland*. Göttingen: Wallstein.
Esposito, John, and Francois Burgat, eds. 2003. *Modernizing Islam: Religion in the Public Sphere in the Middle East and Europe*. New Brunswick, NJ: Rutgers University Press.
Esslinger Zeitung. 2002. "Muslime kritisieren Polizeieinsatz." 23 December. Accessed 26 June 2012. http://www.zentralrat-muslime.de.
Ewing, Katherine Pratt. 2006. "Between Cinema and Social Work: Diasporic Turkish Women and the (Dis)Pleasures of Hybridity." *Cultural Anthropology* 21(2): 265–294.
———. 2008a. "Emine: Muslim University Student in Berlin." In *Muslim Voices and Lives in the Contemporary World*, edited by Frances Trix, John Walbridge, and Linda Walbridge, 71–84. New York: Palgrave MacMillan.
———. 2008b. *Stolen Honor*. Stanford, CA: Stanford University Press.
Fadil, Nadia. 2006. "We Should Be Walking Qurans: The Making of an Islamic Political Subject." In Jonker and Amiraux 2006, 53–78.
Färber, Alexa. 2006. "Mieten, kaufen, (um)bauen; Zur urbanen Kompetenz islamischer Gemeinden." In *Islamisches Gemeindeleben in Berlin*, edited by Riem Spielhaus and Alexa Färber, 93–98. Berlin: Der Beauftragte des Senats für Integration und Migration.
Faerber, Peer-Uli. 1988. *Der Stadtinspektor*. Stuttgart: Engelhorn Verlag.
Faist, Thomas, and Eyüp Özveren, eds. 2004. *Transnational Social Spaces: Agents, Networks and Institutions*. Aldershot, UK: Ashgate.
Faltin, Thomas, and Hilke Lorenz. 2011. *Unser Stuttgart*. Stuttgart: Belser Verlag.
Fawaz. Mona. 2009. "Hezbollah as Urban Planner? Questions to and from Urban Planning." *Planning Theory* 8(4): 323–334.
Fenske, Hans. 1980. "International Migration: Germany in the Eighteenth Century." *Central European History* 13(3): 332–347.
Ferguson, James, and Akhil Gupta, eds. 1992. "Special Issue: Space, Identity, and the Politics of Difference." *Cultural Anthropology* 7(1): 6–23.
Fetzer, Joel, and J. Christopher Soper. 2005. *Muslims and the State in Britain, France, and Germany*. Cambridge: Cambridge University Press.
Filter, Cornelia. 2008. *Mein Gott ist jetzt Allah und ich befolge seine Gebote gern*. Munich: Piper.
Finkelstein, Kerstin. 2006. *Eingewandert*. Berlin: Links Verlag.
Fischer, Johan. 2009. "Halal, Haram, or What? Creating Muslim Space in London." In Pink 2009, 3–22.
FitzGerald, Nora. "Headscarf in Schools Divides Germany." *New York Times*, 21 October 2003.
Flyvbjerg, Bent, Nils Bruzelius, and Werner Rothengather. 2003. *Megaprojects and Risks*. Cambridge: Cambridge University Press.
Focus Online. 2010. "Der Islam gehört zu Deutschland." 3 October. Accessed 12 October 2012. http://www.focus.de/politik/deutschland/20-jahre-wende/christian-wulff-der-islam-gehoert-zu-deutschland_aid_558481.html
Foley, Michael and Dean Hodge. 2007. *Religion and the New Immigrants: How Faith Communities Form Our Newest Citizens*. Oxford: Oxford University Press.
Foucault, Michel. 1980. *Power/Knowledge: Selected Interviews and Writings 1972–1977*, edited by Colin Gordon. New York: Pantheon.
———. 1984. "Space, Knowledge, and Power." In *The Foucault Reader*, edited by Paul Rabinow, 239–256. New York: Pantheon Books.

———. 1986. "Of Other Spaces." *Diacritics* 16(1): 22–27.
———. 1991. "Governmentality." In *The Foucault Effect*, edited by Graham Bruchell, Colin Gordon, and Peter Miller, 87–104. Chicago: University of Chicago Press.
Frankfurter Allgemeine Zeitung. 2008. "Der Islam ist längst Teil unseres Landes." 1 March. Accessed 10 October 2012. http://www.faz.net/aktuell/politik/inland/schaeuble-der-islam-ist-laengst-ein-teil-unseres-landes-1516144.html.
———. 2010a. "Christian Wulff: Vielfalt schätzen—Zusammenhalt fördern." 3 October. Accessed 27 October 2012. http://www.faz.net/aktuell/politik/die-rede-im-wortlaut-christian-wulff-vielfalt-schaetzen-zusammenhalt-foerdern-11054288.html.
———. 2010b. "Muslime keine Bürger zweiter Klasse." 4 October. Accessed 27 October 2012. http://www.faz.net/aktuell/politik/inland/reaktionen-auf-wulff-rede-muslime-keine-buerger-zweiter-klasse-11053327.html.
———. 2010c. "CSU-Politiker: Islam nicht Teil unserer Kultur." 5 October. Accessed 11 October 2012. http://www.faz.net/aktuell/politik/inland/debatte-nach-wulff-rede-csu-politiker-islam-nicht-teil-unserer-kultur-11057331.html.
Fraser, Nancy. 1992. "Rethinking the Public Sphere." In *Habermas and the Public Sphere*, edited by Craig Calhoun, 109–142. Cambridge, MA: MIT Press.
Freudenreich, Josef-Otto, ed. 2008. *Wir können alles: Filz, Korruption und Kumpanei im Musterländle*. Tübingen: Klöpfer und Meyer Verlag.
———. 2009. "Porsche und Zuffenhausen: Zwei Welten, die nicht zueinander kommen." *Stuttgarter Zeitung*, 26 January.
Friedrich, Susanne, and Ulrich Kull. 2004. "Vor- und Frügeschichte." In Gühring 2004a, 41–66.
Gale, Richard. 2005. "Representing the City: Mosques and the Planning Process in Birmingham." *Journal of Ethnic and Migration Studies* 31(6): 1161–1179.
Gans, Herbert. 1962. *The Urban Villagers*. New York: Free Press.
Garbin, David. 2012. "Marching for God in the Global City: Public Space, Religion and Diasporic Identities in a Transnational African Church." *Culture and Religion* 13(4): 425–447.
———. 2013. "The Visibility and Invisibility of Migrant Faith in the City: Diaspora Religion and the Politics of Emplacement of Afro-Christian Churches." *Journal of Ethnic and Migration Studies* 39(5): 677–696.
Gazzah, Miriam. 2010. "Maroc-Hop: Music and Youth Identities in the Netherlands." In Herrera and Bayat 2010, 309–324.
Geber, Bernhard. 2010. "Pro-Völklingen jetzt im Viererpack. *Saarbrücker Zeitung*. 29 September.
Gerlach, Julia. 2006. *Zwischen Pop und Dschihad*. Berlin: Ch. Links Verlag.
Geulen, Christian. 2004. "Symmetrie und Politik: Überlegungen zur Theoriegeschichte des Öffentlichen." Göle and Ammann 2004, 45–68.
Ghannam, Farha. 2002. *Remaking the Modern: Space, Relocation, and the Politics of Identity in a Global Cairo*. Berkeley: University of California Press.
Ghodsee, Kristen. 2010. *Muslim Lives in Eastern Europe*. Princeton, NJ: Princeton University Press.
Gliemann, Katrin, and Gerold Caesperlein. 2009. "Von der Eckkneipe zur Teestube: Urbaner Wandel im Alltag: Dortmund-Borsigplatz." In Mattausch and Yildiz 2009, 119–136.
Göle, Nilüfer. 1996. *The Forbidden Modern: Civilization and Veiling*. Ann Arbor: University of Michigan Press.
———. 2004. "Die sichtbare Präsenz des Islam und die Grenzen der Öffentlichkeit." In Göle and Ammann 2004, 11–44.

Göle, Nilüfer, and Ludwig Ammann, eds. 2004. *Islam in Sicht*. Bielefeld: Transcript.
Grimm, Fatima. 1995. *Die Erziehung unserer Kinder*. Munich: Islamisches Zentrum.
———. 1999. *Frauen und Familienleben im Islam*. Munich: Islamisches Zentrum.
———. 2000. *Der Islam mit den Augen einer Frau*. Munich: SKD Bavaria Verlag.
Gühring, Albrecht, ed. 2004a. *Zuffenhausen*. Stuttgart: Verein zur Förderung der Heimat- und Partnerschaftspflege sowie Judgend- und Altenhilfe.
———. 2004b. "Konrad Vaut." In Gühring 2004a, 105–112.
———. 2004c. "Vom Regierungsantritt Herzog Christophs bis zum Ausbruch des Dreissigjährigen Kriegs." In Gühring 2004a, 139–180.
———. 2004d. "Krieg und Frieden im 17: Jahrhundert (1618–1692)." In Gühring 2004a, 227–256.
———. 2004e. "Im Einflussbereich von Ludwigsburg." In Gühring 2004a, 257–272.
Gülen, Fethullah M. 2006. *Hin zu einer globalen Kultur der Liebe und Toleranz*. Offenbach: Fontäne Verlag.
Günnewig, Jenna. 2008. "Offene Moschee statt Hinterhof." *Wdr.de*. 26 October. Accessed 30 April 2011. http://www.wdr.de/themen/kultur/religion/moschee_duisburg/081024.jhtml.
Gür, Metin. 1993. *Türkische-islamische Vereinigungen in der Bundesrepublik Deutschland*. Frankfurt: Brandes & Aspel.
Guggenheim, Michael, and Ola Söderström, eds. 2010. *Reshaping Cities: How Global Mobility Transforms Architecture and Urban Form*. London: Routledge.
Gupta, Akhil, and James Ferguson. 1992. "Beyond 'Culture': Space, Identity, and the Politics of Difference." *Cultural Anthropology* 7(1): 6–23.
Habermas, Jürgen. 1990 [1962]. *Strukturwandel der Öffentlichkeit*. Frankfurt: Suhrkamp.
———. 2006. "Religion in the Public Sphere." *European Journal of Philosophy* 14(1): 1–25.
Haddad, Yvonne. ed. 2002. *Muslims in the West: From Sojourners to Citizens*. Oxford: Oxford University Press.
Haddad, Yvonne, and John L. Esposito, eds. 2002. *Muslims on the Americanization Path?* Oxford: Oxford University Press.
Haenni, Patrick. 2005. *L'islam de marché*. Paris: Éditions du Seuil at La République des Idées.
Hanselmann, Ulrich. 2011. "Zweite Moschee für Sindelfingen." *Stuttgarter Nachrichten*, 14 April.
Hamann, Jörg. 2000a. "Nun auch OB für Wohnraum statt Moschee." *Stuttgarter Nachrichten*, 14 June.
———. 2000b. "Heslach gegen islamisches Kulturzentrum." *Stuttgarter Nachrichten*, 4 March.
———. 2000c. "Bürgerforum gegen Moschee gegründet." *Stuttgarter Nachrichten*, 3 March.
Häusler, Alexander, ed. 2008. *Rechtspopulismus als Bürgerbewegung*. Wiesbaden: VS Verlag für Sozialwissenschaften.
Hagel, Jürgen. 2002. *Cannstatt und seine Geschichte*. Tübingen: Silberburg Verlag.
Haider, Gulzar. 1996. "Muslim Space and the Practice of Architecture: A Personal Odyssey." In Metcalf 1996, 31–45.
Hajer, Marten, and Arnold Reijndorp. 2001. *In Search of New Public Domain*. Amsterdam: NAI Publishers.
Harb, Mona. 2010. "On Religiosity and Spatiality: Lessons from Hizballah in Beirut." In AlSayyad and Massoumi 2010, 283–302.
Harb, Mona, and Lara Deeb. 2011. "Culture as History and Landscape: Hizballah's Efforts to Shape the Islamic Milieu in Lebanon." *Arab Studies Journal* 29(2): 10–41.
———. 2013. "Contesting Urban Modernity: Moral Leisure in South Beirut." *European Journal of Cultural Studies* 16(6): 725–744.

Harms, Eric. 2009. "Vietnam's Civilizing Process and the Retreat from the Street: A Turtle's Eye View from Ho Chi Minh City." *City and Society* 21(2): 182–206.
Harvey, David. 1989. *The Condition of Postmodernity*. Cambridge, MA: Basil Blackwell.
———. 2006. *Spaces of Global Capitalism*. New York: Verso.
Hayden, Dolores. 1996. *The Power of Place*. Cambridge, MA: MIT Press.
Heine, Peter. 1997. *Halbmond über deutschen Dächern*. Munich: List Verlag.
Henkel, Heiko. 2007. "The Location of Islam: Inhabiting Istanbul in a Muslim Way." *American Ethnologist* 34(1): 57–70.
Herbert, Ulrich. 1999. *Fremdarbeiter: Politik und Praxis des Ausländereinsatzes in der Kriegswirtschaft des Dritten Reiches*. Bonn: Dietz.
Herbert, Ulrich. 1990. *A History of Foreign Labor in Germany, 1880–1980: Seasonal Workers, Forced Labor, Guestworkers*. Ann Arbor: University of Michigan Press.
Herrera, Linda, and Asef Bayat, eds. 2010. *Being Young and Muslim: New Cultural Politics in the Global South*. Oxford: Oxford University Press.
Hervieu-Léger, Danièle. 2002. "Space and Religion: New Approaches to Religious Spatiality in Modernity." *International Journal of Urban and Regional Research* 26(1): 99–105.
Hippler, Jochen, and Andrea Lueg. 2001. *Feindbild Islam*. Hamburg: Konkret Literatur Verlag.
Hirschkind, Charles. 2006. *The Ethical Soundscape*. New York: Columbia University Press.
Höfert, Almut, and Armando Salvatore, eds. 2000. *Between Europe and Islam. Shaping Modernity in a Transcultural Space*. Brussels: P.I.E. Peter Lang.
Höfle, Nicole. 2008a. "Moscheengemeinden wachsen." *Stuttgarter Zeitung*, 21 February.
———. 2008b. "Im Hinterhof wird fünfmal am Tag zu Allah gebetet." *Stuttgarter Zeitung*, 27 March.
———. 2008c. "Afrikanische Predigten auf dem Frauenkopf." *Stuttgarter Zeitung*, 13 June.
———. 2009. "Gemeinde will kleine Moschee bauen." *Stuttgarter Zeitung*, 29 June.
Höfle, Nicole, and Jochen Brand. 2007. "Stadt verhindert Moschee in Wangen." *Stuttgarter Zeitung*, 6 December.
Höfle, Nicole, and Hildegund Osswald. 2002a. "Islamischer Verein will Schülerwohnheim in Zukunft legal betreiben." *Stuttgarter Zeitung*, 15 May.
———. 2002b. "Moscheeklage vor Gericht." *Stuttgarter Zeitung*, 9 July.
Höfle, Nicole, and Erik Raidt. 2007. "Ebru und Ayse trällern Weihnachtslieder." *Stuttgarter Zeitung*, 28 March.
Hofmann, Murad Wilfried. 1995. *Der Islam als Alternative*. Munich: Diederichs.
———. 1996a. "Muslims in Germany: The Struggle for Integration." In *Islam and the Question of Minorities*, edited by Tamara Sonn, 55–71. Atlanta, GA: Scholars Press.
———. 1996b. *Reise nach Mekka: Ein Deutscher lebt den Islam*. Munich: Eugen Diederichs Verlag.
Holod, Renata, and Hasan-Uddin Khan. 1997. *The Contemporary Mosque*. New York: Rizzoli.
Holoch, Helmut. 1987. *Stuttgart im Wandel der letzten 80 Jahre*. Stuttgart: J.F. Steinkopf Verlag.
Holston, James. 2008. *Insurgent Citizenship*. Princeton, NJ: Princeton University Press.
Holub, Renate. 2002. "Intellectuals and Euro-Islam." In AlSayyad and Castells 2002, 167–192.
Horrocks, David and Eva Kolinsky, eds. 1996. *Turkish Culture in Germany*. Providence, RI: Berghahn Books.
Hubbert, Jennifer. 2010. "Spectacular Productions: Community and Commodity in the Beijing Olympics." *City and Society* 22(1): 119–142.
Hüttermann, Jörg. 2006. *Das Minarett: Zur politischen Kultur des Konflikts um islamische Symbole*. Weinheim: Juventa Verlag.

Hunter, Shireen, ed. 2002. *Islam, Europe's Second Religion: The New Social, Cultural and Political Landscape*. Westport, CT: Praeger.
Huus, Kari. "Quest for the Muslim Market Niche." *MSNBC*, 3 October 2003. Accessed 9 May 2003. http://msnbc.msn/id/3130288/print/1/displaymode/1098/.
Idriz, Benjamin. 2010. *Grüss Gott Herr Imam! Eine Religion ist angekommen*. Munich: Diederichs.
Ingram, Mark. 2009. "The Artist and the City in 'Euro-Mediterranean' Marseille: Redefining State Cultural Policy in an Era of Transnational Governance." *City and Society* 21(2): 268–292.
Isenberg, Michael. 2008. "Konflikt um grillende Kleingärtner." *Stuttgarter Nachrichten*, 21 June.
Isin, Engin F., ed. 2000. *Democracy, Citizenship and the Global City*. London: Routledge.
Islam.de. 2002. "Die kamen hereingestürmt, als ob wir im Krieg sind." 16 December. Accessed 26 June 2012. http://islam.de/960_print.php?.
Islamoğlu, Mustafa. 2009. *The Kingdom of Heart*. Istanbul: Denge Yayinlari.
Ismail, Salwa. 2006. *Political Life in Cairo's New Popular Quarters*. Minneapolis: University of Minnesota Press.
Jackson, Vicki C. 2009. "Citizenship, Federalism, and Gender." In *Migrations and Mobilities: Citizenship, Borders and Gender*, edited by Seyla Benhabib and Judith Resnik, 439–486. New York: New York University Press.
Jenkner, Carolin. 2008. "Warum das Wunder von Marxloh funktioniert." *Spiegel Online*, 26 October. Accessed 30 April 2011. http://www.spiegel.de/politick/deutschland/0,1518,druck-586613,00html.
Jentsch, Ulli. 2008. "Pro-Aktivitäten in Berlin und Brandenburg." In Häusler 2008, 94–103.
Jeung, Russell. 2004. *Faithful Generations: Race and New Asian American Churches*. New Brunswick, NJ: Rutgers University Press.
Jonker, Gerdien. 2002. *Eine Wellenlänge zu Gott: Der "Verband Islamischer Kulturzentren" in Europa*. Bielefeld: Transcript.
———. 2005. "The Mevlana Mosque in Berlin-Kreuzberg: An Unsolved Conflict." *Journal of Ethnic and Migration Studies* 31(6): 1067–1081.
———. 2006. "Islamist or Pietist? Muslim Responses to the German Security Framework." In Jonker and Amiraux 2006, 123–150.
Jonker, Gerdien, and Valérie Amiraux, eds. 2006. *Politics of Visibility: Young Muslims in European Public Spaces*. Bielefeld: Transcript.
Jonker, Gerdien, and Andreas Kapphan. 1999. *Moscheen und islamisches Leben in Berlin*. Berlin: Die Ausländerbeauftragte der Stadt.
Jonuz, Elizabeta, and Erika Schulze. 2011. "Vielfalt als Motor städtischer Entwicklung: Das Beispiel der Keupstrasse in Köln." In *Neue Vielfalt in der Urbanen Stadtgesellschaft*, edited by Wolf-Dietrich Bukow, Gerda Heck, Erika Schulze, and Erol Yildiz, 33–48. Wiesbaden: Verlag für Sozialwissenschaften.
Jouili, Jeannette. 2008. "Re-Fashioning the Self Through Religious Knowledge: How Muslim Women Become Pious in the Germany Diaspora." In *Islam and Muslims in Germany*, edited by Ala Al-Hamarneh and Jörn Thielmann, 465–488. Leiden: Brill.
Jouili, Jeannette, and Schirin Amir-Moazami. 2006. "Knowledge, Empowerment and Religious Authority among Pious Muslim Women in France and Germany." *The Muslim World* 96(4): 617–642.
Kalmbach, Hilary, and Masooda Banu, eds. 2012. *Women, Leadership and Mosques: Changes in Contemporary Islamic Authority*. Leiden: Brill.
Kandemir, Hülya. 2005. *Himmelstochter*. Munich: Pendo Verlag.
Kanna, Ahmed. 2010. "Flexible Citizenship: Neoliberal Subjectivity in the Emerging 'City-Corporation.'" *Cultural Anthropology* 25(1): 100–129.

———. 2011. *Dubai: The City as Corporation*. Minneapolis: University of Minnesota Press.
Karakasoğlu, Yasemin. 1996. "Turkish Cultural Orientations in Germany and the Role of Islam." In *Turkish Culture in Germany*, edited by David Horrocks and Eva Kolinski, 181–190. Providence, RI: Berghahn Books.
Karaman, Hayrettin. 2005. *Erlaubtes und Verwehrtes*. Ankara: Publikationen der Türkischen Religionsstiftung/54.
Katznelson, Ira. 1982. *City Trenches*. Chicago: University of Chicago Press.
Kaya, Ayhan. 2001. *Sicher in Kreuzberg: Constructing Diasporas; Turkish Hip-Hop Youth in Berlin*. Bielefeld: Transcript.
Keaton, Trica Danielle. 2006. *Muslim Girls and the Other France*. Bloomington: Indiana University Press.
Kepel, Gilles. 1987. *Les banlieues de l'Islam*. Paris: Édition du Seuil.
———. 1997. *Allah in the West: Islamic Movements in America and Europe*. Stanford, CA: Stanford University Press.
Kessner, Iris. 2004. *Christen und Muslime—Nachbarn in Deutschland*. Gütersloh: Gütersloher Verlagshaus.
Khaled, Amr. 2004. *Muhammad (s) . . . mit den Gläubigen gütig, barmherzig*. Karlsruhe: Andalusia Verlag.
———. 2005a. *Integration im Islam*. Karlsruhe: Andalusia Verlag.
———. 2005b. *Allahs Liebe zu den Menschen*. Karlsruhe: Andalusia Verlag.
———. 2006. *Die Liebe zum Paradies*. Karlsruhe: Andalusia Verlag.
Khosravi, Shahram. 2008. *Young and Defiant in Tehran*. Philadelphia: University of Pennsylvania Press.
Khosrokhavar, Farhad. 1997. *L'islam de jeunes*. Saint-Amand-Montrond: Flammarion.
Killian, Caitlin. 2006. *North African Women in France. Gender, Culture and Identity*. Stanford, CA: Stanford University Press.
Killguss, Hans-Peter, Jürgen Peters, and Alexander Häusler. 2008. "PRO KÖLN—Entstehung und Aktivitäten." In Häusler 2008, 55–71.
Klausen, Jytte. 2005. *The Islamic Challenge*. Oxford: Oxford University Press.
Klausing, Kathrin. 2009. "Gegen die Wand: Frauen machen in Moscheengemeinden nicht selten negative Erfahrungen." *Islamische Zeitung*, 25 February.
Klee, Ernst, ed. 1975. *Gastarbeiter: Analysen und Berichte*. Frankfurt: Suhrkamp.
Knippenberg, Hans. 2006. "The Political Geography of Religion: Historical State-Church Relations in Europe and Recent Challenges." *GeoJournal* 67(4): 253–265.
Knott, Kim. 2005. *The Location of Religion*. London: Equinox.
Köhler, Joachim. 1990. *Katholiken in Stuttgart und ihre Geschichte*. Ostfildern: Schwabenverlag.
Kömeçoğlu, Uğur. 2004. "Neue Formen der Geselligkeit: Islamische Cafés in Istanbul." In Göle and Ammann 2004, 147–177.
Kong, Lily. 1993. "Negotiating Conceptions of 'Sacred Space': A Case Study from Singapore." *Transactions of the Institute of British Geographers* 18(3): 342–358.
———. 2001. "Mapping 'New' Geographies of Religion: Politics and Poetics in Modernity." *Progress in Human Geography* 25(2): 211–233.
———. 2010. "Global Shifts, Theoretical Shifts: Changing Geographies of Religion." *Progress in Human Geography* 34(6): 755–776.
Korn, Salomon. 2008. "Zu schwach, um Fremdes zu ertragen?" *Qantara.de*, 18 November. Accessed 4 December 2008. http://de.qantara.de/webcom/show_article.php?wc_c=468&wc_id=1056&printmode=1.
Kosnick, Kira. 2004a. "'Extreme by Definition': Open Channel Television and Islamic Migrant Producers in Berlin." *New German Critique* 2 (Spring/Summer): 21–38.

———. 2004b. "Good Guys and Bad Guys: Turkish Migrant Broadcasting in Berlin." In *Transnational Social Spaces: Agents, Networks, and Institutions*, edited by Thomas Faist and Eyüp Ozveren, 189–210. Aldershot: Ashgate.
———. 2007. *Migrant Media*. Bloomington: University of Indiana Press.
Kraft, Sabine. 2002. *Islamische Sakralarchitektur in Deutschland*. Münster: LIT Verlag.
Krane, Jim. 2009. *City of Gold: Dubai and the Dream of Capitalism*. New York: St. Martin's Press.
Kugelmass, Jack. 1999. "Moses of the South Bronx: Aging and Dying in the Old Neighborhood." In Orsi 1999, 231–256.
Kuppinger, Petra. 1998. "The Giza Pyramids: Accommodating Tourism, Leisure and Consumption." *City and Society* (Annual Review 1998): 105–119.
———. 2001. "Cracks in the Cityscape: Traditional Spatial Practices and the Official Discourse on Informality and Terrorism." In *Muslim Traditions and Modern Techniques of Power*, edited by Armando Salvatore, 185–207. Hamburg: Lit Verlag.
———. 2004. "Exclusive Greenery: New Gated Communities in Cairo." *City and Society* 16(2): 35–61.
———. 2006a. "Globalization and Exterritoriality in Metropolitan Cairo." *The Geographical Review* (July 2005) 95(3): 348–372.
———. 2006b. "Pyramids and Alleys: Global Dynamics and Local Strategies in Giza." In *Cairo Cosmopolitan*, edited by Diane Singerman and Paul Amar, 313–344. Cairo: American University in Cairo Press.
———. 2008. "Mosque in Stuttgart: Struggling for Space." *ISIM Review* 21 (Spring): 48–49.
———. 2009. "Barbie, Razanne, and Fulla: A Global Tale of Culture, Economy and Religion." In Pink 2009, 170–215.
———. 2010a. "Factories, Office Suites, Defunct and Marginal Spaces: Mosques in Stuttgart, Germany." In *Reshaping Cities*, edited by Michael Guggenheim and Ola Söderström, 83–99. London: Routledge.
———. 2010b. "Jung, deutsch und muslimisch: Neue Lebenswelten." In *Facebook, Fun und Ramadan: Lebenswelten Muslimischer Jugendlicher*, edited by Stephan Bundschuh, Birgit Jagusch, and Hanna Mai, 12–15. Düsseldorf: Informations und Dokumentationszentrum für Antirassismusarbeit (IDA) e.V.
———. 2011a. "Between Anti-Globalization and Islam: Cultural, Political and Religious Debates in the German Muslim *Islamische Zeitung*." *Contemporary Islam* 5(1): 59–79.
———. 2011b. "Vibrant Mosques: Space, Planning and Informality in Germany." *Built Environment* 37(1): 78–91.
———. 2011c. "*Himmelstochter* or New German Muslim Lifeworlds." *Journal of Middle East Women's Studies* 7(2): 27–55.
———. 2012. "Women, Leadership, and Participation in Mosques and Beyond: Notes from Stuttgart, Germany." In *Women, Leadership and Mosques*, edited by Hilary Kalmbach and Masooda Bano, 323–344. Leiden: Brill.
———. 2014a. "Cinderella Wears a *Hijab*: Neighborhoods, Islam, and the Everyday Production of Multi-Ethnic Urban Cultures in Germany." *Space and Culture* 17(1): 29–42.
———. 2014b. "Flexible Topographies: Muslim Spaces in a German Cityscape." *Social and Cultural Geography* 15(6): 627–644.
———. 2014c. "One Mosque and the Negotiation of German Islam." *Culture and Religion* 15(3): 313–333.
———. 2014d. "A Neighborhood Shopping Street and the Making of Urban Cultures and Economies in Germany." *City and Community* 13(2): 140–157.
———. 2014e. "Mosques and Minarets: Conflict, Participation and Visibility in German Cities." *Anthropological Quarterly* 87(3): 793–818.

———. 2014f. "The Stuttgart Crescent: Muslim Mobilities and Spiritual Geographies in Germany." In *Managing Muslim Mobilities: Between Spiritual Geographies and the Global Security Regime*, edited by Anita Fábos and Riina Isotalo, 153–170. New York: Palgrave MacMillan.

Kurz, Jörg. 2005. *Nordgeschichte(n)*. Stuttgart: Gulde Druck.

Kurzlechner, Werner. 2008. "Tag der offenen Moschee: Kommen um zu streiten." *Der Tagesspiegel*, 30 November. Accessed 28 April 2011. http://www.tagesspiegel.de/berlin/tag-der-offenen-moschee-kommen-um-zu-streiten/.

Landes, Joan. 1988. *Women and the Public Sphere in the Age of the French Revolution*. Ithaca, NY: Cornell University Press.

Landeshauptstadt Stuttgart, ed. 2006. *Datenkompass Stadtbezirke Stuttgart*. (Ausgabe 2006/2007) Statistik und Informationsmanagement.Themenheft 4/2006.

———. 2012/13. *Datenkompass Stadtbezirke Stuttgart*. Stuttgart: Statistisches Amt. http://service.stuttgart.de/lhs-services/komunis/documents/6432_1_Datenkompass_Stadtbezirke_Stuttgart_2012_2013___Gesamtstadt__Erlaeuterungen__Definitionen_und_Nachweise.PDF.

Landeszentrale für politische Bildung Baden-Württemberg, ed. 2001. *Islam in Deutschland*. Stuttgart: Landeszentrale für politische Bildung.

Landman, Nico and Wendy Wessels. 2005. "The Visibility of Mosques in Dutch Towns." *Journal of Ethnic and Migration Studies* 31(6): 1125–1140.

Lang, Jeffrey. 1994. *Struggling to Surrender*. Beltsville, MD: Amana Publications.

Landler, Mark. 2003. "A German Court Accepts Teacher's Head Scarf." *New York Times*, 29 May.

———. 2007. "German Splits over a Mosque and the Role of Islam." *New York Times*, 5 July.

Langer, Bernd. 1994. *Gemeinnütziger Wohnungsbau um 1900: Karl Hengerers Bauten für das Wohl der arbeitenden Klassen*. Stuttgart: Klett-Cotta.

Lauterbach, Burkhart, and Stephanie Lottermoser. 2009. *Fremdkörper Moschee?* Würzburg: Königshausen & Neumann.

Lefebvre, Henri. 1991 [1974]. *The Production of Space*. Oxford: Blackwell.

Leggewie, Claus and Zafer Şenicak, eds. 1993. *Deutsche Türken—Türk Alamanlar*. Hamburg: Rowolt.

Lemmen, Thomas. 2001. *Muslime in Deutschland: Eine Herausforderung für Kirche und Gesellschaft*. Baden-Baden: Nomos.

Lemmen, Thomas, and Melanie Miehl. 2001. *Miteinander leben: Christen und Muslime im Gespräch*. Gütersloh: Gütersloher Verlagshaus.

Levitt, Peggy. 2008. "Religion as a Path to Civic Engagement." *Ethnic and Racial Studies* 31(4): 766–791.

Lewis, Philip. 1994. *Islamic Britain: Religion, Politics and Identity among British Muslims*. London: I.B. Tauris.

———. 2006. "From Seclusion to Inclusion: British 'Ulama and the Politics of Social Visibility." In Jonker and Amiraux 2006, 169–190.

Lin, Jan. 1998. *Reconstructing Chinatown*. Minneapolis: University of Minnesota Press.

Livezey, Lowell, ed. 2000. *Public Religion and the Urban: Faith in the City*. New York: New York University Press.

Lösch, Volker, Gangold Stocker, Sabine Leidig, Winfried Wolf, and Walter Sittler, eds. 2010. *Stuttgart 21—Oder: Wem gehört die Stadt?* Cologne: PapyRossa Verlag.

Loukaitou-Sideris, Anastasia, and Renia Ehrenfeucht. 2009. *Sidewalks*. Cambridge, MA: MIT Press.

Low, Setha M. 1996. "The Anthropology of Cities: Imagining and Theorizing the City." *Annual Review of Anthropology* 25: 383–409.

———. 2004. *Behind the Gates*. London: Routledge.
Low, Setha M., and Denise Lawrence-Zunuga, eds. 2003. *The Anthropology of Space and Place*. Malden, MA: Blackwell.
Lubeck, Paul. 2002. "The Challenge of Islamic Networks and Citizenship Claims: Europe's Painful Adjustment to Globalization." In AlSayyad and Castells 2002, 69–90.
Lucassen, Jan. 1987. *Migrant Labour in Europe: 1600–1900*. London: Croom Helm.
———. 1998. "The Great War and the Origin of Migration Control in Western Europe and the United States." In *Regulation of Migration*, edited by Anita Böker, Kees Groenendijk, Tetty Havinga, and Paul Minderhoud, 45–72. Amsterdam: Het Spinhuis Publisher.
Mack, Daniela. 2000. "Grosses islamisches Zentrum gestoppt." *Stuttgarter Zeitung*, 7 April.
Mack, Daniela, and Martin Honecker. 2000. "Wir sind zum Gespräch und zu Kompromissen bereit." *Stuttgarter Zeitung*, 29 March.
Macklin, Audrey. 2009. "Particularized Citizenship: Encultured Women and the Public Sphere." In *Migrations and Mobilities: Citizenship, Borders and Gender*, edited by Seyla Benhabib and Judith Resnik, 439–486. New York: New York University Press.
Mahmood, Saba. 2005. *Politics of Piety*. Princeton, NJ: Princeton University Press.
Malik, Iftikhar Haider. 2004. *Islam and Modernity: Muslims in Europe and the United States*. London: Pluto Press.
Malik, Nadeem. 2000. *The East London Central Mosque: Organising in Action*. Leicester: The Islamic Foundation.
Mamdani, Mahmoud. 2004. *Good Muslim, Bad Muslim*. New York: Random House.
Manço, Ural, and Meryem Kanmaz. 2005. "From Conflict to Co-operation between Muslims and Local Authorities in a Brussels Borough: Schaerbeek." *Journal of Ethnic and Migration Studies* 31(6): 1105–1123.
Mandel, Ruth. 1990. "Shifting Centres and Emergent Identities: Turkey and Germany in the Lives of Turkish *Gastarbeiter*." In *Muslim Travellers*, edited by Dale F. Eickelman and James Piscatori, 153–171. Berkeley: University of California Press.
———. 1996. "A Place of Their Own: Contesting Spaces and Defining Places in Berlin's Migrant Community." In Metcalf 1996, 147–166.
———. 2008. *Cosmopolitan Anxieties*. Durham, NC: Duke University Press.
Mannitz, Sabine. 2006. *Die verkannte Integration*. Bielefeld: Transcript.
Marechal, Brigitte. 2003. *Muslims in the Enlarged Europe*. Leiden: Brill.
Markert, Sandra. 2008. "Islamisches Schülerwohnheim kämpft gegen Vorurteile." *Stuttgarter Nachrichten*, 29 May.
Marx, Hannelore. 2004. *Stuttgart, Riga, New York: Mein jüdischer Lebensweg*. Horb: Staudacher Verlag.
Massey, Doreen. 1992. Politics of Space/Time. *New Left Review* 196: 65–84.
———. 1994. *Space, Place, and Gender*. Minneapolis: University of Minnesota Press.
Mattausch, Birgit, and Erol Yildiz, eds. 2009. *Urban Recycling: Migration als Grossstadt Ressource*. Basel: Birkhäuser.
Maududi, Sayyid Abul A'la. 2001. *Als Muslim leben*. Karlsruhe: Cordoba-Verlag.
Mazawi, André Elias. 2010. "'Also the School Is a Temple': Republicanism, Imagined Transnational Space and the Schooling of Muslim Youth in France." In Herrera and Bayat 2010, 177–188.
McCloud, Aminah. 1996. "'This is a Muslim Home': Signs of Difference in the African American Home." In Metcalf 1996, 65–73.
McDonogh, Gary. 2011. "Learning from Barcelona: Discourse, Power and Praxis in the Sustainable City." *City and Society* 23(2): 135–153.

McLennan, Gregor. 2010. "The Postsecular Turn." *Theory, Culture and Society* 27(4): 3–20.
McLoughlin, Seán. 2005. "Mosques and the Public Space: Conflict and Cooperation in Bradford." *Journal of Ethnic and Migration Studies* 31(6): 1045–1066.
McMurray, David. 2000. *In and Out of Morocco*. Minneapolis: University of Minneapolis Press.
Meier-Braun Karl-Heinz, and Reinhold Weber, eds. 2005. *Kulturelle Vielfalt: Baden-Württemberg als Einwanderungsland*. Landeszentrale für politische Bildung Baden-Württemberg. Schriften zur politischen Landeskunde Baden-Württembergs. Band 32. Stuttgart: Landeszentrale für politische Bildung.
Mele, Christopher. 2000. *Selling the Lower East Side: Culture, Real Estate and Resistance in New York City*. Minneapolis: University of Minnesota Press.
Merry, Sally Engle. 2001. "Spatial Governmentality and the New Urban Social Order: Controlling Gender Violence through Law." *American Anthropologist* 103(1): 16–29.
Messerschmidt, Richard. 1957. *Zuffenhausen einst und heute*. (Heimatgeschichtlicher Arbeitskreis Stuttgart-Zuffenhausen, ed.) Stuttgart-Zuffenhausen: Hornung.
Metcalf, Barbara Daly, ed. 1996. *Making Muslim Space*. Berkeley: University of California Press.
Meyle, Wolfgang. 2004. "Zuffenhausen von den 1980er-Jahren bis zum Beginn des 21. Jahrhunderts." In Gühring 2004a, 529–557.
Mitchell, Don. 2003. *The Right to the City*. New York: Guilford Press.
Modan, Gabriella. 2007. *Turf Wars*. Cambridge: Wiley Blackwell.
———. 2008. "Mango Fufu Kimchi Yucca: The Depoliticization of 'Diversity' in Washington, D.C. Discourse." *City and Society* 20(2): 188–221.
Modood, Tariq. 2005. *Multicultural Politics: Racism, Ethnicity, and Muslims in Britain*. Minneapolis: University of Minnesota Press.
———. 2007. *Multiculturalism*. Cambridge: Polity Press.
Modood, Tariq, and Pnina Werbner, eds. 1997. *The Politics of Multiculturalism in the New Europe: Racism, Identity and Community*. London: Zed Books.
Molendijk, Arie, Justin Beaumont, and Christoph Jedan, eds. 2010. *Exploring the Postsecular: The Religious, the Political and the Urban*. Leiden: Brill.
Monshipouri, Mahmood. 2010. "The War of Terror and Muslims in the West." In Cesari 2010a, 45–66.
Müller, Roland. 2004. "Krise, Diktatur, Krieg und die Folgen in Zuffenhausen." In Gühring 2004a, 411–476.
Müller, Ulrich. 1990. *Fremde in der Nachkriegszeit. Displaced Person—Zwangsverschleppte Personen—in Stuttgart und Württemberg-Baden 1945–51*. Stuttgart: Klett-Cotta. Veröffentlichungen der Stadt Stuttgart Bd.49.
Mutlu, Dilek Kaya. 2009. "The Cola Turka Controversy: Consuming Cola as a Turkish Muslim." In Pink 2009, 101–122.
Muzenhardt, Petra. 2009. "Musliminnen schwimmen ohne Scham." *Stuttgarter Nachrichten*, July 30.
Negt, Oskar, and Alexander Kluge. 1972. *Öffentlichkeit und Erfahrung*. Frankfurt: Suhrkamp.
Newman, Andrew. 2011. "Contested Ecologies: Environmental Activism and Urban Space in Immigrant Paris." *City and Society* 23(2): 192–209.
Nökel, Sigrid. 2002. *Die Töchter der Gastarbeiter und der Islam*. Bielefeld: Transcript.
———. 2004. "Muslimische Frauen und öffentliche Räume." In Göle and Ammann 2004, 283–308.
Nomani, Asra. 2005. "Hijab Chic: How Retailers are Marketing to Fashion-Conscious Muslim Women." slate.com. 27 October. Accessed 29 April 2006. http://www.slate.com/toolbar.aspx?action=print&id=2129906.

Nonnemann, Gerd, Tim Noblock, and Bogdan Szajkowski, eds. 1996. *Muslim Communities in the New Europe*. Reading, UK: Ithaca Press.
N-TV. 2006. "Islam Teil Deutschlands." 28 September. Accessed 12 October 2012. http://www.n-tv.de.
Numrich, Paul. 2000. "Change, Stress, and Congregations in an Edge-City Technoburb." In Livezey 2000, 187–212.
Oestreich, Heide. 2004. *Der Kopftuchstreit*. Frankfurt: Brandes und Apsel.
Özdemir, Cem. 1997. *Ich bin Inländer: Ein anatolischer Schwabe im Bundestag*. Munich: DTV.
———. 2002. *(K)eine Frage der Kultur: Sorun Gercekten Kültür Mü?* Freiburg: Belchen Verlag.
———. 1999. *Deutsch oder nicht sein: Integration in der Bundesrepublik*. Bergisch Gladbach: Bastei Lübbe.
Özelsel, Michaela. 2005. *Pilgerfahrt nach Mekka*. Freiburg: Herder.
Özyürek, Esra. 2009. "Convert Alert: German Muslims and Turkish Christians as Threats to Security in the New Europe." *Comparative Studies in Society and History* 51(1): 91–116.
———. 2015. *Being German. Becoming Muslim*. Princeton: Princeton University Press.
Olson, Elizabeth, Peter Hopkins, Rachel Pain, and Giselle Vincett. 2013. "Retheorizing the Postsecular Present: Embodiment, Spatial Transcendence, and Challenges to Authenticity among Young Christians in Glasgow, Scotland." *Annals of the Association of American Geographers* 103(6): 1412–1436.
Orsi, Robert. 1985. *The Madonna of 115th Street*. New Haven, CT: Yale University Press.
———. 2005. *Between Heaven and Earth*. Princeton, NJ: Princeton University Press.
———, ed. 1999. *Gods in the City*. Bloomington: Indiana University Press.
Osswald, Hildegund. 2000a. "Islamisches Zentrum sorgt für Aufregung." *Stuttgarter Zeitung*, 27 January.
———. 2000b. "Bei Moscheeentscheidung soll OB Schuster für Klarheit sorgen." *Stuttgarter Zeitung*, 24 February.
———. 2000c. "Acht Einsprüche gegen Moscheepläne." *Stuttgarter Zeitung*, 15 March.
———. 2000d. "Moscheepläne in Heslach: Neues Baugesuch ohne Internat." *Stuttgarter Zeitung*, 11 August.
———. 2001a. "Nein zu grossem Gebetszentrum in Heslach." *Stuttgarter Zeitung*, 31 January.
———. 2001b. "Weiter Streit um Gebetszentrum." *Stuttgarter Zeitung*, 31 January.
———. 2001c. "Moschee: CDU fordert neue Suche nach Alternativen." *Stuttgarter Zeitung*, 6 February.
———. 2004. "50 neue Stadtwohnungen statt Moschee." *Stuttgarter Zeitung*, 7 October.
Osswald, Hildegund, and Nicole Höfle. 2002. "Moscheeklage vor Gericht." *Stuttgarter Zeitung*, 9 July.
Ostertag, Roland, ed. 2008. *Die entzauberte Stadt*. Stuttgart: Peter Grohmann Verlag.
Partridge, Damani. 2012. *Hypersexuality and Headscarves: Race, Sex, and Citizenship in the New Germany*. Bloomington: Indiana University Press.
Pazarkaya, Utku. 2002. "Heslacher Moscheen-Streit: Stadt ist am Zug." *Stuttgarter Nachrichten*, 18 March.
Peach, Ceri, and Richard Gale. 2003. "Muslims, Hindus, Sikhs in the New Religious Landscape of England." *Geographical Review* 93(4): 469–490.
Penninx, Rinus. 2004. *Citizenship in European Cities: Immigrant, Local Politics and Integration Policies*. Burlington, VT: Ashgate.
Peraldi, Michel. 2009. "Marseille: Der Geist der Krise und die Ökonomie des Basars." In Mattausch and Yildiz 2009, 82–99.
Peter, Frank. 2010. "Welcoming Muslims into the Nation: Tolerance, Politics and Integration in Germany." In Cesari 2010a, 119–144.

Peters, Jürgen, Tomas Sager, and Alexander Häusler. "2008 PRO NRW und Pro-D—Entwicklung, Struktur und Methodik." In Häusler 2008, 72-87.
Pile, Steve. 2010. "Emotions and Affect in Recent Human Geography." *Transactions of the British Institute of British Geographers* 35(1): 5-20.
Pink, Johanna, ed. 2009. *Muslim Societies in the Age of Mass Consumption: Politics, Culture and Identity between the Local and the Global.* Cambridge: Cambridge Scholars Press.
Pond, Christian. 2006. "The Appeal of Sami Yusuf and the Search for Islamic Authenticity." *Arab Media and Society/TBS Journal* 16 (Summer). http://www.arabmediasociety.com/countries/index.php?c_article=65.
Prantl, Herbert. 2010. "Der Islam ist Teil Deutschlands." *Süddeutsche Zeitung,* 17 May. Accessed 11 October 2012. http://www.sueddeutsche.de.
Presse- und Informationsamt der Landeshauptstadt Stuttgart, ed. 2002. *Stuttgart und seine Geschichte.* Stuttgart: Presse- und Informationsamt der Landeshauptstadt Stuttgart.
Quayson, Ato. 2010. "Signs of the Times: Discourse Ecologies and Street Life on Oxford St. in Accra." *City and Society* 22(1): 72-96.
Rabinow, Paul, ed. 1984. *The Foucault Reader.* New York: Pantheon Books.
Raidt, Erik. 2006. "Zwischen Couscous und Maultaschen." *Stuttgarter Zeitung,* 21 November.
———. 2011. "Liebe Königstrasse!" *Stuttgarter Zeitung,* 26 June.
Räntzsch, Andreas M. 1987. *Stuttgart und seine Eisenbahnen.* Heidenheim: Uwe Siedentop Verlag.
Ramadan, Said. 1996. *Das islamische Recht: Theories und Praxis.* Marburg: Muslimische Studenten Vereinigung in Deutschland.
Ramadan, Tariq. 1998. *To Be a European Muslim.* Leicester: The Islamic Foundation.
———. 1999. *Muslims in France.* Leicester: The Islamic Foundation
———. 2003a. *Western Muslims and the Future of Islam.* Oxford: Oxford University Press.
———. 2003b. *Die Muslime im Westen.* Berlin: Green Palace.
———. 2004. *Islam, the West and the Challenges of Modernity.* Leicester: The Islamic Foundation.
Rey, Terry, and Alex Stepick. 2009. "Refugee Catholicism in Little Haiti: Miami's Notre Dame d'Haiti Catholic Church." In *Churches and Charity in the Immigrant City,* edited by Alex Stepick, Terry Rey, and Sarah J. Mahler, 72-91. New Brunswick, NJ: Rutgers University Press.
Rieger, Abu Bakr. 2007. *Islam in Deutschland.* Freiburg: Spohr.
Reidegeld, Abdelrahman. 2005. *Handbuch Islam.* Freiburg: Spohr.
Rogers, Alisdair, and Jean Tillie. 2001. *Multicultural Policies and Modes of Citizenship in European Cities.* Burlington, VT: Ashgate.
Rotenberg, Robert, and Gary McDonogh, eds. 1993. *The Cultural Meaning of Urban Space.* Westport, CT: Bergin & Garvey.
Rouse, Carolyn Moxley. 2004. *Engaged Surrender.* Berkeley: University of California Press.
Roy, Olivier. 2004. *Globalized Islam: The Search for a New Umma.* New York: Columbia University Press.
Sage, Tomas, and Jürgen Peters. 2008. "Die Pro-Aktivitäten im Kontext der extremen Rechten." In Häusler 2008, 115-128.
Said, Edward. 1979. *Orientalism.* New York: Vintage Books.
———. 1981. *Covering Islam.* New York: Vintage Books.
Said Nursi, Bediüzzaman. 2004. *Die Wunder Muhammads.* Istanbul: Sözler.
Saint-Blancat, Chantal, and Ottavia Schmidt di Friedberg. 2005. "Why are Mosques a Problem? Local Politics and Fear of Islam in Northern Italy." *Journal of Ethnic and Migration Studies* 31(6): 1083-1104.

Saktanber, Ayşe. 2002. "'We Pray like You Have Fun': New Islamic Youth in Turkey between Intellecualism and Popular Culture." In *Fragments of Culture*, edited by Denise Kandiyoti and Ayşe Saktanber, 254–276. London: I.B. Tauris.

———. 2010. "Performance, Politics and Visceral Transformation: Post-Islamist Youth in Turkey." In Herrera and Bayat 2010, 259–272.

Salvatore, Armando. 2007. *The Public Sphere: Liberal Modernity, Catholicism, Islam*. New York: Palgrave Macmillan.

Sassen, Saskia. 1991. *The Global City: New York, London, Tokyo*. Princeton, NJ: Princeton University Press.

———. 1998. *Globalization and its Discontents*. New York: The New Press.

———. 1999. *Guests and Aliens*. New York: The New Press.

———. 2000. "The Global City. Strategic Site/New Frontier." In Isin 2000, 48–61.

———. 2001. *The Global City*. Princeton, NJ: Princeton University Press.

Sassen, Saskia, ed. 2002. *Global Networks. Linked Cities*. London: Routledge.

Sattler, Fariba. 2007. "Hindus müssen ihren Tempel im Westen räumen." *Stuttgarter Zeitung*, 11 June.

Sauer, Paul. 1994. *Das Werden einer Grossstadt: Stuttgart zwischen Reichsgründung und dem Ersten Weltkrieg*. Tübingen: Silberburg.

Sawalha, Aseel. 2010. *Reconstructing Beirut*. Austin: University of Texas Press.

Schäfer, Annette. 2001. "Zwangsarbeiter in den Kommunen." *Vierteljahreshefte für Zeitgeschichte* 49(1): 53–75.

Scheld, Suzanne. 2007. "Youth Cosmopolitanism: Clothing, the City and Globalization in Dakar, Senegal." *City and Society* 19(2): 232–253.

Schiffauer, Werner. 1987. *Die Bauern von Subay*. Stuttgart: Klett-Cotta.

———. 1991. *Die Migranten aus Subay: Türken in Deutschland*. Stuttgart: Klett-Cotta.

———. 1992. "The Fall Akar—eine Fallstudie zu den psychosozialen Konsequenzen der Arbeitsmigration für die zweite Generation." *Hessische Blätter* 29: 145–153.

———. 1997. *Fremde in der Stadt*. Frankfurt: Suhrkamp.

———. 2000. *Die Gottesmänner*. Frankfurt: Suhrkamp.

———. 2001. "Auf der Suche nach Anerkennung im Spagat zwischen zwei Kulturen." In *Islam in Deutschland*. Landeszentrale für politische Bildung Baden-Württemberg, ed. Pp. 226–232.

———. 2008. *Parallelgesellschaften*. Bielefeld: Transcript.

———. 2010. *Nach dem Islamismus*. Berlin: Suhrkamp.

Schiffer, Sabine. 2005. *Die Darstellung des Islam in der Presse*. Würzburg: Ergon.

———. 2008. "Islam in German Media." In *Islam and Muslims in Germany*, edited by Ala Al-Hamarneh and Jörn Thielmann, 423–440. Leiden: Brill.

Schilder, Peter. 2008. "Lautlos in Marxloh." *Frankfurter Allgemeine*, 26 October. Accessed 30 April 2011. http://www.faz.net/sRubFC06D389EE76479E9E76425072B196C3/Doc.

Schmid, Hansjörg, Ayşe Almile Akça, and Klaus Barwig, eds. 2008. *Gesellschaft gemeinsam gestalten. Islamische Vereinigungen als Partner in Baden-Württemberg*. Baden-Baden: Nomos Verlag.

Schmitt, Thomas. 2003. *Moscheen in Deutschland*. Flensburg: Deutsche Akademie für Landeskunde.

Schorlau, Wolfgang, ed. 2012. *Stuttgart 21: Die Argumente*. Cologne: Kiepenheuer and Witsch.

Schukraft, Harald. 1999. *Wie Stuttgart wurde was es ist*. Tübingen: Silberburg Verlag.

Schuster, Wolfgang. 2006. *Wir sind Stuttgart. We are Stuttgart*. Leipzig: Hohenheim Verlag.

Schwarz, Konstantin. 2000. "Islamisches Kulturzentrum einhellig abgelehnt." *Stuttgarter Nachrichten*, 23 February.

———. 2001a. "Moschee-Pläne in Heslach könnten vor Gericht enden." *Stuttgarter Nachrichten*, 16 January.
———. 2001b. "Sackgasse." *Stuttgarter Nachrichten*, 31 January.
Sciorra, James. 1999. "'We Go Where the Italians Live': Religious Processions as Ethnic and Territorial Markers in a Multi-Ethnic Brooklyn Neighborhood." In Orsi 1999, 310–340.
Semyonov, Moshe; Anya Glukman, and Maria Krysan. 2007. "Europeans' Preferences for Ethnic Residential Homogeneity." *Social Problems* 54(4): 434–453.
Şenocak, Zafer. 1993. *Atlas des tropischen Deutschland*. Berlin: Babel Verlag.
———. 1998. *Gefährliche Verwandtschaft*. Munich: Babel.
Serageldin, Ismaïl (with James Steele), ed. 1996. *Architecture of the Contemporary Mosque*. London: Academy Editions.
Serageldin, Ismaïl. 1996a. "Introduction: Background Study." In *Architecture of the Contemporary Mosque*, edited by Ismaïl Serageldin, 8–11. London: Academy Editions.
Sevindi, Nevval. 2008. *Contemporary Islamic Conversations: M. Fethullah Gülen on Turkey, Islam, and the West*. Albany: SUNY Press.
Sezgin, Hilal. 2006. *Typisch Türkin*. Freiburg: Herder.
Shah, Bindi, Claire Dwyer, and David Gilbert. 2012. "Landscapes of Diasporic Religious Belonging in the Edge-City: The Jain Temple at Potters Bar, Outer London." *South Asian Diaspora* 4(1): 77–94.
Shaheen, Jack. 2008. *Guilty: Hollywood's Verdict on Arabs after 9/11*. Ithaca, NY: Olive Branch Press.
———. 2009. *Reel Bad Arabs: How Hollywoods Vilifies a People*. 2nd ed. Ithaca, NY: Olive Branch Press.
Shavit, Uriya, and Frederic Wiesenbach. 2012. "An 'Integrating Enclave': The Case of Al-Hayat, Germany's First Islamic Fitness Center for Women in Cologne." *Journal of Muslim Minority Affairs* 32(1): 47–61
Shooman, Yasemin, and Riem Spielhaus. 2010. "The Concept of the Muslim Enemy in the Public Discouse." In Cesari 2010a, 198–228.
Sieber, Tim, Gracia Indias Cordeiro, and Ligia Ferro. 2012. "The Neighborhood Strikes Back: Community Murals in Boston's Communities of Color." *City and Society* 24(3): 263–280.
Silverstein, Paul A. 2004. *Algeria in France: Transpolitics, Race and Nation*. Bloomington: University of Indiana Press.
Smith, Jonathan. 1987. *To Take Place*. Chicago: University of Chicago Press.
Smith, Michael Peter. 2001. *Transnational Urbanism*. Malden, MA: Blackwell.
Somunçu, Serdar. 2004. *Getrennte Rechnungen*. Bergisch Gladbach: Gustav Lübbe Verlag.
Sorkin, Michael, ed. 1992. *Variations on a Theme Park*. New York: Hill and Wang.
Soysal, Yasemin Nuhoğlu. 1994. *Limits of Citizenship: Migrants and Postnational Membership in Europe*. Chicago: Chicago University Press.
Spielhaus, Riem. 2011. *Wer ist hier Muslim? Die Entwicklung eines Bewusstseins in Deutschland zwischen Selbstidentifikation und Fremdzuschreibung*. Würzburg: Ergon Verlag.
———. 2013. "Vom Migranten zum Muslim und wieder zurück—Die Vermengung von Integrations- und Islamthemen in Medien, Politik und Forschung." In *Islam und die deutsche Gesellschaft*, edited by Dieter Halm und Hendrik Meyer, 169–194. Wiesbaden: Springer Fachmedien.
Spielhaus, Riem, and Alexa Färber, eds. 2006. *Islamisches Gemeindeleben in Berlin*. Berlin: Der Beauftragte des Senats für Integration und Migration.
Spohr, Hagar. 1998. *Die Reise nach Mekka*. Bonndorf: Gorski and Spohr.

Starrett, Gregory. 1998. *Putting Islam to Work: Education, Politics and Religious Transformation in Egypt*. Berkeley: University of California Press.
———. 1999. "Muslim Identities and the Great Chain of Buying." In *New Media in the Muslim World*, edited by Dale F. Eickelman and Jon W. Anderson, 57–79. Bloomington: University of Indiana Press.
Statistisches Bundesamt. 2013. *Bevölkerung und Erwerbstätigkeit: Bevölkerung mit Migrationshintergrund; Ergebnisse des Mikrozensus 2012*. Wiesbaden: Statistisches Bundesamt.
Stepick, Alex, Terry Rey, and Sarah J. Mahler, eds. 2009a. *Churches and Charity in the Immigrant City*. New Brunswick, NJ: Rutgers University Press.
———. 2009b. "Religion, Immigration and Civic Engagment." In *Churches and Charity in the Immigrant City*, edited by Alex Stepick, Terry Rey, and Sarah J.Mahler, 1–38. New Brunswick, NJ: Rutgers University Press.
Stowasser, Barbara Freyer. 2002. "The Turks in Germany." In *From Sojourners to Citizens*, edited by Yvonne Haddad, 52–72. Oxford: Oxford University Press.
Stuttgarter Nachrichten. 2000a. "Widerstand gegen Moschee in Stuttgart." 11 February.
———. 2000b. "Moschee: Bürgerforum sucht Gespräch mit OB." 3 May.
———. 2002. "Heslach: Wohnungen statt Moschee." 18 September.
———. 2011a. "Integrationspreis." 14 October.
———. 2011b. "Information zum Moscheen-Streit: Pro Heslach hält Stammtisch." 15 November.
Stuttgarter Zeitung. 2000a. "Muslime: Verzicht auf Klage." 19 April.
———. 2000b. "Moschee: Stadt will Haus kaufen." 13 December.
———. 2001a. "Moschee verstösst nicht gegen Baurecht." 1 March.
———. 2001b. "Angst vor Radikalisierung." 12 December.
———. 2001c. "Moschee: Stadt kann Planung fortführen." 19 December.
———. 2010. "Sichere Jobs, gute Aussichten." 21 July.
Südkurier. 2002. "Doppelkritik und Polizei-Razzia." 17 December. Accessed 26 June 2012. http://www.suedkurier.de/region/schwarzwald-baar-heuberg/schwarzwald-baar-kreis/Doppelkritik-an-Polizei-Razzia;art372502,190267.
Supp, Barbara. 2006. "Die Integrierten." *Der Spiegel* No. 27: 58–63.
Tagesschau.de. 2009. "Schweizer stimmen für Minarett-Verbot." 29 November. Accessed 1 December 2009. http://www.tagesschau.de/ausland/schweiz144.html.
Tarlo, Emma. 2010. *Visibly Muslim: Fashion, Politics, Faith*. Oxford: Berg.
Taylor, Charles. 1989. *Sources of the Self*. Cambridge, MA: Harvard University Press.
———. 2004. "Die Religion und die Identitätskämpfe der Moderne." In Göle and Ammann 2004, 342–378.
TAZ (Die Tageszeitung). 2010. "Islam ist ein Teil Deutschlands." 3 October. Accessed 12 October 2012. http://www.taz.de/!59216/.
ter Haar, Gerrie. 1998. *Halfway to Paradise: African Christians in Europe*. Cardiff: Cardiff Academic Press.
Ternisien, Xavier. 2002. *La France des Mosques*. Paris: Albin Michel.
Thelen, Sybille. 2007. "Musste das sein mit dem Pinguinvergleich?" *Stuttgarter Zeitung*, 2 June.
———. 2010. "Zeigen, dass Sarrazin unrecht hat." *Stuttgarter Zeitung*, 9 September.
Thielmann, Jörn. 2012. "Competing Spaces, Contested Places: Muslims' Struggles for Place, Space and Recognition at a German University." In *Prayer in the City*, edited by Patrick Desplat and Dorothea Schulz, 171–184. Bielefeld: Transcript.
Tietze, Nikola. 2001. *Islamische Identitäten: Formen muslimischer Religiosität junger Männer in Deutschland und Frankreich*. Hamburg: Hamburger Edition.

Trix, Frances, John Walbridge, and Linda Walbridge, eds. 2008. *Muslim Voices in the Contemporary World*. New York: Palgrave Macmillan.
Tweed, Thomas. 2002. *Our Lady of Exile: Diasporic Religion at a Cuban Catholic Shrine in Miami*. Oxford: Oxford University Press.
———. 2008. *Crossing and Dwelling: A Theory of Religion*. Cambridge, MA: Harvard University Press.
Uhlemayr, Nebiye. 2010. *Parwana*. Norderstadt: Books on Demand.
Uhlmann, Fred. 1992. *Erinnerungen eines Stuttgarter Juden*. (Veröffentlichungen des Archivs der Stadt Stuttgart, Band 56.) Stuttgart: Klett Verlag.
Urry, John. 2007. *Mobilities*. Cambridge: Polity Press.
Van der Veer, Peter, and Hartmut Lehmann, eds. 1999. *Nation and Religion*. Princeton, NJ: Princeton University Press.
Van Nieuwkerk, Karin. 2006. *Embracing Islam: Gender and Conversion in the West*. Austin: University of Texas Press.
Venel, Nancy. 2004. *Musulmans et citoyens*. Paris: Presses Universitaires de France.
Verkaaik, Oskar. 2012. "Designing the 'Anti-Mosque': Identity, Religion, and Affect in Contemporary Mosque Design. *Social Anthropology* 20(2): 161–176.
———. 2013. *Religious Architecture*. Amsterdam: University of Amsterdam Press.
Verstraete, Ginette. 2010. *Tracking Europe: Mobility, Diaspora and the Politics of Location*. Durham, NC: Duke University Press.
Vertovec, Steven. 1992. Community and Congregation in London Hindu Temples. *Journal of Ethnic and Migration Studies* 18(2): 251–264.
Von Denffer, Ahmad. 1983. *Islam für Kinder*. Aachen: Haus des Islam.
———. 2000. *Kopftuch und Kleidung*. Munich: Islamisches Zentrum.
———. 2003. *Über islamisches Verhalten*. Munich: Islamisches Zentrum.
———. 2005. *Ulum al-Qur'an: Einführung in die Koranwissenschaften*. N.p.: Deutscher Informationsdienst über den Islam.
Vowinkel, Heike. 2005. Kopftuch statt Popkarriere. *Welt Online*. 9 October. Accessed 23 August 2010. http://www.welt.de/print-warms/article133246/Kopftuch_statt_Popkarriere.html.
Wadud, Amina. 1999. *Qur'an and Woman: Rereading the Sacred Text from a Woman's Perspective*. Oxford: Oxford University Press.
———. 2006. *Inside the Gender Jihad: Women's Reform in Islam*. London: One World.
Waghorne, Joanne Punzo. 1999. "The Hindu Gods in a Split-Level World: The Sri Siva-Vishnu Temple in Suburban Washington, D.C." In Orsi 1999, 103–130.
Walley, Christine. 2013. *Exit Zero: Family and Class in Postindustrial Chicago*. Chicago: The University of Chicago Press.
Warner, Michael. 2002. *Publics and Counterpublics*. New York: Zone Books.
Warner, Stephen, and Judith Wittner, eds. 1998. *Gatherings in Diaspora: Religious Communities and the New Immigration*. Philadelphia: Temple University Press.
Wedam, Elfriede. 2000. Catholic Spirituality in a New Urban Church. In *Public Religion and the Urban*, edited by Lowell Livezey, 213–238. New York: New York University Press.
Wein, Eberhard. 2008. "Wolf erhebt Vorwürfe gegen Moschee." *Stuttgarter Zeitung*, 17 June.
Wellershoff, Dieter. 2007. "Wofür steht die Kölner Moschee?" *Frankfurter Allgemeine Zeitung*. 14 June. Accessed 2 November 2010. http://www.faz.net/aktuell/feuilleton/debatten/debatte-wofuer-steht-die-koelner-moschee-1435869.html.
Welt Online. 2008. "Moschee im Wohngebiet—und keiner regt sich auf." 12 August. Accessed 30 April 2011. http://www.welt.de/politik/deutschland/article8955395-moschee-im-wohngebiet.

Welzbacher, Christian. 2008. *Euroislam—Architektur. Die neuen Moscheen des Abendlandes*. Amsterdam: SUN Publishers.
Wentzel, Abd al-Hafidh. 2004. *Die Sunna: Texte zum Verständnis der unverzichtbaren Bedeutung der prophetischen Tradition im Islam*. Freiburg: Spohr.
Werbner, Pnina. 2002. *Imagined Diasporas among Manchester Muslims: The Public Performance of Pakistani Transnational Identity*. Oxford: James Currey.
White, Jenny. 2002. *Islamist Mobilization in Turkey: A Study in Vernacular Politics*. Seattle: University of Washington Press.
Wiktorowicz, Quintan. 2005. *Radical Islam Rising*. Lanham: Rowman and Littlefield Publishers.
Wilford, Justin. 2009. Sacred Archipelagos: Geographies of Secularization. *Progress in Human Geography* 34(2): 328–348.
Wilson, Elizabeth. 1992. *The Sphinx in the City: Urban Life, the Control of Disorder, and Women*. Berkeley: University of California Press.
Wilson, G. Willow. 2010. *The Butterfly Mosque*. New York: Grove Press.
Winston, Diane. 1999. *Red-Hot and Righteous: The Urban Religion of the Salvation Army*. Cambridge, MA: Harvard University Press.
Wohlrab-Sahr, Monika. 1999. *Konversion zum Islam in Deutschland und den USA*. Frankfurt: Campus.
Yahya, Harun. 2002. *Honigbienen: Perfekte Wabenbauer*. Istanbul: Okusan Verlag.
———. 2003a. *Die Allianz der Tugendhaften*. Istanbul: Okusan Verlag
———. 2003b. *Die Unvernuft der Gottlosigkeit*. Munich: SKD Bavaria Verlag und Handels GmbH.
Yeğenoğlu, Meyda. 2012. *Islam, Migrancy, and Hospitality in Europe*. New York: Palgrave MacMillan.
Yildiz, Erol. 2009. "Als Deutscher ist man hier ja schon integriert: Alltagspraxis in einem Kölner Quartier." In Mattausch and Yildiz 2009, 100–118.
Yıldız, Yasemin. 1999. "Keine Adresse in Deutschland? Adressierung als politische Strategie." In *AufBrüche*, edited by Cathy Gelbin, Kader Konuk, and Peggy Piesche, 224–236. Sulzbach: Ulrike Helmer Verlag.
———. 2009. "Turkish Girls, Allah's Daughters, and the Contemporary German Subject: Itinerary of a Figure." *German Life and Letters* 62(4): 465–481.
Yorgason, Ethan, and Veronica della Dora. 2009. "Geography, Religion, and Emerging Paradigms: Problematizing the Dialogue." *Social and Cultural Geography* 10(6): 629–637.
Yurdakal, Gökce. 2006. "Secular versus Islamist: The Headscarf Debate in Germany." In Jonker and Amiraux 2006, 151–168.
Zaidan, Amir. 1999. *Al-'Akida*. Offenbach: ADIB Verlag.
Zaimoglu, Feridun. 1998. *Koppstoff*. Hamburg: Rotbuch.
———. 2000. *Kanak Sprak: 24 Misstöne vom Rande der Gesellschaft*. Hamburg: Rotbuch.
———. 2003. *Abschaum: Die wahre Geschichte von Ertan Ongun*. Hamburg: Rotbuch Verlag.
———. 2005. *Zwölf Gramm Glück*. Cologne: Kiepenheuer & Witsch.
Zielcke, Adrian. 2000. "Verstecken hilft nicht weiter. Eine Moschee für Stuttgart." *Stuttgarter Zeitung*, 29 March.
Zöller, Katharina. 2012. "Arenas of Contest? Public Islamic Festivals in Interwar Dar es Salaam." In Desplat and Schulz 2012, 137–170.
Zukin, Sharon. 1991. *Landscapes of Power*. Berkeley: University of California Press.
———. 1995. *The Cultures of Cities*. Cambridge: Blackwell Publishers.
———. 2010. *Naked City*. Oxford: Oxford University Press.

City Archives Stuttgart

Baurechtsamt D4701
Kasten 35.
    E 1 (Mappe) Vereine, Vereine Allgemein
Kasten 36 B-E
    E 2 Vereine
Kasten 38 H-K
    Vereine
Repertorium Depot B
    C IV A 4 Bd.9 Nr.27
    Stadterweiterungsprojekt 1894
    (Haupt- und Residenzstadt Stuttgart. Städtisches Tiefbauamt. Begleitschrift zum projectierten Stadterweiterungsplan 1895.)

Index

9/11, 3, 14, 15, 27, 28, 41, 54, 58, 76, 81, 102, 109, 132, 134, 139, 141, 154, 147, 180, 186, 215

Abitur, 113,187, 214
Afghanistan, 15, 16, 41, 139, 145, 204, 205, 226, 235n15
Ahmadi community, 42
Akgün, Lale, 33n25
Akin, Fatih, 33n25
Aladdin, 141–42
Albania, 229
Al-Banna, Hassan, 76, 143
alcohol, 70, 72, 73, 80–82, 148, 149, 158, 188, 215, 232
Alevi, 131, 228
Algeria, 97, 223–24
'alim, 119
alms, see also *zakat*, 60, 72, 102
Al-Qaradawi, Yusuf, 76, 95–97
Al-Sherbini, Marwa, 235n10
Ammar114, 77, 97
Anatolia, 16, 179
Ankara, 10
anti-Islamic sentiments, anti-Muslim sentiments, see also Islamophobia, 31, 35, 43, 49, 54, 141
anti-Semitism, 148
Asad, Muhammad, 99n3
asylum seekers, 13
Ausländer, 14, 32n16, 41
ausländische Mitbürger, 15, 239
Ausländerausschuss, 119
Austria, 85, 100n12, 127, 133, 137n7, 165, 167, 171, 243
Australia, 175
authenticated Islam, 71, 97

background of migration, see also *Migrationshintergrund*, 15, 24, 29, 33n22, 45, 163, 205
backyard mosque, see also *Hinterhofmoschee*, 9, 24, 42, 61, 238
Baden-Württemberg, 3, 9, 14, 128, 146, 156
Baghdad, 116, 117
Baghdad University, 116
Bangladesh, 27
Bauman, Zygmunt, 21, 211
Bavaria, 52, 153, 167, 204, 205, 209, 211
bayram, 133
Bebauungsplan, see also master plan, 52
Beethoven, Ludwig van, 14
Beinhauer-Köhler, Bärbel and Claus Leggewie, 42
Beirut, 6
belonging, 12–14, 39, 89, 120–124, 134, 151–53, 163, 189
  national belonging, 161
  quest for belonging, 218
  sense of belonging, 196, 234
Berlin, 8, 24, 42, 223
  Berlin-Kreuzberg, 17, 33n21, 198
  Berlin-Neukölln, 17
  Berlin-Prenzlauer Berg, 198
Bezirk, 33n22, 45, 161, 204
Bezirksamt, 162
Bezirksbeirat, see also local council, 34, 156
Bezirksvorsteher, 46, 164, 182
Bild Zeitung, 150, 152–53, 155n7
Böblingen, 166
Bölsche, Jochen, 45, 63n5
Bosnia, 16, 25, 28, 83, 164, 193, 204, 205
Bowen, John, 4, 73
Breuer, Rita, 148–49, 155, 155n3
Buddhism, 70, 80

Buddha statues 145
building code, 35, 48–49, 53, 174
Bukhara, 176
Bundesamt für Verfassungsschutz, 142–47
Bürgerhaus, 126, 240
Burger King, 83

Calhoun, Craig, 107
Cairo, ix, 29
call for prayer, 74, 145
Catholic Church, 1, 9, 19, 74, 78, 79, 128, 165, 169, 171, 202
    and Italian migrants, 32n6
    as *Körperschaft des öffentlichen Rechts*, 175
    Catholic migrants, 9, 128
    Catholic preschool, 157, 202
celebration, see also festival, 1–3, 23–24, 32n2, 64, 149, 156, 183, 226–27, 230–31
Ceylan, Rauf, 13
chaplain, 117, 119
Christian Democratic Union (CDU), 13, 14, 47, 49, 50, 54, 154
Christian-Muslim dialogue, 28, 115, 120
    Christian-Muslim dialogue association, 75, 119, 127, 135, 181, 182, 240
    Christian-Muslim dialogue event, 61
Christian preschool, 121, 164
Christianity, 33n18, 78, 80, 151
    Position of Islam vs. Christianity, 44
    Christianity in GDR after 1989, 220
Christlich-Islamische Gesellschaft Stuttgart e.V., 28
Christmas, 121, 129, 130, 134, 164, 179, 218, 227, 239
church, churches 1, 2, 20, 68, 122, 150, 158, 159, 166, 189, 190, 209
    Church assembly, 167–68
    church community, 42, 105
    church group, 157
    church official/representative, 164, 182
    church service, 1, 2, 113
    defunct churches, 42
    storefront church, 38
citizen, 104–105
    equal citizens, 140
    naturalized citizen, 143
    Muslim German citizens, 41, 47, 50, 126, 142, 219–224
citizenship, 12–14, 23, 35, 41, 44, 109–10, 123, 137n3, 161
    active citizenship, 23, 109–10
    cultural citizenship, 23
    citizenship law, 13, 15–16
    citizenship test, 4
    definition of, 3, 150
    German citizenship, 13–15, 41, 161, 204
    performing citizenship, 137n3
    social citizenship, 23
    urban citizenship, 234n6
city council, see also *Gemeinderat*, 10, 35, 47, 48, 52–56
civic associations, see also *Verein*, 11, 36, 61, 76, 156, 159, 180, 191
    mosques as civic associations, 40
civic center, 93, 240
civic engagement, 85, 89, 134
civic participation, 2–5, 15, 23, 36, 43, 68, 225, 245
    banned from civic participation, 76,
    civic participant, 31, 41–42, 134–136
    civic rights, 35, 191n9
    mode of civic participation, 105, 169
    Muslim civic participation, 35, 45, 109
    religiously inspired civic participation, 18
    urban civic participation, 234n6
Cologne, 24, 25, 47, 52, 144, 145, 175, 192n16
    Cologne Mosque, 42, 62
    Pro-Cologne, 49
conversion to Islam, 68, 71, 77, 81–82, 99n3, 101, 121–123, 128–30, 221
    public conversion, 78
    formal conversion, 98
    conversion on www.youtube.com, 100n10
conversion to Catholicism, 80–81
convert (to Islam), 11, 41, 68–71, 76–77, 80, 86, 98, 110n8, 100n10, 137n8, 146, 193, 242–43
    converts and the headscarf, 89
counterpublic, 107–09
    Muslim counterpublic 108
cultural alienation, see also *Überfremdung*, 47, 57

cultural production, 2–3, 5, 18, 22, 24, 30, 35, 44, 105, 197–99, 231–34, 241, 245

dating, 80, 86, 97–98, 136
da'wa, 77, 146
Day of the Open Mosque, 74, 180–81, 241
De Certeau, Michel, 37–38
Deeb, Lara, 6, 71
Deutsche Islamkonferenz, 154
Deutscher Gewerkschaftsbund, 175
discrimination, 4, 6, 12, 22, 69, 72, 89, 106, 148, 216
DİTİB, 10, 26, 28, 176
diversity (cultural, ethnic, and religious) 7, 23, 38, 105, 126, 133, 150, 169, 195, 230, 233 235n18
dome (of mosque), 8, 26, 36, 41–42, 50
Dublin, 25, 32n8
Duisburg, 25
    Duisburg-Hochfeld, 17
    Duisburg-Marxloh, 42

East Germany, GDR, 42, 150, 204–05, 211, 220, 222–23
Eaton, Gai, 126, 137n8
Egypt, ix, 27–28, 45, 76, 86, 96, 144
Eid, 121, 226–28
    Eid el-Fitr, 32n8, 226
    Eid Al-Adha, 173
Elyas, Nadeem, 149
Erbakan, Necmettin, 10–11, 144
Esslingen, 76
ethnic ghetto, 6, 17
ethnic segregation, 136
ethnic shopping street, 198–200
ethnicity, 16–18, 31, 43, 65, 97, 105, 124, 126–27, 133–34, 136, 163, 182, 196, 201, 201, 229–30, 234, 240
ethos, 94, 97, 233
    communal ethos, 93, 98
European Council for Fatwa and Research, 76
exclusion, 15, 106–7
    exclusionary incorporation, 33n23
    lines of exclusion, 14, 15, 123
    processes of exclusion, 22
    stories of exclusion, 69

Fachhochschule, 215
Fachhochschulreife, 120, 124

faith, 9, 18, 30, 72, 81, 87, 89, 104, 113, 125, 127, 186, 188, 207, 215, 218
faith-based organization, 19–20
fatiha, 80, 81
fear, 5, 16, 34, 48, 52–53, 55, 138–55
    fear of Islam/Muslims, 14, 23, 31, 43, 45, 56, 138–155, 186
    irrational fears of Islam/Muslims, 15, 47–48, 57, 154–55, 186
    fear of immigrants, 29
    fostering fears of Islam, 33n19
    fear of "over-alienation", 47, 57, 63n7
    fear of radicalization, 53
    fear of discrimination, 89
    fear of rejection, 237
Federation of Muslim Organizations in Europe, 76
festival, see also celebration, 156, 181
    summer festival season, 156
    neighborhood festival, 156, 184, 203, 230–33, 156–58
forced labor/forced labor camps, 170–72
foreigner, 14, 41, 80, 82, 119–20, 134, 161
freedom of religion, 42, 47, 58, 153
France, 4, 166, 211
Frankfurt, 24, 100n12, 166
Fraser, Nancy, 106–07
Freudenreich, Josef-Otto, 172, 192n4
Friedrich, Hans-Peter, 153
Fulla doll, 146–47, 155n3

Gastarbeiter, see also guest worker, 14–16, 39, 41, 42, 51, 122, 239
Gazzah, Miriam, 63n2
Gemeinderat, see also city council, 10, 48, 52
gender,
    gender blindness, 106,
    gender mixing, 72, 104, 182
    gender relations, 71, 178
    gender segregation, 27, 72, 75, 93, 97, 115, 182
gentrification, 33n21, 198
German Constitution. *See under Grundgesetz*, 3, 6, 139
German President, 31, 140, 155n8
Gesellschaft für Christlich-Islamische Begegnung und Zusammenarbeit e.V., 28, 181
Giordano, Ralph, 154

globalization, 36, 70, 151, 179
Goethe, Johann Wolfgang von, 14, 151
Graf Eberhard, 165
Greece, 8, 205, 210
Greek Orthodox Church, 9, 172
Green Party, 13, 32n14, 33n17, 52, 54, 154
Grimm, Fatima, 146
Grundgesetz, 3, 5, 41, 44, 51, 52, 143, 153
Gühring, Albrecht, 190–91
guest worker, see also *Gastarbeiter*, 9, 12, 209
Gymnasium, 235n16
Gysi, Gregor, 154

H&M, 83
Habermas, Jürgen, 106
hadith, 66, 87, 126, 220, 224
hajj, 60, 82–84, 88, 113
halal, 5, 72, 92, 93, 239
    halal foods, 11, 108, 148
    halal slaughtering, 148, 222
Hamburg, 8, 24
    Hamburg-Wilhemsburg, 17
haram, 73, 89, 148
Hare Krishna temple, 74
Hauptschule, 125, 197, 214, 235n13
headscarf, see also *hijab*, 4, 18, 22, 81–85, 88–89, 94, 99, 101–03, 109, 112–14, 122, 125, 128–29, 146, 148, 157, 163, 181, 183–84, 214, 216–19, 221, 227, 230, 232, 234n9. 239, 242
heaven, 87–88
Hechingen, 42
hell, 87–88
Herzog Eberhard Ludwig, 168
Herzog Friedrich II, 166
Herzog Ulrich, 165–66
hijab, see also headscarf, 4, 65–67, 89, 93–94, 121–22, 128–29, 134, 215, 219, 221
Hinduism, 20
    Hindu temple, 63n4, 73–74
himar, 219–21
Hinterhofmoschee, 9, 39–40, 61
Hizballah, 144, 147
hoca, 132, 187
Hofmann, Murad, 77
Hohenlohe, 164, 205–07, 211, 213, 233
Holocaust, 161, 172, 192n11
Holod, Renata and Hasan-Uddin Khan, 25
Hungary, 150

ibadat, 72
identity, 5–8, 12–14, 16–18, 21, 71–72, 107–8, 120–24, 134–36, 194, 196, 199, 200, 205, 232, 234
    identity construction, 100n7
    markers of identity, 211
    Muslim identity, 17, 144, 201, 218
    new identity, 72, 129
    pious identity, 85
    quest for identity, 123, 135
iftar, 30, 75, 127, 147, 183, 227, 233
    public *iftar* cycle/events, 28, 181
IGD, 11, 27, 75–77, 100n7, 100n8, 144
IGMG. See under Milli Görüş,
Imam, 1–2, 6–7, 10, 18, 23–24, 26, 65, 74, 77–78, 86, 102, 132, 138, 157, 174, 187–88, 238, 243
inclusion, 151, 158–59, 190
    civic inclusion, 31, 158
    inclusion of immigrant culture, 3
    inclusion of mosque community, 158–59, 179, 191
    inclusion of Muslims, 2–3, 14, 19, 24, 147, 180
    resented inclusion, 22–24, 33n23
India, 177
industrialization, 161, 167–68, 172
    industrializing cities, 161, 233
Innsbruck, 165
interfaith dialogue, 52, 75, 115–20,
Internet, 108, 127
    youth and Internet, 28, 97, 108, 127, 180, 189
    Internet resources (theological), 201, 240
invisibility/invisible, 114
    invisible barriers, 216
    invisible contribution, 205
    invisible individual, 104, 114, 130, 145, 237
    invisible mosque/community 43, 45, 189–90
Iran, 8, 67
Iraq, 15, 16, 41, 112, 115–120, 139, 141, 146, 204
    Christians in Iraq, 117
Islam,
    basics of Islam, 126, 132
    construction of German Islam, 11
    Islam as a foreign religion, 152

Islam as a German religion, 22, 31, 41, 46
debates about Islam, 3, 5, 8, 14, 19, 28, 41, 44, 47, 200
debating Islam, 86–93, 98, 147–49
learning about Islam, 69–70, 82, 85, 92, 121, 125, 128
negative image of Islam, 133
political Islam, 5
representing/representation of Islam, 139, 141–42
radical Islam, 59
"talking Islam", 69, 72
traditional, popular Islam, 71
Islam and urban transformations, 19
"Islam ist ein Teil Deutschlands", 140, 149–154
Islam, Yusuf (Cat Stevens), 70
Islamic,
    Islamic ambiance, 73, 95,
    Islamic banking, 93, 148
    Islamic dress/fashion, 108, 148, 163, 225
    Islamic instruction, 40, 59, 60, 135,
    Islamic knowledge, 68, 85, 99, 178
    Islamic networks, 99,
    Islamic piety, 68, 82, 96–97
    Islamic politics, 11, 44
    Islamic practices, 31, 69, 91, 98, 121, 178
    Islamic products, 97,
    Islamic religious instruction at public schools, 193
    Islamic sensitivities, 81,
    Islamic space, 93–94
    Islamic spatiality, 93,
    Islamic sociality, 93,
    Islamic state, 17
    Islamic studies, 26, 75, 77, 85, 94, 184–86, 189, 193, 234n1, 240, 243
    Islamic tradition, 71, 89,
    Islamic utopia, 95,
Islamische Zeitung, 77
Islamism, 6, 138–47
    politicial Islamism, 140
    militant Islamism, 140
Islamist, 31, 138–47
    Islamist politics, 44,
Islamization, 6, 17, 33n20, 45,
Islamoğlu, Mustafa, 146, 155n4

Islamologisches Institut, 81, 85, 93, 125–27, 240, 242–43
Islamophobia, 15, 22, 28, 31, 141, 154
Islamrat für die Bundesrepublik Deutschland, 153, 176
Islam Week, 127, 146, 241–43
Islamwoche, see also Islam Week, 78, 112, 241–43
Ismail, Salwa, 45
Istanbul, 177, 215
Italy, 8, 9, 205

Jacobite, 117
Jain Temple, 63n3, 63n9
Jesus, 79, 220
Jewish community, 20, 62
Jews, Jewish, 116, 154, 172, 175, 192n24, 234n2, 241
Jihad, 17, 145
Jonker, Gerdien and Valérie Amiraux, 62
Jordan, 76
Judaism, 33n18, 151
Judeo-Christian tradition/history, 150, 151
Jugendamt, 55, 138, 185–86
jus sanguinis, 13, 15
jus solis, 13, 15

Kandemir, Hülya, 77, 97
Karlsruhe, 243
Katznelson, Ira, 199
kermes, 112, 114, 136, 180, 183–84, 241
Khaled, Amr, 76, 96–97
khalif, 173
Khan, Sharukh, 163
King Friedrich Wilhelm I, 8
Kirchensteuer, 175
Kizilkaya, Ali, 153
Klausen, Jytte, 33n25
Klausing, Kathrin, 92
Kong, Lily, 19
Koordinationsrat der Muslime, 175
Koordinationsrat des christlich-islamischen Dialogs e.V., 28
Kurd, Kurdish, 203, 230, 236

laicism, 177
Landes, Joan 106
Lebanon, 76, 92
Leitkultur, 13–14
Lefebvre, Henri, 37

liberal democracy, 16, 44, 71
Liberal Party (FDP), 54
LIDL, 83
lifestyle, 7, 37, 72, 82, 122, 129, 198, 222
    changing lifestyles, 68, 70, 85
    creating lifestyles, 83, 97
    Islamic/Muslim lifestyles, 71–72, 78, 85, 91, 98, 185, 224, 244
    new lifestyle, 83, 97
    secular lifestyles, 70
lifeworld,
    construction of lifeworld, 82
    dominant lifeworld, 40, 45
    everyday pious lifeworld, 84–86
    individual lifeworld, 3, 62, 70, 136, 237
    Muslim German lifeworld, 69, 148, 244
    Muslim lifeworld, 2–3, 5, 8, 30–31, 105, 130, 149, 232
    multi-ethnic and multi-religious lifeworld, 140
    pious Muslim lifeworld, 84–86, 98, 105, 124, 127, 146, 232, 240
    urban lifeworld, 4, 110, 200
die Linke, Left Party, 154
local council, 31, 48, 55, 160, 190
    head of the local council,
    local council member, 47
localization,
    localization of Islam/Muslims, 2–3, 6, 24, 35–36, 47, 61, 69, 104, 133, 148, 196, 236, 238
    localization of other religions, 19
    processes of localization, 31, 160, 182
    successful localization, 159, 190
    localization of mosque community, 159, 174
London, 63n3, 145, 147
Ludin, Fereschte, 217, 234n9
Ludwigsburg, 76, 167, 201, 208
Luther, Martin, 165
LVIKZ, see also VIKZ, 28, 52, 175, 189

Madrid, 145
Mannheim, 25, 51
master plan, 58
Maududi, Abul Ala, 143
Mayor (of the city of Stuttgart), 35, 50, 51–53, 56, 58, 60

Mazyek, Ayman, 77, 153–54
Mecca, 82, 113–14, 137n6, 221
media, 35, 40, 42–45, 52, 106, 110, 133, 138–39, 140, 159
    dominant media, 17, 110
    media experts, 5
    media hype, 139–40
    media images, 2, 7, 57
    popular media, 5, 160
Merkel, Angela, 153
Merz, Friedrich, 13
migration, 8–12, 14–16, 36, 70
    migrant experiences, 211–213, 219–224
    seasonal migration 161
    temporary migration, 160
Migrationshintergrund, 15, 24, 32n16, 33n26
mihrab, 25, 60, 74
minaret, 8, 26, 36, 41–42, 44, 50, 227
minbar, 25, 60, 74, 173
minority, 152, 204, 219, 224
    Muslim minority contexts, countries, 4, 12, 25, 70, 96, 99
    religious minority, 49, 52
Milli Görüş, 10–11, 27–28, 63n10, 144, 153, 183
Mittlere Reife, 122, 187, 214
mobility, 32, 36, 236–245
    immobility, 237, 245
    long-distance mobility, 236
    urban mobility, 236
Morocco, 8, 32n4, 205, 244
mosque,
    local/Stuttgart mosque-scape, 10, 62, 183, 240
    mosque community, 10–11, 40–44, 54, 62–62, 64–100, 108, 134, 217, 237–38, 156, 192
    mosque complex, 30, 34–63
    mosque conflict/controversy, 34–63
    mosque construction, 3, 19–20, 25, 45
    mosque hopper/hopping, 127, 236, 239–41, 245
    mosque opponent, 35–36, 44–45, 49, 57–59
    purpose built mosque, 25, 26, 43, 51, 56
    warehouse mosque, 38

mosque association, 10–12, 26, 30, 32n13, 34–63, 76, 126, 139, 160, 180
    national mosque association, 27, 109, 138–39, 180, 192n6, 243
    mosque association official/representative/board members, 42, 182, 158–60
    mosque association politics, 126
    mosque association president, 30, 139
    regional mosque association, 243
Mosul, 116–17, 119
mu'amalat, 73
Mulid An-Nabi, 64
multi-ethnic working-class quarter/neighborhood, 1–2, 21, 26, 31, 128, 159, 161–64, 193–235
Munich, 24, 100n8
municipality, 44, 58, 61
    municipal authorities/officials, 11, 57
    municipal politics, 35
Muslim Brotherhood, 11, 76, 143–44
Muslim
    Muslim law, 91
    Muslim majority contexts/countries, 4, 7, 16, 19, 25, 72, 95, 97, 99, 143
    Muslim politics, 119,
    Muslim public sphere, 12, 18, 28, 30, 43, 99, 106, 109, 124, 241, 245
Muslim Youth in Germany, *Muslimische Jugend in Deutschland* (MJD), 76, 77, 123, 240
Muslimische Studenten Union (MSU), 78, 243

nafs, 218
Naqshband, Baha-uddin, 176
Naqshbandi Order, 176–79
nation-state, 12, 15, 161
    consolidating German nation-state, 167
Negt, Oskar and Alexander Kluge, 106
neighborhood, 156–192, 193–235
    immigrant neighborhood, 194
    multi-ethnic neighborhood, 23, 24, 29, 43, 59, 121, 199, 232
    multi-ethnic working class neighborhoods, 2, 21, 31, 162, 195, 198
    multi-religious neighborhood, 45, 196

neighborhood culture, 32, 129, 194, 197–200, 224–31
neighborhood festival/celebration, 156–58, 183–84, 230–32
neighborhood spaces, 21, 196
neo-Nazi groups/politics, 49, 148
Netherlands, 63n2, 133
New York, 147
nihak misyar, 89–90
niqab, 146
Nökel, Sigrid, 109
noise (complaints about), 40, 44, 51, 57, 164, 174
Nurçuluk community, 10

OBI, 83
Orsi, Robert, 19
Ottoman Empire, 177
Özdemir, Cem, 33n17, 33n25

Pakistan, 120–21
Palestine, 76, 117, 119
paradise, 87–88, 92, 113
Parallelgesellschaft, see also parallel society, 17
parallel society, see also *Parallelgesellschaft*, 17, 22, 24, 45, 68, 148, 152
parking, parking spaces (complaints about), 39, 40, 44, 47, 49, 51, 57, 164, 174
Partridge, Damani, 33n23,
patriarchy, 91, 129
    social patriarchy, 71, 91, 98, 223
Pfeiffer, Eduard, 234n2
Pietist/s, 74, 168
piety, 30, 64–100, 115, 119, 101–37, 176, 217
    pious circles/circuits/networks, 81, 96, 244
    pious identity, 11, 69, 85, 124
    pious knowledge, 85
    pious lifestyle, 78, 85, 91, 98, 124, 127, 134
    pious modes of public engagement/participation, 1, 30, 36
    pious practices, 32, 68, 69, 71, 72, 98, 102, 123, 125, 240
    pious self, 30, 71, 78, 82, 93–95, 97, 113, 128, 130
    pious spaces, 94,

282 | Index

pious subjectivities, 69, 93, 95, 106, 109
pious trajectory, 82, 85, 104, 134–35, 239–41
pious transformation, 83, 105
quest for piety, 85
pilgrimage, see also *hajj*, 87, 114
place-making, 20, 36–39
Poland, 12, 150, 209
police, 27, 28, 55, 76, 186, 189
pork, 82, 102, 117–18, 120–21, 158, 164, 232
Porsche, 171–72, 191n8
Portugal, 9, 205
post-secular city, 20, 200
prayer, 84, 87, 92
    Friday prayer, 93, 174
    daily prayer, 102
prayer room, 8, 9, 26, 40, 47, 61, 173, 184, 189
    men's prayer room, 27, 60–61, 74–75, 92, 115
    women's prayer room, 60, 64, 75, 86, 94
preacher, 71, 72
    popular preacher, 96
prejudice, 2–5, 12, 22, 31, 34, 43, 56–58, 139, 141–42, 155, 159–60, 179
principal/school, 1, 194, 218, 224–25
Pro-Heslach, 49–53
Prophet Muhammad, 27, 64–67, 72, 92, 103, 112, 132, 176–77, 242
Protestant Church, 166, 171, 202, 241
    and Greek migrants, 9
    as *Körperschaft des öffentlichen Rechts*, 175
    President of the national Protestant Church, 154
    Protestant preschool, 164, 202
    Protestant service, 166
public,
    emerging public, 110,
    public circuits, 124, 127, 133, 180
    public culture, 199–200
    public debate, 3,5, 16, 30, 34–36, 41, 45, 86, 109, 110, 119,140, 152, 155, 182, 200
    public event, 28, 30, 75, 78, 99, 101, 134, 142, 173, 189, 214

public engagement/participation, 30, 40, 78, 88, 98, 104, 107, 109, 181
public persona, 71, 72, 78, 82, 85,
public space, 6, 31, 127, 136, 196, 199–200, 245,
public sphere, 5, 22, 27, 31, 82, 85, 103–04, 105–109, 134, 157, 161, 181, 189, 200, 222
    dominant public sphere, 109
    bourgeois public sphere, 106,
    national Muslim public sphere, 241
    secular public sphere, 31,
public transportation, 21, 73, 81, 83, 94, 127, 195, 216
Qur'an, 47, 71–74, 80, 91, 95, 101–03, 112–15, 120, 132–33, 145, 149, 155, 173, 178, 215, 223
    Qur'an recitation, 64, 74, 116, 145
    Qur'an study group, 72, 75, 77–78, 81, 86–93, 114, 126, 128, 224, 240, 243
Qutb, Sayid, 143

radicalization, 53, 57
railroad/railways, 12, 11, 167–68, 194–214
    railroad/railways facilities, 195, 201–3, 207
    railroad workers housing, 195, 201–2, 204
Ramadan, 70, 75, 81, 87, 88, 112, 117, 147, 149, 181–82, 226–228, 232, 236, 239
    annual public Ramadan *iftar* series, 75, 127
Ramadan, Said, 76
Ramadan, Tariq, 76,
Realschule, 169, 181, 214
recognition, 3–4, 23, 110, 206
    fight for recognition, 57
    public recognition, 8, 11, 25, 57, 58, 110,
    recognition of mosque/communities, 179
    recognition of Muslims, 104
    urban recognition, 36–39, 43
refugee, 13–16, 157, 160–61, 171–72, 177, 190, 204–05, 209, 211, 236
Reidegeld, Abdelrahman, 85, 125, 242
religion,
    freedom of religion/religious freedom, 42, 58

immigrant religion, 3
public religion, 200
urban religion, 4, 8, 18–20, 200
religiosity, 5–8, 16–18, 43, 62, 64–100, 101–137, 148, 183–88, 195, 201, 215, 218, 240
religious,
   religious choice, 70
   religious community, 20, 34, 36, 70, 200
   religious geography/topography/landscape, 4, 6–7, 19–20, 196, 236–37, 241
   religious identity, 16, 97
   religious instruction, 59–60, 151, 173–74, 179, 184–88, 193, 209, 220, 234n1, 237, 243
   religious needs, 36, 38, 40, 42, 46, 200
   religious practices, 5, 20, 47, 68–72, 81, 94, 148, 224, 239–40
   religious space, 9–10, 74,
   religious symbol, 239
resentment, 2–4, 14, 16, 34, 36, 42, 47, 76, 89, 109, 138–155, 159, 186, 222, 230,
   anti-Islamic resentment, resentment against Islam/Muslims, 43, 44, 49
   popular resentment, 237
   public resentment, 105,
re-unification, 149–50, 153
reversion (to Islam), 71, 108, 121–123
   revert, 71, 77, 95
Rida, Rashid, 143
right-wing groups/politics, 44, 49, 51, 56, 159
ritual purity, 116
ritual washing, *wuduu*, 84, 102, 126, 132
Romanian-Orthodox Church, 164
Rotterdam, 25
Russia, 150, 157, 231

Said, Edward, 141
Salafi, 27, 109, 222
Sarrazin, Thilo, 32n3
Sassen, Saskia, 12, 160
Saudi-Arabia, 52, 59, 90, 96, 220–21
Schäuble, Wolfgang, 154
Schengen Agreement, 15
Schorndorf, 26
Schuster, Wolfgang, Mayor of Stuttgart, 50, 52, 56
Schwarz, Konstantin, 54

secular,
   concept of the secular, 20, 23
   secular (civic) association, 19, 239
   secular city, 5, 19, 20, 68, 200
   secular (public) platform, 108, 134
   secular space, secular public/urban space, 31, 37, 93
   secular state, 14
   secular vocabularies, 108
secularism, 2
Serbian Orthodox Church, 172
sermon, 65, 66, 72, 96
   Friday sermon, 75, 77
shahada, 66, 78, 95, 121, 220
sharia, 17, 144, 146
soccer, 14, 105, 130–32, 149, 157, 188, 194–96, 213, 233
Spain, 8, 9, 120, 205
Shi'a, 6, 8, 144
Sikh community, 164
Sindelfingen, 25, 26
Social Democratic Party (SPD), 13, 32n14, 49, 52, 54, 154
Somonçu, Serdar, 33n25
Soviet Union, 141, 204, 209
Spielhaus, Riem, 32n15
spirituality, 72, 101–03, 124–27
   spiritual experiences, 102
   spiritual geography, 32, 236
      Muslim spiritual geography, 239
   spiritual needs, 85
   spiritual search, 85
sports club, 157, 158, 171, 210
   Muslim women's sports club, 78
state security, see also *Verfassungsschutz*, 11, 27, 55, 76, 142–47, 186
Stiftskirche, 166
Strasbourg, 113, 166
student dormitory, 47, 51–56, 58, 173, 184–89
Stuttgart, 24–28
   Muslim Stuttgart, 24–28
   Stuttgart-Bad Cannstatt, 17, 26, 29, 165–66, 191
   Stuttgart-Botnang, 33n28,
   Stuttgart-Degerloch, 26, 163
   Stuttgart-Feuerbach, 26, 169
   Stuttgart-Hallschlag, 17
   Stuttgart-Heslach, 34–63, 158–59, 185

Stuttgart-Killesberg, 26, 204, 234n4
Stuttgart-Nordbahnhof, 1–2, 23, 24, 29, 31, 110, 111, 193–235
Stuttgart-Rot, 161, 171, 191n3
Stuttgart-Sillenbuch, 26, 164
Stuttgart-Süd, 26, 45,
Stuttgart-Wangen, 26, 63n10,
Stuttgart-Zuffenhausen, 17, 26, 31, 156–192
Stuttgart 21, 54, 63n8, 203, 208
Stuttgarter, 24, 31, 97, 123
    Catholic Stuttgarter, 205, 206–11, 234
    Jewish Stuttgarter, 192n11
    Muslim Stuttgarter, 32, 99, 133, 205, 213–19, 234, 245
subsidiary public (sphere), 107–09
    Muslim subsidiary public, 108
Sufi, 26, 176–79, 243
suhur, 117, 226
Sunna, 72, 91, 103, 220, 223
Swabia, Swabian, 45, 51, 130
    Swabian accent/dialect, 58, 115, 127–28, 130
Sweden 81
swimming lessons/school, 148, 224–26, 235n16
Switzerland, 85, 100n12, 127, 137n7, 166, 167, 170, 243
Syria, 16, 76

tafsir, 80, 220
takbir, 66–67, 95
tawhid, 146, 220
television/TV, 112
    German TV, 111
    television preacher, 96, 113
    satellite TV, 97, 112, 146
    Turkish TV, 112,
terrorism, 4, 5, 188, 188
    global terrorism, 139
    terrorist attacks, 144–45, 147
theology, 11, 16, 78, 92, 103, 112–13, 118, 126, 148, 177–78, 240, 243
    female theologian, 10, 26, 113
    theologian, 71, 78, 85, 112, 113, 241–42
    theological books/texts/literature, 72, 97, 108, 112, 116, 188, 220
    theological debate, 98
    theological knowledge, 78, 81, 103, 125–26
    theological question, 27, 92, 112
    theological terms, 146
Tunahan, Suleyman, 47–48, 177–79
Tunisia, 8, 205
Turkey, 8, 10–11, 55, 102, 111–14, 124, 131, 155n1, 164, 174, 178–79, 185, 205, 214–16, 236
Turkish Consulate, Turkish Consul, 10, 46, 47, 50
Turkish government, 48
Turkish Republic, 177
Turkishness, 217

Überfremdung, 47, 63n7
Ulfkotte, Udo, 33n19
ummah, 7–8, 11, 69, 94, 97–98, 108, 146
umra, 60, 219–21
unemployment/unemployed, 24–26, 82, 130, 163, 197, 221
United States, 28, 150, 161, 175, 199, 233
university, 8, 113, 117
    university students, 97
University of Göttingen, 117
University of Stuttgart, 78, 102, 112, 113, 124, 241, 242, 244
University of Tübingen, 116
urban,
    urban authenticity, 39
    urban beginnings, 38–39, 60–62, 104, 110
    urban district, see also *Bezirk*,
    urban garden/gardener 203, 207, 209, 211, 230, 231
    urban public, 12, 61, 98, 120, 159
    urban public culture, 38, 158, 199
    urban public sphere, 3, 35–36, 38–39, 43, 58, 61, 62, 68, 89, 120, 136, 236, 245

Verein, see also civic association, 26, 40, 175
Verfassungsschutz, see also state security, 76
VfB Stuttgart, 194
Vienna, 85, 100n12
VIKZ, 10, 27, 30, 34–63, 112, 156–192
visibility/visible, 9, 12, 27, 35, 37, 45, 110, 157, 239

becoming more visible, 36, 43, 62, 238
visible engagement/participation, 3, 106, 120, 136, 157
visible piety, 82–84, 122, 128
visible presence, 58, 179, 224
visible spaces, 22, 43
Vogel, Pierre, 100n11
von Denffer, Ahmad, 80, 100n8

Walley, Christine, 234n8
war, 70, 80, 83, 118, 160
    Cold War, 141
    Gulf Wars, 141
    World War I, 169
    World War II, 8, 157, 161, 172, 202, 206–08, 211
        post-World War II, 160–62, 190, 237
        post-World War II industrial expansion, 171

Warner, Michael, 107
Württemberg/Kingdom of, 165–67
Wulff, Christian, see also German President, 140, 149–55, 155n8

xenophobia, xenophobic, 22, 44, 49, 50, 53

Yıldız, Yasemin, 32n15
Yugoslavia, 8, 15, 80, 171, 205
Yusuf, Sami, 76, 97

zaghrata, 67, 95
Zaidan, Amir, 85, 125
Zaimoğlu, Feridun, 33n25
zakat, 102, 227
Zentralrat der Juden in Deutschland, 175
Zentralrat der Muslime in Deutschland (ZMD), 11, 76, 119, 120, 134, 154, 176
Zielcke, Adrian, 51
Zukin, Sharon, 38–39, 198–200

www.ingramcontent.com/pod-product-compliance
Lightning Source LLC
Chambersburg PA
CBHW070912030426
42336CB00014BA/2385